THE PHILOSOPHY OF SCHOPENHAUER

THE PHILOSOPHY

OF

SCHOPENHAUER

by

BRYAN MAGEE

'It is far easier to point out the faults and errors in
the work of a great mind than to give a clear and full
exposition of its value.'

Schopenhauer: *Criticism of the
Kantian Philosophy*

CLARENDON PRESS · OXFORD
OXFORD UNIVERSITY PRESS · NEW YORK
1983

Oxford University Press, Walton Street, Oxford OX2 6DP

London   Glasgow   New York   Toronto
Delhi   Bombay   Calcutta   Madras   Karachi
Kuala Lumpur   Singapore   Hong Kong   Tokyo
Nairobi   Dar es Salaam   Cape Town
Melbourne   Auckland

and associates in
Beirut   Berlin   Ibadan   Mexico City   Nicosia

Oxford is a trade mark of Oxford University Press

Published in the United States by
Oxford University Press, New York

British Library Cataloguing in Publication Data

Magee, Bryan
The philosophy of Schopenhauer.
1. Schopenhauer, Arthur
I. Title
193   *B3148*

ISBN 0-19-824673-0

Library of Congress Cataloging in Publication Data

Magee, Bryan.
The philosophy of Schopenhauer.

Includes bibliographical references and index.
1. Schopenhauer, Arthur, 1788–1860.   I. Title.
B3148.M27   1983   193   82-22523
ISBN 0-19-824673-0

Printed in Great Britain by
Thomson Litho Ltd, East Kilbride, Scotland

to
Patrick Gardiner

Contents

Prefatory Note

Since this book is written in English, and most people in the English-speaking world are unable to read German, my references to Schopenhauer's writings are to English translations. Readers who wish to consult the original passages will find them easy to trace via these translations, so I have not felt justified in weighting my book down with duplicate footnotes in German. The readers in question will, I hope, understand and forgive. They will find, by the way, that the German edition of Schopenhauer's works to be preferred is that edited by Arthur Hübscher and published in Wiesbaden over the years 1946–1950.

The English translations to which I refer are:

On the Fourfold Root of the Principle of Sufficient Reason. Translation by E. F. J. Payne; published by the Open Court Publishing Company, La Salle, Illinois, 1974.

The World as Will and Representation. Translation in two volumes by E. F. J. Payne; first published by The Falcon's Wing Press, Colorado, in 1958; republished by Dover Publications, New York, 1966.

On the Will in Nature. Translation by Mme Karl Hillebrand, published in one volume with her translation of *On the Fourfold Root of the Principle of Sufficient Reason* under the joint title *Two Essays by Arthur Schopenhauer* by George Bell & Sons, London, 1889; revised edition 1891.

Essay on the Freedom of the Will. Translation by Konstantin Kolenda; published by Bobbs–Merrill, Indianapolis and New York, 1960.

On the Basis of Morality. Translation by E. F. J. Payne; published by Bobbs–Merrill, Indianapolis and New York, 1965.

Parerga and Paralipomena. Translation in two volumes by E. F. J. Payne, published by The Clarendon Press, Oxford, 1974.

In a few cases I have changed a word or two in quotations from these sources where it seemed to me that a significant point had not been brought out clearly enough. I have also, occasionally, changed the punctuation where it seemed to me un-English or unidiomatic. The instances are trivial, but I mention them so that anyone taking a Schopenhauer quotation direct from this book is warned that it may not correspond in every particular to the reference cited for it.

However one tries to expound a system of thought whose every part is interconnected with every other, one cannot avoid introducing propositions early on which are at that stage under-supported and under-explained in terms of the system as a whole, and whose full justification does not emerge until later. I have tried to minimize the effects of this by separating my discussion of the presuppositions of Schopenhauer's system (Chapters 2–5) from my exposition of the system itself (Chapters 6–9), thus making possible an exposition of the system in terms of statements that carry their credentials with them. This still means, though, that the earlier chapters contain statements whose full substantiation in Schopenhauer's terms does not appear until later, and for this I can only beg the reader's patience.

Chapter 1

Schopenhauer's Life as Background to his Work

Schopenhauer always believed that he would not have been able to accomplish his life's work if he had not inherited financial independence. He was born into a rich Hanseatic merchant family in Danzig (now renamed Gdansk) on 22 February 1788. The Schopenhauers had been prominent in Danzig for generations. When Peter the Great and his Empress Catherine had visited the city in 1716 they had stayed overnight with the philosopher's great-grandfather Andreas. The story is told that Andreas, inspecting his guests' room at the last moment and finding the air in it a trifle chilly, ordered brandy to be poured all over the floor and set alight, thus introducing instant warmth and a luxurious aroma into the room immediately before his guests' arrival, but leaving the floor bone dry. The family, whose motto was *Point de bonheur sans liberté* ('Without freedom there can be no happiness'), seems to have been accustomed to conduct its relations with emperors and conquerors in a spirit of independence. Frederick the Great once spent two hours in private with the philosopher's father, Heinrich Floris Schopenhauer, in an attempt to induce him to leave Danzig and settle in Prussia. Heinrich Floris did indeed leave Danzig eventually, but not until after Frederick's death, and then the point of his going was to turn his back on Prussian occupation of his native city.

Besides this grand-seigneurial spirit of independence, another family characteristic was a cosmopolitanism rare in its day. As a young man Heinrich Floris Schopenhauer had been sent out into the world by his father to gain experience, and had lived for many years in France and England. During those years he developed a lasting enthusiasm for contemporary French literature, above all the works of Voltaire, and an admiration for English ways of life, private as well as public. After his return to Danzig he read an English and a French newspaper every day, and he encouraged his son from boyhood to read *The Times* — from which, he told him, 'one could learn everything'. The philosopher, like his father, read *The Times* every day for most of his adult life.

Before his son was even born, Heinrich Floris was active in planning for him the same sort of cosmopolitan upbringing as he himself had received. Having uncompromisingly settled in his own mind what the child's sex was to be, he chose the name 'Arthur' on the ground that it was not only common to Germany, France and England but had the same spelling in all three languages. He then made arrangements for the boy to be born in England so that he should have the rights of a British citizen for life. This part of the plan came adrift, however, because his wife's illness in pregnancy prevented her from making the necessary journey. Arthur had to be born in Danzig.

When Arthur had just turned five, in March 1793, Danzig was invaded by Prussian troops. Within twenty-four hours Heinrich Floris had abandoned his ancestral city for good, taking his family with him, though they had to leave more than a tenth of their total wealth behind. They settled, deliberately, in another free city and great Hanseatic seaport, Hamburg; and this remained their home until Heinrich Floris's death in 1805, when Arthur was seventeen. Heinrich Floris had been through a period of depression and strange irascibility before he was found drowned in the canal that flowed outside the family firm's warehouse. Everyone suspected suicide, but no one could be sure. The philosopher was subsequently to evince a great interest in, and insight into, suicide, and it is probable that the death of his father had something to do with this.

Arthur Schopenhauer may be said, then, to have grown up in Hamburg, though I suspect that Hamburg was more of a base than a home. His parents travelled almost perpetually, and always took him with them. When he was nine, after a journey through France, they left him in the care of a business friend at Le Havre for two years, there to be educated in the bosom of a French family who had a son of the same age. In later life he looked back on those two years as the happiest of his childhood. They were lived in the French language, which he mastered almost to perfection. When he got back to Hamburg he had a considerable amount of catching-up to do on his German vocabulary.

In the light of his later development the most significant feature of his pre-university education was its worldliness. This was its chief point as far as his father was concerned, its purpose being to groom him to take over an international business. But in his early teens Arthur began to ask his father for an academic future of Gymnasium and University. Heinrich Floris, who had a low opinion of academics in business, refused. However, the boy's pleading became insistent, and in the end Heinrich Floris offered him a choice: either he could have two years or more of international travel, to be followed by entry into the family firm, or else a higher education, in which case he would have to spend those two years at home studying. The offer was disingenuous. Arthur chose to travel, as his father knew he would. And thus he completed the form of education which by this time could be said to be traditional in the family, an education whose express aim was to turn a boy into a man of the world.

From the age of fifteen to seventeen his parents, in fulfilment of their promise, took him travelling for another period of over two years, this time on an extended tour of Belgium, France, Switzerland, Germany and England. In England they left him in a boarding-school in Wimbledon for three months while they toured the North. Two of his special activities here, both of which were to be daily pursuits throughout adult life, were flute-playing and physical fitness; but, much more important, as had been the case in France, the living of daily life at an impressionable age in a foreign language in which he had already received some formal tuition resulted in a mastery of it which never left him. For the rest of his life he spoke and wrote English almost like a native — could indeed sometimes pass as one for his first few minutes with an English stranger. The English prose he was to write in adult life, though containing minor blemishes of grammar and syntax, had the same highly distinctive character as his German, though this is perhaps less surprising when one remembers that his adult German prose had an English model. Despising as he did the pretentiousness so characteristic of German writing — and the long, convoluted sentences that went with it — and seeing nothing in the language itself that called for these things, he consciously set out to write German in the way Hume wrote English.

By the time he was seventeen he was almost equally at home in three languages, and had been set for some years to the task of getting to know Europe from the Alps to London. His accustomed way of life, together with his expectations for his personal future, were those prevailing in rich Hanseatic merchant families. The world he saw himself as belonging to was an international one of trade and practical affairs, with the long-distance communications that go with these; a world of big houses and many servants at home, and of well-appointed, frequently visited hostelries in other countries; a world of cosmopolitan hospitality given and received; of theatre, concerts, opera and other civilized pursuits in cities all over Europe; of interest in public affairs; of visits to the famous. ('As a child he was acquainted with many celebrities, such as Baroness Staël, Klopstock, Reimans, Madame Chevalier, Nelson, and Lady Hamilton': Helen Zimmern, *Arthur Schopenhauer: His Life and His Philosophy*, p. 17.) Socially, for the rest of his life, he was fully at ease only with people who could also have been at ease in such a world. In his later, adult contempt for academics there lay, I believe, a residuum of the rich, clever, cosmopolitan man-of-affairs's contempt for the limited social as well as intellectual horizons of middle-class professors.

His upbringing saved him from some of the consequences of what he later came to see as the chief drawback of formal education, namely that it reverses the proper order of experiences and concepts. Concepts have content and significance, he was later to believe, only in so far as they derive from experience and can be cashed back into it. And the trouble with formal education is that it pre-empts experience in this regard by giving us our first knowledge of many of the most important aspects of life not through experience, from which we then abstract and generalize, but through concepts based on other people's abstractions and generalizations, to which nothing in our own experience corresponds or can be opposed. Some of this is unavoidable, but by no means all of it, and in consequence there are unnecessarily large elements in our conception of the world which are not rooted in anything we ourselves have ever observed, experienced, felt or thought. Even when these are accurate they are still not fully authentic, for they are not truly and inwardly *ours*. So for all of us the clear-eyed perception of, and spontaneous emotional response to, reality is bound to be to some extent impeded by them; and so, therefore, is truly original thinking and insight.

Schopenhauer's work all his life was to be distinguished by an unmistakable, often almost physical, rootedness in lived thought and experience. As regards philosophy, he came to feel that the most important difference between academic philosophers and real ones was that the former encountered and acquired their philosophical problems conceptually, by study, and the latter existentially, by involuntary reflection on their own existence and experience. For the former, philosophy is entirely a verbal activity, a matter of reading and writing, of talking and listening: for the latter, the most important parts of it are rooted in non-verbal being and living, and have something profoundly in common with creative art. For the former, philosophy is an illuminating interest and an enjoyable, serious pursuit: for the latter it is inseparable from life itself, and may be a matter of life and death. The former might make good teachers, but only the latter are likely to make original contributors to the subject.

Without driving the point too hard, I think Schopenhauer's upbringing encouraged in him a tendency, which was no doubt there already, to reflect and learn by spontaneous response to his own experience rather than by imbibing the notions of others. Perhaps more significantly, in relation to the way his formative years were spent, this sense of existential involvement permeates his prose style, which is distinctly non-literary and non-academic, colloquial, concrete, idiomatic, direct, and much more remarkable for being these things in German than would be the case in English. He himself attributed its individual character to the fact that he had grown up more on French and English literature than on German. It manages to combine lucidity with musicality, sharp-edged precision with haunting metaphor, torrential energy with logical rigour. He has been regarded by many since his day as the greatest writer of modern German prose. Even in translation the quality of his writing is unmistakable. Above all, there is a man speaking: a whole man, a whole life, a whole way of seeing the world are embodied before us on those pages, in those sentences. No writer is more 'there', more with you, almost tangibly and audibly present when you read him.

A further connection between Schopenhauer's upbringing and his work lies in the fact that the only kind of writing he produced in any quantity apart from philosophy consists of what one might call — to use a treacherous term — worldly wisdom. There is no accepted label for it, but there is a mode of writing with which we associate such names as Montaigne, Vauvenargues, Rochefoucauld, Lichtenberg and Nietzsche, which may shock us or make us laugh — or both — but in any case liberates our perceptions by unmasking the difference between reality and what we like to think about it, especially with regard to ourselves. The literary forms employed are usually short — seldom longer than essays, often no more than maxims or aphorisms. One of the finest books of such aphorisms, *The Oracle* by Gracian, was translated from Spanish into German by Schopenhauer, who produced a good deal of such writing on his own account. I am in no doubt that what was already a natural bent for it was strengthened by his upbringing as a clear-eyed and precociously intelligent child in a world of worldly adults.

Intellectually, as in other ways, he was an early developer, but this was disguised at first by the scrappiness of his schooling, then later by his involvement with his father's firm. His doctorate thesis, written in his middle twenties and published with the title *On the Fourfold Root of the Principle of Sufficient Reason*, is a minor philosophical classic; and the first edition of his masterpiece, *The World as Will and Representation*, was completed while he was still in his twenties. Yet at the age of nineteen he still had no secure grasp of any academic subject apart from modern languages. This was in part because, when scarcely seventeen, he had given up schooling altogether and gone to work in his father's office. At that age he had sincerely intended to buckle down to a career like his father's; and even after Heinrich Floris's death, and the subsequent selling of the family's interest in the firm, he felt still bound by the promise he had made to work in it. For another year or more he did so. But his intellectual interests began to assert themselves: he played truant from the office to attend Gall's lectures on phrenology, and behind a smokescreen of busy-ness with office letters and ledgers he started to put his thoughts on paper. Increasingly, as he did so, he became depressed by the prospect of lifelong frustration to which he was beginning to feel he had committed himself. His letters to his mother became embittered. At this point, because his needs chimed so exactly with hers, she responded to him with sympathetic understanding. It was probably the only time she ever did. But it was decisive.

For Johanna Schopenhauer, Heinrich Floris's death had been a liberation which opened up a new and entirely unanticipated life. She found herself all at once with the freedom and the means to gratify social, literary and intellectual ambitions which had been frustrated for years by domesticity. She left her son in Hamburg and, with her daughter Adele — Arthur's only sibling, and eight years younger than he — moved her residence to Weimar, where there were more literary lions to be found than anywhere else in Germany. In scarcely any time at all she established herself as hostess of *the* salon. Goethe, the brothers Grimm, the brothers Schlegel, Wieland and others of international fame frequented her house. One of her poems was set to music by Schubert. Not content with all this, she embarked on a literary career which was eventually to bring her international fame as a romantic novelist (and was to have the incidental consequence that until he was well into middle age, and for years after he had published his greatest work, Arthur Schopenhauer was not uncommonly thought of and referred to as 'Johanna Schopenhauer's son' — a fact which, needless to say, incensed him). The transformation in her was astounding, not least in its speed, and was unmistakably triggered off by her husband's death. So when her son, in those letters of his from Hamburg, started to complain that the future was being crushed out of him by his obligations to his dead father, an unaccustomed empathy seems to have stirred in her. She consulted the celebrities of her Weimar salon about the boy's chances of being able to get back into the academic system at his age, after such a gap, and then make up the lost time. And on their advice she wrote to him with full encouragement and support for doing so.

For him the release was like an explosion. He threw up everything in Hamburg and rushed to Gotha, where he became a pupil at the Gymnasium and hurled himself almost ferociously into study. At once he began to make his mark. His writing in German had self-evident distinction from the beginning. His progress in Latin and Greek, which he took in private lessons, was so remarkable that his tutors began to predict a distinguished future for him as a classical scholar. After six months he moved to private lodgings in Weimar, where for two more years, under private tutors, he 'laboured day and night at Greek, Latin,

Mathematics and History, allowing nothing to divert his attention'.[1] Then in 1809, at the age of twenty-one, he matriculated into the University of Göttingen as a member of the medical faculty.

During his first year at University he continued his voracious reading, and attended lectures on Physics, Mineralogy, Natural History and Botany. In his second year he moved into the philosophy faculty and specialized in Plato and Kant, but also attended lectures on Physiology, Astronomy, Meteorology, Ethnography and Jurisprudence. This omnivorousness might arouse suspicions of superficiality, but suspicion is laid to rest by a study of his student notebooks, which survive. The passionate involvement is unmistakable: each subject is treated with application and concentration, and taken as far as one could reasonably expect it to be by a student of his age and situation. In no subject was he a passive learner: his notes on each are studded with his own observations, comments and criticisms, which are acute from the beginning, and become rapidly more original.

It was during these two years that his vocation became clear to him. As he remarked not long afterwards to the elderly Wieland: 'Life is a wretched business. I've decided to spend it trying to understand it.' He remained a passionate student for the rest of his life, chiefly of philosophy, but to an important degree of the sciences too, and also of literature in seven languages — Latin, Greek, French, English, German, Italian and Spanish. (I have browsed through his library in the Schopenhauer archive in Frankfurt and found that it was his custom to make marginal notes, often extensive, in the same language as the book he was reading. These notes, unfailingly penetrating, are sometimes written with such vehemence that the pencil has almost pierced the paper.) His great leisure pursuits were music, the theatre, walking and conversation. To one or other of these activities, along with his writings, it can almost be said that he devoted not merely every day of a long adult life but every hour of every day. Though never really an academic in the professional sense once his student days were over, he became arguably the most erudite of the great philosophers. Not having to teach or earn his living, he studied only what he felt prompted to in following his own bent, and as a result his massive erudition, far from overlaying his personality, was an authentic expression and extension of it. He was not just at ease with it, he was at one with it, and this helps to explain the pungent sense of personality conveyed by his writings.

At the time when Schopenhauer found his vocation the philosopher of the hour in Germany was Fichte, who was teaching at the University of Berlin. So in 1811 Schopenhauer changed universities and went to

---

[1] Helen Zimmern, *Arthur Schopenhauer: His Life and His Philosophy*, p. 32.

Berlin. His gargantuan appetite for work grew even larger, and while studying philosophy he continued to steep himself in the physical and biological sciences. From the beginning he went to Fichte's lectures, and in his second year he attended Schleiermacher's too. With Fichte, at least, he became deeply disillusioned. Confronted by the man himself, he developed towards him the same attitude as he was later to extend to Hegel — and, in lesser degree, Schelling — namely, that this man was not impersonally devoted to philosophy but was exploiting it to make a mark, and that his mode of utterance was calculatedly oracular both in order to impress and in order to conceal the banality of such little thought in it as there was. The student Schopenhauer conducted a mountingly angry dialogue with the lecturer in his notebooks, in the course of which he began to formulate increasingly important ideas of his own. (Perhaps that was why he went on going to the lectures.) His rejection of Schleiermacher was less contemptuous but still sweeping — perhaps the chief point here is summed up in his note: 'No one who is religious gets as far as philosophy; he does not need it.' But he did admire, and in later life often quoted, Schleiermacher's remark that the only thing any student gets to know at university is what it is he is going to have to learn afterwards.

After completing his second year at Berlin, and thus his fourth at university, Schopenhauer took himself off to a quiet country spot to work on a doctorate thesis. Most of the year 1813 was spent by him in an inn in Rudolstadt in the Thüringian forest. The thesis he wrote there was submitted to the University of Jena, which duly made him a Doctor of Philosophy. He paid to have it published in volume form and took it with him to Weimar, where he presented a copy to his mother. She accepted it with the comment that a book called *The Fourfold Root* of something must presumably be intended for apothecaries. He observed hotly that his book would still be available when all the rubbish she was publishing had been forgotten. She agreed with him, saying sweetly that the entire first printing of his book would, indeed, still be available.

The relationship between Schopenhauer and his mother is of great significance for one particular effect it had on his work. To us in the twentieth century it appears an obvious and extreme example of what is now termed 'maternal deprivation'. Johanna Schopenhauer was one of those brittle, socially oriented personalities who are almost totally devoid of true feeling. Writing, in his *Memoirs* published in 1852, of her as she was in 1815, Anselm von Feuerbach described her as 'without heart and soul' — a judgement specifically endorsed by the elderly Schopenhauer. Of her marriage to her husband she herself wrote: 'I as little feigned ardent love for him as he demanded it of me.' It was into an unusually loveless domestic atmosphere that Schopenhauer was

born. What is worse, those decisive early years were spent mostly alone
with his mother on the family's remote estate at the eastern limit of
Danzig's territory while his father stayed in the city for most of the
week. We know from Arthur himself that the happiest years of his
childhood were those spent away from his mother. Never, at any age,
was he able to get on with her, and after his father's death 'the bitter
antipathy between him and his mother, which on Schopenhauer's side
seems to have had some profound psychological origin in deprivation
or fear, only grew more extreme, expressing itself in violent disagree-
ments and quarrels'.[2] She rejected him in a manner which was both
direct and brutal. When he was about to leave the Gymnasium in
Gotha to continue his studies in Weimar, where she was by this time
living, she wrote to him: 'It is needful to my happiness to know that you
are happy, but not to be a witness of it. I have always told you it is
difficult to live with you; and the better I get to know you, the more I
feel this difficulty increase, at least for me. I will not hide it from you: as
long as you are what you are, I would rather make any sacrifice than
consent to live with you.' It was in consequence of this letter that he
moved into lodgings in Weimar instead of into her house.

But — to begin with, anyway — he visited her frequently, and
attended her salons, where he met many famous people. It was now
that he really got to know Goethe well, though they had met before —
at a previous meeting Goethe had remarked of him: 'Eventually he'll
out-top us all.' But relations remained bad between Schopenhauer and
his mother. In 1813 he tried moving back under her roof for what was
intended as only a short stay, but it was a disastrous step, and it ended
in a break which was final: she threw him out altogether in the spring of
1814, and they never saw each other again during the remaining
twenty-four years of her life.

For someone of Schopenhauer's force of temperament to have, as his
very first experience of life, total dependence on a human being so
violently rejecting — or, at the least, for the first object of those volcanic
emotions to have been so glacially indifferent and unresponsive — was
evidently a traumatic experience for him in the literal sense of that
term. According to today's textbooks of child psychology, maternal
rejection is likely to result in a neurotic distrust of people in general
which has three common consequences: first, a lowered if not depressed
view of the world, and of the kind of behaviour to be expected from the
people in it; second, a cut-offness from people, an inability to form and
maintain close relationships with anyone; third, a neurotic sense of
personal insecurity, whether in the form of anxiety attacks, or phobias,

---

[2] Patrick Gardiner, *Schopenhauer*, p. 13.

or hypochondria, or a permanent conviction that catastrophe is imminent. Every one of these afflictions was suffered by Schopenhauer in extreme degree. His first English biographer,[3] writing many years before Freud, says of him: 'He was naturally nervous. Whenever the postman brought a letter he would start at the thought of possible evil. He confessed, "If I have nothing that alarms me I grow alarmed at this very condition, as if there must still be something of which I am only ignorant for a time. 'Misera conditio nostra' ". At the outbreak of the wars of liberation he was pursued with the fear of being forced to serve. He was easily angered, suspicious and irritable. "It's safer trusting fear than faith", was one of his favourite quotations. As a child of six he had once persuaded himself that he was abandoned by his parents, and was found in a passion of tears on their return from a long walk. The slightest noise at night made him start and seize the pistols that always lay ready loaded. He would never trust himself under the razor of a barber, and he fled from the mere mention of an infectious disease. He carried a little leathern drinking-cup about with him if he dined in a public place, to avoid possible contagion, and his pipes and cigar [holders] were carefully locked away after use lest another person should touch them. Accounts or any notes regarding his property were never entrusted to the German language; his expenses were written in English, his business affairs in Greek or Latin. His valuables were hidden in the strangest places, he even labelled them with deceptive names to avert the suspicion of thieves, thus, his [share] coupons as "Arcana medica". He hid bonds among old letters, and gold under his inkstand. This inborn nervousness caused him much torture, and was bitterly regretted, but appears to have been quite unconquerable . . . Periods of blind terror would seize him at various times during his life, and then nothing would do but to submit. Thus he fled from Naples when the small-pox broke out there, and thus at Verona was he haunted by the idea that he had imbibed poisoned snuff. As a youth he was pursued by the fear of lawsuits; for years he dreaded a criminal prosecution about the housekeeper business;[4] while a student he had

---

[3] Helen Zimmern's *Arthur Schopenhauer: His Life and His Philosophy* was published in 1876, only sixteen years after its subject's death. The first passage quoted here comes from pp. 89–90, the second from pp. 147–8.

[4] [In the lodgings where Schopenhauer was staying in Berlin in 1821 the servant women working in the house were in the habit of congregating in the semi-private little hallway outside his rooms and holding conversations there. He complained, but they persisted. No doubt this was a genuine nuisance to someone doing his kind of work, but over and above that he had a nervous aversion to noise and was apt to lose control of his temper when subjected to it. One day he asked a group of three chattering women to remove themselves. Two did, but the third refused. He became threatening. She obstinately refused to budge. He started pushing her, and a tussle ensued which ended

imagined himself consumptive. These panics, heightened by a lively imagination, made such periodical attacks of horror a burden to him.'

In the light of present-day knowledge there can be little doubt that Schopenhauer's despairing view of the world, above all his conviction of the terribleness of existence *as such*, were in some degree neurotic manifestations which had their roots in his relationship with his mother. Neither here nor elsewhere in this volume do I propose to attempt an analysis of this: I am not qualified to do it, and in any case the right place for it would be a biography, which this book is not. What I am concerned with are Schopenhauer's ideas, and like all ideas they are logically independent of the psychological processes by which they were arrived at. Nevertheless there is a point to be made here which is fundamental to what I have to say later. In most people's minds the indentifying feature of Schopenhauer's thought has always been its pessimism. Indeed, his name is more closely associated with pessimism than any other writer's. Even professional philosophers tend to see him in this light, as is evidenced by the title of Frederick Copleston's book *Arthur Schopenhauer: Philosopher of Pessimism*. Yet this is odd, because it is an elementary point in logic that no truth claim can entail a value-judgement. If a valid argument has a value-judgement anywhere in its conclusions this can mean only that the same value-judgement was already to be found somewhere in the premises: you cannot derive an 'is bad' from an 'is'. No general philosophy — no ontology, epistemo-logy or logic — can entail pessimistic conclusions. Professional philo-sophers ought always to have known, without having to read Schopenhauer to discover it, that in this sense his pessimism is logically independent of his philosophy; and so it is. It is true that he was a pessimist, no one more so. And it is true that his pessimism is com-patible with his philosophy — but that is only because the two are, of necessity, logically unconnected. Non-pessimism is equally compatible with his philosophy. The traditional identification of him in terms of his pessimism is largely irrelevant to a serious consideration of him as a philosopher: I am tempted to say that it is a view of his writings which leaves his philosophy out. The point is so rudimentary that it is hard to see how it can have been so widely overlooked. Perhaps it happened because the pessimism is so all-pervading in the way the philosophy is articulated — in the prose, the metaphors, the illustrations, the ref-erences, the selection of quotations — all this combined with the

with his throwing her down the stairs. She took him to court. He fought the case, and kept it going for nearly five years. In the end he was ordered to compensate her for her injuries by paying her 60 thalers a year for the rest of her life — which turned out to last a further 26 years. When finally she died, and he was sent a copy of her death certificate, he scrawled across it *Obit anus, abit onus*. ('The old woman dies: the burden is lifted').—B.M.]

extraordinary vividness of the writing and the dramatic force of the vision it conveys.

I remember as a child having the difference between optimism and pessimism explained to me in a way that illustrates perfectly their separability from fact and their inseparability from vision. Two men who are drinking together shoot simultaneous glances at the bottle they are sharing, and one thinks to himself: 'Ah good, it's still half full' while at the same moment the other thinks: 'Oh dear, it's half empty already.' The point is, of course, that they would have no argument about how much wine there is in the bottle, or about the accuracy of any measurement, photograph or drawing, and yet the same fact is being not only seen but responded to in two all-pervadingly different ways. This all-pervadingness makes the whole world of the optimist different from that of the pessimist, and our two men would describe differently almost everything that there is — in significantly different language, that is to say, albeit with the same factual content. (This is the import of Wittgenstein's 'The world of the happy man is a different one from that of the unhappy man'.)[5]

I would not so labour this point about the independence of philosophical argument from optimism or pessimism if it were not for the fact that most of what has been written about Schopenhauer has been vitiated by a disregard of it. His whole philosophy is expressed in a vocabulary of pessimism, yet all of it except for some of those parts that deal with ethics and aesthetics could be formulated with equal accuracy in a vocabulary of optimism, or in a vocabulary agnostic as between the two. Some of it would be untenable however it were formulated, but much of it is of great profundity and insight, and appreciation of this should not be overlaid — as more often than not in recent decades it has been — by responses relevant only to the pessimism-saturated terms in which he writes.

During the period of Schopenhauer's final stay with his mother, the winter of 1813–1814, he came in contact with two people who were to have a formative effect on his life. One was Friedrich Majer, the orientalist, who introduced him to Hinduism and Buddhism. It was not before the early nineteenth century that German translations of the classic texts of these religions began to appear in any number, opening up what seemed to most people a wholly new world of thought. The book with which Schopenhauer fell in love was a Latin translation of a Persian translation of the Upanishads, which he referred to always as *the Oupnekhat*. Perhaps he was, as has been claimed,[6] the first German

[5] *Tractatus Logico-Philosophicus*, 6. 43.

[6] e.g. by Dorothea W. Dauer in *Schopenhauer as Transmitter of Buddhist Ideas* (European University Papers, Bd./vol. 15, Berne 1969)

who thoroughly understood the Upanishads. Certainly his insight into them, despite the double barrier of translations, was profound. For most of his life he read a few pages of the Oupnekhat every night before going to sleep. Of it he wrote: 'With the exception of the original text, it is the most profitable and sublime reading that is possible in the world; it has been the consolation of my life and will be that of my death.'[7]

To this day Schopenhauer remains the only great Western philosopher to have been genuinely well versed in Eastern thought and to have related it to his own work. However, the nature of the relationship has been commonly misunderstood: his philosophy is often said to have been *influenced* by Eastern thought, and that is not correct in the sense in which it is usually meant. He did not begin to make the acquaintance of Eastern thought until the end of 1813, when he met Majer, and by this time *The Fourfold Root of the Principle of Sufficient Reason* had been written and published. As he was later to write (in a marginal note dated 1849): '. . . already in 1814 (my twenty-seventh year) all the dogmas of my system, even the subordinate ones, were established.' And this is true, as can be verified from the notebooks. What happened is that, working entirely within the central tradition of Western philosophy — before all else continuing and completing, as he believed, the work of Kant — he arrived at positions which *he then almost immediately discovered* were similar to some of the doctrines central to Hinduism and Buddhism. The discovery came to him as a revelation, and throughout his subsequent writings he made play with the parallels. But the relationship is not one of influence. Indeed, in his mind the most important point lay in the fact that there was no influence: the profoundest thinkers of East and West, working unknown to each other in virtually unrelated traditions and languages — evolved quite separately over huge stretches of time, indeed in different historical epochs and completely different kinds of society — had been led to the same fundamental conclusions about the nature of the world.

Another relationship at this time which was to matter to Schopenhauer for the rest of his life was with Goethe. He had known Goethe for some while, but it was only during this period that the two of them became friends. Goethe had recently, in 1810, published his three-volume work *The Theory of Colour*, which he was inclined to regard as the greatest of all his achievements, and he had since then been struck by the similarity to his own ideas of some of Schopenhauer's in *The Fourfold Root of the Principle of Sufficient Reason*. He now tried to engage the young man's interest in his optical theories. He invited Schopenhauer

[7] *Parerga and Paralipomena*, ii. 397.

to his house, where they spent long evenings in discussion together, during which Goethe demonstrated his experiments. The older man also lent the younger his apparatus to repeat the experiments on his own. 'Goethe educated me anew', Schopenhauer was to write later. From many such declarations we know that the influence of Goethe on Schopenhauer was very great — and yet, as is so often the case with influence, it is not easy to say precisely what it consisted in, apart from the theory of colour and perhaps some encouragement of a prose style whose frame of reference was life itself and not chiefly the world of books. I suspect that the truth is something of the following kind. Schopenhauer was to come to regard himself, if he did not already, as one of the outstanding figures in the history of mankind; and in the whole of his life the only other such person he got to know really well was Goethe. Some years later he wrote in his notebook: 'I have lifted the veil of truth higher than any mortal before me. But I should like to see the man who could boast of a more miserable set of contemporaries than mine.' A Gulliver condemned to live out the whole of his life in Lilliput, and in the course of it to meet only one other human being, might well have felt in relation to him the same complicated and intense feelings of empathy, gratitude and a powerfully reinforced sense of his own identity as I think Schopenhauer felt in relation to Goethe. Goethe, on the other hand, was sixty-four, and, in addition to having lived through his famous friendship with Schiller, had met the greatest figures of the age, from Beethoven and Napoleon downwards, so he could scarcely have been expected to feel in the same way about the twenty-five-year-old Schopenhauer — though he certainly saw potential greatness in him, and talked of it to others. The point is that Schopenhauer was enjoying the only close relationship with an equal he was ever to experience; and it was understandable, therefore, that a sense of special community with Goethe should have stayed with him for the rest of his life. His tendency, decades after Goethe's death, to refer to him as if he were a friend with whom he had been in conversation only a few hours previously is based on this sense, and is not at all calculated: it is not mere pride in the acquaintance, and it is certainly not name-dropping. In any case Schopenhauer was perfectly clear-sighted about Goethe's failings. 'It is foolish to lose inwardly for the sake of outward gain, i.e. to give up entirely, or in great part, leisure and independence, for the sake of splendour, position, show, titles, and honour. This is what Goethe did. My genius has drawn me strenuously in the other direction.' Indeed, each saw the other's decisive flaw quite plainly. When Schopenhauer left Weimar in the spring of 1814 to take up residence in Dresden, Goethe composed this couplet for him:

Willst du dich des Lebens freuen,
So musst der Welt du Werth verleihen.[8]

The first thing Schopenhauer wrote in Dresden was a pamphlet *On Vision and Colours*. Goethe received it with mixed feelings: Schopenhauer, though remaining a disciple, was venturing to develop ideas of his own on the same subject, and to criticize his master in print. From then on they began to drift apart. Goethe's later account of this was: 'We dealt with many things in mutual agreement, but at last a certain division became inevitable, as when two friends who have hitherto gone together say goodbye — the one, however, wanting to go north, the other south, so that they very speedily lose sight of each other.'

Schopenhauer remained in Dresden for the four years 1814–1818, and it was there and then that he wrote *The World as Will and Representation*. His notebooks describe its creation in these terms: 'The work grows, takes substance gradually and slowly, like the child in the womb. I do not know what originated first, what last. I discern one member, one vessel, one part after another; that is to say, I write them down without troubling myself about the unity of the whole, for I know that all has sprung from one source. Thus arises an organic whole . . .' He did not go into seclusion to write the book, but spent his evenings with friends, either in talk or at the theatre. Sometimes during the day he would visit an art gallery, or make a trip into the beautiful country-side around Dresden. He also, as he did throughout the prime of his life, had affairs with women. It was not until much later that he became the misanthropic and misogynistic recluse that he is now generally thought of as having been. There is an important discrepancy here between posterity's image of him and the man who actually wrote the book for which he is famous. The familiar portraits of him — in the English-speaking world they are those in the standard reference books, and on the covers of his main work — show him as a mustily dressed, grim-faced old man with a bald dome and shocks of white hair sprouting at the sides, his skin dry and his mouth a sunken, lipless line. And naturally we think of his philosophy as having been produced by this man. But such is not the case. His masterpiece was the product of his late twenties, and the only portrait we have of him from that period of his life tells not just a different but an opposite story. It is the portrait of

---

[8] 'If you want to get pleasure out of life you must attach value to the world.' Goethe inscribed these lines in Schopenhauer's album. Beside them in the margin Schopenhauer set a quotation from Chamfort: '*Il vaut mieux laisser les hommes pour ce qu' ils sont, que les prendre pour ce qu'ils ne sont pas.*' ('Better to leave men for what they are than take them for what they are not') — adding as his own comment: '*Rien de si riche qu'un grand soi-même*' ('No wealth can equal the possession of greatness in oneself').

a sensually good-looking, intelligent, highly sensitive young man. The most striking feature is the mouth, almost voluptuous in its fullness and redness, the lips thick and deeply curved. (The later change of shape was due to nothing other than the mundane fact that he lost his teeth.) This young man is expensively and fashionably dressed. His complexion is fresh; his high forehead is framed in tight curls of dark hair; and the slight protuberance of his eyes gives to his whole face a look of alertness that borders perhaps on the anxious but certainly on the vulnerable. Somehow, in the portrait, a sense is conveyed of pent-up drive, of energy straining beneath the surface.

As regards his personal appearance and character, a general resemblance which it became commonplace to draw in the late nineteenth century, when the renown of both as culture-heroes was at its height, was between Schopenhauer and Beethoven — though again this was based on portraits of the philosopher when he was older. Born only eight years apart, both men were North Germans of Flemish or Dutch descent, and physically they were strikingly similar in middle life. (Visitors to my study who see the materials for this book lying around quite often mistake Schopenhauer's portrait for Beethoven's.) Each was of barely medium height, stocky and muscular, with a huge head and short neck set in bull shoulders. Both were bustlingly energetic and alarmingly vehement, irascible, truculent, suspicious. Both were marked out above all by (apart from genius) a disconcerting independence and forcefulness of personality which was accompanied by a propensity to declare home truths roundly regardless of circumstances, fashion or persons. Both were profoundly musical yet deaf from early manhood. (Schopenhauer's deafness was less extreme than Beethoven's, but always troublesome.) Both had a powerful heterosexual drive yet never married: they lived as solitaries, subsisting on a thin and intermittent sexual diet of shallow, casual relationships, probably with recourse to prostitutes in their younger days and servant girls later. Both longed for acceptance and love, yet fiercely drove everyone away from them, persistently living in a self-created isolation which they bitterly resented and for which they misanthropically blamed mankind.

These points of resemblance are indeed striking. But the differences are striking too. To take the most superficial first, Beethoven was slovenly in dress, boorish in manner and squalid in his personal and domestic habits, whereas Schopenhauer was conspicuously the opposite in all three respects. Beethoven's daily life was chaotic, Schopenhauer's obsessionally ordered. Beethoven knew little about anything but music: Schopenhauer was a polymath. Beethoven was humourless, albeit with something like the humourlessness of the saint:

Schopenhauer was blisteringly funny. Verbally, Beethoven was not very adept at all, and not merely because he was a great composer — Rossini was renowned for his wit, and Wagner for his torrential loquacity — whereas Schopenhauer was an artist with words. Beethoven believed in God, Schopenhauer did not. Beethoven embraced the proclaimed political values of the French Revolution: Schopenhauer was a counter-revolutionary, reactionary in the strict sense of that word — once, on the occasion of a political riot, he invited the soldiery into his home to shoot at the mob from the vantage point of his windows; and when he died he left his money to a fund for the maintenance of soldiers disabled in the suppression of the 1848 revolution, and for the widows and orphans of those killed. Beethoven's work grew artistically more radical the older he became: Schopenhauer devoted the whole of his adult life to working out the consequences of the system he had produced in his twenties. In sum, although both men were prodigies of energy and endowment, and certainly had a great many things in common, the similarities mislead if pursued too relentlessly.

Whereas Beethoven poured out a lifelong spate of independent masterpieces, Schopenhauer produced only one such work, *The World as Will and Representation*. It was published in December 1818 (with the date 1819 on the title-page, hence the common but mistaken ascription of it to the latter year). It contained four parts which set forth in succession the author's epistemology, ontology, aesthetics, and what might be dubbed his metaphysics of the person, by which I mean a realm of thought embracing not only ethics but all considerations of the self and human character and behaviour, including sex, death, and the vanity of life. These four books were followed by a long appendix (which is logically the starting-point of the work) containing Schopenhauer's critique of Kant. Like a number of other great philosophers,[9] he was convinced that in his masterpiece he had finally solved the fundamental problems of philosophy — indeed, as he put it: 'Subject to the limitation of human knowledge, my philosophy is the real solution of the enigma of the world.' He retained this opinion for the remaining forty-two years of his life.

As soon as he had sent his manuscript to the publisher he left for Italy in the quiet conviction that he had secured immortality. But when December came and the book appeared it went very nearly unsold, unreviewed and unread. Nearly seventeen years later, when, 'in 1835, he made enquiries concerning the sale of the book he was informed that there was no sale — a somewhat exasperating thought to a man who

[9] e.g. Wittgenstein in his Preface to *Tractatus Logico-Philosophicus*: '. . . the *truth* of the thoughts that are here set forth seems to me unassailable and definitive. I therefore believe myself to have found, on all essential points, the final solution of the problems.'

believed that he had unveiled the mystery of the world'.[10] This neglect continued until his old age, and was thus the dominating feature of his experience of life. It needs to be considered along with maternal rejection in explaining his profound misanthropy and pessimism. It placed him, more than it would have done most other philosophers, in an impossible situation, for if you are convinced that you have solved the riddle of life, and your achievement is then not noticed sufficiently even to be disputed, what are you to do next? The task is not one which there is any sense in, or even possibility of, repeating, and there could be no other task of comparable worthwhileness to move on to. In the event, he published nothing at all for seventeen years after the first edition of *The World as Will and Representation*. And during that period he had to suffer the superimposition of insult on injury by watching an older contemporary whom he regarded as a charlatan and a betrayer of the Kantian inheritance — Hegel — elevated to the position which he regarded as rightfully his own. It was insupportable. He became more and more frustrated and enraged by his situation, more and more contemptuous of the stupidity of mankind, more withdrawn, more isolated, as the years went by.

At first he thought he would counteract the neglect of his book by becoming a university teacher and propagating his ideas through lectures, with the advantage of having a young and receptive audience. So, after two years in Italy, he went to teach at the University of Berlin, where Hegel and Schleiermacher were now at the height of their celebrity. He chose, deliberately, to give his lectures at the same time as Hegel's. The result was disastrous. Nobody came — with the result that he was unable to deliver the lectures at all. He abandoned the course, and with it his career as a university teacher.

For two years more he stayed on in Berlin in the hope of somehow or other being able to draw attention to his ideas; but he failed, and, not surprisingly, grew to hate the place. So in 1822 he returned to Italy. For the next three years he lived a peripatetic life — after Italy he stayed for a time in Switzerland, then in various towns in Germany, including a year in Munich, where he seems to have been both isolated and ill. (Because of his solitariness, and his abstention from writing, the documentation for this period of his life is sparse.) In 1825 he returned to Berlin, and put his name on the lecture list once more — though without, this time, making any attempt to give the lectures.

The six years of residence in Berlin which then followed were in some ways the nadir of his life. In terms of his age they were the years from thirty-seven to forty-three, commonly in men a period of mid-life crisis.

---

[10] Frederick Copleston: *Arthur Schopenhauer: Philosopher of Pessimism*, p. 31.

The neglect of his work was total, his youth was over, he was rootless and lonely, and, quite simply, he did not know what to do. He read, as always, hungrily, but was still at a loss what to write. This being so, his thoughts reverted more and more to the idea of translating the works of his most important precursors. He had already abandoned a project for translating Hume into German (he had written the preface to the translation but not the translation itself). Now he conceived the idea of translating Kant into English. The dark night in which British philosophy lay invisible had been brought on, he believed, by Britain's persisting ignorance of Kant. Of his own unique qualifications for dispelling this darkness he wrote to an English publisher, in self-recommendation for the task: 'A century may pass ere there shall again meet in the same head so much Kantian philosophy with so much English as happen to dwell together in mine.' But the publisher had himself in mind for the job, so what would have been one of the most remarkable books in the English language never came into being. The only book-length translation Schopenhauer completed was that from Spanish into German of Gracian's *The Oracle*, and this was found among his papers only after his death, and was published posthumously.

In 1831 Berlin was hit by a cholera epidemic. Among those killed in it was Hegel. Schopenhauer fled to Frankfurt, where he sank into what was evidently a depression in the clinical sense of the term: for several weeks he could not be got to speak to anyone at all. His doctor seems virtually to have commanded him to change his surroundings, so he moved to the neighbouring town of Mannheim, and spent a whole year there. But in June 1833, at the age of forty-five, he moved back to Frankfurt, and remained in Frankfurt for the rest of his life. He died there of a heart attack in 1860 at the age of seventy-two. Among his posthumous papers was found an account book dating from the Mannheim year on whose cover he had listed, in English, the pros and cons as between Mannheim and Frankfurt as places to settle in permanently. Mannheim scored with superior intellectual and artistic circles, 'a better foreign bookseller' and 'a better table'. But against that Frankfurt offered 'better plays, operas, concerts', 'more Englishmen', 'an able dentist, and less bad physicians', and, perhaps decisive for a depressive, 'the gaiety of the place, and everything about it'.

Once settled permanently in Frankfurt he began, at last, to write for publication once more. Because he was a deeply reflective man a problem had been solved for him by the mere passage of time: he had acquired worthwhile things to say about his earlier work which neither repeated nor repudiated it but reinforced and enriched it. The first new book to come from his pen was intended to show that the central thesis of *The World as Will and Representation* had been confirmed by developments in the natural sciences. This was *On the Will in Nature*, published in 1836, a book which he described as 'small in volume but rich and weighty in content'.[11] In 1839 he was awarded a prize by the Scientific Society of Trondheim, Norway, for a long essay on *The Freedom of the Will*; and a year or two later he was refused a prize (despite the fact that his was the only entry) by the Royal Danish Academy of the Sciences for an even longer essay on *The Foundations of Morality*. In 1841 he published these two essays together in a single volume under the title *The Two Fundamental Problems of Ethics*.

All these works were supplements to *The World as Will and Representation*, and Schopenhauer explicitly said so[12] — *On the Will in Nature* was supplementary to part two, the other two essays to part four. He then prepared a second edition of the original book, and this was published in 1844. Even leaving the separately published essays aside, the amount of new matter to be incorporated exceeded the entire length of the first edition. Instead of revising the book throughout into something differing all the way through from its original self he hit on a simple, brilliant alternative: he republished the first edition almost without alteration (except for the appendix on Kant) as Volume One of a two-volume work, and accompanied this with a larger Volume Two in the form of a section-by-section and chapter-by-chapter commentary on Volume One. These two volumes, each with a different, highly distinctive structure and tone of voice, create through their identity of subject-matter a new and greater whole within which the original work retains its discernible lineaments. In sending this revised version to the publisher Schopenhauer wrote: 'This second volume has important advantages over the former one, and stands in relation to it as the finished picture to the mere sketch. For it has the thoroughness and riches of thought and knowledge which can only be the fruit of a whole life spent in constant study and meditation. At any rate it is the best thing I have ever written. Even the first volume will only now declare its real significance.' All editions of the work that have been published since have retained this form: a large volume accompanied by a somewhat larger commentary on itself. Schopenhauer issued a third edition

---

[11] *The Fourfold Root of the Principle of Sufficient Reason*, p. 62. What is now the standard edition of *The Fourfold Root* is a revised one published in 1847 — hence the reference to a book published in 1836, well after *The Fourfold Root* had originally appeared. In his Preface to this revised edition of his first book Schopenhauer writes: 'Many a reader will get the impression that he is listening to an old man reading a young man's book which is frequently put down so that the old man may indulge in his own digressions on the subject.'

[12] *The World as Will and Representation*, ii. 191 and 461.

in 1859, the year before his death, which contained 136 pages of additional material, but it kept to the framework established by the second edition. Editions published after his death either reproduce the third edition or, preferably, incorporate into it all or some of the notes made by Schopenhauer in the last year of his life in preparation for a fourth edition.

He published only one book apart from those already mentioned. The 1840s were a period of fecundity for him, and in addition to all the new material contained in the second edition of *The World as Will and Representation* he poured out a spate of separate notes and essays. The range of topics was almost as wide as life itself, yet, even so, most of this writing stood in a clearly discernible relationship to his central philosophy. In an ideal, unconfined edition of *The World as Will and Representation* it would all have been included.[13] As things were, he gathered it together and published it in 1851 in two large volumes, with a title which has no doubt done a great deal to reduce the number of its readers: *Parerga and Paralipomena*.[14] These two words are from Greek: *parerga* is the plural of *parergon*, which means something subordinate to the main task, an ancillary part of the business; *paralipomena*, also a plural noun, comes from the Greek for 'to omit', and applies to things left out of the main body of a work. The main work referred to by both words is, of course, *The World as Will and Representation*.

As is thoroughly clear by now, Schopenhauer was a one-book writer in the sense that everything else he wrote is a preparation for, or reflection on, or enrichment of, or pendant to, *The World as Will and Representation*. He never saw reason to abandon any important aspect of the view of reality which he formed in his twenties and expounded in the first edition of that book. Later writings have, at their best, a greater richness, maturity and depth, qualities of insight and wisdom altogether unavailable to the younger man, but they constitute always an extension of his early vision, never a shift of it. In consequence, the work of his whole life is unitary in a way that makes it best understood — understandable only, indeed — as a single, organic whole. That is how he saw it himself, and how he wanted it to be seen; and that is how I have approached it in this book. It is perversely unfortunate that Schopenhauer — more than any other philosopher, because of the pointed brilliance of his writing — has had the living body of his work

---

[13] Preface to the Third Edition, *The World as Will and Representation*.

[14] I do not think it is too far fetched to say that Schopenhauer's choice of titles has been a contributory factor in the neglect of his work. *On the Fourfold Root of the Principle of Sufficient Reason* is almost as unenticing as *Parerga and Paralipomena*. And the title of *The World as Will and Representation* has led to perpetual misunderstandings about its contents.

butchered for aphorisms and epigrams, juicy extracts and dramatic quotations torn out of context, and these bleeding chunks wrapped in paper and served to the public as if they were books by him.

As my outline of it shows, Schopenhauer's adult life falls into two clearly contrasted halves. The first, up to the age of forty-five, was spent perpetually on the move, much of the travel being undertaken for its own sake, and the last seventeen years of this period producing no writing for publication. The second, from the age of forty-five to his death at seventy-two, was spent unbudgingly in Frankfurt, writing every day, and producing as a result most of his published work. This half was spent in two simply furnished rooms overlooking the river Main. His daily routine was an adaptation of Kant's to his own needs. He would get up between seven and eight o'clock in the morning, take a cold bath followed by a cup of coffee, and then sit down and write until noon, at which time he would finish writing for the day. He then relaxed for half an hour by playing the flute, after which he would dress in tailcoat and white tie and go out to lunch. He always wore clothes of the same style and cut, of the kind that had been high fashion in his youth, and always ate at the same place, a hotel called the Englischer Hof. After lunch he would return to his rooms and read until four. Then, regardless of the weather, he would go out for a two-hour walk. His route would bring him to the doors of the library at six, and he would go into the reading-room and read *The Times*. Almost every evening he would go on to either a theatre or a concert. After that he would eat a light, cold supper at the Englischer Hof. If the company was rewarding (in those days table d'hôte meant what it said: the guests all sat at a large table, and there was general conversation) he was prepared to stay up talking late into the night; but usually he would go home between nine and ten. In bed he would read a few pages of the Oupnekhat before going to sleep.

He was, by all accounts, a prodigious conversationalist — zestful, wide-ranging, well-informed and witty. His reputation for this spread, and strangers would come and eat at the Englischer Hof just to see him and listen to him talk. The first impression such visitors would get of him — with his patrician manners and expensive, old-fashioned dress, his obvious enjoyment of the food and wine, his stimulating talk nourished by a daily reading of the foreign Press and nightly theatre-going, his reactionary social views expressed with self-confident, biting wit — was of a brilliant man of the world of the old school holding court in the grand manner and keeping the company entertained in percep-tive, forceful and amusing style. He would, of course, have been at much his most animated at the Englischer Hof, for this was his chief — at some periods his only — contact with other human beings.

At first sight there seems to have been a lifelong disparity between the content of what Schopenhauer said, particularly on paper, and the way he said it. The content was so often negative — corrosive, sarcastic, derisive, pessimistic, sometimes almost despairing — yet the manner was always positive, indeed exhilarating. Its gusto and verve both express and impart a *joie de vivre* which is almost gargantuan. These differences are reflected in his responses to his own work. While writing *The World as Will and Representation* he noted: 'The outcome of this knowledge is sad and depressing, but the *state* of knowing, the acquisition of insight, the penetration of truth, are thoroughly pleasurable — and, strange to say, add a mixture of sweetness to my bitterness.' Any lover of wisdom, however dark or painfully acquired, will understand this. But another part of the underlying explanation is, I believe, psycho-dynamic. Schopenhauer's behaviour pattern was one which is now familiar to psychiatrists: the solitary who responds to others with unusual intensity and animation, and is sparkling in general company; who eats all his meals out, finding a special solace in food and drink; who goes almost nightly to some public entertainment; who, in short, is always stimulating and yet always himself undergoing stimulation. It is the flight from depression of the self-isolated.

In the sunset of his life he had the pleasure, for him exquisite, of witnessing the dawn of his fame. It began only a couple of years after he had completed his life's work, that is to say after he had published what was intended to be, and was, his final book. On this latter point, it is important to realize that he was a totally fulfilled man as regards the content and quality of his work: the world's refusal to take any notice of it for most of his life embittered him, but the work itself was everything he wanted it to be, and he had a profound sense of accomplishment. With the completion of *Parerga and Paralipomena* he wrote: 'I will wipe my pen and say "the rest is silence".' After it was published he wrote: 'I am deeply glad to see the birth of my last child, which completes my mission in this world. I really feel as if a load, that I have borne since my twenty-fourth year, and that has weighed heavily upon me, had been lifted from my shoulders. No one can imagine what that means.' In this connection the point needs be made that there was one very important sense in which he was not a pessimist, and did not believe in the ultimate cruelty or indifference of the world, nor in the ultimate dishonesty and wickedness of mankind: his faith that truth would always prevail in the end was total and invariant throughout his life, and so therefore was his confidence that nothing could stop his philosophy from coming into its own in the end, if only after his death. His pessimism, if held consistently, would have made such a faith impossible.

The first light of his reputation broke in England — not unfittingly, since in his view her people 'surpass all others in intelligence'.[15] In April 1853, in one of only ten issues of the *Westminster Review* to be edited by George Eliot, there appeared an unsigned article with the title *Iconoclasm in German Philosophy*. It dealt solely with Schopenhauer, but in a way that made it clear that the anonymous author[16] was interested in his philosophy not primarily for its own sake but as a stick with which to beat the Hegelians — the very title reflects this. However, far from offending Schopenhauer this delighted him. He seems either not to have perceived or not to have cared that his expositor, though clearly understanding his main ideas and reproducing them accurately, does not agree with them. The article wears well and still appears an impressive piece of work, trenchantly written, its quotations especially well chosen and stylishly translated. It rated Schopenhauer's prose superior to his philosophy, and rightly noted that 'there are many points of affinity between Schopenhauer and Fichte, notwithstanding the former's strong abuse of the latter'. It gratified Schopenhauer nevertheless. More to the point, it was published in German translation in the *Vossische Zeitung* and read more widely in Germany than it had been in England. Somehow it seems to have broken the dam. In 1854 in neighbouring Denmark, which in those days was something of a cultural dependency of Germany, Kierkegaard noted in his journal that 'all the literary gossips, journalists and authorlings have begun to busy themselves with S'.

'A similar service was accorded to the philosopher in France by Saint-René Taillandier in an article (*L'Allemagne Littéraire*) in the *Revue des Deux Mondes* for August 1856, while in December, 1858, Francesco De Sanctiis published his *Schopenhauer e Leopardi* in the *Rivista Contemporanea* of Turin. Richard Wagner sent the philosopher a copy of *Der Ring des Nibelungen* in 1854, "in admiration and gratitude", while in 1853 E. Erdmann had given him an extended notice in his *Die Entwicklung der deutschen Spekulation seit Kant*, protesting against the oblivion into which he had unjustly fallen. Moreover, the fact that the philosophical faculty of Leipzig University offered a prize in 1856 for an exposition and criticism of Schopenhauer's system showed clearly (whatever motives may have led to the institution of the competition) that the philosopher could no longer be ignored, and by 1857 lectures were being delivered

---

[15] *Parerga and Paralipomena*, i. 16 n.

[16] John Oxenford, an example of the Victorian man of letters at his most redoubtable: dramatic critic of *The Times*, successful playwright, distinguished translator, genuine scholar. His English translation, published three years earlier, of Eckermann's *Conversations with Goethe* is still, for all its shortcomings, in print, getting on for a century and a half later.

on his philosophy in the universities of Bonn, Breslau and Jena . . .
Visitors came from all sides, from Vienna, from London, from Russia,
from America . . . on his birthday flowers, gifts, compliments, verses,
were showered upon him: his portrait was painted (thus the French
painter Jules Lutenschütz painted at least three portraits in oils, in
1855, 1858 and 1859): Elizabeth Ney, a descendant of Napoleon's
Marshal, came from Berlin to make a marble bust . . .'.[17]

Sometimes, understandably, the comments Schopenhauer made on
this were caustic. 'After one has spent a long life in insignificance and
disregard they come at the end with drums and trumpets and think that
is something.' But on the whole he basked in the international acclaim
which he had always believed would accrue to his name, even if for
most of his life he had feared it would not begin until after his death.
What was happening had, in truth, been prefigured by him in his final
book, perhaps not altogether unconsciously. 'If a man lives to see a
fame that is to be posthumous, this will rarely occur before he is old . . .
A confirmation of this is furnished by the portraits of men who have
become famous through their works, for in most cases they were taken
only after their subjects had become celebrated. As a rule, they are
depicted as old and grey, especially if they are philosophers.'[18]

[17] Frederick Copleston: *Arthur Schopenhauer: Philosopher of Pessimism*, p. 41.
[18] *Parerga and Paralipomena*, i. 400–1.

Chapter 2

The Ends of Explanation

If there is to be any point in my looking for something, I need to have some idea how I shall know if I find it. Schopenhauer, clear about this from the start, realized that before it could make sense to embark on the search for an explanation of the world the question had to be confronted of what would, or could, constitute such an explanation. What, indeed, is an explanation, any explanation? An attempt to answer that question is the natural starting-point of his enquiry, and as such the subject of his first book. A better title for it than *On the Fourfold Root of the Principle of Sufficient Reason* would probably have been — and it is what the title refers to anyway — *The Nature of Explanation*. The phrase 'the principle of sufficient reason' had been introduced into the common currency of modern philosophy by Leibniz, but Schopenhauer used it in a way of his own which will be the subject of this chapter. The nature of necessary connection, and hence the nature of explanation, is a subject to which he reverted frequently in his later writings, and the account I am about to give of his view of it is a synoptic one. At this point I need no more than mention the fact that even his first book, considering as it does the concept and procedures of explanation, goes also into the nature of what it is that requires to be explained, namely the structure of our experience as a whole; and that his view of this from the beginning is essentially a Kantian one, albeit critically revised and strengthened. This will be gone into in later chapters.

It is possible for us to pose some sort of *Why?* question with regard to anything. As Schopenhauer puts it: 'The validity of the principle of sufficient reason is so much involved in the form of consciousness that we simply cannot imagine anything objectively of which no "why" could be further demanded.'[1] This point can be expressed in many different ways, among others logically, psychologically and epistemologically. To put it logically, anything that can be formulated can be questioned. To put it psychologically, the status of anything that can be perceived, or thought, or understood, can be queried. In terms of epistemology — and this rather than something psychological is Schopenhauer's point about 'the form of consciousness' — it is a

---

[1] *The World as Will and Representation*, i. 483.

necessary pre-condition of our being in anything that can be called a world at all that, whatever the elements in our experience may be, they must have intelligible relationships with each other, or at least relationships in which intelligibility can be sought. And it is the unfolding of such an intelligible relationship in a particular context that we are asking for when we ask for an explanation — not for just any information about the object, state of affairs or event under consideration, but for such as will account for its being as it is. We want to be told enough for whatever it is that requires explanation to be seen to follow. In short, we want a sufficient reason.

However, the request for sufficient reason raises a new and fundamental question. What is it for something to be a sufficient reason for something else? What counts as sufficient reason for what? Since Schopenhauer there have been philosophers who believed that the central core of philosophy must be contained in the answer to that question, since it would give us the prescribed forms of all intelligibility.[2] Schopenhauer says that his own answer constitutes 'the substructure for the whole of my system'.

His central thesis (hence his title) is that sufficient reasons are not all of one logical type but fall into four main categories (I have rearranged his order so as to bring out more clearly the way they follow from each other):

1. In the physical world, sufficient reasons take the form of causes: event A causes event B. In the world of organic matter we may in some cases dub these causes 'stimuli' — event A *stimulates* event B — but stimuli can be regarded as a special subclass of causes, the defining difference being that the action of all other kinds of cause is quantitatively equal to the reaction, e.g. in the amount of energy released, whereas the action of a stimulus may be smaller or greater than the response to it. Schopenhauer is insistent that the cause of an event can be only another event: it cannot be an object or a state of affairs. Objects and states of affairs are brought into and pushed out of existence by sequences of causally interconnected events which, taken all

---

[2] As an example, see the exchange on p. 62 of *Modern British Philosophy* (ed. Bryan Magee):

'AYER: . . . this fits in, I suppose, with my general conception of philosophy, which I more and more come to regard as being, if you like, the study of *proof*; and what I'm doing is applying this in various fields . . .

MAGEE: When you say philosophy is the study of proof, what do you mean?

AYER: I mean really the study of what is a valid reason for what. If I had to sum up philosophy in a sentence I'd say that philosophy is the theory of the form of the proposition "*p* supports *q*". . . .'.

together, constitute the ongoing history of the natural world, which is to say the whole physical universe. This is causal connection as conceived in Newtonian science and in biology.

2. This ongoing history takes place in a framework of time and space. Every point in time is absolutely determined with respect to every other, and from this fact can be derived the whole of arithmetic. Similarly every point in space is absolutely determined with respect to every other, and from this fact can be derived the whole of geometry. The history of the universe, then, takes place in a framework whose forms are mathematical — indeed, whose a-priori forms give us our a-priori mathematics (which is why mathematics fits the world in the way it does). So whereas in the ongoing history sufficient reasons are causal, in the framework of time and space they are mathematical. Thus a second sense in which A can be a sufficient reason for B is that A can be a mathematical determination or demonstration of B.

3. There is a special class of organic physical objects which can be moved in space and time not only from without — by causes, including stimuli — but also from within, by motives. Any given such object, with its unique set of determinate characteristics, can, in any unique set of circumstances, react to any one motive in only one way. So the actions of these agents, though internally motivated, are as determined as natural events: motives are causes experienced from within. Thus a third way in which A can be sufficient reason for B is that A can be a motive and B the action motivated. (In the late twentieth century the analysis of the problem of the freedom of the will which seems to be more widely accepted among philosophers than any other — for example, that to be found in most of the standard textbook expositions — is the same as Schopenhauer's, to which there is a great deal more than appears at first sight in the foregoing simplification. This being so, in holding over a full consideration of it until a later chapter I am not asking my readers to make any particularly special waivers.)

4. The medium (internal to these animate physical objects) through which motives operate is mind. In the mind judgements are formed, and judgements guide action. At this point, for the first time, we encounter the notion of truth, for judgements may be (indeed must be — see 4.d.iii below) either true or false. The fourth sense, then, in which A can be sufficient reason for B is that A can entail the truth of proposition B. There are in turn four distinguishable ways in which the truth of a proposition can be entailed.

a. It can be entailed by direct observation or experience, in which case it is an empirical truth.

b. It can be one of the necessary presuppositions of experience (see Chapters 3 and 4). Such, for instance, are a-priori propositions about space, time and indeed the whole of mathematics; or about causality and the indestructibility of matter. These are transcendental truths.

    c. It can follow from the truth of another proposition, according to the laws of logic, in which case it is a logical truth. If it follows logically from a true empirical statement we often call it a material truth.

    d. It can itself be one of the laws of logic, in which case it is a metalogical truth. Of those there are four:

      i. The law of identity.

      ii. The law of contradiction.

      iii. The law of excluded middle.

      iv. The principle that truth consists in correspondence to reality.

Thus, to sum up, the four kinds of necessary connection to which Schopenhauer refers in the title of his book are causation as understood in science, in mathematical determination, in logical entailment and in motivated action: according to him, all examples of necessary connection must fall into one of these four categories. Within any given chain of logical explanation the links need not be all of the same logical kind. I may offer a material statement as sufficient reason for the truth of another material statement, but if repeatedly challenged I shall be pushed back to empirical statements, and, if challenged further, to causal statements. Furthermore the line of explanation can go back or forth in either direction: I can 'explain' something either by showing how it is put together internally or by showing how it connects up externally. For instance, if someone were to ask me how a carburettor works I could answer him in one of two ways, either by explaining what its components are and how they go together to make up the carburettor, or by explaining what a carburettor's function is in an internal combustion engine and how it thus helps to drive a car. Taken in isolation the question 'How does a carburretor work?' is ambiguous. It could equally well be asking for either kind of explanation, and only its context can tell us which.

The traditional and familiar terms for these two opposite 'directions' of explanation are 'analysis' and 'synthesis'. At first sight it seems obvious that a full explanation of anything would need to be double-barrelled in the sense of including both. But as soon as we pursue any such full explanation we run into paradox. Every explanation I give of anything can be challenged, and an explanation — what we might call Explanation 2 — can be demanded of the terms of Explanation 1. In meeting this demand I am compelled to introduce new terms, otherwise Explanation 2 is circular. But that means that an Explanation 3 can then be demanded of the new terms in my Explanation 2 of what I said in Explanation 1. In analysis, at least, this can obviously go on to infinity. This being so, only one of two things can happen. Either I (and others) will continue adding explanation to explanation without end, or — depending on the practical needs of the situation, such as the satisfaction or exhaustion of my hearer's curiosity — I will stop somewhere. In either case my explanation will be incomplete, in the former case by definition and in the latter because, at the point at which I stop, I am using explanatory terms which are not themselves explained. Thus the nature of explanation is such that any explanation of anything is necessarily and always incomplete. In practice we can be satisfied, but in theory never. In practice our wants and our curiosity are nearly always limited: either they have a specific object which achieves satisfaction, whereupon they wane, or else they grow stale and then seek a change of focus. If neither of these things happens, and our wants and curiosity go on not being satisfied, a point is reached when we begin to feel that life will become intolerably frustrating unless we can learn to accept this withholding from us of something which, it seems, we are not going to get, and at that point we usually try to force ourselves to *stop demanding*. The adaptive mechanism at work is at bottom biological. Curiosity that persists beyond it is rare. Of its nature it is bound to be strong, and likely to be disconcerting, perhaps even to the point of distress: but, disconcerting or not, it constitutes a drive so powerful that, precisely because it cannot be satisfied, the life of anyone who feels it cannot but be driven by it.

Having charted the available forms of explanation, what Schopenhauer does in the next stage of his investigation is to identify the location in each one at which, in practice, explanations characteristically stop, these being points at which important philosophical questions arise. Considering first the 'direction' of analysis, and taking the four forms of the principle of sufficient reason in the order in which we have considered them, there is first the domain of the natural sciences. Ultimate explanations here are usually given and accepted in terms of matter, natural forces and scientific laws. The matter may itself be further analysed in terms of chemical formulae, the table of elements, fundamental particles and the rest. The natural forces working on or through it are such as energy, gravitation, magnetism, electricity and so on. And the laws of science state the known regularities of matter in motion under the impulse of these natural forces. But if someone says to the scientist: 'All right, but what *is* matter? What *is* energy? What *is* a scientific law?,' the scientist gestures in the direction of the philosopher and bows out, for reduction to this level of concepts *is* what constitutes explanation in science. The scientist goes no deeper: the most he can do by way of explaining his ground-floor concepts is to shed light on their relationships with each other. He can tell you, for example, that what is meant by the energy contained in matter is permanently equivalent to the product of the matter's mass with the square of the velocity of light. To explicate concepts in terms of each other like this may tell you a prodigious amount more about them than you knew before, and enable you to do all manner of practical things; and yet, as Schopenhauer puts it, it is as if I were to meet a group of persons each of whom was introduced to me as a relative of one of the others — this one was that one's sister, that one was this one's cousin — so that by the end of the introductions I understood precisely how they were all related to each other, but was left saying to myself: 'That's all very well, but who on earth are they all? And how do I stand in relation to the whole lot of them?' This ground-floor level of explanation in science is, in a serious sense of the term, occult, in that it explains everything else without itself being explained. This is one of the things that precludes science from ever giving us ultimate insight into the mystery of the world: its explanations shift the locus of that mystery but they do not remove it. These shifts are of enormous importance and value, because they constitute the growth of our knowledge within the world of phenomena. But even if it could be shown that all explanations can be reduced ultimately to those of science, and even if all the reductions were then to be carried out, the mystery of the world *as such* would be as great at the end of the process as it had been at the beginning.[3]

In mathematics a not dissimilar situation exists: the entire edifice of demonstration has to be built on a foundation of axioms and rules which are not themselves demonstrated, but are assumed. And, of course, since every position and every moment is both determined and determining with respect to every other, and since space and time are alike unbounded, the number of possible demonstrations is infinite, so one can simply follow another without any stopping place ever being reached. As for the laws of logic: like the basic concepts of science, and the axioms and rules of mathematics, any attempt to justify them must involve circularity, since they themselves generate the justification procedures in their universe of discourse. Logical justification is, by definition, a demonstration that the laws of logic have been followed and not contravened. Justified thought can no more not embody them than the human body can bend its limbs against its joints. In *that* sense they are not only laws of logic but laws of thought.[4]

In the case of motives, the mind presents the will with the necessary

---

[3] Cf. 'We feel that even when *all possible* scientific questions have been answered, the problems of life remain completely untouched.' Wittgenstein: *Tractatus Logico-Philosophicus*, 6. 52.

[4] See also *The World as Will and Representation*, i. 454.

information and the will decides. But how does the will decide? We find ourselves unable to give any further definition or description of what willing is, since it is itself what is most directly given to us in self-consciousness — there simply is nothing more immediately known to us than it, and therefore no terms in which we could make it more intelligible to ourselves than it already is. 'The identity of the subject of willing with that of knowing, by virtue of which the word "I" necessarily indicates and includes both, is the nodal point of the world, and as such is inexplicable ... An actual identity of the knower [the knowing] with the willer [the known], and hence of the subject with the object, is *immediately given.* But whoever really grasps the inexplicable nature of this identity will term it, as I do, the ultimate miracle.'[5]

Thus, in identifying the point at which explanation characteristically comes to a halt on each of its available paths, Schopenhauer has located the sites on which fundamental problems of philosophy arise, and shown why they arise. In each case it is because explanation up to that point 'explains things in reference to one another, but it always leaves unexplained something that it presupposes. In mathematics, for example, this is space and time; in mechanics, physics, and chemistry, it is matter, qualities, original forces, laws of nature; in botany and zoology it is the difference of species, and life itself; in history, it is the human race with all its characteristics of thought and will. And in all these it is the principle of sufficient reason in the form appropriate to each. *Philosophy* has the peculiarity of presupposing absolutely nothing as known; everything to it is equally strange and a problem, not only the relations of phenomena, but also those phenomena themselves.'[6] He does not claim to provide further explanations at every such point. Indeed, 'two things are absolutely inexplicable, in other words, do not lead back to the relation expressed by the principle of sufficient reason. The first of these is the principle of sufficient reason itself, in all its four forms, because it is the principle of all explanation, which therefore has meaning only in reference to it; the second is that which is not reached by this principle, but from which arises that original thing in all phenomena; it is the thing-in-itself, knowledge of which is in no wise subject to the principle of sufficient reason. Here for the present we must rest content not to understand the thing-in-itself, for it can be made intelligible only by the following book,[7] where we shall also take up again this consideration of the possible achievements of the sciences. But there is a point where natural science, and indeed every branch of knowledge, leaves things as they are, since not only its explanation of

---

[5] *On the Fourfold Root of the Principle of Sufficient Reason*, pp. 211–12.
[6] *The World as Will and Representation*, i. 81.
[7] [This remark applies in the context of my book too — BM.]

them, but even the principle of this explanation, namely the principle of sufficient reason, does not go beyond this point. This is the real point where philosophy again takes up things and considers them in accordance with its method, which is entirely different from the method of science.'[8]

Notwithstanding these questions which are inherently unanswerable, Schopenhauer considers that his philosophy makes the solution possible of all important philosophical problems that have solutions. The great bulk of his philosophy is devoted to a systematic exposition of these. But to be equipped to follow him on his journey we need to be aware of what he has to say about the other 'direction' of explanation, namely synthesis.

Whereas analysis faces the choice of either going on for ever or calling an arbitrary halt, synthesis appears to be in no such case. By processes of synthesis we could, on the face of it, go on relating things to other things until we had drawn all the relations there are between everything there is, and at that point we would come to a natural and necessary end: there would be nothing left to which anything could be related, and nothing left to relate to it. The totality of things would then stand before us as a perspicuous whole, with all its internal relations exhibited. So there appear not to be the same theoretical problems with regard to synthesis as there are with regard to analysis. It is true that throughout the human past a powerful demand has been expressed for a further explanation of this *everything*, of this totality of human experience, of this world as a whole. And because, by definition, there is nothing else to which this everything can be related, the almost inevitable recourse has been had to an explanation outside the world, in terms of the transcendental: the known has been explained in terms of the unknown, or rather the knowable in terms of the unknowable. But because the unknowable *is* unknowable, no such explanation can ever be validated. It is not so much that such explanations ask us to take them on faith (or authority, which involves faith in the authority): they *can* only be taken on faith, there is no other basis they could have. There have, of course, been many such explanations — one thinks, for instance, of most of the world's religions. But they are incompatible with each other. And this means that when any two of them come into conflict there is no way of deciding between them — except, again, faith or authority.

This is one of the areas where Schopenhauer parts company with Kant. Kant had shown that it was impossible to understand the world

[8] *The World as Will and Representation*, i. 81. An echo of this passage reverberates — and I suspect that the allusion was conscious — in Wittgenstein's much-quoted assertion that philosophy leaves everything as it is.

by use of reason alone, which had been what the great rationalist philosophers such as Spinoza and Leibniz had tried to do. So far, Schopenhauer agreed. But Kant saw this as opening the door to religion: if it is possible for a transcendental explanation of the world to be accepted only on faith then there is nothing self-contradictory or irrational in doing so — on the contrary, the irrational thing is to claim certainty, whether theistic or atheistic, in an area where there can be only unsecured belief. That was Kant's view, and he was himself a Christian. Schopenhauer remained more consistently agnostic. Any attempt to explain the known in terms of the unknown seemed to him an inversion of intelligible procedure, and any attempt to explain the knowable in terms of the unknowable a flight into Cloud-Cuckooland. Both procedures were bound to make matters less clear, a great deal less clear, than they already are, and what kind of explanation is that? Still worse, both procedures must involve the making of statements about what is unknown or unknowable, and this is a recipe for, at best, self-indulgence if not self-deception, and, at worst, charlatanry or madness. Schopenhauer is insistent that we really must face the full implications of the fact that our human powers of apprehension are limited: whether or not there is anything that is permanently inaccessible to them is permanently unknowable to us. Furthermore, the nature of any such something would be incomprehensible to us even if a being with higher powers than our own were to try to explain it to us. So 'the nature of things before and beyond the world is open to no investigation'. The most honest conclusion to be drawn from this has been put in its best-known form by Wittgenstein in the final sentence of the *Tractatus*. Having said, a couple of pages previously, that 'the sense of the world must lie outside the world', Wittgenstein concludes: 'What we cannot speak about we must remain silent about.'

Of his own work Schopenhauer declares roundly and robustly: 'The present philosophy, at any rate, by no means attempts to say *whence* or *for what purpose* the world exists, but merely *what* the world is.'[9] He expands this by saying: 'My philosophy does not presume to explain the ultimate causes of the world. It confines itself to the facts of inner and outer experience, which are accessible to everybody, and points out the true and intimate connection between these facts, without, however, concerning itself with that which may transcend them. It refrains from drawing any conclusions concerning what lies beyond experience. It merely explains the data of sensibility and self-consciousness, and strives to understand only the immanent essence of the world.'

[9] *The World as Will and Representation*, i. 82.

There is, he argues, one way in which enigmatic wholes can be elucidated which it is reasonable to accept and unreasonable not to accept, in spite of its not being logically unassailable. He gives as his paradigm example any form of code-breaking. If, by assuming a particular set of equivalents as a key, a man finds he has made sense of a coded message which was hitherto hermetic, the possibility remains that his postulated equivalents are not the correct ones and that he has decoded the message wrongly. In the early stages of simple trial-and-error code-breaking this occurs unsurprisingly. But logically it is a possibility which cannot be eliminated at any stage: however many examples of a code a key fits, and however detailed, consistent, germane, truthful and useful the messages thus yielded turn out to be, it could still be sheer coincidence that these equivalents apply in these particular cases, and the real key — and hence the true meaning of all the messages — could be quite different. Without recourse to something *beyond* the messages there is no way of proving that this is not the case. With a cryptogram as elaborate as the Rosetta Stone — with its two languages and three scripts, the deciphering of which unlocked the secret of Egyptian hieroglyphics which had baffled Western man for centuries — we might in practice dismiss as an obvious crackpot anyone who denied that it had been deciphered, yet we could not prove him wrong. His charge against us that all our validation procedures were circular would be correct: they *are* circular. To his question: 'How then can you be sure your key is the right one?' we could only reply: 'Because it is inconceivable — given that it makes such relevant and convincing sense of everything, not to mention all the rest of the historical and other manifold considerations involved — that it should not be.' But in logic that is not an answer. And if he were to snort back: 'Well it isn't inconceivable to *me*', we should be close to impasse. We might say to him: 'Are you denying that it is possible for anyone ever to crack a code, then?', but his reply would be: 'No, I am merely denying that it is possible for him ever to know for certain on internal evidence alone that he has got it right.' Yet the fact is that we do *know* we have deciphered the Rosetta Stone in any normal sense of the word 'know'. Similarly, if any coded message is long and elaborate enough, and we find a key that makes detailed and consistent and relevant sense of it in all its parts — and of every part in relation to every other part — and then turns out to be just as successful with other examples of the same code, then we are certain down to the very depths of our intuition that our key is the right one. We do not regard it as merely a probability, however high. We are as sure of it as we are of anything, and this despite the fact that any attempt to demonstrate it must be logically inconclusive.

Now all this is what Schopenhauer claims for the relationship between his philosophy and the structure of experience as a whole — that the former solves the riddle posed by the latter in precisely this sense. He appeals to nothing outside or beyond the world, and he makes no false logical claims, yet he is confident that his system makes such manifestly coherent sense of the enigma of the world in all its details and through all their interrelationships that anyone who really understands it will be as sure as he can be of anything that it is correct. And beyond that there is simply nowhere left to go. So in the final resort, this is the basis on which Schopenhauer's philosophy commends itself. But it is important for its readers to realize as clearly as does its author that this is not because of any shortcoming on the part of the philosophy: no firmer basis is theoretically possible for any view of experience as a whole.

A central characteristic of Schopenhauer's writing is that he is not only himself aware of the status and limitations of whatever arguments are available, and also of the one he happens to be using, but he keeps the reader well reminded of them too. In general he is a scrupulous and interesting arguer, and he argues everything, not taking anything on trust and not expecting us to do so either. However, he has a firm practical grasp of what the limitations are of argument as such. And although this is something which all serious students of philosophy are familiar with theoretically, nearly all of them tend to forget about it in practice to a quite astonishing degree. The central point here, put baldly, is that no argument can add to our information. Any valid argument or proof, however long and interesting, can tell us only that its conclusions follow from its premises: *if* A, *then* B, but if not B, then not A . . . It makes explicit in the conclusion what was already fully implicit, if not fully perspicuous, in the premises; but it gives us no information to which we did not at that point already have access. In this sense valid arguments and proofs are the empty vessels of reason. They are prodigiously useful, because they enable us to catch and hold all the implications of whatever we start out from, but they do not *add* empirically to what we start out from.

Every argument has to have premises — or, to be precise, has to have an absolute minimum of one premiss and one rule of procedure — before it can begin, and therefore begin to be an argument, at all. So every argument has to rest on at least two undemonstrated assumptions, for no argument can establish either the truth of its own premisses or the validity of the rules by which it itself proceeds. These can be established only by direct experience (in the case of empirical premisses) or direct intuition (in the case of logical, or otherwise formal, premisses) or as the conclusions of other arguments — and if it is the last of these the same considerations then apply all over again. Now if we consider together the two points that have just been made — the point that no argument can add to the content of its premisses, and the point that all arguments have to rest in the end on unproven premisses — it becomes clear that the widely accepted notion that every truth needs to be proved, and that only what has been demonstrated is true, is the opposite of what is actually the case: in fact every proof must rest on foundations whose truth is not demonstrated, must go back eventually to something which is not the conclusion of an argument. We may be inclined, for as long as we do not think about it, to suppose that human knowledge about the world has come into existence through chains of reasoning, and is embodied in their conclusions, but in reality all the information we have is already embodied in the premisses from which those very chains of reasoning begin — if we know anything about the world we know it not because it has been demonstrated or proved but because it has been directly experienced or perceived, or else because it follows *by logical processes which contribute nothing at all in the way of empirical content* from what has been directly experienced or perceived. In this fundamental sense, all knowledge precedes all demonstration. 'It must be possible in some way to know directly, without proofs and syllogisms, every truth that is reached through syllogisms and communicated by proofs.'[10]

This being so, it has always seemed to me that in practice most people professionally concerned with philosophy grossly exaggerate the importance of arguments. Perhaps, as Schopenhauer rather wickedly suggests, 'proofs are generally less for those who want to learn than for those who want to dispute. Those latter obstinately deny directly established insight . . . we must therefore show such persons that they admit under one form, and indirectly, what under another form, and directly, they deny.'[11] It *cannot* be the case that what is most important about what a philosopher has to convey to us is introduced by his arguments, unless his problems are primarily technical ones of logic: it must lie already in the insights, judgements, perceptions, points of view, choices, formulations and so on that stock his premisses. True, it is only by means of argument that he can lay before us the full implications of what he is saying — and for that matter it is probably only by such chains of reasoning that he can expect to work them out even for himself— so in practice it is usually only by argument that he can get fully to understand his own position, and get us fully to understand it too, and can hope to persuade us of its cogency. But

[10] *The World as Will and Representation*, i. 65.
[11] Ibid. i. 68.

these, and only these, are the chief functions of argument. Therefore it is not absolutely essential to philosophy. Indeed, there are philosophers who dispense with it, giving us only their formulations of their insights, and leaving us to understand these and their implications as best we may. The supreme example, over large areas of his work, at least, is Wittgenstein, who had a clear and conscious grasp of the inessential nature of the role of argumentation in philosophy, derived no doubt from Schopenhauer. Such people are notoriously difficult to understand — the lack of explication, of any indication of what the implications are of what is being said, means that one needs to be already on the same wavelength before one can understand — but, although this may make such philosophers exasperating, to dismiss them as being 'not philosophers' because of their lack of concern with argument would be a complete mistake. Argument is the great vehicle of insight (I leave aside the arts, which we shall come to in due course) and as such is to be prized above rubies; but to be prized more highly still is the insight of which it is the vehicle, and this is not itself an argument, nor could it have been arrived at by argument, and nor of course does it need to be conveyed by argument. It is this insight, not the arguments that usually convey it, that philosophy is ultimately for, or about. But this, I fear, has been lost sight of by many, if not most, professional philosophers.

Although professional philosophers nowadays are often highly skilled in matters of argument, it is in the nature of things that not many of them can be expected to have original insights. The outcome is hundreds upon hundreds of books which are well argued but have little or nothing to say that has not been said before. And because the quality of the argumentation is the only distinguished thing about them, and also the thing their readers as well as their writers are best at, it becomes the object of interest, and hence the criterion by which they and their authors are judged. In consequence, many professional philosophers and their students slide unthinkingly into proceeding as if philosophy is *about* arguments, and they lose sight of the fact that it is really about insights. So when a philosopher comes along who really does have something new to contribute, he tends to be judged more by the quality of his arguments than by the quality of his insights — and if the former is unremarkable the latter may go unappreciated. However, such is not the case with Schopenhauer, fortunately. Although he understood every bit as clearly as his follower Wittgenstein that the substantive content of philosophy is not introduced by its arguments, he treasured argument as a supreme clarifier and communicator. Wittgenstein does not seem to have been particularly interested in clarification or communication — indeed, one occasionally has the opposite suspicion, that he was tempted to try to confine understanding of his work to within a closed circle, and therefore to appear as something of a mystery-monger to the world at large. Schopenhauer argues nearly everything he can to the hilt, so as to see, and so as to get us to see, the full implications of it, and also so as to demonstrate its compatibility with what is already accepted, and thereby to persuade us to add it to what we already accept.

The various forms of reasoning and argument which we have been discussing all take place in the same medium, the medium of concepts, usually embodied in language or some other equivalent symbolism, such as the symbolisms of mathematics or logic. But the direct perceptions and experiences on which they all depend for their empirical content are not concepts. On the contrary, concepts are *derived from* experiences and perceptions, and are formed to enable us to handle them in certain ways. Concepts stand to experiences and perceptions in the relation of general to particular, abstract to concrete. Each actual experience or perception is immediate, specific, unique. For that reason it cannot itself be retained or communicated. So if we are to be able to remember it when it is no longer present we must retain, and therefore we need to form, something that will stand for it in its absence, namely a symbol of some kind. By the same token, if we are to communicate the experience to others we need to be able to present to them a symbol which they can then interpret by relating it to something they are already acquainted with. Thus in order both to retain and to communicate our experiences and our perceptions we abstract from them and generalize their content into concepts. It is this faculty of forming, storing and using concepts that the term 'reason' denotes. It is what enables us to think about, and thus relate ourselves to, places other than where we are, and to the past and the future as well as to the present (and, by combining these, to envisage things that do not exist at all). It is what makes possible language, and consequently our ability to formulate and carry through complicated projects in co-operation with each other — and consequently the whole of social organization. It makes all the forms of thought possible which have been discussed in this chapter. From its uses and their consequences flows all that essentially differentiates man from the animals — and thus, adds Schopenhauer, 'gives rise to all that makes man's life so rich, artificial and terrible'.[12]

The fact that concepts are formed by a process of abstraction and generalization from experience means that what is uniquely particular to any individual experience has perforce to be left out of the concept

---

[12] *On the Fourfold Root of the Principle of Sufficient Reason*, p. 146.

used to convey it. This means, among other things, that concepts never precisely match experience. 'Concepts always remain universal, and so do not reach down to the particular; yet it is precisely the particular that has to be dealt with in life.'[13] The need for concepts to be communicable, and therefore separable and negotiable, and therefore detachable, gives them a character which is categorially different from that of the continuum and flux of experience in which they have their origin, with the result that — with whatever subtlety and refinement they may have been formulated, and may be used — they stand in the same sort of relation to living experience as a copy in mosaic to a painting in oils. 'However fine the mosaic may be, the edges of the stones always remain, so that no continuous transition from one tint to another is possible. In the same way, concepts, with their rigidity and sharp delineation, however finely they may be split by closer definition, are always incapable of reaching the fine modifications of perception.'[14]

From the fact that concepts inevitably fail to match precisely the experiences from which they are derived, plus the fact that what they contain must inevitably be *less* than the experiences from which they are derived, spring fundamental problems about communication, and about the relation of language to reality. Concern with this relation — based on the central realization that, so to speak, the map is not the landscape — has come close to dominating philosophy in the twentieth century, and this makes Schopenhauer's understanding and treatment of the subject look remarkably prescient, indeed 'modern'. Nor is this coincidental: he was the first great — and perhaps to the end the greatest — intellectual influence on Wittgenstein, so the causal connection with the philosophy of our day is direct. Schopenhauer saw clearly that empirical concepts not only cannot have the full empirical content of the experiences from which they are derived but also that they cannot contain anything empirical which is *different* from the content of the experiences from which they are derived. It is true that higher-order concepts can be formed by abstracting and generalizing exclu-

---

[13] *The World as Will and Representation*, ii. 74. This sentence of Schopenhauer's articulates what was virtually the central doctrine of Søren Kierkegaard. Kierkegaard, who died in 1855, did not discover Schopenhauer until 1853 or 1854, and reacted powerfully when he did so. His diary for 1854 contains an extensive discussion of Schopenhauer, a discussion whose main theme is stated in its first sentence. 'A.S. is unquestionably an important writer; he has interested me very much and I am astonished to find an author who, in spite of complete disagreement, touches me at so many points.' To Schopenhauer's initials at the beginning of this sentence Kierkegaard appends a footnote which reads 'Curiously enough I am called S.A. and we probably stand in an inverse relation to one another.'

[14] Ibid. i. 57.

sively from lower-order ones, but the entire pyramidal structure thus created can rest only on a base of direct experience, and can have only part but not all of *that* experience as its total empirical content. 'It must therefore be possible for us to go back from every concept, even if through intermediate stages, to the perceptions from which it has itself been directly drawn . . . Therefore these perceptions furnish us with the real content of all our thinking, and wherever they are missing we have had in our heads not concepts but mere words. In this respect our intellect is like a bank of issue which, if it is to be sound, must have ready money in the safe in order to be able, on demand, to meet all the notes it has issued; the perceptions are the ready money, the concepts are the notes.'[15] . . . 'Concepts and abstractions that do not ultimately lead to perceptions are like paths in a wood that end without any way out.'[16]

This doctrine plays a role of the utmost importance in Schopenhauer's philosophy. It is not, of course, original to him. On the contrary, it is central to that whole section of the great tradition that runs from Locke through Berkeley and Hume to Kant. And it goes much further back. Aristotle is credited with having said: 'There is nothing in the intellect that was not previously in sense-perception.'[17] However, in Schopenhauer's opinion most philosophy has been vitiated by its neglect. 'Philosophy has been for the most part a *continued misuse of universal concepts*, such as, for example, "substance", "ground", "cause", "the good", "perfection", "necessity", "possibility", and very many others. A tendency of minds to operate with such abstract and too widely comprehended concepts has shown itself at almost all times. Ultimately it may be due to a certain indolence of the intellect, which finds it too onerous to be always controlling thought through perception . . . Even the whole of Spinoza's method of demonstration rests on such uninvestigated and too widely comprehended concepts. Here Locke's very great merit is to be found; in order to counteract all that dogmatic unreality he insisted on an investigation of the *origin of concepts*, and thus led back to what is *perceptive* and to *experience*. Before

[15] *The World as Will and Representation*, ii. 71. Cf. A. J. Ayer in *Men of Ideas*, p. 132: 'William James had a phrase in which he asked for the "cash value" of statements. This is very important. The early Logical Positivists were wrong in thinking that you could still maintain the gold standard — that if you presented your notes you could get gold for them — which of course you can't. There isn't enough gold. And there are too many notes. But nevertheless there has to be some backing to the currency. If someone makes an assertion, well, all right, perhaps you can't translate it out into observational terms — but it still is important to ask how you would set about testing it. What observations are relevant? This, I think, still holds good.'

[16] Ibid. ii. 82.

[17] Quoted by Schopenhauer in *The World as Will and Representation*, ii. 82.

him Bacon had worked in a similar sense, yet with reference to physics rather than metaphysics. Kant pursued the path prepared by Locke in a higher sense and much further . . . With me perception is throughout the source of all knowledge . . . It is true that universal concepts should be the material *in* which philosophy deposits and stores up its know-ledge, but not the source *from* which it draws such knowledge; the *terminus ad quem*, not *a quo*. It is not, as Kant defines it, a science *from* concepts, but a science *in* concepts.'[18]

'It is actually a *petitio principii* of Kant, which he expresses most clearly in §1. of the *Prolegomena*, that metaphysics may not draw its fundamental concepts and principles from experience. Here it is assumed in advance that only what we know prior to all experience can extend beyond possible experience. Supported by this, Kant then comes and shows that all such knowledge is nothing more than the form of the intellect for the purpose of experience, and that in consequence it cannot lead beyond experience; and from this he then justifiably infers the impossibility of all metaphysics. But does it not rather seem posi-tively wrong-headed that, in order to solve the riddle of experience, in other words, of the world which alone lies before us, we should close our eyes to it, ignore its contents, and take and use for our material merely the empty forms of which we are *a priori* conscious? Is it not rather in keeping with the matter that the *science of experience in general and as such* should draw also from experience? Its problem is itself given to it empirically; why should not its solution also call in the assistance of experience? Is it not inconsistent and absurd that he who speaks of the nature of things should not look at the things themselves, but stick only to certain abstract concepts? It is true that the task of metaphysics is not the observation of particular experiences; but yet it is the correct explanation of experience as a whole. Its foundation, therefore, must certainly be of an empirical nature.'[19]

We have now seen quite separately that both the forms of our reasoning and the concepts they employ can have no cognitive content other than what is derived from direct perception. For both these reasons, there-fore, the entire edifice of human knowledge — all language, common-sense knowledge, science, scholarship, and the rest — can have no more content than is contained already in the sum of the experiences and perceptions from which the concepts themselves were formed and to which all reasoning must lead back. So it must be an error to attempt to add to it by taking logic or concepts as our subject-matter, for no addition is to be made by developing chains of logical reasoning whose

[18] *The World as Will and Representation*, ii. 39–41.
[19] Ibid. ii. 180–1.

cognitive content can never increase, nor by pursuing concepts through higher and higher orders of generality which must indeed have ever-diminishing content, nor by elucidating concepts in terms of one another. Our task is to add, if we can, to the content of the experience in which all concepts and all chains of reasoning have their beginning. This can be done not only quantitatively but also qualitatively — not only can we add to the number of, we can also enrich the quality of, or deepen our insight into, our direct perceptions and intuitions. 'To perceive, to allow the things themselves to speak to us, to apprehend and grasp new relations between them, and then to precipitate and deposit all this into concepts, in order to possess it with certainty; this is what gives us new knowledge ... The innermost kernel of every genuine and actual piece of knowledge is a perception; every new truth is also the fruit of such a perception . . . If we go to the bottom of the matter, all truth and wisdom, in fact the ultimate secret of things, is contained in everything actual, yet certainly only *in concreto* and like gold hidden in the ore. The question is how to extract it.'[20]

If we want to acquire a deeper understanding of the world, then, we have somehow to find a way of getting under the outer skin of our direct experience. The mystery lies in what is, and it is into our direct perceptions of what is that we need to dig. Many if not most philosophers have regarded the actual as banal, and concepts as much more interesting — they have seen our individual perceptions and experiences as trivial, concepts as somehow 'higher' — and have therefore tried to deepen our understanding of the world by examining concepts. In doing this they are like a man who empties a box so as to be able to look inside and see what is in it. In Schopenhauer's view it is a characteristic defect of the academic type of person that he tries to live his life and relate to reality, including other people, much too much in terms of concepts — by contrast with the man in the street, or the administrator, or the man of action, or the artistic type of person, all of whom live more in terms of spontaneous response to the uniquely specific, and thus more in terms of direct experience. The most radical personal implications for intellectuals of all kinds follow from the fact that the value of what comes out of any valid process of reasoning is comprised of the validity and quality of the experiences, perceptions and judgements from which it begins. If these are defective or weak, no amount of skill in the handling of concepts, or virtuosity in argument, can increase their substance. Yet fine perception calls for a high degree of sensibility, and penetrating judgement calls for independence of mind, and the conjunction of these characteristics is rarer than intellec-

---

[20] *The World as Will and Representation*, ii. 72.

tual ability — indeed, not many intellectually able people have it, not even among the ranks of philosophers; for, as Geoffrey Warnock has recently said: 'Philosophers tend very much to take up the subject in the state in which they find it, and to swim contentedly along in the way the stream is going.'[21] Here lies the key to the fact that so many brilliant people, in universities and elsewhere, produce little or nothing that is of lasting value. They may have high IQs, remarkable powers of reasoning, and a genuine devotion to their work, but if the material with which they start out is unremarkable — if their perceptions lack subtlety, depth, or above all authentic independence (for instance, if their judgements are too influenced by the intellectual fashions prevailing in their professions) — no amount of cleverness, ingenuity or dedication can transubstantiate it. In creative thought, as in creative art, the quality of the original material is most of the story, and in determining this it is personal originality and independence, insight and imagination that count, not intellectual power — though intellectual power certainly comes into what the individual then *does* with his material. Even so, technique, for all its usefulness, is auxiliary, and many are the masters of technique who have little to say. Such people tend honestly to overrate the importance of technique, not only because it is what they can do, and do well, but because it is what they can improve at, and what they can teach. Some may be great teachers; yet however able they are they will have no original contribution of much lasting significance to make to the subject. And they will often be baffled as to why this is so, especially when they see people whom they know to be both less clever and less technically proficient than themselves producing work which is better.

The categorial difference between concept and direct experience bears on all of the most important questions of life, since the more important the experience the more important the distinction. Schopenhauer draws out its implications with marvellous richness. 'I wanted in this way to stress and demonstrate the great difference, indeed opposition, between knowledge of perceptions and abstract, or reflected, knowledge. Hitherto this difference has received too little attention, and its establishment is a fundamental feature of my philosophy; for many phenomena of our mental life can be explained only from this difference. The connecting link between these two such different kinds of knowledge forms the *power of judgment . . .*'.[22] From this distinction he derives fundamental insights into the nature of, on the one hand, philosophy, logic and mathematics, and on the other, art and

---

[21] *Modern British Philosophy* (ed. Bryan Magee), p. 88.
[22] *The World as Will and Representation*, ii. 88.

ethics. It provides him with a theory of wit and humour. It pervades his essays on worldly matters, and gives him illuminating things to say about, among other things, the many different forms of mental character in human beings — stupidity, silliness, levity, prudence, pedantry, learning, wisdom, genius, and so on.

One point that Schopenhauer makes in this connection is that *in practice* nearly all intellectual activity, nearly all art, and nearly all moral behaviour, take their starting-point from concepts and not from authentic individual perceptions and judgements, and therefore do not have in them the stuff of life, namely autonomous independence. They fit the time, because the received concepts are those of the time, but they have no separate life with which to outlive it. 'With most books . . . the author has *thought*, but not *perceived*; he has written from reflection, not from intuition. It is just this that makes them mediocre and wearisome . . . [But] where *a perception or intuition* was the basis of the author's thinking, it is as if he wrote from a land where his reader has never been, for everything is fresh and new, since it is drawn directly from the primary source of all knowledge.'[23] . . . '*Perception* is not only the *source* of all knowledge, but is itself knowledge *par excellence*; it alone is the unconditionally true genuine knowledge, fully worthy of the name. For it alone imparts *insight* proper; it alone is actually assimilated by man, passes into his inner nature, and can quite justifiably be called *his*, whereas the concepts merely cling to him.'[24] . . . 'For the man who studies to gain *insight*, books and studies are merely rungs of the ladder on which he climbs to the summit of knowledge. As soon as a rung has raised him one step, he leaves it behind. On the other hand, the many who study in order to fill their memories do not use the rungs of the ladder for climbing, but take them off and load themselves with them to take away, rejoicing at the increasing weight of the burden. They remain below for ever, since they are carrying what ought to have carried them.'[25]

What Schopenhauer lived for was to gain insight, and it is the aim of his philosophy to impart it. Yet he himself could not escape the problems posed by the fact that the insights of the philosopher can be imparted only in concepts. All through his writings he tries to relate his formulations to concrete perceptions: for instance he makes a practice of, as soon as he has finished making a point, transfixing the nub of it with a striking image, such as the one at the end of the foregoing paragraph about the rungs of the ladder. Once read, some of these images are never forgotten, and enter permanently into one's way of

[23] *The World as Will and Representation*, ii. 72.
[24] Ibid. ii. 77.   [25] Ibid. ii. 80.

seeing things.[26] But they do demand from the reader an imaginative response which is almost poetic. The vital connection between image and reality, concept and perception, exposition and insight, remains in the end, in some crucial sense, external to both, and is one which only the reader can make. 'Only the poorest knowledge, abstract secondary knowledge, the concept, the mere shadow of knowledge proper, is unconditionally communicable. If perceptions were communicable, there would then be a communication worth the trouble; but in the end everyone must remain within his own skin and his own skull, and no man can help another. To enrich the concept from perception is the constant endeavour of poetry and philosophy.'[27] It was Schopenhauer's constant endeavour, and his success in it is one of the reasons for his special appeal, unsurpassed by that of any other philosopher since, to so many great creative artists.

[26] The image of the ladder was not forgotten by Wittgenstein — see *Tractatus Logico-Philosophicus*, 6. 54: 'My propositions serve as elucidations in the following way: anyone who understands me eventually recognizes them as nonsensical, when he has used them — as steps — to climb up beyond them. (He must, so to speak, throw away the ladder after he has climbed up it.)'

[27] *The World as Will and Representation*, ii. 74.

Chapter 3

The Great Tradition

A sense of wonder was identified by Aristotle as the experience with which the impulse to philosophize originates, whether in the history of mankind or in the development of the individual.[1] It may be that he was consciously echoing Socrates, who had already been quoted by Plato as saying: 'This sense of wonder is the mark of the philosopher. Philosophy indeed has no other origin.' (*Theaetetus*, section 155.) The assertion has been re-echoed down subsequent generations: Montaigne's 'Wonder is the foundation of all philosophy' (*Essays*, book iii, Chapter 11), Bacon's 'Wonder — which is the seed of knowledge' (*Advancement of Learning*), or, in our own century, Whitehead's 'Philosophy is the product of wonder' (*Nature and Life*, Chapter 1) are a few instances only. Schopenhauer believed passionately that wonder, felt to the point of bafflement, was what motivated philosophy. 'The philosopher always becomes such as the result of a perplexity from which he is trying to disengage himself.[2] . . . What distinguishes ungenuine from genuine philosophers is that this perplexity comes to the latter from looking at the world itself, to the former merely from a book, a philosophical system that lies in front of them.'[3] He believed that most human beings experience this sense of wonder no more than dimly or fleetingly — a fact which he felt to be at the heart of his sense of isolation from his fellow men. 'The lower a man is in an intellectual respect, the less puzzling and mysterious existence itself is to him; on the contrary, everything, how it is and that it is, seems to him a matter of course.'[4] But in fact the attribute at issue is not one of intellect only. There are plenty of intelligent people who largely lack this sense of wonder: many if not most men of affairs, for instance — merchants, lawyers, soldiers, politicians and the rest (in so far as they are intelligent, and many of

---

[1] Aristotle: *Metaphysics*, i. 982: 'It is owing to their wonder that men both now begin and at first began to philosophize'; quoted by Schopenhauer in *The World as Will and Representation*, ii. 160.

[2] This sentence states succinctly the root presupposition of the later philosophy of Wittgenstein. See *Philosophical Investigations*, 309: 'What is your aim in philosophy? — To show the fly the way out of the flybottle.'

[3] *The World as Will and Representation*, i. 32.

[4] Ibid. ii. 161.

them undoubtedly are — some highly so). To such as these, the world is like a perfectly fitting garment: although it touches them at every point they are not conscious of it, nor self-conscious in it. Such people are often, for that reason, incapable of apprehending the world as strange, still less as astonishing, except perhaps in rare moments; or else they segregate what sense of wonder they have into a little ghetto of their time — say, an hour every Sunday.

In Schopenhauer's opinion most professional philosophers were, as such, worldlings. It is important to remember that, in his time and place, university teachers were employees of the state, and their jockeyings for academic promotion often involved ingratiating themselves with government officials. Furthermore, up to his time only one great philosopher since the ancient Greeks had been a professional academic, namely Kant. Descartes, Spinoza, Leibniz, Locke, Berkeley, Hume — none of these were professional academics. Academic philosophers were then, and are now, most of them, led to philosophy not by a sense of wonder but by the education system. Their first encounter with philosophical problems is as students, through the works of others — which, being intelligent, they may be good at understanding, reproducing and discussing. If they distinguish themselves at this, academic life offers them the possibility of making it a career. So philosophy as an academic subject comes to be the means whereby they are provided with a living for themselves and their families, a post in a respected social institution, a professional reputation, prestige, a pension, even administrative authority and power over subordinates. It becomes one way among others of living a life in society, of making one's way in the world. But all this is in response to external, not internal, stimuli — to teaching syllabuses, lecture schedules, examination subjects, and beyond that to job requirements, and what is admired and rewarded by the most eminent of one's colleagues (or, failing them, a more general and less discriminating public, if only, at worst, one's students). With such people there would be no danger of their career prospects being sacrificed to their dedication to philosophy, since those prospects are the aim of that dedication. And however intellectually able such people may be, there is no likelihood of their work's having lasting value, since it answers no deep-rooted need (or, if it does, the need is not a philosophical one). It does not stand in independent relationship to its ostensible subject-matter. It does not grow out of a strongly motivated, direct and fundamental questioning of, and insight into, experience, but derives from the study of — and from responses to — other people's work.

However, the true philosopher is not one who retains a merely childlike sense of wonder. On the contrary, as children we all start out by being as unselfconscious as the animals and taking our being in the world for granted. We are intensely curious, but at first it is the world, not ourselves, that we are curious about. Self-consciousness emerges slowly in the course of our growing up; and only with that, if at all, does a sense of wonder at one's own existence develop. It may develop further into — and it is at this point that it gives rise to the metaphysical impulse — a sense of astonishment that anything exists at all. Why is there something rather than nothing?[5] That there should be anything is not, to use an Irishism, what one would have expected. *Nothing* is what one would have expected . . . 'In fact, the balance wheel which maintains in motion the watch of metaphysics that never runs down is the clear knowledge that this world's non-existence is just as possible as is its existence'[6] — a recognition, as Schopenhauer is quick to point out, which is implicit in any belief in a God as creator of the world: 'it infers the world's previous non-existence from its existence; thus, it assumes in advance that the world is something contingent'.[7]

Existence, then, precisely because it is contingent, presents philosophizing man with a problem which is fundamental in a literal sense: it could not have been taken for granted a priori, yet it is prior to all other issues. Indeed, even given the fact of existence, everything else could have been quite other than it is. What *is* just happens to be. 'In endless space countless luminous spheres, round each of which some dozen smaller illuminated ones revolve, hot at the core and covered over with a hard cold crust; on this crust a mouldy film has produced living and knowing beings: this is empirical truth, the real, the world. Yet for a being who thinks, it is a precarious position to stand on one of those numberless spheres freely floating in boundless space, without knowing whence or whither, and to be only one of innumerable similar beings that throng, press, and toil, restlessly and rapidly arising and passing away in beginningless and endless time.'[8] To see this as a vast riddle pressing on the human mind for solution is something that happens occasionally, in glimpses, to most people, I suppose. But a few are bewitched and engrossed by it. Among these are some of the great artists, great philosophers, great religious thinkers — and these comprise, in Schopenhauer's assessment, 'the noblest portion of mankind in every age and in every country'.[9]

If we were indestructible, and this existence of ours simply went on

[5] The first explicit formulation of this question appears to be Leibniz's in his *Résumé of Metaphysics* (*c.*1697). See p. 145 of *Leibniz Philosophical Writings*, Everyman edition, 1973.
[6] *The World as Will and Representation*, ii. 171. (Cf. Wittgenstein: 'It is not how things are in the world that is mystical, but that it exists.' *Tractatus Logico-Philosophicus*, 6. 44.)
[7] *The World as Will and Representation*, ii. 171.
[8] Ibid. ii. 3.   [9] Ibid. ii. 171.

and on without end, any explanation of it which we might be able to arrive at could do no more than feed curiosity, avid though that might be. It could have no practical significance of a fundamental kind, for there would be no way in which the forms of our existence could be changed by it, or in the light of it, and no possibility of our ever having any other form of existence to which it might relate. So if we knew we were simply going to go on going on, as we are, whatever happened, few would feel strongly the pressure of what would in those circumstances be a purely detached and impersonal curiosity. In addition, we should be faced with the fact that any aspects of reality with which our human intellectual or sensory apparatus could not make contact must forever remain beyond all possibility of apprehension, since we were destined to remain forever the beings we are, with the apparatus we have. The very question whether most, part, or none of reality was inaccessible to human faculties would itself lie permanently outside any possibility of answer.

However, none of this is necessarily so. And what makes it not necessarily so is the fact of death. Each one of us is faced with the certainty of an end to his human life, and, although the knowledge of this frightens us so much that most of us avoid thinking about it, it has all-pervading consequences for us as metaphysical animals. It makes our search for a meaning in existence a matter of practical significance, and gives it an edge of urgency and anguish, since our future being or annihilation hangs on what the truth is in answer to these questions. At the same time it opens the possibility of certain types of answer that would otherwise be ruled out. For the fact that our human existence must end carries with it the possibility that we may then participate in some other mode of existence that is not bounded by human nature. And from outside the limits of human nature something might be apprehensible which is not accessible to humans. So death, which impels us to hope that our being in the world has a significance which is not bounded by our human lot, is at the same time a *sine qua non* of the possibility that this may be the case.

This, however, gives rise in turn to a temptation which is nearly overpowering and yet has to be resisted, the temptation to believe what we want to believe on the ground that it could be true. Ignorance is ignorance, not a licence to believe what we like. All we know, at least to begin with, is that the possibility of there being aspects of reality which are outside the limits of human experience — and of our being at some point connected with such aspects of reality — cannot be ruled out. We do not know whether this possibility is realized or not. *A fortiori* we do not know anything about what — if the possibility is, unknown to us, realized — such reality consists in. All theistic religions fall into the error of proceeding as if they know what cannot be known. Schopenhauer believes that such religions owe their chief origins and appeal to the fear of death. 'We find that the interest inspired by philosophical and also religious systems has its strongest and essential point absolutely in the dogma of some future existence after death. Although the latter systems seem to make the existence of their gods the main point, and to defend this most strenuously, at bottom this is only because they have tied up their teaching on immortality with it, and regard the one as inseparable from the other; this alone is really of importance to them. For if we could guarantee them their dogma of immortality in some other way, the lively ardour for their gods would at once cool; and . . . if continued existence after death could be proved to be incompatible with the existence of gods — because, let us say, it presupposed originality of mode of existence — they would soon sacrifice these gods to their own immortality, and be hot for atheism.'[10]

Schopenhauer did not believe in God, nor did he believe in a personal survival of death. He regarded these notions as radically incoherent, in the sense that they are impossible to formulate without self-contradiction. What *can* meaningfully be said in the light of the fact that the limits of what is intelligible to us are not necessarily the limits of what there is is a question to which he addresses himself with great insight, but he never falls into the error of trying to speculate at length about what cannot be thought about, still less of trying to say the unsayable, or to express the inexpressible. He leads us, as it were, to the edge of the abyss, and then not only declines to make more than the briefest of comments about what might lie beyond it but insists that there are no possible terms in which such talk could be properly conducted, or even understood by us if conducted by some other kind of being with greater knowledge than ours.

With one vital qualification, which is the starting-point of his original contribution to philosophy, Schopenhauer accepts Kant's cartology of the bounds of sense. He is clear that the possibility of human understanding is limited by those bounds, and that the validation of any statement, argument, explanation or interpretation must come from within them if it is to *be* a validation. The aim of his work is to push our understanding to the full extent of those limits without falling over into nonsense by transgressing them; and moreover to do this in terms of concepts that can be cashed against the gold standard of experience, and by means of arguments that carry their own credentials with them.

[10] *The World as Will and Representation*, ii. 161–2.

On this last point: he divides into two broad kinds the thought-systems that have been put forward to meet man's need for metaphysics. There are those that try to justify themselves in terms of observation and argument, providing — or attempting to provide — good reasons for everything they say, and resting their claims on the merits of the case they are able to put before us; and there are those which, appealing to some authority, demand our credence on other than rational grounds. As he puts it, there are those that claim validation from within themselves, and those that claim validation from without. Among systems of the second kind are those which 'are known under the name of religions, and are to be found among all races, with the exception of the most uncivilized of all. As I have said, their evidence is external, and, as such, is called revelation, which is authenticated by signs and miracles. Their arguments are mainly threats of eternal, and indeed also temporal, evils, directed against unbelievers, and even against mere doubters. As *ultima ratio theologorum* we find among many nations the stake.'[11] These systems are, he thinks, 'for the great majority of people who are not capable of thinking but only of believing, and are susceptible not to arguments but only to authority. These systems may therefore be described as popular metaphysics . . .'.[12] He is not disposed to combat their existence, for he thinks that, meeting as they do a basic human need, something of their sort is bound to exist. Intellectually their level is low, and throughout history they have tried to silence criticism by force. They have also usually sought to indoctrinate the defenceless young. 'If only they are imprinted early enough, they are for man adequate explanations of his existence and supports for his morality. Consider the Koran, for example; this wretched book[13] was sufficient to start a world-religion, to satisfy the metaphysical need of countless millions for twelve hundred years, to become the basis of their morality and of a remarkable contempt for death, and also to inspire them to bloody wars and the most extensive conquests. In this book we find the saddest and poorest form of theism. Much may be lost in translation, but I have not been able to discover in it one single idea of value.'[14]

Only thought-systems of the alternative kind, those that claim validation from within, are philosophies in the true sense of the word. They try as far as they can to rest their arguments on sufficient reason, and in doing so they call on each man to judge their credentials for himself. However, in the case of intellectually serious philosophies this

[11] *The World as Will and Representation*, ii. 164–5.   [12] Ibid. ii. 164.

[13] [Cf. Hume's characterization of the Koran as 'that wild and absurd performance' in his essay *Of the Standard of Taste*. B.M.]

[14] *The World as Will and Representation*, ii. 162.

is unavoidably difficult, because of the complexity of what it is they are trying to explain. Their proper comprehension calls for prolonged study and reflection. Only people who have not just the necessary level of intelligence but also the necessary time are in a position to pursue an interest in them, even if they have one. Such people are in a minority, and likely to remain so. Therefore even if it were possible for man to arrive at a philosophy which was the one true philosophy — and, as such, qualified to displace religion — nine-tenths of mankind would still have to take it on trust, so for them it would still remain a body of faith which they accepted on someone else's say-so.

Yet religious wielders of intellectual authority and social power have always coveted the legitimation which they themselves felt validation from within would bestow on their ideas. For a thousand years natural theologians have maintained that the existence of God, the soul and immortality could be established by rational argument alone, without recourse to authority; and even after Kant had demonstrated the permanent impossibility of this they still went on trotting out their 'proofs'. Whenever the Church has been in a position to, it has imposed on philosophers the demand that their conclusions accord with its doctrines.[15] Schopenhauer mocks this magnificently. 'Why should a religion require the suffrage of a philosophy? Indeed, it has everything on its side — revelation, documents, miracles, prophecies, government protection, the highest dignity and eminence (as is due to truth), the consent and reverence of all, a thousand temples in which it is preached and practised, hosts of sworn priests, and, more than all this, the invaluable prerogative of being allowed to imprint its doctrines on the mind at the tender age of childhood, whereby they become almost innate ideas. With such an abundance of means at its disposal, for it still to desire the assent of wretched philosophers it would have to be more covetous — or still to attend to their contradiction it would have to be more apprehensive — than appears compatible with a good conscience.'[16]

Even more — indeed most of all — does Schopenhauer despise those so-called philosophers who truckle to religious or civil authority, or to intellectual fashion, or who use philosophy as a means to some other worldly end. Among his contemporaries he regarded the arch-offenders as Fichte, Schelling and Hegel, whom he saw as acquiring professor-

---

[15] The reasoning on which this demand is based is crisply exemplified in the dismissal of Schopenhauer's philosophy by the Jesuit Frederick Copleston, towards the end of his book *Arthur Schopenhauer, Philosopher of Pessimism* (p. 210): 'If Schopenhauer's philosophy were true, then Christianity would be false: if Christianity is true, as it is true, then Schopenhauer's philosophy is, in the main, false.'

[16] *The World as Will and Representation*, ii. 166.

ships and patronage in the state-run universities by teaching political
ideas which were pleasing to officialdom; flattering the religious sus-
ceptibilities of the time by reconstituting under such names as 'the
Absolute' the factitious entities of natural theology which had been
reduced to rubble by Kant; deceiving the public as to what they were
doing by deliberately cloaking it all in mystifying, oracular language;
and, through all this, debauching the intellectual development of their
students. He had no time to waste on controversy with them or with
any of their protégés. 'It enters my mind as little to mix in the philosophic disputes of the day as to go down and take part when I see the
mob having a scuffle in the street' (*Notebooks*). What he regarded as his
natural company among philosophers was quite different; it was that
nobler portion of mankind in every age whose lives are lived in thrall to
their sense of philosophic wonder and devoted to the pursuit of truth —
a community of fellow spirits, stretching back to the pre-Socratics, who
have been passing the same torch from one to another down the
darkness of centuries. As one of those, 'it occurs to me as little to
acquaint myself with all the philosophic essays of my contemporaries
as it would occur to a man, travelling from capital to capital on
important business, to seek acquaintance with the dignitaries and
aristocrats of each little town *en route*' (*Notebooks*).

Schopenhauer's view of the great tradition to which he saw himself
as belonging is made clear in his *Fragments for the History of Philosophy*,
the most substantial item in either volume of *Parerga and Paralipomena*.
Over a hundred pages long, it is almost a book in itself, or perhaps
rather an unusually full and detailed synopsis for a book. The successive section headings tell a story: 'Pre-Socratic Philosophy', 'Socrates',
'Plato', 'Aristotle', 'Stoics', 'Neo-Platonists', 'Gnostics', 'Scotus
Erigena', 'Scholasticism', 'Francis Bacon', 'The Philosophy of the
Moderns', 'Some Further Observations on the Kantian Philosophy',
'Some Observations on My Own Philosophy'. I shall not make any
attempt to retrace the whole of this journey, but something will have to
be said about that part of it which is covered in the last three sections,
namely Schopenhauer's view of his place in modern philosophy —
which is to say, philosophy since Descartes — and, in particular, his
relationship to Kant. This is also the subject of the only item in *Parerga
and Paralipomena* which precedes *Fragments for the History of Philosophy*, a
paper called *Sketch of a History of the Doctrine of the Ideal and the Real*.

In Schopenhauer's view, the fact that Descartes (1596–1650) is
generally taken to be the founder of modern philosophy is fully justified, for three reasons above all others. The first is that for hundreds of
years before him thinkers of all kinds had tried to validate claims to
knowledge by citing authority, usually the authority of ancient texts —

whether human, like those of Aristotle, or supra-human, like those of a divinely inspired bible — whereas Descartes made it an article of method not to do this. Thus he was the first philosopher of consequence since the ancient world to turn his back on forms of argument claiming validation from without, and to make a conscious and systematic effort to use only arguments which carried their own credentials. In the course of this attempt he established — and this was his second great achievement — that, far from the objective being certain and the subjective uncertain, the sole certainty we have consists in what is immediately given to us in subjective experience. Any other knowledge we lay claim to must involve inference, and therefore be liable to error. Third, following directly on from this, he formulated the problem which more than any other has been central to Western philosophy ever since: What can I know? And how can I know that I know it?

The challenge presented by Descartes was taken up by Locke (1632–1704), who described the purpose of his *Essay Concerning Human Understanding* as being 'to inquire into the original, certainty and extent of human knowledge, together with the grounds and degrees of belief, opinion, and assent' (I. i. 2). The explanatory model at which he arrived — very much under the influence of Descartes, but also of the new physics in general from Galileo to Boyle (with which Descartes was closely involved, both as scientist and as mathematician — being, among other things, the inventor of analytic geometry) — was something like this. We live in a universe of material objects existing in boundless space and time. These objects impinge on our sensory apparatus in various ways, for instance by reflecting light rays to our eyes; or by creating, when touched, sound-waves which travel through the air and strike on our ear-drums; or by pressing our skin against our nerve ends. In ways like this, through our senses, we acquire notions like red, green, loud, quiet, hard, soft, hot, cold, bitter, sweet. These stimuli come in regular combinations which we learn from experience to associate with particular objects as their sources — for instance, relative to the other contents of the world, apples all come within a tiny range of size, of shape, of colour, of consistency, and so forth, and as children we soon learn to identify any bundle of combined such characteristics from within these ranges as an apple. (Of course, our perceptions remain fallible: on some particular occasion the object may be a piece of wax fruit, or a different kind of real fruit, or we might be deceived in some other way — by the light, perhaps, or the distance, or our own inattention.) From innumerable such experiences we generalize to form concepts which enable us to think about objects when they are not present to direct experience. This decisive step liberates us from animal enslavement to the here and now, and enables us to build up a picture of a world which extends forward and backward from our own location in time, and in all directions beyond our horizons in space. Nevertheless, all our knowledge derives originally from experience, and that is both its guarantee of reliability and the only such guarantee it could have. This direct experience is ultimately of two categories: sensation and reflection. By reflecting on our sensations, and by being self-aware when we reflect, we learn about the operations of our own minds, and acquire such concepts as perceiving, knowing, thinking, reasoning, believing, doubting, and so on.

Even now, after three hundred years, this account tends at first to strike many people as a straightforward picture of reality which is so obviously true as to be dull. Yet it bristles with difficulties, some of which seem to defy solution, and others of which Locke himself recognized and moved on to deal with. It needs little reflection, he added, to tell us that the world around us cannot bear a simple one-to-one relationship with the picture of it we build up in our heads. Sensory qualities like colour and smell, for instance, could not exist independently of sensation, and must therefore require an experiencing subject before they can come into being. To the unreflecting, the apple's colour may seem to inhere in it, to be as much a constituent of it as its shape and size, but this cannot be so, for its shape and size, thought Locke, could exist in exactly the form in which we perceive them if there were no perceiving subjects in the universe, yet its colour could not. For there to be colour, he says, an interaction is required between an object and a subject such as is not involved in the case of shape or size. Obviously there is a plain sense in which objects do have different colours — some apples are red and some are brown, some are green, some are yellow — but for an object to have a certain colour is for it to have a propensity to cause experiences of a certain kind in the consciousness of an observer. It may well be that this process always has its origin in the object, and differs according to which object it originates in, but it cannot operate without a subject, and therefore cannot be something that just *is*, in the object, independently. Examples of other such properties, besides all the colours, are all the tastes and all the smells, and all varieties of such relative characteristics as hot and cold, light and dark, soft and hard. The term Locke uses for them is 'secondary qualities'. 'Primary qualities', by contrast, are all those attributes which 'would be really in the world, as they are, whether there were any sensible being to perceive them or not'.[17] Examples of primary qualities are weight, shape, dimensions and movement. This distinction be-

[17] Locke, *Essay Concerning Human Understanding*, II. xxi. 16 — quoted by Schopenhauer in *Parerga and Paralipomena*, i. 16.

tween primary and secondary qualities was not invented by Locke, but it was expounded by him at unprecedented length and strength: it was he who made it fully operational in philosophy, and it is still associated with his name more than with anyone else's.

A second set of problems arising out of Locke's model has its origins in the double role played by causality. The model postulates, first, the physical causation of sensations in us by objects outside us, followed by, second, a process of causal inference whereby we who are in receipt of these sensations translate them back into a world of physical objects perceived by us as being in a space around us. So although the simple act of looking at an object may feel to me as direct and unmediated as can possibly be, this is an illusion, for it is a process comprised of not one but two chains of cause and effect, the first operating physically between objects (one of which is my body), the second operating inside me as a perceiving subject. In the course of either of these processes, primary and secondary qualities alike can get distorted. Every colour looks different in different lights. Distant objects look smaller than they are. From every angle of vision except one a circle looks not circular but elliptical — indeed, from every angle except one all two-dimensional shapes and surfaces appear different from what we know them to be. In these and many other ways, objects in the external world are not as our senses present them to us. How, that being so, are we to know what they are really like? Does 'really' have any meaning in this context? If it does, can we ever know things as they really are? And if we can, how will we know when we know?

By this route, Locke arrived at his own formulation of Descartes's fundamental problem. In this form it became central to the empiricist tradition in philosophy, and has remained so ever since. Personally, I am inclined to think that, on empiricist assumptions, a question presented in any such form as *How can I know whether, or to what extent, the real world existing in space outside me corresponds to the picture of it I have in my head?* poses a problem which cannot be solved. For the only satisfactory way of testing the accuracy of a picture is by comparing it with the original: and if we question the accuracy of perception itself we have no access to the original except via the picture — indeed, the very existence of the original is an inference from the picture, and is therefore open to doubt. We can never stand outside experience as such and make an independent comparison of it with its objects (which would then have to be apprehended by us independently of experience, which is self-contradictory). Given the empiricist model, then, what the world is like independently of experience is a permanently unanswerable question — with the consequence that human knowledge as such presents a permanently insoluble problem.

Berkeley (1685–1753) met this situation with an observation simple in itself but epoch-making in its consequences for philosophy. We have to concede, he said, that all that can ever be present to our conscious awareness is experience. This being so, in inferring from our experiences the existence of entities of a categorially different nature — namely physical objects, which are not experiences — we are putting forward a hypothesis for which we shall never be able to provide justification, and which indeed could make no difference to us even if it were true. What is more, we cannot so much as render intelligible to ourselves the notion of objects as existing in terms other than the experiences we have of them. Why, then, do we balk at the obvious inference? *What there is is experience, and experiencing subjects.* We know this positively, because we know ourselves in the most direct and undeniable way to be experiencing subjects that have experiences. And we know it negatively, because the existence of nothing else can ever be established, and perhaps not even envisaged. (To say that experience must be experience *of* something is to make an elementary confusion between language and logic: there is no reason in logic why experiencing subjects and their experiences should not be all there is.) Berkeley, like Descartes, was enough a child of his time to bring God into the argument. To such a question as: 'Does your philosophy mean that no object exists unperceived — so that, for example, the cooking utensils in my kitchen pop into and out of existence as observers pop into and out of the kitchen?' his answer was: 'The question does not arise, because there is one observer who perceives everything all the time, namely God — so the world of experience actually does persist in time in the way we ordinarily take it to do, because it is sustained in the mind of God.' He might have added, but did not think to, that people who have no difficulty in understanding what it means to say that the world exists in the mind of God ought to have no difficulty in understanding what it means to say that the world exists in the minds of men.

Fortunately, when God is brought in to a good argument it does not seem to be too difficult to get him out again. Berkeley's immediate successor in the great tradition, Hume (1711–1776), had little difficulty in demonstrating that on Berkeley's own showing the existence of God was as unwarrantable an inference from direct experience as the existence of an independent world of matter. More interestingly, he applied the same argument to one of the two entities in terms of which Berkeley had explained all human experience, namely the experiencing subject — the point being that this cannot be located in experience, and therefore cannot be known directly. 'Pain and pleasure, grief and joy, passions and sensations succeed each other, and never all exist at the same time. It cannot therefore be from any of these impressions, or from any other, that the idea of self is derived; and consequently there is no such idea.'[18] In different guises this argument has reappeared over and over again in the writings of empiricist philosophers down to our own day.[19] If it is accepted, and the concept of the experiencing self is dropped, the pure empiricist's answer to the basic Cartesian or Lockean question becomes: '*Yes, there is indeed something which is known for certain, and that is that there are experiences. To assert the existence of anything else is to make an inference which cannot be proved. Known reality consists of experience, and experience alone.*'

Thus a consistently held-to line of empiricist argument leads away from any form of Cartesian dualism — away from a view of the known world as containing two radically different kinds of entity, one physical, the other mental — to a neutral monism, a world in which everything is of one stuff, experience. To say, as has been said so often, that a thoroughgoing empiricism thus leads us inexorably into a thorough-going idealism is false, and misses the point that what it actually leads us to is a nullification of the distinction. If known reality consists of experience alone it is merely a matter of linguistic preference whether we describe it in the language of material objects and scientific concepts or in the language of subjective sense impressions and thoughts. No issue about the nature of reality is at stake, for it is the same reality that is being described in either case: the question is merely which of two ways of talking we find the more serviceable. (This argument constitutes the central thesis of A. J. Ayer's *The Foundations of Empirical Knowledge*.) This step leads only too easily to the removal from philosophy of the age-old argument about the nature of the world, and its replacement by discussion of alternative ways of describing experience — and this is indeed the way empirical philosophy has developed in the twentieth century.

Hume's characteristic mode of critical argument was to show that a

[18] *A Treatise of Human Nature*, Book I, pp. 238–9 (Everyman Edition).
[19] See, for instance, Bertrand Russell: *The Problems of Philosophy*, p. 19:

'When I look at my table and see a certain brown colour, what is quite certain at once is not "I am seeing a brown colour", but rather, "a brown colour is being seen" . . . So far as immediate certainty goes, it might be that the something which sees the brown colour is quite momentary, and not the same as the something which has some different experience the next moment.'

And Wittgenstein: *Tractatus Logico-Philosophicus*, 5. 631:

'The thinking, perceiving subject does not exist.'

And A. J. Ayer: *Language, Truth and Logic*, 2nd edition, p. 126:

'Our reasoning on this point, as on so many others, is in conformity with Hume's.'

And Gilbert Ryle: *The Concept of Mind*, VI (7), the whole section headed 'The Systematic Elusiveness of "I" '.

certain concept was not derived from experience, was therefore without
empirical justification, and must therefore be regarded by any consistent empiricist as empty. So far we have mentioned two of his applications of it, to God and to the self; but he applied it most disconcertingly
of all, and with the greatest historical consequences, to the concept of
causality. According to the new (by this time Newtonian) science, all
the motions of matter in space, which in aggregate constitute the
ongoing history of the physical world, take place in accordance with
causal laws. And according to Locke's new way of ideas, human
observation of this world involves both of the causal processes described a moment ago in connection with his account of perception.
Furthermore, to the direct experience we thus acquire, we apply the
(again) causal connections of inductive inference in order to formulate
concepts — and then again, using concepts at a higher level, to formulate scientific laws. At every level, causal connection is seen as being the
all-integrating connecting tissue of the world, and also of our knowledge, and furthermore as being what connects those two to each other.
It is what at every level, therefore, provides cohesion and coherence. It
is why there is a world. It is why there is not chaos.

Hume's greatest insight, as astounding as Berkeley's, was that causal
connection is not something that can be met in experience. His
argument begins by subjecting the concept 'cause' to analysis and
showing that it connotes not only a conjunction of two states of affairs
but their *necessary* conjunction: not just 'A happened and then B happened' but 'A happened, therefore B happened'; not just 'B happened
after A' but 'B happened because of A'. He then goes on to show that
whereas the successive states of affairs can be observed, there is no
observable third entity in the form of a link between them which
establishes the necessity of their conjunction. It may be arguable that
we are able to 'think' such a connection, but it is certain that however
hard we look we cannot locate it in observation.

The critic might say: 'Ah yes, but we can distinguish between states
of affairs which are causally connected and those which are only
fortuitously connected by the fact that the former invariably occur
together.' That will not do. First, many states of affairs occur together
invariantly in a conjunction which is not fortuitous but also not causal:
for instance, day has invariably followed night, and night day, but
neither is the cause of the other. Second, there is no reason why a
fortuitous conjunction should not be invariant. For all I know there
might be, somewhere in the world, a person who, every time I cough
(and only when I cough), sneezes. This is perfectly possible, and
unknown to us both it may have been going on like this since the day we
were both born, and may continue to the day we both die. In that case

the conjunction between my coughs and his sneezes will have been totally invariant. But it is not causal. And the fact is that in a universe as vast and complex as ours there are practically bound to be things which recur together in constant conjunction without being causally connected.

So, however often we observe that in certain circumstances an event of type A is accompanied or immediately followed by an event of type B, that does not prove that the two are causally connected. But this, Hume pointed out, knocks the bottom out of inductive support for scientific laws. However often we observe that, say, a body of gas increases in volume when it is heated, our observations do not prove that the heating causes the expansion, and therefore do not logically justify the expectation that next time we heat a body of gas it will necessarily expand. If we observe the succession often enough, you may say, we shall come to take it for granted and expect it in advance. Hume would reply that if what you say is a fact then it is a fact about human psychology and not about the logic of the situation, which remains as described. Furthermore, since causal connection cannot be established by observation in a single case, still less can unrestrictedly general causal statements be validated by observations, however numerous. Yet all scientific laws consist of such statements — for instance Boyle's law that at a constant temperature the volume of a given quantity of any gas is inversely proportional to the pressure of the gas. The same is true of descriptive generalizations that do not contain any causal elements at all: however often water has been encountered and found to be wet it does not follow that all water is wet. We know that some liquids are not wet, for instance mercury, and it could be that unwet water awaits us in some as-yet unencountered place or time. So even statements like 'water is wet' cannot be validated by observation. Yet it is impossible to formulate any account of experience generally — in other words to frame any conception of the world, indeed any conception of *a* world — without the use of such general notions.

Hume showed, in short, that the world picture of Newton and Locke — down-to-earth, commonsensical, scientifically demonstrated though it appears — is (a) built up by means of inductive inference for which it is impossible to give a logical justification, and (b) erected on a foundation of assumptions about causality whose validity cannot be demonstrated. These arguments had a revelatory effect on Kant (1724–1804), whom, in his famous phrase, they woke from dogmatic slumber. Until he came across them, which seems to have been in early middle age, he had regarded the foundations of Newtonian science as utterly secure. His own studies in it were profound and original — at the age of thirty-one he had become the first person to publish a physical theory

which accounted for the history of the universe in terms of its having
evolved, as against its having always had more or less its present form.
His more strictly philosophical writings had been talented but conventional, the sort that meet only the felt needs of the day and bring a man
the kind of renown that dies with his pupils. When he experienced the
intellectual shock of reading Hume he did not go so far as to doubt that
the physical world was as Newton described it. It was proved to be, he
thought, by the accuracy of all known predictions based on Newton's
laws — whether as applied to the solar system, the tides, ballistics,
machinery, or whatever else. It would be simply false to say that we do
not have all this knowledge. We do. The point, in the light of Hume's
arguments, is: How is it *possible* for us to have it? The twin bases on
which Kant had always supposed it to rest — the observation of causal
connection, and induction — had turned out not to be sustaining it.
What, then, was? How is it possible for us to have knowledge of the
world which is accurate and yet not supplied to us *by* the world? Where
does it come from? How do we get it? The question is not primarily
about the workings of the world, it is about the nature of knowledge,
and thus turns out on analysis to be about the workings of the human
mind. And Kant's attempts to solve the problem in this hitherto
unperceived form led him to look at the human intellect in an entirely
new way. By the end of his investigations he was ascribing to the mind
things which everyone before him had ascribed to the world 'outside'
us. The shift of viewpoint was one which seemed to him as radical and
as all-revealing as Copernicus's discovery that the motions of the
heavenly bodies suddenly make sense if we look at them from the point
of view of the sun and not the earth as our centre of reference.

The natural starting-point of the Kantian argument is the observation that what we can perceive, experience or know must inevitably
depend not only on what there is to perceive, experience and know but
also on whatever apparatus we have for perceiving, experiencing and
knowing. As one might put it now, our bodies happen to be equipped to
receive and interpret electro-magnetic waves of some frequencies but
not others — light waves and heat rays, but not radio waves or X-rays.
If we had another sort of physical equipment we would apprehend
objects in other terms. Anyone who has discussed vision with the
congenitally blind will know that it is radically impossible for them to
get any inkling of what seeing is, however intelligent or imaginative
they may be and however much they may yearn to understand. We
can, all of us, conceptualize objects only in terms of the modes of
apprehension we have. It is this that gives its fullest force to the
empiricist doctrine that all knowledge is derived from experience. The
very opening sentence of the Introduction to *The Critique of Pure Reason*

is: 'There can be no doubt that all our knowledge begins with experience.' Empiricist philosophers before Kant had viewed this in terms of its positive implications only, but Kant realized that what was *ruled out* by the doctrine, delineating as it does the limits of all possible human knowledge, had yet more fundamental implications for our understanding of the world.

Let us take, as an example, our apprehension of a small and simple object in nature such as an apple. We may see it, and identify its location in space relative to ourselves and any number of other objects, up to the rest of the known physical universe. We may also locate in time the moment of our seeing it relative to any number of other events, up to the whole of history: 'My eye fell on that apple just as the clock struck one on the afternoon of the 16th February, AD 1982.' Using our sense of sight more concentratedly we can look closely at its colour and texture. We can note its exact shape, measure its exact dimensions, weigh it. Bringing into play our sense of touch we can feel the weight in our hands, and the apple's degree of hardness, the degree of its coldness against our skin, the balance of its mass as we aim it as if for a throw. Using other senses still we can smell it, taste it, and listen to the different sounds it gives off when struck or touched by different sorts of objects. We can break it open and repeat all these operations on its innards, noting also new entities, such as pips, and other kinds of attribute such as consistency and moisture. We can make our description of the apple as full and detailed as we like, to the extent of giving exhaustive accounts of its biophysical structure and its biochemical constitution. But every single one of the operations I have listed is dependent on our having the particular perceiving apparatus we have, and yields its information in forms which cannot exist separately from that apparatus, namely in terms of visual, tactile, olfactory, gustatory and aural data, and the concepts derived ultimately from these, and the operations with those concepts that constitute thought. There simply are no other ways in which we can experience contact with the apple, or form any conception of it. If we try a thought-experiment and attempt to 'think away' from the apple all these sense-dependent and mind-dependent attributes which we associate with it, in order to arrive at what it 'really' is *in itself* independently of our experience of it, what we actually arrive at is indistinguishable from nothing at all. It might seem that 'out there' beyond our sense-dependent experiences there must lie some entity which causes these experiences in us and which we differentiate in English by the word 'apple' from other entities which give us other experiences; but what it is like independent of all actual and possible experiences is something of which we can form not the ghostliest conception. Our position with respect to that is the same as the congenitally blind man's with respect to vision. Inescapably, the whole world as we experience it is mediated through our sensory and mental apparatus. Consequently this world of our experience is not at all a world of things as they are in themselves but a world of sense-dependent and mind-dependent phenomena. To things as they are in themselves we have simply no access.

Up to this point Kant's argument may seem like a richer, more powerful and sophisticated version of Berkeley's. Certainly, he had more in common with Berkeley that he was prepared to admit, even to himself. (Schopenhauer regarded the second edition of *The Critique of Pure Reason* as a mutilation of the first, perpetrated by Kant with the mistaken aim of emphasizing his differences from Berkeley.) However, from this point in the argument Kant moves on to consider the role which our minds, as distinct from our senses, have to play in perception, and here his arguments become altogether more original and profound. As a small, straightforward instance of an act of immediate perception than which it would be hard to pick anything simpler or more direct, let us take again the case of simply looking at an apple. For me to have the experience I describe as 'seeing an apple' the following three conditions, at the very least, have to be satisfied: I must (1) be in receipt of some visual datum; (2) be in possession of the concept denoted by the word 'apple'; (3) be able to categorize the visual datum as falling (or as not falling) under the concept. Unless I can do at least these three things I cannot see an *apple*. But only the first is sensory, and only the first is solely a matter of immediate activity; the other two are mental, and depend on my bringing prior dispositions to bear on the sensory situation. It turns out, then, that even the simplest act of direct perception is by no means solely a matter of immediate experience but is more mental than sensory, and involves as great a contribution from my brain as from the object seen. By this token there can be no such thing as *immediate experience*. We readily assume that, for me to see an apple, there has to be an apple. But — equally necessary — there have also to be those mental pre-conditions which make my having the experience [which I can identify as seeing an apple] possible. Some of Kant's profoundest pages are devoted to an investigation of what these pre-conditions are. On reading them one feels he is opening up a whole floor beneath what had always been taken for the basement level in our analysis of experience: Locke had been led by his investigation of experience to consider its pre-conditions, but Kant's investigation of those pre-conditions leads him to consider *their* pre-conditions.

Kant goes on to point out that the mind makes another contribution to perception of a different order. Our percepts present themselves to us not in a chaos or jumble or torrent but as elements in an interconnected structure which we may refer to as either 'the world' or 'experience'. The dimensions of this structure are space and time. The phenomena so structured are in continuous change — but again these processes are coherent, not chaotic, owing to the causal interconnectedness of successive states of the phenomena. But if the phenomena of our experience cannot exist in the way we experience them independently of our experience of them, and therefore independently of our apparatus for experiencing, then nor can the frameworks which are nothing but the forms of their interconnectedness in our experience — spatial, temporal, causal. The notions of an absolutely empty space, an absolutely empty time, and a causality that does not connect anything with anything else at all, are without content; space, time and cause are not 'things' which have some separate existence, they are ways in which objects and events relate to one another. This being so, there is no imaginable sense in which, as disembodied and empty forms, they could walk into our heads from outside and be filled up there by having the world of phenomena pumped into them by our senses. Indeed, there is no way in which they could exist 'outside' us at all, separate from the phenomena whose interrelatedness they are the forms of. So time, space and causal connection — those constituents of the irreducibly necessary structural framework of the world of phenomena — must, like the phenomena themselves, be mind-dependent: they must have their origins in that massive mental apparatus of ours which provides the necessary pre-conditions of experience.

Appropriately, the philosophy of which these are the central doctrines is called 'transcendental idealism'. It is Kant's main teaching, and constitutes the core of what Schopenhauer took from him. To some people it seems to appear self-evidently wrong, even if difficult or impossible to confute. So, for that matter, do the much simpler doctrines of Berkeley. One of the most famous passages in Boswell's *Life of Johnson* contains an assertion of this. 'After we came out of the church, we stood talking for some time together of Bishop Berkeley's ingenious sophistry to prove the non-existence of matter, and that everything in the universe is merely ideal. I observed, that though we are satisfied his doctrine is not true, it is impossible to refute it. I shall never forget the alacrity with which Johnson answered, striking his foot with mighty force against a large stone, till he rebounded from it, — "I refute it *thus.*" '

It is the crassest possible misunderstanding of Kant, as of Berkeley, to suppose that he was in any way denying empirical reality. On the contrary, both philosophers were insisting on it with a specificity that others had not seen the need for, or possibility of. Neither of them was super-subtly rejecting the validity of our ordinary everyday experiences of stones and apples. What Berkeley was denying was the existence of a duplicate world of objects corresponding to these experiences yet categorially different from them and subsisting independently of them. Kant, by contrast, supposed that the objects of our experience must have some substratum of independent existence — in other words, that there must be things in themselves, independently of our experience of them — but that what they thus were in themselves was something which we could form no conception of, since *everything* about the way we can conceptualize them is experience-dependent. To express this, as Schopenhauer tends to, by saying that the whole world of phenomena is a world of appearances only, is misleading, because it seems to imply that these appearances are illusory. This is not what is being said. On the contrary, on a consistent Berkeleian view the world of phenomena is all the reality there is, and on the Kantian view the world of phenomena is the entire world of experience, created by interaction between transcendentally existent subjects and transcendentally existent objects, neither of which is able to figure in it because it is something to which they give rise between them. But by the same token, although this subject in itself and this object in itself are metaphysical and unknowable, they are nevertheless known to exist, because they are necessary presuppositions of the experiences we have.

Locke had already familiarized us with the proposition that secondary qualities, though they appeared to us to exist 'out there' in the objects of the external world, required certain predispositions in a perceiving subject before they could have being. He did not, of course, suggest that we were conscious of possessing such predispositions, still less of bringing and applying them to perception situations. He would have agreed that if we sought to locate them in ourselves or in our perceptions we would not be able to do so. Nevertheless, they were shown by analysis to be necessary pre-conditions of the experience we have: 'if the conditioned is given, then the totality of its conditions must also be given'.[20] Thus what Kant did was to extend to all experience what Locke had tried to establish with regard to secondary qualities — and to extend it not only to primary qualities but to the very framework itself: to causality, without which it is impossible for us to conceive of any intelligible experience at all; and to the forms of space and time, without which it is impossible for us to conceive of any material object as existing. But although the Kantian view transcends the distinction between primary and secondary qualities, it provides us with a rationale of it. Locke's primary qualities were those which we could not conceive of any object as not possessing: and the real reason why we

[20] *The World as Will and Representation*, i. 481.

could not so conceive is that they relate to the pre-conditions of our being able to have any apprehension of an object at all. Likewise, a solution is provided to the problem of causality which seemed insoluble to Hume. The reason why we cannot locate causal connections anywhere within our experience of the world, and yet at the same time are unable to make the very notion of any such experience intelligible to ourselves without it, is that it is a necessary *pre-condition* of there being any experience of a world at all.

Kant's conclusions opened up pathways of a completely new kind to the frontiers of human knowledge and understanding. Before him, it had been assumed that if there were any limits to human knowledge we should eventually come up against them in our investigations of the world. Some people even believed that it would be possible for us to go on finding out more and more until there was nothing left to find out. But Kant introduced a hitherto undreamt of possibility, that the limits of possible human knowledge could be determined by investigating the limits of our own faculties. If it could be established with certainty what the pre-conditions are that need to be met with within our own faculties before we can have any experience or any knowledge at all, we should have succeeded in establishing in general terms the limits of all possible experience and knowledge. What particular experience or knowledge we then actually acquired within those limits would depend on circumstances, but there would be no circumstances in which we could acquire experience or knowledge outside them. This is not to say that there could *be* nothing outside them, but only that nothing outside them could be a possible object of experience or knowledge *for us*.

In the course of this argument Kant showed that there were whole areas of intellectual activity in which claims to knowledge transgressed the bounds of sense — for instance traditional metaphysics, theology and rational psychology; or, to give examples, 'proofs' of the existence of God, and the soul, and 'proofs' of immortality. He did not, it must be stressed, regard himself as having disproved immortality or the existence of the soul, or of God,[21] but as having shown these things to be beyond all possibility of proof or disproof, since they were beyond all possibility of experience or knowledge, and thus forever *incapable of being known*. His arguments to this effect reduced to rubble much of the

---

[21] Indeed, he himself believed in all three. In the context of his philosophy this can be defended as rational. Where the truth or falsehood of a proposition can be ascertained, it is superstitious to rest on faith, but where it cannot, it is equally superstitious to adopt an attitude of certainty either way. In such a case the only rational alternatives are either to hold what is acknowledged to be a fallible opinion on one side, or else to suspend judgement. Myself, I should have thought that the straightforward conclusion to draw is the agnostic one; but faith, in the circumstances, is not counter-rational.

philosophizing and theologizing of centuries. It was for this that he earned from Moses Mendelssohn (the grandfather of the composer, and not only one of the most famous philosophers of his century but an important pre-critical influence on Kant) the epithet *Der Alleszermalmer* — the all-pulverizer. Schopenhauer, on the other hand, though he thought very highly of Kant's destructive accomplishments, saw his supreme achievement as being the liberation of human understanding from the age-old and fundamental error of realism, the almost irresistible belief that the world exists outside us independently of our perception of it and yet pretty much as we perceive it. The piercing of this illusion by arguments validated from within seemed to Schopenhauer the most significant advance in the history of human thought. And he saw his own philosophy as realizing the revolutionary possibilities opened up by it. 'Kant's teaching produces a fundamental change in every mind that has grasped it. This change is so great that it may be regarded as an intellectual rebirth. It alone is capable of really removing the inborn realism which arises from the original disposition of the intellect . . . In consequence of this, the mind undergoes a fundamental undeceiving, and thereafter looks at all things in another light. But only in this way does a man become susceptible to the more positive explanations that I have to give.'[22] . . . 'My line of thought, different as its content is from the Kantian, is completely under its influence, and necessarily presupposes and starts from it.'[23]

Schopenhauer's first book opens with the words 'Plato the divine, and the astounding Kant . . .', and his writings from then on are studded with expressions of awe at Kant's achievement, and also a sense of personal indebtedness to him for it. Kant's 'meditations are the profoundest that ever entered into man's mind'.[24] He is 'one for whose profound wisdom I have the greatest reverence and admiration; one to whom, indeed, I owe so much, that his spirit might truly say to me, in the words of Homer: "I lifted from thine eyes the darkness that covered them before" . . .'.[25] The effect [Kant's] words produce in the mind to which they really speak is very like that of an operation for cataract on a blind man.'[26] Working entirely from within the central tradition of Western philosophy, Kant had carried the mainstream of its development to the point at which, without his even knowing it, it made contact

---

[22] *The World as Will and Representation*, i. xxiii. Schopenhauer's explanation of why the original disposition of the intellect is to realism is given in the footnote on page 88 and discussed in Chapter 7.

[23] Ibid. i. 416–17.   [24] Letter dated 21 December 1829.

[25] *On the Fourfold Root of the Principle of Sufficient Reason*, Hillebrand translation, pp. 109–10. (See Payne tr., p. 133.)

[26] *The World as Will and Representation*, i. xv.

with the insights which lie at the heart of Hinduism and Buddhism. He had thus, without its having been any part of his intention — and though he died without knowing he had done it — connected Western with Eastern thought at the most fundamental level. All this was part of the position from which Schopenhauer saw himself as having made a decisive, not to say conclusive, advance. It is therefore essential for a grasp of Schopenhauer's philosophy to understand how he saw the Kantian revolution as having drawn together all the most important developments in the history of human understanding before him. The following quotation will, I hope, make this clear.

Now as Kant's separation of the phenomenon from the thing-in-itself, arrived at in the manner previously explained, far surpassed in the profundity and thoughtfulness of its argument all that had ever existed, it was infinitely important in its results. For in it he propounded, quite originally and in an entirely new way, the same truth, found from a new aspect and on a new path, which Plato untiringly repeats, and generally expresses in his language as follows. This world that appears to the senses has no true being, but only a ceaseless becoming; it is, and it also is not; and its comprehension is not so much a knowledge as an illusion. This is what he expresses in a myth at the beginning of the seventh book of the *Republic*, the most important passage in all his works, which has been mentioned already in the third book of the present work. He says that men, firmly chained in a dark cave, see neither the genuine light nor actual things, but only the inadequate light of the fire in the cave, and the shadows of actual things passing by the fire behind their backs. Yet they imagine that the shadows are the reality, and that determining the succession of these shadows is true wisdom. The same truth, though presented quite differently, is also a principal teaching of the *Vedas* and *Puranas*, namely the doctrine of Maya, by which is understood nothing but what Kant calls the phenomenon as opposed to the thing-in-itself. For the work of Maya is stated to be precisely this visible world in which we are, a magic effect called into being, an unstable and inconstant illusion without substance, comparable to the optical illusion and the dream, a veil enveloping human consciousness, a something of which it is equally false and equally true to say that it is and it is not. Now Kant not only expressed the same doctrine in an entirely new and original way, but made of it a proved and incontestable truth through the most calm and dispassionate presentation. Plato and the Indians, on the other hand, had based their contentions merely on a universal perception of the world; they produced them as the direct utterance of their consciousness, and presented them mythically and poetically rather than philosophically and distinctly. In this respect they are related to Kant as are the Pythagoreans Hicetas, Philolaus, and Aristarchus, who asserted the motion of the earth round the stationary sun, to Copernicus. Such clear knowledge and calm, deliberate presentation of this dreamlike quality of the whole world is really the basis of the whole Kantian philosophy; it is its soul and its greatest merit. He achieved it by taking to pieces the whole machinery of our cognitive faculty, by means of which the phantasmagoria of the objective world is brought about, and presenting it piecemeal with marvellous insight and ability. All previous Western philosophy, appearing unspeakably clumsy when compared with the Kantian, had failed to recognize that truth, and had therefore in reality always spoken as if in a dream. Kant first suddenly wakened it from this dream; therefore the last sleepers called him the all-pulverizer. He showed that the laws which rule with inviolable necessity in existence, i.e. in experience generally, are not to be applied to deduce and explain *existence itself*; that their validity is therefore only relative, in other words, begins only after existence, the world of experience generally, is already settled and established; that in consequence these laws cannot be our guiding line when we come to the explanation of the existence of the world and of ourselves. All previous Western philosophers had imagined that these laws, according to which all phenomena are connected to one another, and all of which — time and space as well as causality and inference — I comprehend under the expression of the principle of sufficient reason, were absolute laws conditioned by nothing at all, *aeternae veritates*; that the world itself existed only in consequence of and in conformity with them; and that under their guidance the whole riddle of the world must therefore be capable of solution. The assumptions made for this purpose, which Kant criticizes under the name of the Ideas of reason, really served only to raise the mere phenomenon, the work of Maya, the shadow-world of Plato, to the one highest reality, to put it in the place of the innermost and true essence of things, and thus to render the real knowledge thereof impossible, in a word, to send the dreamers still more soundly to sleep. Kant showed that those laws, and consequently the world itself, are conditioned by the subject's manner of knowing. From this it followed that, however far one might investigate and infer under the guidance of these laws, in the principal matter, i.e., in knowledge of the inner nature of the world in itself and outside the representation, no step forward was made, but one moved merely like a squirrel in his wheel. We therefore compare all the dogmatists to people who imagine that, if only they go straight forward long enough, they will come to the end of the world; but Kant had then circumnavigated the globe, and had shown that, because it is round, we cannot get out of it by horizontal movement, but that by perpendicular movement it is perhaps not impossible to do so. It can also be said that Kant's teaching gives the insight that the beginning and end of the world are to be sought not without us, but rather within.[27]

[27] *The World as Will and Representation*, i. 419–21.

Chapter 4

More Arguments for Transcendental Idealism

Transcendental idealism was at the core of what Schopenhauer took over from Kant, and it needs to be accepted at least provisionally, if only for the sake of the argument, if the development of his philosophy is to be followed. But for many people even this constitutes an obstacle, since their attitude to it is uncompromisingly dismissive. So before we proceed, there is need to give more discussion to transcendental idealism, not with a view to persuading the reader of its truth but with a view to persuading him that it is not beneath serious consideration. People are most commonly impeded in giving it this by two things: first, the doctrine is widely misunderstood, and therefore widely misrepresented, especially in the English-speaking world, as being something that *is* beneath serious consideration; second, both the doctrine and the standard misrepresentation of it are deeply counter-intuitive. Let us start by getting these two obstacles out of the way.

I have often heard professional philosophers in Britain, including gifted ones, assert that according to transcendental idealism 'everything exists in a mind, or in minds' or 'existence is mental'. This is a radical error. It is not what Kant or Schopenhauer were saying, nor is it what they believed. On the contrary, both of them believed that the abiding reality from which we are screened off by the ever-changing surface of our contingent and ephemeral experiences exists in itself, independent of minds and their perceptions or experiences. If reality had consisted only of perception, or only of experience, then it would presumably have been possible for us to encompass it exhaustively in perception or experience, to know it through and through, without remainder. But that is not so, and the chief clout of transcendental idealism is contained in the insight that while it is possible for us to perceive or experience or think or envisage only in categories whose possibility, nature and limits are determined by our own apparatus, whatever exists cannot in itself exist in terms of those categories, because existence as such cannot be in categories at all. This must mean that in an unfathomably un-understandable way whatever exists independently of experience must be in and throughout its whole nature different from the world of our representations. But because the world of our representations is the only world we know — and the only world we can ever know — it is almost irresistibly difficult for us not to take it for the world *tout court*, reality, what there is, the world as it is in itself. This is what all of us grow up doing, it is the commonsense view of things, and only reflection of a profound and sophisticated character can free us from it.

It is a tautology to say that the world as we perceive and conceive it is solely something that exists in terms of sense-dependent and mind-dependent categories. For that reason, far from anyone dismissing it as nonsense, everyone ought to feel compelled to accept its truth. The question is, is there anything other than our perceptions and conceptions? The commonsense realist says, Yes, there is an independently existing material world to which our perceptions and conceptions correspond. Berkeley says: There are only our, and God's, perceptions and conceptions. Kant and Schopenhauer systematically differentiate themselves from both: they say, Our perceptions and conceptions cannot be all there is, but cannot be 'like' what exists in addition to them, so what else there is cannot consist of an independently existing world which corresponds to them; however, since they constitute the limits of what we can envisage, we cannot form any notion of what there is besides. I suspect that we have lying before us here the chief elements in the explanation of why a radical misconception of transcendental idealism has been absorbed so thoroughly into the empirical tradition. It is a tradition which prides itself on being founded on observation and commonsense: it incorporates the commonsense view of the world, and hence the primal error of realism with which we all grow up. This being so, it is easy to see how, when the transcendental idealist insists on what is actually an analytic truth, namely that our whole conception of the world is in mind-dependent categories which could not possibly apply to anything independently of awareness, an empiricist who believes that the world of actual and possible experience is everything there is can take him to be saying that nothing has any existence independently of our minds. This interpretation is reinforced by the fact that transcendental idealists use terms like 'empirical world' and 'physical object' in accordance with their own presuppositions and not those of empiricists: by 'empirical world' they mean not the totality of what there is but the totality of actual and possible experiences, which is a decidedly more accurate use of terms; and whereas many empiricists would argue that it comes to the same thing, transcendental idealists specifically think it does not. And when they speak of a 'physical object' or 'material object' they mean an object as it figures in the empirical world in *their* sense of that term. So on their use of terms the whole world of material objects is indeed mind-dependent — but only tautologically. Transcendental idealists write in this vein as a matter of course; but only if they were to share presuppositions of the empiricists which they do not share would they be meaning what the empiricists take them to mean. An empiricist's tendency to misinterpretation is likely to be yet further reinforced if the only idealist philosopher with whose work he has a scholarly acquaintance, and hence the one from whom his only solidly based notions of idealism derive, is the one thrown up by his own tradition, namely Berkeley. But far from Kant's having been a Berkeleian of any sort, the need — which he was made increasingly aware of by the way the first edition of *The Critique of Pure Reason* was misunderstood — to dissociate his philosophy much more clearly from Berkeley's than he had yet done was the chief thing that motivated him to revise the book as radically as he did for the second edition. In other words, that famous revision was aimed at counteracting precisely the sort of misunderstanding that has nevertheless become perennial.

After two hundred years, empiricist philosophers still usually give the impression of proceeding on the assumption that, by and large, reality must roughly correspond to our conception of it. For most of the time they make no effective distinction between the world and our system of the world, except in so far as they commonly, and as an article of method, treat discussion of the latter as doing for discussion of the former. They are familiar with the Argument from Illusion,[1] of course,

---

[1] This is the name traditionally given to arguments designed to show that things are not, and cannot be, always as we perceive them. In most circumstances objects look smaller to us the further away from us they are, yet we know their size to be constant; the church tower looks red in the sunset, yet we know it to be grey; from all directions except one a circle looks like an ellipse; and so on. There is an inexhaustible supply of such examples, most of them in themselves trivial, but what they show is not trivial, namely that the world is not 'really' as it presents itself to us in experience. And even a philosopher who is unequivocally located within the empiricist tradition will find, if he pursues this line of reflection far enough, that it carries him into the domain of the incommunicable. For instance, Bertrand Russell: 'It is sometimes said that "light *is* a form of wave-motion", but this is misleading, for the light which we immediately see, which we know directly by means of our senses, is *not* a form of wave-motion, but something quite different — something which we all know if we are not blind, though we cannot describe it so as to convey our knowledge to a man who is blind. A wave-motion, on the contary, could quite well be described to a blind man, since he can acquire a knowledge of space by the sense of touch; and he can experience a wave motion by a sea voyage almost as well as we can. But this, which a blind man can understand, is not what we mean by *light*: we mean by *light* just that which a blind man can never understand, and which we can never describe to him.

'Now this something, which all of who are not blind know, is not, according to science, really to be found in the outer world: it is something caused by the action of certain waves upon the eyes and nerves and brain of the person who sees the light. When it is said that light *is* waves, what is really meant is that waves are the physical cause of our sensations of light. But light itself, the thing which seeing people experience

and agree that things are not in all respects as they appear to us, but they tend to believe that the discrepancies are in principal all susceptible of a rational explanation, and that apart from such discrepancies the world must be pretty much as we perceive it, otherwise we should not be able to function in it as successfully as we do. What has still not been taken on board, even after all this time, is that there is no intelligible sense in which our system of the world can be said to be 'like' the world as it is in itself because the former can exist only in terms of mind-dependent and sense-dependent categories *and there are no other kinds of category in terms of which any comparison between those and the world could be made by us.* And even leaving aside the impossibility of comparison, categories as such are applicable only to experience, they are forms of experience: they *categorize* perceptions, conceptions, and whatever else may be available to us in consciousness or awareness: what they are is such that there is no way in which they could be features of things as those are in themselves, independent of consciousness or awareness. The main conclusion to which such considerations drive us — that reality in itself cannot be what we all grow up taking it to be, but that whatever it is independently of what we take it to be is something radically unconceptualizable by us — is, it seems to me, inescapably true, and is the nub of transcendental idealism, but neither of these things seems to have been properly grasped by empiricists.

I take the notion that everything exists in a mind, or in minds, or that existence as such is mental, to be incredible — indeed, not to be coherently statable — and certainly to be counter-intuitive. It is that notion that is the standard misrepresentation of transcendental idealism. But the doctrine correctly understood is also counter-intuitive. Although the arguments for it can be coherently stated, and may be assented to by the understanding, to look at total reality as if it really is as the doctrine says it must be is almost impossibly difficult for most of us for most of the time. However, far from being a peculiarity of transcendental idealism, this is something which it has in common with a consistent empiricism. There is a famous passage towards the end of Hume's exposition of his epistemology in which he writes: 'The *intense* view of these manifold contradictions and imperfections in human reason has so wrought upon me, and heated my brain, that I am ready to reject all belief and reasoning, and can look upon no opinion even as more probable or likely than another. Where am I, or what? From what causes do I derive my existence, and to what condition shall I return? Whose favour shall I court, and whose anger must I dread? What

and blind people do not, is not supposed by science to form any part of the world that is independent of us and our senses. And very similar remarks would apply to other kinds of sensations.' (*The Problems of Philosophy*, pp. 28–9.)

beings surround me? and on whom have I any influence, or who have any influence on me? I am confounded with all these questions, and begin to fancy myself in the most deplorable condition imaginable, environed with the deepest darkness, and utterly deprived of the use of every member and faculty. Most fortunately it happens, that since reason is incapable of dispelling these clouds, Nature herself suffices to that purpose, and cures me of this philosophical melancholy and delirium, either by relaxing this bent of mind, or by some avocation, and lively impression of my senses, which obliterate all these chimeras. I dine, I play a game of backgammon, I converse, and am merry with my friends; and when, after three or four hours' amusement, I would return to these speculations, they appear so cold, and strained, and ridiculous, that I cannot find in my heart to enter into them any further.'[2] Even so, as Hume himself would always insist ('A true sceptic will be diffident of his philosophical doubts, as well as of his philosophical convictions'[3]) we must never let the fact that something is counter-intuitive lead us into assuming it to be false. Counterintuitiveness is itself something that calls for philosophical investigation — especially since it plays such an important *de facto* role in everyone's approach to metaphysical questions.

Among the most elementary features of the human situation are such facts as that we are living on the surface of a giant ball that is spinning on its axis, and at the same time hurtling through space; that on the opposite side of the ball from some of us are others who, relative to us, are upside-down; that 'up' feels the same to them as it does to us, yet is in the opposite direction; and that in space *as such* there can be no 'up' or 'down' at all. I do not suppose there is a single one of my readers who will want to dispute any of these propositions. Yet they are deeply counter-intuitive — all of them notoriously difficult, if not impossible (especially the last one) for us to grasp in determinately imagined terms. Throughout most of human history the possibility of nothing like any of them seems to have occurred to anyone. The individuals who began to put them forward — or put forward the theories which led to them — were often persecuted as subverters of religious and other established order, or else derided as cranks and fantasists. Copernicus was dismissed by Luther as 'this fool [who] wishes to reverse the entire science of astronomy'. Even Bacon, a philosopher-scientist of genius, regarded the doctrine of the rotation of the earth as self-evident rubbish unworthy of serious consideration.

Yet such new theories as these gave birth not only to modern science

---

[2] David Hume: *A Treatise of Human Nature*, vol. i (Everyman Edition), pp. 253–4.
[3] Ibid., pp. 257–8.

but to modern philosophy — the whole distinctive tradition of modern Western thought developed out of the new view of the world of which they were part. What may seem to us now the bluff, plain, commonsensical, down-to-earth empiricism of Locke incorporates ideas which earlier in Locke's own century had been unintelligible to men of genius. At several important subsequent stages in the development of the same tradition there were forward strides which were likewise dismissed by eminent contemporaries as steps into fantasy. In short, what we are inclined to regard as the most hard-headed and practical of all the intellectual traditions to which we are heir is rooted in ideas which, when they were new, were as counter-intuitive as any justified innovations have ever been. Furthermore, although we may now suppose it to be obvious why those ideas were so counter-intuitive at first, the obviousness is dispelled by reflection. This is the point of a famous anecdote. 'Meeting a friend in a corridor, Wittgenstein said: "Tell me, why do people always say it was *natural* for men to assume that the sun went round the earth rather than that the earth was rotating?" His friend said: "Well, obviously, because it just *looks* as if the sun is going round the earth." To which the philosopher replied: "Well, what would it have looked like if it had looked as if the earth was rotating?" '[4] Actually the state of affairs is even more puzzling still, because we now know that the earth is rotating, and yet it still remains virtually impossible for us to see or feel much of our experience in terms of the reality of that knowledge. The result is that in our unreflecting day-to-day thinking most of us go on imputing the same geocentricity to our total environment as our remote ancestors did who knew no better.

There are multiple parallels between the conceptual revolutions advocated by Copernicus and Kant which Kant himself was the first to draw. To those he drew, similar parallels could be added between the way the two theories were received. Transcendental idealism has met with the same snorting dismissal from intelligent people, the same openly declared assumption that it is so blatantly counter-intuitive that it can be agreed to be untrue without discussion; and even when it is respected and grasped — indeed, even if it is believed — it remains intractably difficult to feel that one is *actually* experiencing matters as the theory says one is. From these parallels, obviously, it does not follow that, because the heliocentric theory of our planetary system turned out to be correct, transcendental idealism is also correct; but it does follow that these particular considerations against it do not constitute good arguments. It simply may be the case that the truth about any feature of our situation is almost insuperably counter-intuitive. In

---

[4] Tom Stoppard: *Jumpers*, p. 75.

fact we now *know* that a considerable number of fundamental truths — perhaps, in a sense, most of them, including those I have already itemized — are. Schopenhauer offers an explanation of why this is so which we shall come to in due course. Meanwhile, if a prima-facie case is made out for a counter-intuitive theory's being worthy of our serious consideration — and surely Kant has done at least that — then serious consideration it must receive.

This may sound obvious, but in practice it is surprisingly difficult to get transcendental idealism taken seriously, even by many good philosophers. Once, in Karl Popper's living-room, I asked him why he rejected it, whereupon he banged his hand against the radiator by which we were standing and said: 'When I come downstairs in the morning I take it for granted that this radiator has been here all night' — a reaction not above the level of Dr Johnson's to Berkeleianism. Some of the best of empiricist philosophers have regarded transcendental idealism as so feeble that they have spoken patronizingly of Kant for putting it forward — from James Mill's notorious remark about his seeing very well what 'the poor man would be at'[5] to passages in P. F. Strawson's *The Bounds of Sense* in which the author calls transcendental idealism names[6] without bothering to argue seriously against it, and toys playfully with the question whether Kant was perhaps having us all on in putting it forward. Strawson's book is especially interesting in this context because of its merits, which are considerable. It succeeds in a twofold task: first, to show that Kant's programme of constructive metaphysics is for the most part an admirable programme which can still provide us with great illumination; second, to show that it is not logically interdependent with transcendental idealism (as Kant clearly thought it was), thereby enabling us to embrace the former while rejecting the latter — an aim which emerges as the chief purpose of the book. That we should want to reject transcendental idealism is never questioned, still less argued. Strawson appears from the outset to take it as having been already agreed between himself and his readers that transcendental idealism is some sort of risible fantasy, and therefore that Kant's constructive metaphysics will merit our attention only on condition that it can be shown to be logically independent of transcendental idealism. That we might take both these aspects of Kant's thought seriously is a possibility which seems not to have entered Strawson's head.

Just in passing, the point may be made that Kant is not alone in being almost universally hailed as one of the very greatest of philo-

---

[5] Quoted by Leslie Stephen in *The English Utilitarians*, vol. II, p. 288.
[6] 'Preposterous' . . . 'a doctrinal fantasy' . . . 'a phantasmagoria' . . .

sophers yet having his central doctrine subjected to this kind of dis-
missal-without-discussion by analytic philosophers. Even Plato is subjected to similar treatment. Anthony Quinton puts the point with
characteristic trenchancy and succinctness when he says: 'Who would
deny, after all, that Plato was a genius, yet who could seriously believe
Plato's view of the Universe — that what really exists is abstract
timeless entities, and that the world of things in space and time is a sort
of shadowy appearance? One can recognize the genius of a philosopher
without accepting very much of what he says.'[7] The short answer to
Quinton is that the view he dismisses, or something recognizably
similar to it, has been held by most of the people whom he would regard
as the greatest philosophers there have ever been, and also by countless
millions of others, including all the believers in the world's main
religions. In other words, most of the human beings who have lived
since the beginning of civilization, including most of the ablest ones,
have held it. This does not make it correct — that, I trust, goes without
saying — but to talk as if it is generally agreed to be so obviously false
that it can be dismissed without discussion is mistaken.

There is a double fault in this no-nonsense approach. The tradition
to which all the contemporary philosophers I have quoted regard
themselves as belonging began with the new science, and — in addition
to the fact, which I have already stressed, that the beginnings of that
were as counter-intuitive as anything in transcendental idealism — the
world view it has led to in our own day is counter-intuitive to an even
greater degree. It would be difficult to imagine anything much more
counter-intuitive than either of the two outstanding advances in twentieth-century physics, namely relativity theory and quantum mechanics. No one understands what quantum mechanics even so much as
means, and there is serious discussion as to whether we may not have to
revise our standards of intelligibility to accommodate it.[8] So the self-
consciously commonsensical approach of some contemporary philosophers could scarcely be more at odds with the current state of the
scientific tradition to which they pay lip-service. If the truth be told,
their attitudes are now commonsensical in precisely the way in which
Luther's and Bacon's attitudes to Copernicus were commonsensical.
In addition to all this there is the point — which we shall discuss more
fully when we come to Schopenhauer's pioneering version of it — that

[7] *Men of Ideas*, ed. Bryan Magee, pp. 114–15.

[8] See, for instance, Hilary Putnam in *Men of Ideas*, p. 230: 'We want to say: "Quantum mechanics works, and the very fact that it works means there's something
fundamentally right about it." And, with respect to its intelligibility, we're willing to
say, in part, that maybe we have the wrong standards of intelligibility, that we have to
change our intuitions.'

what is counter-intuitive is largely biology-dependent. Furthermore, such of it as is not biology-dependent is largely culture-dependent. Schopenhauer was fond of pointing out that Hinduism and Buddhism — whose adherents, he usually went on to say, number together more than those of any other religion — incorporate a version of transcendental idealism, so that the doctrine would seem neither new nor odd to educated people in large parts of the world. He ought in fairness to have added that it has always been accepted in those religions that it takes an individual years of study and reflection before he is able to pierce the veil of phenomena with his intellectual imagination and stop mis-taking the world of experience for the world as it is in itself. Yet here again there is a parallel: students of Kant, to an extent unmatched by those of any other Western philosopher, are prone to say that it took them years of study and reflection before they understood him.

I would go so far as to say that there is now no seriously entertainable theory about the nature of the objects of immediate experience which is not counter-intuitive. As far back as 1912 Bertrand Russell wrote in *The Problems of Philosophy* (p. 38 — his italics): '. . . common sense leaves us completely in the dark as to the true intrinsic nature of physical objects, and if there were good reason to regard them as mental, we could not legitimately reject this opinion merely because it strikes us as strange. The truth about physical objects *must* be strange.' *Must* indeed. There is no major branch of human thought, whether philosophical or scientific, by which the material world of subjective experience is not now regarded as something in the nature of a surface which is sustained and presented to our senses by a more permanent, underlying order of things which itself is invisible. In the case of science this is the world internal and external to the surfaces of matter, a world of cells and molecules and atoms and subatomic particles, of chemical structure and transmission, of electricity, magnetism and gravitation, of mass and energy, waves and gases. Much of this is counter-intuitive in the highest degree. Most of what we already know about it was undreamt of and unimaginable until only yesterday in human history; yet to disbelieve in the existence of this world of almost entirely imperceptible entities all around us and within us would be taken today as a sign of ignorance, or stupidity, or lack of imagination, or perhaps even of slight madness by way of crankiness — just as it would be so taken to disbelieve in the rotation of the earth.

If the truth about physical objects *must* be strange, any pursuit of it is bound to make demands on the imagination as well as on the intellect. The common assumption that to grasp a theory one need only be sufficiently intelligent is misplaced. Over and over again, as in examples I have given, men of the highest intelligence fall into an imaginative, not an intellectual, shortcoming in the way they fail to grasp a theory, or in the point-missing way they criticize it; indeed this happens only too often to every one of us. Consequently, the need for self-awareness and self-criticism is as great at the imaginative as at the intellectual level — perhaps, for philosophers, greater, because they tend to be preselected for intellectual rather than imaginative qualities, and also because so much of their normal activity (consisting as it does in attempts to make distinctions, especially fine ones, perspicuous) involves a disciplined and scrupulous insistence on literalness and exactitude — and this activity, like any other, tends to attract to itself people whose cast of mind makes it congenial. Our imaginative limitations are probably taxed more severely today by transcendental idealism than by any major doctrine in the central tradition of philosophy. In our consideration not only of Kant's transcendental idealism but of Schopenhauer's philosophy in general we shall need all the imaginative resources we can draw on, for the imaginative depth of both is very great.

For reasons which have been set forth notably by Karl Popper, and which I have discussed elsewhere,[9] I do not believe that it is possible to demonstrate the truth of a theory, but I do think it may be possible to demonstrate that one theory is nearer to the truth than another; and, like Popper, I see this as being the case not only with theories which are falsifiable, and may therefore be regarded as scientific, but also with some theories which are unfalsifiable, and have therefore to be regarded as metaphysical. And for reasons which I hope this chapter will make clear, I think transcendental idealism must be nearer to the truth than transcendental realism. This, I repeat, is not to say that I regard transcendental idealism as the whole truth. On the contrary, I suspect there may be room for a better theory, and in Chapter 10 I shall have something to say that bears on this. All that matters for the present, and indeed for purposes of following Schopenhauer's arguments, is whether or not Kant's central doctrines represent an advance on Hume's; and it seems to me clear that they do. I am also convinced that to react to their shortcomings by returning to, or staying with, transcendental realism is regressive. It is usually dangerous to accuse other people of not understanding, but I really do think, as Schopenhauer has put it, that 'in spite of all that may be said, nothing is so persistently and constantly misunderstood as idealism, since it is interpreted as meaning that the empirical reality of the external world is denied. On this rests the constant return of the appeal to common sense, which appears in many different turns and guises ...'[10] To

---

[9] Bryan Magee: *Popper* (Fontana, London, 1963).
[10] *The World as Will and Representation*, ii. 7.

anyone who has grasped the essentials of transcendental idealism —
and I have to confess it took me years of wrestling with it before I came
anywhere near to doing so — it is uncomfortably clear that the familiar
criticisms of it from empiricist and positivist standpoints are made
prior, not posterior, to any such process of understanding. They are
shallow, and they rest on mistakes about what it is that is being said. Of
course transcendental idealism may be wrong, but it cannot be wrong
for *those* reasons.

The crux of what the transcendental idealist needs to say to the
empiricist is this: 'None of your experience is being doubted, still less
denied. *None.* Your feelings to the contrary are misleading you. What is
being denied is the validity of your inference from what you experience
to what you do not experience, indeed to what you could never experience. It is an inference which your own philosophers have been
trying and failing to justify these three hundred years. And your
present-day philosophers who applaud Kant's demonstration of the
vacuity of all those so-called empirical concepts whose content is not
among the possible objects of experience do not seem to cotton on to the
fact that in doing this Kant demonstrated the vacuity of the concept of
independently existing things. It is transcendental idealism, not
empiricism, that has the merit of starting from immediate experience,
and then proceeding only by steps which it can justify. Empiricism, in
spite of its name, does neither of these things: it starts from an assumption, which it then finds impossible to validate. Most of its perennially
insoluble problems are rooted in the fact that it cannot justify what it
presupposes. Its most fundamental error is that it systematically mistakes an epistemology for an ontology: it ascribes sense-dependent or
mind-dependent properties to independently existing things. This
means, in other words, that it ascribes independent existence to entities
which are sense-dependent or mind-dependent, and thus does unawares the very thing which it mistakenly accuses transcendental idealism of doing. It does this because, for reasons which it is tautologous to
state (and if it is tautologous it must be true), there are no terms in
which we can have any apprehension of whatever exists other than
through the categories made available to us by what we are — the
categories of human sense, feeling, thought and so on, and these are
epistemological categories. Of what exists as it is in itself, independent
of us and our categories, we have no way of forming any conception.
Thus we cannot *help* constructing our ontological notions in epistemological terms. And thus we all grow up assuming that things *are* in
the terms in which we *perceive* them. It requires an undeceiving of a
categorially fundamental character for us to realize that it cannot be
so, except in the sense (if there is a sense) in which Beethoven's Fifth

Symphony is like the groove on a disc of black vinyl which is a record of it.'

Transcendental idealism sets out from a realization which empiricism has never come to terms with, except in the person of Berkeley, and which induced in Hume something akin to intellectual despair, namely the realization that our commonsense belief in an independent world of material objects that exist around us in space and time cannot be legitimated by experience, nor by logic, nor by any combination of the two. This being so, our everyday belief in such a world is a metaphysical belief: the commonsense view of the world is a primitive and pre-critical metaphysics. Our acceptance of it is an unvalidatable leap of faith. This fact, so counter-intuitive, is extraordinarily difficult to grasp — and, as Hume stressed, difficult to retain even after it has been grasped — but it is a fact nevertheless. Unlike Hume, though, transcendental idealism offers a solution to the problem. It points out that many of the apparently insoluble difficulties and paradoxes and contradictions which we encounter in our realistic thinking about the world of experience dissolve when the unvalidatable postulate of its independent existence is given up. A point which Schopenhauer, like Berkeley, repeatedly makes, and which the realist persistently misunderstands, is that experience is what it is and not another thing. The realist has somehow got it into his head that experience is being denied when, on the contrary, it is being insisted upon. Experience is experience is experience: it is not something else. The whole world of experience is precisely what it seems: this is what Schopenhauer is saying, and he says it several times. In that it is the realist who wants to make unjustified inferences to the independent existence of a duplicate world of material objects of which our experiences are supposed to be representations — and the transcendental idealist who points out that these inferences cannot validly be made — it is transcendental realism, not transcendental idealism, that is the fantasy. To understand this it is essential for us to be clear that what the transcendental idealist is saying is not that the empirical world does not 'really' exist: of course it exists. 'To dispute about its reality can occur only to a mind perverted by over-subtle sophistry.'[11] The point is that the world of experience cannot exist independently of experience. Therefore it cannot exist independently *full stop*. It is not an autonomous, hermetically sealed and self-contained realm. Therefore it cannot be all there is. Furthermore, for us to have the experiences we do have, something has to be the case in addition to those experiences and the processes of experience (we shall come to Schopenhauer's arguments for this in the

---

[11] *The World as Will and Representation*, i. 15.

next chapter), and therefore they cannot exist independently of whatever that is, either. So the empirically real is presented by transcendental idealists *not* as something whose existence is illusory, and *not* as a
realm which stands over against the transcendentally ideal and somehow in conflict with it, but as a realm which is exactly what it seems to
us to be, neither more nor less, and the conditions of whose possibility
are contained in (perhaps indeed comprise) the transcendentally ideal.
In other words the transcendentally ideal and the empirically real are
complementary, the two components of total reality, and without the
former the latter could not exist. There is nothing at all — nothing
necessarily, that is — religious about this view, still less mystical, and
less still occult: on the contrary, it has been arrived at solely by the
processes of reason. For myself, I should say that it is more rigorously
arrived at, and better sustainable logically, than transcendental realism.

The history of ideas, including philosophy, develops to an indispensable degree on the basis of criticism. *A* puts forward a theory, and is
then followed by *B*, who perceives not only its value but some of its
shortcomings, and puts forward a new theory which subsumes what is
good in *A*'s without containing its perceived faults. Then along comes
C, who does exactly the same with *B*'s theory. And so it goes on
indefinitely — albeit untidily, with interruptions, detours, zig-zags,
journeys up blind alleys and garden paths, waves of reaction, and so on.
There are always last-ditch defenders of *A* against *B* who, when *C*
comes along and effectively criticizes *B*, claim *C*'s efforts as justifying
their own pertinacities. We are all under a temptation to stay put in the
most forward resting-place that is felt by us to be comfortable, and to
return to it after unsuccessful attempts to advance from it. This urge to
return to, or stay with, an earlier one in a long line of failed solutions has
its roots deep in human psychology, and is found in every field of
human activity: in politics it is one of the many reasons why conserva-
tive attitudes are perennial. In philosophy it is why there are not just
Cartesians and Lockeans but also Platonists and Aristotelians. One is
tempted to infer that every position that has ever been occupied is still
occupied by someone. Of course, if all individuals behaved like this
there would be no intellectual history, but that cannot be held as an
intellectual objection: if a theory could be 'correct' it would be wrong,
or at least unnecessary, to change it, and resistance to change —
however temperamental, or psycho-emotional, or self-interested its
basis — would be intellectually justifiable. But in reality there does not
seem ever to have been a philosophy that was open to no valid criticism.
It has never yet happened that all *S*'s criticisms of *R* have been nullified
by *T*'s criticisms of *S* (at least where *R*, *S* and *T* were all well-known

philosophers). What has always been required is a forward movement, not a backward one — a new synthesis, or an innovating theory, which incorporates the old ones while at the same time superseding them by providing acceptable solutions to problems which they were unable to solve.

As we saw in the last chapter, this is how modern philosophy developed from Descartes, through Locke, Berkeley and Hume, to Kant. But at that point the mainstream becomes a delta. Because of the counter-intuitiveness of transcendental idealism, defenders of the empirical tradition have seized on the faults in Kant as a justification for remaining within their own tradition. In consequence they have never really got beyond Hume, who provides (as Kant himself would have agreed) the best established position before Kant. Many of their outstanding representative figures have acknowledged this, some in despair, others with good cheer. An example of the latter is A. J. Ayer, who, in talking about logical positivism (otherwise known as logical empiricism), has made the point frequently and contentedly — for instance: 'It is indeed remarkable how much of the doctrine that is now thought to be especially characteristic of logical positivism was already stated, or at least foreshadowed, by Hume.'[12] An example of the former is Bertrand Russell, who begins the chapter on Hume in his *History of Western Philosophy* with this despairing paragraph:

> 'David Hume (1711–76) is one of the most important among philosophers, because he developed to its logical conclusion the empirical philosophy of Locke and Berkeley, and by making it self-consistent made it incredible. He represents, in a certain sense, a dead end: in his direction, it is impossible to go further. To refute him has been, ever since he wrote, a favourite pastime among metaphysicians. For my part, I find none of their refutations convincing; nevertheless, I cannot but hope that something less sceptical than Hume's system may be discoverable.'

Russell says here that a thoroughgoing empiricism is not credible, but if it is taken to embrace — as it almost always is — the doctrine of

---

[12] *Logical Positivism*, ed. A. J. Ayer, p. 4. Such utterances from Ayer abound: see for instance the quotation on p. 61 of the present volume; or the passage on p. 49 of *Modern British Philosophy* (ed. Bryan Magee) which begins:

'MAGEE: ... The central doctrines of *Language, Truth and Logic* were baldly and clearly stated. What were they?
AYER: They were very simple. They derived very much from Hume ...'.

Or: 'Not only did Hume exclude metaphysics for very much the same reasons as the Viennese positivists were to give but he can also be seen as having anticipated their famous principle of verifiability ...'. (*Part of My Life*, A. J. Ayer, p. 116.)

transcendental realism, I would go further and say that it is not coherently statable. Therefore if transcendental idealism is rejected, some third doctrine is required. It may be that this is the next step forward, the next great act of innovating genius that lies ahead of us in the history of philosophy.

It is not fortuitous that the profoundest questions to which enquiry within the empirical or realistic traditions penetrates are at the level of epistemology — *What can we know? And how can we know we know?* — for this is the deepest level at which questions can coherently be formulated on the basis of empiricist assumptions. Questions of existence as such cannot be handled on the basis of those assumptions because, for reasons put forward in the previous chapter, there is no way in which the existence of things *as such*, independent of our knowledge of them, can be coherently characterized or conceptualized; and — as, ironically, Kant was the first to realize and show — what we can know cannot extend beyond the limits of what we can ask. However, in the very asking of the basic empiricist questions an ontology has already been passed over. The fact that there is any possibility of 'knowing' at all, anything that may conceivably know or be known — that state of affairs, *whatever it may be*, which is accepted as given — *this* is the biggest mystery of all. However, any attempt to ask questions about it is branded by empirical philosophers, consistently with their presuppositions, as futile, because the questions themselves either are nonsensical or could not possibly have answers.

If, for the sake of argument, we were to allow an empirical philosophy to presuppose an ontology without question, I can think of at least one which would give rise naturally to a fully coherent empiricist epistemology as regards our knowledge of objects. It would not be refutable by epistemological analysis, and therefore not refutable within a philosophical tradition whose deepest level of penetration was the epistemological level. It could thus, within such a tradition, appear as a true account of our knowledge, with the qualification only that its presuppositions could not be established. To put this another way, it would be obviously possible for it to be true, but it would not be possible for us to prove it to be true. It would go roughly as follows. If the material world exists independently of any sentient being's experience of it, then the degree of success which living entities at any evolutionary level will achieve in surviving in it must relate to their success in adapting themselves to it. Realism in this everyday sense of the word might not alone be enough to guarantee survival, but unrealism beyond a certain point must inevitably bring destruction. At the higher levels, the levels of sentient and animate species, survival must involve, among other things, the reliability and speed with which food, shelter, enemies and escape routes can be identified and seized. A creature would therefore need to have a specific, detailed and accurate representation of its environment immediately available to it, on the basis of which it could act with sufficient realism in our everyday sense to survive. It is difficult for us not to envisage any such representation in visual terms — the very words 'envisage' and 'representation' have the visual metaphor built into them — but it could in principle take any number of forms. Bats identify the precise location and shape of objects in their environment by a sophisticated yet accurate interpretation of the reflections back to them of sounds which they themselves emit — a sort of natural radar. The forms of sense involved are not the decisive factor: it is the accuracy and usefulness of the information gained that count. From what we know of evolution it could be said to be virtually certain that those species alone have survived which, among other things, have a sensory apparatus which supplies them with detailed accurate representations of those aspects of their environment that matter to their survival, and that such apparatus in each case was evolved as a survival mechanism through millions of years of natural selection. This would explain why the physical world is so closely and refinedly akin to what we humans at our highly selected level of the evolutionary process perceive it to be, and yet still not exactly the same.[13] For on this account there are indeed two worlds, one of things in themselves, the other a representation of that world in the senses and minds of conscious beings who are able to make contact with it only through images and concepts which are inside their own bodies and which were developed for that purpose; and discrepancy between the two worlds must always be both a logical and a practical possibility. Even so, for all the reasons given in the foregoing chapter, we could never have the independent-of-experience access to objects which alone would enable us to test the validity of our 'knowledge' by directly comparing our perception of reality with reality itself. So this plausible epistemological model, derived from evolutionary biology — even though it seems to provide an explanation which, if true, really does explain — cannot be put to the test. (I am leaving aside the notorious difficulties involved in testing the theory of evolution itself:[14] my point

---

[13] It would also provide a plausible explanation of counter-intuitiveness as a characteristic of some aspects of reality (see pp. 156–8). Schopenhauer came close to supplying this whole argument in his explantion of why it is that our intellects are such defective instruments for apprehending the larger questions of existence, namely that they were not evolutionarily developed for that purpose but for a quite different one, the promotion of our animal survival — and for *that* purpose they have proved to be outstandingly effective. We shall return to this in Chapter 7.

[14] See, for instance, Ch. 27 of Karl Popper's *The Poverty of Historicism*.

here is confined to epistemology.) Up to this point, then, it remains the case that with this, as with any theory of perception which incorporates the assumptions of transcendental realism, a leap of faith is required: it may be true, but it is not testable, and it is therefore a metaphysical system of belief. However, if that were the only drawback to it, it would be possible for someone to be a realist without self-contradiction, provided he acknowledged the logical status of his faith and did not claim it as knowledge.

I say 'if that were the only drawback to it' because in the words with which I introduced this example I allowed, in order simply to let the argument be put, two assumptions that cannot be permitted to stand. The first, impermissible because it begs the main question, was the existence of the natural order as given. The second, impermissible because it is demonstrably false, was that the only requirement of a coherent epistemology is that it should explain our knowledge of objects. By now there should be no need for me to explain the first of these objections. As for the second, a coherent epistemology needs to give an account not only of our knowledge of objects but also of the spatio-temporal framework within which they are perceived as existing. And as Kant saw clearly — it is the natural starting-point of his refutation of transcendental realism, and his exposition of it has indeed become a *locus classicus* in the history of philosophy — this cannot be done on the basis of consistent empiricist assumptions. Here we come to a new, and this time devastating, objection to transcendental realism, an objection which concerns the limits of a framework which transcendental realism cannot avoid postulating. If material objects, which cannot be conceived of as other than extended in space and persisting in time, exist independently of experience, then their spatio-temporal interrelationships must also exist independently of experience. In that case, are time and space unbounded? If they are not, did time have a beginning, and will it have an end? If it had a beginning, are we precluded from asking what was the case before that? May we not ask what will be the situation after it ends? Indeed, can the notion of time as starting or stopping be even so much as coherently formulated without our having to postulate a meta-time for it to start or stop *in* — and could not the same questions then be asked about the meta-time? Corresponding antinomies also arise with regard to causal connections between events in the empirical world. If the present state of affairs is the causal outcome of whatever preceded it, and that of whatever preceded that, and so on, was there ever a first state of affairs? If so, what brought it about? If there is any answer *at all* to that question, then it was not the first state of affairs but the causal product of something before it. But if there is no answer, let us consider just a moment what it is we then find ourselves trying to envisage: a world not merely unexplained but *by definition* inexplicable, coming instantaneously into existence out of nothing (and not created by a God either, since that would be a causal explanation — of which we would then have to ask: 'And how did *He* get there?'). As with time and causality, yet again with space: if space has limits, am I precluded from asking what lies beyond them? If so, what, in principle, could prevent a rocket from continuing on a straight course for ever? Would it eventually bump up against something? If so, what? Would that something itself exist in a space? If so, one could ask what lies beyond it, and it would then not constitute a limit — but if it did not, how could it constitute an obstacle?

All these seemingly insoluble problems arise on the assumption that time, space, and sequences of causal interconnection have limits. If they do not — or if we try to bypass the problems by assuming that they do not — what we find is that we then run into another set of problems which are equally insoluble. Let us assume that the spatio-temporal framework must be unbounded, must be one of unlimited space, and of beginningless and endless time, within which all chains of causally connected events are without beginning. As Schopenhauer was fond of pointing out, the present moment could not exist, and we could not exist in the present, if it were necessary for infinite time to have elapsed before *now* was reached. The same point applies to any beginningless causal chain of events. And as for space, the universe cannot be infinite in extent and still *be*: for, to exist, an entity must have identity, and there cannot be identity without limits. By the same token there cannot be an infinite number of objects in the universe. Infinite series can be constructed in mathematics and then put to practical use — the series of whole numbers is the most obvious and useful example — so the point is not that the concept of infinity does not have meaning or usefulness (it has both) but that it can characterize only what Kant called 'mere ideas'. To count without stopping is something which can be set as a task — it can be thought of, ordered, understood, attempted, symbolized in mathematical and other ways — only it cannot be *done*. An endless series cannot, by definition, be completed, and therefore cannot exist as an entity. In other words, infinity can characterize an object of thought, but cannot characterize anything *as it is in itself* independently of thought: therefore it can be a property of a transcendentally ideal world but not of a transcendentally real one.

In sum, then: if we postulate the world as existing independently of our experience of it there is no way in which we can make fully and determinately intelligible to ourselves the thought of its having come into existence out of nothing, and yet no way in which we can make intelligible to ourselves the thought of its not having had a beginning;

similarly, there is no way in which we can coherently formulate the notion of the space in which it exists as being bounded, and yet no way of conceiving it as unbounded; and there is no way in which we can think of time itself as beginningless, nor yet of it as having had a beginning. So the presuppositions of realism cannot be formulated. Thus realism is an incoherent doctrine.

The blight which has descended on empirical philosophy since Hume results ultimately from the attempt to carry on as if these problems either had not been formulated or had been satisfactorily dealt with. Empiricist philosophers have simply plunged on without facing up to the fact that their realist assumptions are incoherent. This is especially culpable in that one of the main tasks of philosophy is the excavation and critical investigation of the presuppositions of our thinking. Philosophers, of all people, have no excuse for refusing or neglecting to engage in that. And it is especially ironical when such people, of all people, mock at transcendental idealism for what they allege to be its incoherences. It ill behoves philosophers who have opted to rest in a world-view whose presuppositions are riddled with anti-nomies which they choose to refrain from investigating to deride alternative world-views in which the fissures are, to say the least of it, no more monstrously gaping. If a man may accept transcendental realism it is hard to see on what ground transcendental idealism can be denied serious consideration. Indeed, if a man may accept transcendental realism it is difficult to imagine what a man may not accept.

We have seen how Schopenhauer, who regarded knowledge of Kant as the beginning of wisdom and saw clearly that the British philosophy of his day was benighted because it remained in ignorance of Kant, actually tried to rectify this by getting himself commissioned to translate *The Critique of Pure Reason* into English. Alas, even when — eventually, and by other hands — Kant's chief work was translated, his metaphysics was not properly absorbed by the Anglo-Saxons, only his ethics. Between Kant's day and ours the only systems of metaphysics from outside the empiricist tradition to secure any appreciable foothold in the Anglo-Saxon world have been those of 'that intellectual Caliban'[15] Hegel and his philosophical successors, notably Marx. Justified disillusionment with these has resulted in an unjustified rejection of metaphysics as such, followed usually by a flight back to the discredited solutions of unreconstructed empiricism. In the 1940s and 1950s the commonest response of empiricist philosophers to the challenge of the antinomies of time, space and causality was to dismiss them as pseudo-questions, non-questions. The chief reason why they were

[15] Preface to the Second Edition of *The World as Will and Representation*.

said to be unreal questions was that they were not answerable. This wilfully ignored the fact that if the questions appeared unanswerable it might be because they rested on false assumptions, in which case investigation of those assumptions might be an important philosophical task. It also seemed to assume that only questions with determinate answers should be asked — which, if true, would abolish almost the whole of philosophical enquiry, including most of the enquiries on which empiricist philosophers of the forties and fifties were themselves engaged. In the 1960s and 1970s their approach gave way to a more self-aware response which said, in effect: Yes, those questions are real questions, and admittedly fundamental ones, but we do not see how we can even begin to go about finding answers to them; and since there are so many other interesting, if lesser, questions which we can make progress with, and perhaps even find answers to, let us get on with those, in the interests both of advancing the subject and of experiencing a little personal satisfaction rather than intolerable frustration.

This is honest, and modest, but averts its gaze from an unwelcome truth which is acknowledged throughout science, and ought to be acknowledged in philosophy too, namely that if a theory (Newtonian physics is the most obvious case in point) is applicable even across the most prodigious areas and yet eventually reaches limits of applicability at which it begins to break down in paradox and self-contradiction, what this indicates is not that the theory is true and, on the limits of its application, reality weird, but that the theory is defective and needs to be replaced by a better one which will work at least as well over the same area and not break down at the same limits. And people who are philosophers rather than scientists ought even less, without shame, to carry on working on the basis of presuppositions which they do not question yet which none of them can formulate coherently, for it is an evasion of the philosopher's primary responsibility: his task is on the frontiers of intelligibility, and the chief aim of his activity should be to push those frontiers back. Stretches of frontier where reason is perplexed and imagination baffled by problems of a fundamental character are precisely those areas on which philosophical enquiry ought most to concentrate. Philosophers who turn their backs on them in order to concentrate their attentions elsewhere remind me of 'the late Munich comedian Kurt Vallentin — one of the greatest of the rare race of metaphysical clowns — [who] once enacted the following scene: the curtain goes up and reveals darkness; and in this darkness is a solitary circle of light thrown by a street-lamp. Vallentin, with his long-drawn and deeply worried face, desperately looking for something. "What have you lost?" a policeman asks who has entered the scene. "The key to my house." Upon which the policeman joins him in his search. They find nothing; and after a while he enquires: "Are you sure you lost it here?" "No," says Vallentin, and pointing to a dark corner of the stage: "Over there." "Then why on earth are you looking for it here?" "There's no light over there," says Vallentin.[16]

There can be no way round or beyond Kant which does not provide an acceptable resolution of the antinomies of time, space and causality: one cannot both reject Kant's solutions and proceed as if the problems had been solved or did not exist. Transcendental idealism, even if it is to be rejected, has provided us with the great realization that these antinomies are antinomies of realism alone: they arise only from the claim that the spatio-temporal world exists in itself, independently of experience. If spatial, temporal and causal connection are seen, by contrast, as categories of subjective origin, the contradictions melt away. We then start not from a supposedly objective framework for which we immediately find ourselves unable to give determinate co-ordinates: we start from where we actually are. Our standpoint, in other words, is the immediate reality of direct experience. If from that base we project our activities — whether bodily, intellectual or imaginative — forward in time, or outward in space, or project our inferences backward in time, they can indeed continue indefinitely, but the spatio-temporal framework of the activity has no existence separate from the activity, and therefore cannot be said to be or not be, *in itself*, anything — whether bounded, or unbounded, or anything else. The fact that infinities can be constructed but cannot exist independently of the process of their construction is thus seen as the key to the true explanation of time, space and causal connection.

Although Kant's criticism of realism along these lines was of vertiginous originality and depth, it laid him open to a challenge which he was half aware of, and unsure of his ability to deal with. The challenge can be put in this way: how can any form of transcendental idealism account for the fact that human beings live in a shared world? All sane, sighted, serious people who come into this room where I sit at this moment writing this page will agree with me and with each other about the size and shape of the room, and about what the objects in the room are, and where they are. Yet if each one of us is in some sense or other 'constructing' those objects in the process of perceiving them — and not only that, but constructing the spatio-temporal framework in which they are perceived as existing — how does it come about that each of us perceives, in all its details, the same room? The point is reinforced when we consider that there are, after all, such phenomena as dreams. Even realists can agree that dreams are constructed by people in their minds

[16] Erich Heller: *The Disinherited Mind*, p. 172 (Penguin ed.).

— spontaneously, involuntarily and unconsciously — in the process of experiencing them; that the objects and events occurring in any dream need have no existence apart from that process;[17] and that there need be no way in which the objects or events thus occurring in any one dream are related to those occurring in any other, nor any way in which the spatio-temporal framework of one dream is related to that of another. How does the transcendental idealist explain that matters are not like this when we are awake? Berkeley would have said: because each of us, complete with all his experiences, coexists with everyone else in a single mind, namely the mind of God: that is why the world of experience is a shared world. This explanation is indemonstrable and unwarranted, as Kant saw only too well. His own response was to say that we impose the same frameworks on the world because we ourselves have in common the same human nature, and that this is met half-way by the fact that things as they are in themselves (which he called *noumena*) are independent of us, and therefore the same for all of us; and so, since it is they that give rise to our experiences (the world of *phenomena*, the name he gave to all things experienced, or things as experienced, or experiences), we find the world of experience a shared one.

It was clear from the beginning that, for most of the time at least, Kant was thinking of the noumenon as the imperceptible but ultimately real substratum of the object, in which all its perceptible characteristics inhere: what one might call *the objective object*, the object as it is in itself, unexperienced by a subject — and further, that he regarded this noumenon as the cause of our sensations. But if the categories of space and causality are characteristic of experience (and possible experience) only, then there is no sense in which things as they are in themselves can be objects of any sort at all 'out there' in the world, nor is there any sense in which they can give rise to our experience of them — for location in space, and causality, are alike of subjective origin. As I have said, Kant was half-aware of this difficulty. But his dilemma was this: if he were explicitly to admit that physical objects are the causes of our sensations, then objects as we experience them are conceded to be things in themselves, and we are back with Locke's pre-critical empiricism, with all its insoluble problems; but if, on the other hand, he were to dispense altogether with the notion of an objective substratum to experience, then we should be back with Berkeley in a reality which consisted of experiences alone, except that we should not be able to support ourselves with Berkeley's — or, as far as can be seen, any other

[17] Because dreams have this much in common with the empirical world as understood by transcendental idealists the latter are sometimes inclined to dramatize their point by saying things like: 'The world is my dream.' This does their position an injustice, and propagates misunderstanding.

— explanation of the fact that human individuals live in a shared world. And because the latter course was the one he most feared to be thought to have adopted, Kant tended persistently towards the former error — though without ever quite making explicit to himself what it was he was doing. The echoes of this unconscious evasion reverberate throughout his work. At the heart of his epistemology and ontology lies a problem which his whole strategy shows him to have been repressedly aware of and yet which he never acknowledged. He was trying to find a solution without formulating his problem. That is to say, he was unwilling to confront the problem until he was sure he could solve it — and that was a situation he never reached.

Kant's double self-contradiction in allowing things as they are in themselves to appear in his philosophy as independently located entities which cause our sensations was at once apparent to all serious students of his work, as was the nature of the supposed dilemma which had led him into it. All the misdemeanours for which Schopenhauer takes him most relentlessly to task have these as points of common reference, for not only does Schopenhauer berate Kant directly for his illegitimate assumption of the noumenon as a kind of invisible object, spatially located, causing experiences, he also scolds him for his reiteration that 'the empirical content of perception is *given* to us' (Schopenhauer's italics — he nags Kant with a special unforgivingness for this), or, quite differently, for his mutilation of the first *Critique* to make the second. At the central point of all these cruces Kant is wriggling on the same hook, his inability to explain how it is that the perceived world is the same for everyone without either extending the application of causality to things as they are in themselves or else relapsing into Berkeleianism.

The first of his successors to become well known, Fichte, embraced the option which Kant had most fiercely dreaded and avoided, and developed a philosophy in which the entire world is seen as the creation of the subject. This inaugurated the tradition to which the term 'neo-Kantian' is properly applied. It is a term which should never be applied to Schopenhauer. He was not only radically different from, he was directly opposed to, the neo-Kantians. He despised them as travestiers of Kant, first because they had failed to understand Kant's most important achievement, and second because what they did take from him, and put to cynical use, was the lesson that a philosopher who is too obscure for most people to understand will for that very reason be deferred to as profound. It was his view that on account of the first of these two points their thought was developmentally behind Kant's, not ahead of it; and as a result of the second, this fact was obscured by deliberately befuddling rhetoric. The real and only way forward,

Schopenhauer believed, was to accept Kant's central achievement, which was his establishment of the distinction between phenomenon and noumenon, but to correct his central error, which was his false identification of them, particularly of the noumenon. The correct identification and characterization of the noumenon was regarded by Schopenhauer as his own main achievement, and the one which unlocked the secret of the world. It also explained, he thought, how it is that the world is a shared one (but we shall come to that later).

I have shown how, when the mainstream of modern Western philosophy ran up against transcendental idealism, it ceased to flow along a single course and ramified into various channels. This still appears to have been so to most people who look at the past from the standpoint of the 1980s. Perhaps from some position in the future it will be clearly evident that one of those channels — and which one — was the continuation of the great tradition, but no one can claim that this is generally clear as yet. That can be illustrated by the fact that there is general agreement among serious students of philosophy as to who are the great philosophers from Descartes to Kant, but no such agreement on one single figure since Kant. Some may regard the outstanding philosophers in the period of two hundred years since Kant as Hegel and Marx, some as Kierkegaard and Nietzsche, some as Husserl and Heidegger, some as Mill and Russell, some as Frege and Wittgenstein, some as any other selection or combination of these, or of others. Yet each of those I have named would be denied the accolade by a considerable body of serious students of the subject. The distinguished people who taught me philosophy at Oxford in the 1950s openly denounced Hegel and Heidegger as obscurantist charlatans, and asserted that Marx, Kierkegaard and Nietzsche were not philosophers at all. Scarcely any of them had read Schopenhauer, nor had they as yet read much, if any, Husserl or Frege. They were inclined at that time to say that Mill was second rate, just as they are now, thirty years later, inclined to say that Russell and Wittgenstein have been overrated. Yet virtually all of them, without demur, would have agreed then, and would agree now, that the greatest philosophers of the seventeenth century were Descartes, Spinoza, Leibniz and Locke, and of the eighteenth century Berkeley, Hume and Kant. The chief reason why there is no generally agreed continuation of the central tradition of Western philosophy after Kant is, it seems to me, that the revolution which he made has still not been universally accepted and absorbed. This in turn is due to the extraordinary depth and difficulty of his work, combined with the fact that it is not only counter-intuitive but also subversive of a form of realism which for some reason is more deeply entrenched in the mind of Western than of Eastern man.

In the rest of this book we shall be concerned with one of the ways forward from Kant, namely Schopenhauer's way (which has found a continuance in the twentieth century in the work of Wittgenstein). Schopenhauer was perpetually aware of the mainstream behind him, and of the alternative channels running alongside his own, but he was never in any doubt that he, and in his day he alone, was the carrier of the great tradition. His characteristic way of proceeding was to relate each of his arguments to those of the other philosophers in that tradition as if he and they were engaged in a continuing discussion: his essay *On the Freedom of the Will*, to take an instance, discusses penetrating quotations on the subject from most of the great figures of the past. Kant in particular is a stable point of reference: Schopenhauer is inclined to compare or contrast what he has to say on almost any subject with Kant's doctrine or lack of one. There are also, throughout his writings, denunciations of his contemporaries — particularly of realists and empiricists for being sunk in muddled dreams but undisturbable sleep; of neo-Kantians for being mountebanks; and of the public at large for being taken in. All this is interesting and lively — especially the points of comparison and difference with Kant. Time and again he accepts a conclusion of Kant's while rejecting the reasoning with which Kant supported it — for instance: 'Precisely the same thing happened to Kant with the demonstration of the thing-in-itself as with the demonstration of the *a priori* nature of the law of causality; both doctrines are correct, but their proof is false . . . I have retained both, yet I have established them in an entirely different way and with certainty.'[18] In what follows I shall refrain, for the most part, from going into these comparative aspects of Schopenhauer's arguments. Apart from anything else, this book is long enough as it is, without my entering into additional two- or three-way comparisons at each point in the discussion.

One piece of good fortune, however, falls to our lot at the outset. As we embark on the final and main stage of our journey, and follow the development of Schopenhauer's philosophy beyond Kant's, the first argument to present itself for consideration is Schopenhauer's descriptive theory of perception. And here at once some of the most characteristic contrasts between the two philosophers present themselves. Schopenhauer criticized Kant persistently for failing to distinguish adequately between percepts and concepts, and for tending to assimilate the former to the latter. Their two descriptive theories of perception exemplify this difference. Schopenhauer complained that Kant was here describing in purely abstract terms, as if they existed in

---

[18] *The World as Will and Representation*, i. 503.

concepts alone, processes which, if his description were accurate, must also be physical. For if Kant is right, it is the function of our sensory apparatus, nervous system and brain to construct a perceived spatio-temporal world of material objects in the same sort of way as it is the function of our stomach to digest food, or our liver to secrete bile. Correlative to every step in any acceptable philosophical account of perception there must be some optical, neurological or other such physically real process going on in actual biological organs which are lumps of matter, stuff, physical objects performing the functions for which they were evolved. Thus a double-barrelled account of perception, philosophical and scientific, is required, and the two parallel accounts must fit flush at every point.

This realization, and the way Schopenhauer followed it through, illustrates one abiding merit of his philosophy, which is his ever-present awareness of the relevance and claims of science. Although he thought it demonstrably wrong to believe that science could explain everything, he did not at all think that the claims of science could be disregarded. On the contrary, he always asserted that within the empirical realm of inter-subjectively observable phenomena the claims of scientific explanation, and of scientific procedures generally, were paramount. It is true that he regarded some of the questions which science could not deal with as having vastly greater significance than those it could, but he was genuinely interested in both sorts of question, and he took an active interest in science throughout his life. It will be remembered that he entered university as a medical student, and that his first courses were in the natural sciences. After that, and until his death, he took pains to keep abreast of new scientific developments. (One of the last things he read, shortly before he died, was *The Times*'s review of Darwin's *Origin of Species*. The implications of this book for his philosophy are so rich that an active sense of loss is induced by the fact that he was denied the time in which to consider them.) He was always alive to the need for a philosophical position to be not only consonant with direct experience, and consistent within itself, but also not to be at odds with the best of our scientific knowledge. It is characteristic of him that the very first part of his philosophy to be worked out and published — the descriptive theory of perception contained in his doctorate thesis — should make such frequent and detailed references to physiology and optics as to be almost as much a scientific as a philosophical theory. It remains, in a clear sense, Kant's theory, but its substance has doubled: in providing only the philosophical arguments Kant issued coins that were blank on one side until Schopenhauer stamped them into specie. Only three years after the publication of *The Fourfold Root of Sufficient Reason* in 1813, Schopenhauer published his overlapping essay *On Vision and Colours* which was purely physical. And it has to be said that in Schopenhauer's more physical terms the central argument is easier to grasp than it had been in Kant's more abstract terms, and is at the same time more persuasive. Its main outline runs as follows.

Our conscious sense perceptions do not consist of the data conveyed to our brains by our sense organs. On the contrary, in many respects the two are startlingly disparate. For instance, the optical image of objects that our eyes receive is upside-down, and it is only because the brain corrects this by turning the received image upside-down once more that we 'perceive' objects as being the right way up. Our two differently positioned eyes receive two incongruent images of everything they look at, which are then fused into one by the brain. We 'see' objects in perspective, though this does not characterize the optical data. We 'see' most objects as being roughly the size we know them to be, though again this does not characterize the optical data, and we are capable of monstrous error in this regard when the object is strange to us. In all these respects, not to mention others, our conscious perceptions are not just different from, they *contradict* the optical data which occasion them. In view of this, if our percepts were actually to consist of the data, our visual experience would be unimaginably different from what it is, and might even be a chaos. It is easy to establish this with no more than a handful of examples taken from one only of the five senses: if we go on to take into account all the other available instances from all the other four senses, it becomes clear that the role of the brain in perception, as against that of the sense organs, is an all-transforming and all-dominating one. 'The *understanding* is the artist forming the work, whereas the *senses* are merely the assistants who hand up the materials.'[19]

The raw materials are indeed raw — mere primitive, unidentified patches of light and colour, noises, pressures, and so forth. The brain not only identifies them but relates them to each other and weaves them together into the measurelessly detailed, richly textured, multi-dimensional yet homogeneous world that we experience in conscious perception. The relative complexity and importance of the two operations is manifested by the physical apparatus involved. 'The mass of the nerves of sensation of all the sense organs is very small compared with the mass of the brain, even in the case of animals, whose brain, since they do not really think in the abstract, serves merely to produce perception, and yet where this is perfect, as in the case of mammals, has a considerable mass. This is so even after the removal of the

---

[19] *The Fourfold Root of the Principle of Sufficient Reason*, p. 114.

cerebellum, whose function is the regulated control of movement.'[20] In other words, what we are now considering — the organizing of the raw data of sense into a coherent and perceived world — is not some ghostly scenario that has its existence in terms of abstract philosophical analysis only: it is the everyday activity of a physical object, the brain, and it is what the brain is *for* in the same sense as the heart is for pumping blood. It is called by Schopenhauer the understanding, and it is shared by us with the animal kingdom — indeed it (and control of movement) is what differentiates animal from plant life. In humans the brain has developed the additional and higher function of creating, storing and using the abstract concepts which make thinking possible — the faculty of reason — and this has always been rightly held to be what differentiates man from the animals. It also explains why the human brain is so much larger than that of animals, relative to body size. However, even in man the perception-producing function of the brain is primary, both in the development of the species and in the development of the individual. Reason may be 'higher', but it is secondary.

Although in humans the brain is the seat of reason, the 'lower' (in the evolutionary sense) function of perception or understanding carries on in the same autonomous, unselfconscious way as it does in animals, or for that matter as do the functions of our other bodily organs. This point, so difficult to grasp in philosophical terms, is simple when put in physical terms. However keenly and long we concentrate, there is no way in which we can raise to the level of conscious awareness the activity of, say, our hair in growing, or our lymph glands in manufacturing blood corpuscles, or our pylorus muscles in controlling the flow of nourishment from our stomachs into our small intestines. Not only do we not have to make the slightest effort in order that our bodily parts should perform any of these amazing functions: the functions go on whether we like it or not — continuous, automatic, involuntary, and above all inaccessible to our conscious awareness. Most of us, not having studied physiology, do not even know what most of them are. In any case, no amount of theoretical knowledge of them will help our perceptions to catch them at work: they are closed off completely and permanently from any possibility of conscious observation. And so it is with the perceiving functions of our brains. By no effort of will, for instance, can we bring into conscious awareness those upside-down images in our eyes, even though we know they are there — not even for the most fleeting moment, no matter how conversant we are with the science of optics, and therefore with the exact location and character of

[20] *The World as Will and Representation*, ii. 20.

the images. We have the end-product of perception, but the process itself is hermetically sealed off from introspection. However, not only is there no special mystery about this, since it is characteristic of the workings of our bodily organs in general: there is even an additional reason in the case of the brain why it must be so. The function we are discussing is what results in perceptual experience: in other words, it is what needs already to have taken place before there can be a perception of anything. It must therefore be impossible for perception to precede it, or to accompany it.

What follows from this is of the utmost significance for philosophy. The brain no more 'learns from experience' to create a perceived world out of the data transmitted to it by the sense organs than the blood corpuscles 'learn from experience' to take up carbon dioxide from the body's tissues and void it in the lungs. On the contrary, it is necessary for the brain already to have carried out its characteristic function before there can be any experience. So whatever the categories might be (and in this physical version of the argument we have yet to reach the question of what they are) in terms of which the brain constitutes a perceived world out of sensations, those categories would have to originate in us, it being logically impossible for them to originate outside us and then come to us 'through experience'. The *prerequisites* of experience could no more be among the *objects* of experience, and therefore derivable *from* experience, than a camera could directly photograph itself, or an eye could be one of the objects in its own field of vision.

The inaccessibility to us of our own perceptual processes is illustrated dramatically by the case of illusions which we know to be illusions and whose explanations we perfectly well understand, yet which we cannot remove: we go on, willy-nilly, perceiving what we know to be not the case: '. . . the moon that appears to be greater at the horizon; the image formed at the focus of a concave mirror and floating in space exactly like a solid body; the painted relievo regarded as something real; the motion of the shore or of the bridge on which we are standing while a ship is sailing under it; high mountains that appear to be much nearer than they are, owing to a want of atmospheric perspective, this being the result of the purity of the air round their high peaks. In these and a hundred similar instances the understanding assumes the usual cause with which it is familiar. It therefore perceives this at once, although our reasoning faculty has discovered the correct state of affairs in other ways. The understanding, however, is inaccessible to the teaching of reason, since in its knowledge it precedes reason and so cannot be reached by that faculty. Thus *illusion*, i.e. deception of the understanding, persists unmoved, although *error*, i.e. deception of the faculty of reason, is prevented.'[21] . . . 'The illusion remains unshakable in all the cases mentioned, in spite of all abstract knowledge; for the understanding is completely and totally different from the faculty of reason.'[22]

Perception is characterized by two systematic illusions of immediacy, one of immediacy in the sense of instantaneousness (time), the other of immediacy in the sense of direct contact (space). In the former of these two senses, perception feels as if it takes no time at all. It is only through our scientific knowledge that we know it to be made up of elaborate processes in equally elaborate combinations and sequences, all of which take time. However, because we have no conscious awareness of any such processes as having been gone through, we have no conscious awareness of any time as having elapsed. As for the latter of the two senses of immediacy, because we have no awareness of any perceptual apparatus as being in any way 'between' us and what we perceive, we seem to be in immediate contact with the objects of our perceptions. A familiar example of both these illusions of immediacy is provided by pain. I may feel a stabbing pain in one of my toes — and feel it as being located specifically, say, under the toe-nail and a little to one side — yet although the seat of the experience seems to be located at a precise point in a space external to my brain, it must in fact be in the brain itself, for if the nerve message from the toe is impeded at any point on its journey to my brain I do not feel the pain. (This, after all, is how local anaesthetics work.) There are even people who feel precisely located pains in extremities they do not possess. Amputees complain of this: it is caused by the stimulation of the nerves which once had their endings in the amputated limb at the precise point where the pain is now felt as being. Here again, attribution of an object of sensation to a point in a space characterizes an experience whose sole location is in the brain. In a not dissimilar way I am able to see external objects which are not there. When I look up at stars whose light takes millions of years to reach the earth, it may be, for all I know, that any or all of them disintegrated before I was born, or that none of them are now in the positions I see them as occupying. Although the object of my experience seems to me to be directly and manifestly there before me in space, and although I have the sensation of being in immediate contact with it, these experiences are the same whether the star is there or not, because the star of my experience, located in my brain, is the same in either case. Since differences of distance are differences of degree, not of kind, this principle must apply to everything we see, including an

[21] *The Fourfold Root of the Principle of Sufficient Reason*, pp. 103–4.
[22] *The World as Will and Representation*, i. 25. This passage is a direct comment on the one here quoted before it.

object in the same room; we allocate it to a precise position in space, whereupon it seems to us to be self-evidently and unquestionably 'there' at that particular point 'outside' us, just as the pain seemed to be indubitably 'in' my toe. The percept in all such cases can be only in the brain and nowhere else. 'The "outside us" to which we refer objects on the occasion of the sensation of sight, itself resides inside our heads, for there is its whole scene of action; much the same as in the theatre we see mountains, forest, and sea, yet everything remains within the house. From this we can understand that we perceive things with the determination "outside" and yet quite directly . . . .'.[23]

The implications of this are manifold. The most important is that the spatial location of the objects in our experience is a constituent feature of them *as experience*. It is impossible for me to see anything — a star, a house, a tree, a fly, any physical thing at all — without seeing it as being *somewhere*: in other words, I cannot perceive it at all if not as an object in a space which is outside me. Yet the percept itself is in my brain, and has been put together by my brain. The conclusion to which we are led is that the ordering of objects in a space apprehended as external to ourselves is one of the constructive principles involved in the brain's unconscious creation of the world of conscious perception. Space, in other words, must be one of the categories whose necessary existence we acknowledged a moment ago, categories 'in terms of which the brain constitutes a perceived world out of sensations' — categories which, as prerequisites of experience, cannot be derived from experience, and must therefore originate in us.

There is no need for me to go separately through the corresponding arguments for each of the other categories. By parity of reasoning Schopenhauer argues that what the brain contributes to percepts are all those features that go to make up their structure, while what the sense organs contribute are the sensory qualities: 'while the nerves of the sense-organs invest the appearing objects with colour, sound, taste, smell, temperature, and so on, the brain imparts to them extension, form, impenetrability, mobility, and so on, in short, all that can be represented in perception only by means of time, space and causality.'[24] We are back, of course, with the distinction drawn by Locke between secondary and primary qualities. And it was indeed Locke who first identified the characteristics which could not be 'thought away' from the objects of our experience — characteristics without which objects

---

[23] *The World as Will and Representation*, ii. 22.
[24] Ibid. ii. 20. Schopenhauer regarded time, space and causality as the only real a-priori categories of experience, Kant's others being 'blind windows' put in to complete the symmetry of his architectonic — a symmetry by which Kant was obsessed, and his obsession with which led him often astray.

as such were literally inconceivable. This was an achievement of genius. But it was not until philosophy's Copernican revolution that the true philosophical explanation of it became possible. And this was not, as Locke had thought, that the primary qualities are the irreducibly minimal attributes necessary to material objects existing independently of experience, in a space and time which are also independent of experience, but that they are constructive principles in terms of which the mind creates the percepts of conscious experience out of raw material supplied to it (of necessity prior to perception, and therefore not perceived) by the senses.

Schopenhauer was the first person to put forward 'a thorough proof of the intellectual nature of perception [made possible] in consequence of the Kantian doctrine',[25] and was also the first person to marry this philosophical account to its corresponding physical account. These beginnings, after generations of disregard, are currently being re-endorsed by the biology of the second half of the twentieth century. As P. B. and J. S. Medawar put it gingerly in their book *The Life Science* (1977): 'In the light of modern sensory physiology Kant's ideas no longer sound as extravagant as they once did.' Indeed, as the same authors remark on the same page, 'modern sensory physiology [has] a curiously Kantian colour'. Ever since the publication in 1941 of Konrad Lorenz's paper 'Kant's Doctrine of the *A Priori* in the Light of Contemporary Biology' more and more biologists of reputation have stressed the Kantian nature of the view of perception towards which modern science is leading us. This is corroborated also by the work of some of the most distinguished of modern psychologists of perception, such as Richard Gregory and Stuart Sutherland. Through the work of such figures as Noam Chomsky it is even finding its way back into philosophy.

[25] *The World as Will and Representation*, ii. 21.

Chapter 5

Objects and Subjects

Schopenhauer's reformulation of Kant's theory of perception brings out implications of it which Kant touched on without giving them anything like the consideration their importance demanded — and this must mean, I think, that he was not consistently aware of their importance. The first of these is that if all the characteristics we are able to ascribe to phenomena are subject-dependent then there can be no object *in any sense that we are capable of attaching to the word* without the existence of a subject. Anyone who supposes that if all the perceiving subjects were removed from the world then the objects, as we have any conception of them, could continue in existence all by themselves has radically failed to understand what objects are. Kant did see this, but only intermittently — in the gaps, as it were, between assuming the existence of the noumenon 'out there' as the invisible sustainer of the object. He expressed it once in a passage which, because so blindingly clear and yet so isolated, sticks out disconcertingly from his work: 'If I take away the thinking subject, the whole material world must vanish, as this world is nothing but the phenomenal appearance in the sensibility of our own subject, and is a species of this subject's representations.'[1]

We have already mentioned one of the obvious objections to which this view appears to be open, namely the problem about the sharedness of the world. We shall return to that later. Another objection would run: 'Everyone knows that the earth, and *a fortiori* the universe, existed for a long time before there were any living beings, and therefore any perceiving subjects. But according to what Kant has just been quoted as saying, that is impossible.' Schopenhauer's defence of Kant on this score was twofold. First, the objector has not understood to the very bottom the Kantian demonstration that time is one of the forms of our understanding. The earth, say, as it was before there was life, is a field of empirical enquiry in which we have come to know a great deal; its reality is no more being denied than is the reality of the objects of immediate perception. The point is, the *whole* of the empirical world in space and time is the creation of our understanding, which apprehends

---

[1] Quoted by Schopenhauer in *The Fourfold Root of the Principle of Sufficient Reason*, p. 50.

all the objects of empirical knowledge within it as being in some part of that space and at some part of that time: and this is as true of the earth before there was life as it is of the pen I am now holding a few inches in front of my face and seeing slightly out of focus as it moves across the paper. This, incidentally, illustrates a difficulty in the way of understanding which transcendental idealism has permanently to contend with: the assumptions of 'the inborn realism which arises from the original disposition of the intellect' enter unawares into the way in which the statements of transcendental idealism are understood, so that these statements appear faulty in ways in which, properly understood, they are not. Such realistic assumptions so pervade our normal use of concepts that the claims of transcendental idealism disclose their own non-absurdity only after difficult consideration, whereas criticisms of them at first appear cogent which on examination are seen to rest on confusion. We have to raise almost impossibly deep levels of presupposition in our own thinking and imagination to the level of self-consciousness before we are able to achieve a critical awareness of all our realistic assumptions, and thus achieve an understanding of transcendental idealism which is untainted by them. This, of course, is one of the explanations for the almost unfathomably deep counter-intuitiveness of transcendental idealism, and also for the general notion of 'depth' with which people associate Kantian and post-Kantian philosophy. Something akin to it is the reason for much of the prolonged, self-disciplined meditation involved in a number of Eastern religious practices.

Schopenhauer's second refutation of the objection under consideration is as follows. Since all imaginable characteristics of objects depend on the modes in which they are apprehended by perceiving subjects, then without at least tacitly assumed presuppositions relating to the latter no sense can be given to terms purporting to denote the former — in short, it is impossible to talk about material objects at all, and therefore even so much as to assert their existence, without the use of words the conditions of whose intelligibility derive from the experience of perceiving subjects. Again, then, and for a reason that goes deeper than those which had been given the last time this point was made (p. 91), transcendental realism cannot be stated. It is 'the philosophy of the subject who forgets to take account of himself'.[2]

But 'just as there can be no object without a subject, so there can be no subject without an object, in other words, no knower without something different from this that is known . . . A consciousness that was through and through pure intelligence would be impossible . . . For

_____

[2] *The World as Will and Representation*, ii. 13.

consciousness consists in knowing, but knowing requires a knower and a known. Therefore self-consciousness could not exist if there were not in it a known opposed to the knower and different therefrom.'[3] Hume was the first philosopher to realize clearly that, if we search inside ourselves for that perceiving subject which we are so easily inclined to take ourselves to be, we find ourselves coming up against all sorts of objects of consciousness — thoughts, feelings, images, sensations, and the rest — but not against any entity separate from these which has them. Consciousness is intrinsically intensional — it is always consciousness *of* something: it always has an object. You may say that I can contemplate my own consciousness of x and thereby turn it into the object of my consciousness — but who or what, then, is the perceiving subject of this object of consciousness? What is the 'I' that contemplates 'my consciousness of x', and to what does 'my' in the latter phrase refer? Whatever it is, it is systematically elusive — we never grasp it.[4] The subject is never able to appear as an object in the world of its own perceptions. As far as self-awareness goes, the perceiver *is* that which is perceived — and indeed, that is what Hume took the self to be: a bundle of perceptions. Kant, in his celebrated Refutation of Idealism,[5] sought to prove that our awareness of our own existence logically presupposes an awareness of the existence of objects in a space outside us. Schopenhauer's analysis of perception, though radically different from Hume's, re-inforces at least Hume's conclusion that the perceiving self is nowhere to be found in the world of experience. In Schopenhauer's view a metaphysical self exists as the sustainer of that world, and cannot itself enter it. So all three philosophers would have agreed, albeit for different reasons, that if all objects of perception were taken away the self would vanish.

On any of these views, therefore, anyone who supposes that if all the objects of perception were removed from the world the perceiving subjects could carry on in existence all by themselves has failed to understand what subjects are. Subjects and objects are able to exist at all only as correlates of each other. More to the point, Schopenhauer wants to stress, on Kantian grounds, that their *structures* are correlative: the modes of perception constitutive of the perceiving subject correspond to the empirical characteristics constitutive of the object, and vice versa. 'Being subject means exactly the same thing as having an object, and being object means just the same as being known by the subject. In precisely the same manner, with an object *determined in any way*, the

[3] *The World as Will and Representation*, ii. 202.
[4] See Gilbert Ryle, *The Concept of Mind*, pp. 195–8.
[5] pp. 244–7 of *Critique of Pure Reason*, translation by Norman Kemp Smith, London, 1929.

subject also is at once assumed as *knowing in just such a way*. To this
extent it is immaterial whether I say that objects have such and such
special and inherent determinations, or that the subject knows in such
and such ways. It is immaterial whether I say that objects are divisible
into such and such classes, or that such and such different powers of
knowledge are peculiar to the subject.'[6]

What all this comes to is this. Empirical reality is experience, which
does not present itself as a duality, partly mental and partly material,
but as being all of one category. This was Berkeley's great insight, and
it is that which makes him so important as a precursor of Kant and
Schopenhauer, even though with that one thought he had shot his bolt
and made no further contribution to philosophy. Although we always
find on examination that experience is analysable into subject and
object, these are not independent constituents that could be separated
out, but are mutually dependent correlates. They are parallel lines of
analysis: to every point on each there is, and must be, a corresponding
point on the other. The way in which the world is constructed parallels
in detail the way in which the mind works, and this has to be so for
understanding to be possible.[7] Put the other way round, the whole
elaborate structure of our explanatory powers as outlined in Chapter 2,
and therefore of our powers of comprehension, is at the same time a
blueprint of the organization of the world. The ground-plan of both is
the principle of sufficient reason in all its forms, which on the side of the
object is matter and causality (which is the cement of the universe) and
specifies the spatio-temporal framework within which the universe
exists, while on the side of the subject it programmes our understanding and our sensibility, allotting to these alike their tasks and their
limitations. These parallels persist to the vanishing-points of abstraction. If, on the side of the object, we pursue our analysis to the point of
trying to pin down matter, material, stuff itself, independent of all
changing forms and attributes, we find ourselves with a purely inferred
abstraction, a metaphysical substrate — which, precisely because it
could never appear in the world of experience, could not be subject to
its forms, and would have therefore to be timeless, and hence indestructible, no more able to come into existence than to be annihilated.
Correspondingly, if we try to identify the subject independently of its
modes of apprehension we find ourselves with an inferred and metaphysical abstraction which could never appear in the world of experience, could not come under its forms, and would therefore have

---

[6] *The Fourfold Root of the Principle of Sufficient Reason*, pp. 209–10.

[7] Cf. Wittgenstein's view, expressed in the *Tractatus*, that the fact that we can talk
about the world must mean that the structure of the world and the structure of
discourse in language correspond.

to be timeless and indestructible. Thus the indestructibility of matter (or — as the principle has become in modern science with the discovery of the equivalence of matter and energy — the conservation of energy) is the objective correlate of the indestructibility of our inner nature.

To say this is to race a long way ahead of our present argument, though it does give a foretaste of what is to come. Those limiting points of abstraction lie on the edge at which the world of phenomena turns over into the noumenon which is, so to speak, its other side. And that is something we shall have to leave until we come to Chapter 7.

Staying with the present analysis, it has already become clear where most philosophy before Kant had been centrally in error. Quite simply, it had not started from what is given. What is given to us in direct experience are the representations of sense and of thought. Schopenhauer stressed this by adopting the word *Vorstellung* (which is translated in this book as 'representation') as his standard term for the content of experience — a term deliberately chosen by him because it does not smuggle in any hidden material-object or realist presuppositions. Most philosophers before Kant had started not from this, from what is genuinely given, but from two premises each of which involves an unwarrantable inference from the given, namely that there exist in the world independent objects and independent subjects. The problem then became to explain how the latter could reproduce the former within themselves, and how they could possibly have any notion of the degree of accuracy, if any, with which they had done so. This bifurcation of nature, and the insoluble problem to which it gave rise, were regarded by Schopenhauer as having been imported into the central tradition of philosophy by Descartes, and as then having become 'the axis on which the whole of modern philosophy turns'.[8] The explanations of Lockean empiricism, like those of commonsense realism, attempt to solve the problem by starting from the object and showing how this causes representations of itself to appear within the subject. Fichtean philosophy, by contrast, started from the ego and tried to explain how this spins the world of external objects out of itself. Both lines of development are doomed to failure, for reasons which have been considered in earlier chapters, as well as the one provided by the central argument of this. The reason accorded the greatest significance by Schopenhauer is that all such explanations constitute an attempt to establish a causal connection between two sets of entities at least one of which is postulated as existing independently of experience; but causal connection is one of the structural features of experience, and can

[8] *Parerga and Paralipomena*, i. 15.

characterize experience only; therefore such explanations are attempting to bridge a gap which is inherently and of its nature unbridgeable, since on at least one side of it there is nothing with which any such bridge can make contact.

Before Kant there was one great modern philosopher apart from Berkeley who rejected the Cartesian bifurcation of the world, and that was Spinoza. He had maintained that reality consisted of a single substance of which matter and mind were merely different attributes. For this insight Schopenhauer held him in great esteem and was a close student of his work. Where Spinoza ultimately went wrong, Schopenhauer concluded, was in this: the central task of metaphysics is to locate the frontier, and exhibit the connection, between the phenomenal and the noumenal worlds; Spinoza sought ultimately to reduce all explanation to the notions of 'substance' and 'cause' and their interaction; but all this is intelligible only within the world of phenomena; thus Spinoza was drawing his line *within* the world of phenomena, not *between* it and the noumenal world. Nevertheless Schopenhauer regarded him as having in some important respects come closer to the truth than anyone before Kant.

But it is the Lockean tradition which Schopenhauer saw clearly as having issued in Kant. And he also saw clearly that the position into which a Kantian is led by the logic of his own argument is that substance and cause are one and the same. For in the phenomenal world the potential which a physical object has for being the cause of effects on other physical objects comprises the sum total of its attributes. It has mass, inertia, weight; it exerts gravitational pull on all other objects; it is movable in space, which means displacing something else, while at the same time making room for something else; it reflects light-waves and sound-waves to other physical objects, presses up against them, and so on; and when all these and other such features have been enumerated there is simply nothing left that can be stated about the object. The very minimum condition thinkable for anything's being a material object at all is occupancy of space-time, and that clearly has causal implications in that 'it involves the idea of *repulsion*; a body repels other bodies that are said to "contest its space", and to do away with this (causal) idea is to do away with the notion of a material body itself'.[9] (Incidentally, the fact that occupancy of space-time is the minimal condition for anything's being a material object leads Schopenhauer to characterize objects as 'the unity of space and time', and hence to characterize causality in the same way. He also sometimes refers to objects, or causality, as 'occupied space'.) Since what we have

[9] Patrick Gardiner: *Schopenhauer*, p. 101.

now reached is a minimal condition, any attempt to pursue analysis
further leads us on to a purely abstract concept of matter, the metaphysical inference referred to on p. 108 — and even this abstract
matter, if we do indeed pursue the analysis, turns out to be abstract
causality. 'With the concept of matter we think of what is still left of
bodies when we divest them of their form and of all their specific
qualities, a residue which, precisely on this account, must be one and
the same in all bodies . . . If, then, we disregard these forms and
qualities, all that is left is *mere activity in general*, pure acting as such,
causality itself, objectively conceived, thus the reflection of our own
understanding, the outwardly projected image of its sole function, and
matter is throughout pure causality; its essence is action in general.'[10]

The equivalence of matter and causality has profound and far-
reaching implications for our conception of both objects and subjects.
As regards objects, the doctrine that 'bodies are spaces filled with force'
(described by Schopenhauer in *The Will in Nature* as 'a far-famed
Kantian dogma'[11]) has subsequently, like so much else in the Kantian-
Schopenhauerian philosophy, been startlingly vindicated by developments in natural science. We now know on quite other grounds that the
volume occupied by any apparently solid body consists of fields of force
in whose space atoms and molecules unceasingly whirl at velocities

---

[10] *The Fourfold Root of the Principle of Sufficient Reason*, pp. 118–19. The quotation is
worth continuing because it ties together, in a new way and in Schopenhauer's own
words, several of the points being made. 'This is why pure matter cannot be perceived
but only conceived; it is something added in thought to every reality as the basis
thereof. For pure causality, mere action, without a definite mode of action, cannot be
given in intuitive perception, and so cannot occur in any experience. Matter is only
therefore the objective correlative of the pure understanding; thus it is causality in
general and nothing else, just as the understanding is immediate knowledge of cause
and effect in general and nothing else. Now this again is precisely why the law of
causality is not applicable to matter itself; in other words, matter cannot arise or pass
away, but is and remains permanent. For all change and fluctuation of accidents (forms
and qualities) i.e., all arising and passing away, occur only by virtue of causality, but
matter is pure causality itself as viewed objectively. Therefore it cannot exercise its own
power on itself, just as the eye can see everything except itself.' (This last metaphor is a
favourite of Schopenhauer's, from whom it was fruitfully appropriated by Wittgenstein
— see *Tractatus Logico-Philosophicus* 5.633 and 5.6331.) In addition to all this,
Schopenhauer thought we were furnished with a-priori knowledge of the indestructibility of matter because it was entailed by our a-priori knowledge of causality: the
operation of causality as a universal principle in the world would not be possible if the
entities at work could simply disappear at any point in the process, or if new ones could
pop into existence out of nothing and start adding their effects to those already at work.

[11] *On the Will in Nature*, p. 207 of the translation by Mme Karl Hillebrand published in
Bohn's Philosophical Library, together in one volume with her translation of *On the
Fourfold Root of the Principle of Sufficient Reason*, under the joint title *Two Essays by Arthur
Schopenhauer*: George Bell & Sons, London, 1889, revised edition 1891.

approaching that of light; that within the individual atoms similar activity is occurring; and that at the subatomic level what is going on is more readily accountable for altogether in terms of force than of matter — in other words, at that level the very concept of matter is absorbed into that of energy.[12] We now know that 'mass and energy are equivalent in the sense that if *m* units of mass could be made to disappear, mc^2 units of energy would be liberated, *c* being the speed of light'.[13] Perhaps the most astonishing of all the many Kantian-Schopenhauerian anticipations of modern science lies not in the latter's forceful and concise exposition of the central core of Freudianism, nor in his sharp though uncoordinated glimpses of a theory of biological evolution — both of which we shall come to in due course — but in the former's very specific announcement of one of the central doctrines of Einstein's theory of relativity more than a century before Einstein — the doctrine that (as Schopenhauer put it, following Kant): 'force and substance are inseparable because at bottom they are one'.[14] It is an extraordinarily impressive fact that this true, unobvious and amazing conclusion was reached purely by epistemological analysis. When the physicists (who cannot sensibly be blamed for not being familiar with Kant and Schopenhauer) caught up with it over a hundred years later they regarded themselves as intellectual revolutionaries. As one of the central figures of twentieth-century science wrote half a century later still: 'Fifty years ago, when the theory of relativity was formulated, this hypothesis of the equivalence of mass and energy seemed to be a complete revolution in physics, and there was still very little experimental evidence for it.'[15]

Given the Schopenhauerian doctrine of the thoroughgoing correlativity of subject and object, the correct perception of the equivalence of mass and energy (or substance and force) has decisive implications also for the subject. The fact that matter *is* causality means that the world of matter is a world of causality not in the sense that the principle of sufficient reason *characterizes* it but in the sense that the principle of sufficient reason *is* it. This provides the all-important link between the

[12] e.g. 'According to the [field theory of matter] a material particle such as an electron is merely a small domain of the electrical field within which the field strength assumes enormously high values, indicating that a comparatively huge field energy is concentrated in a very small space. Such an energy knot, which by no means is clearly delineated against the remaining field, propagates through empty space like a water wave across the surface of a lake; there is no such thing as one and the same substance of which the electron consists at all times.' Herman Weyl: *Philosophy of Mathematics and Natural Science*, p. 171.

[13] *Encyclopaedia Britannica*, 1973, from the entry on Einstein.

[14] *The World as Will and Representation*, ii. 309.

[15] Werner Heisenberg: *Physics and Philosophy* (1958), p. 105.

world and our perception or understanding or knowledge of the world. 'The subjective correlative of matter or of causality, for the two are one and the same, is the *understanding*, and it is nothing more than this. To know causality is the sole function of the understanding, its only power, and it is a great power embracing much, manifold in its application, and yet unmistakable in its identity throughout all its manifestations. Conversely, all causality, hence all matter, and consequently the whole of reality, is only for the understanding, through the understanding, in the understanding.'[16]

If we turn to consider what the implications of this philosophical point are for what a true physical account of perception needs to be it might seem at a casual first glance as if Schopenhauer has, by implication, conceded a causal explanation of perception of a kind which the rest of his philosophy forbids. But this is not so. He agrees, of course, that material objects excite our physical senses by reflecting light to the retinas of our eyes, and sound-waves to our ear-drums, and that they exert pressure through our skins against our nerve endings, and so on. But that they do these things is a fact which no one would dream of denying. Certainly Schopenhauer never denied it. What he denied was that this impoverished and exiguous input could constitute the measurelessly extensive, rich, beautiful, subtly detailed, almost limitlessly varied yet minutely integrated world, with all its internal consistency and organization, that we experience in perception. (His reasons for doing this, and an outline of what he thought does happen, were given on pp. 99–104, and will not be repeated here.[17]) Furthermore, to say that our bodies are empirical objects in space, and that as such they causally interact with other physical objects, is not to posit a causal connection between entities any of which lie outside the world of experience. Some of these physical interactions trigger off activity of the brain, which does then indeed create the world of perception in accordance with the principle of sufficient reason in all its forms. But the only part of that process at which causal connection is posited is the point at which the brain infers back from the effect on a physical organ of sense to the cause of such an effect in an object which impinges on that organ, and that is to infer causal interaction only between two physical objects in space. So the principles of transcendental idealism are not infringed.

---

[16] *The World as Will and Representation*, i. 11.

[17] In our own day this insistence that our conception of the world is radically unexplainable in terms of the experiential input — and that therefore the notions of learning and knowledge fundamental to empiricism are mistaken — is central to the thought of Noam Chomsky. He has, of course, brought it to bear particularly on our acquisition of language; but he is also concerned to make the general point. (See *Men of Ideas*, ed. Bryan Magee, pp. 218–20.)

The far more disconcerting element of circularity involved in the notion of a sensory input triggering off the intellect's creation of a world which contains and accounts for, along with all else, the sensory input — or for that matter the brain's creation of an empirical world which contains all brains among its objects — will be confronted when the theory is expanded to take account of the noumenon.

Indeed, we have now penetrated just about as far into Schopenhauer's philosophy as it is possible to go without taking its most distinctive constituent, the identification of the noumenon, into account. And even if we were to stop altogether at this point we would be confronted with an impressive and attractive structure of ideas. What we have before us, at this stage, is a handsomely corrected, enriched and clarified Kantianism which could well be regarded as an advance on anything in philosophy that had gone before it. It gives rise to problems and paradoxes, of course — to evade repetition I have not yet pin-pointed those which will become soluble only at a later stage in the discussion — but it does so no more, and if anything rather less, than its predecessor philosophies. Before we proceed to cast it all in the new light of an as yet unconsidered doctrine of the noumenon, it is worth while pausing to take stock of it as we have it in its present form. Here is a recapitulation in Schopenhauer's own words:

One must be forsaken by all the gods to imagine that the world of intuitive perception outside, filling space in its three dimensions, moving on in the inexorably strict course of time, governed at each step by the law of causality that is without exception; but in all these respects merely observing laws that we are able to state prior to all experience thereof — that such a world outside had an entirely real and objective existence without our participation, but then found its way into our heads through mere sensation, where it now had a second existence like the one outside. For what a poor, wretched thing mere sensation is! Even in the noblest organs of sense it is nothing more than a local specific feeling, capable in its way of some variation, yet in itself always subjective. Therefore, as such, this feeling cannot possibly contain anything objective, and so anything resembling intuitive perception. For sensation of every kind is and remains an event within the organism itself; but as such it is restricted to the region beneath the skin; and so, in itself, it can never contain anything lying outside the skin and thus outside ourselves. Sensation can be pleasant or unpleasant — and this indicates a reference to our will — but nothing objective is to be found in any sensation. In the organs of sense sensation is heightened by the confluence of the nerve extremities; it can easily be stimulated from without by the wide distribution and thin covering of these; and, moreover, it is specially susceptible to particular influences, such as light, sound, and odour. Yet it remains mere sensation, like every other within our body; consequently, it is something essentially subjective whose changes directly reach our consciousness only in the form of the *inner* sense and hence of

time alone, that is to say, successively. It is only when the *understanding* begins
to act — a function not of single delicate nerve extremities but of that complex
and mysterious structure the brain that weighs three pounds and even five in
exceptional cases, — only when the understanding applies its sole form, *the law
of causality*, that a powerful transformation takes place whereby subjective
sensation becomes objective intuitive perception. Thus by virtue of its own
peculiar form and so a priori, in other words, *prior* to all experience (since till
then experience was not yet possible), the understanding grasps the given
sensation of the body as an *effect* (a word comprehended only by the understanding), and this effect as such must necessarily have a *cause*. Simultaneously
the understanding summons to its assistance *space*, the form of the *outer* sense
also lying predisposed in the intellect, i.e., in the brain. This it does in order to
place that cause *outside* the organism; for only in this way does there arise for it
an outside whose possibility is simply space, so that pure intuition a priori
must supply the foundation for empirical perception. In this process, as I shall
soon show in more detail, the understanding now avails itself of all the data of
the given sensation, even the minutest, in order to construct in space, in
conformity therewith, the *cause* of the sensation. This operation of the understanding (which, however, is expressly denied by Schelling in the first volume
of his *Philosophische Schriften* of 1809, pp. 237–8, and likewise by Fries in his
Kritik der Vernunft, Vol. I, pp. 52–6 and 290 of the first edition), is not discursive
or reflective, nor does it take place *in abstracto* by means of concepts and words;
on the contrary, it is intuitive and quite immediate. For only by this operation
and consequently in the understanding and for the understanding does the
real, objective, corporeal world, filling space in three dimensions, present
itself; and then it proceeds, according to the same law of causality, to change in
time and to move in space. Accordingly, the understanding itself has first to
create the objective world, for this cannot just step into our heads from
without, already cut and dried, through the senses and the openings of their
organs. Thus the senses furnish nothing but the raw material, and this the
understanding first of all works up into the objective grasp and apprehension
of a corporeal world governed by laws, and does so by means of the simple
forms already stated, namely space, time, and causality. Accordingly, our
daily *empirical intuitive perception is intellectual*.[18]

   The world as representation, the objective world, has thus, so to speak, two
poles, namely the knowing subject plain and simple without the forms of its
knowing, and crude matter without form and quality. Both are absolutely
unknowable; the subject, because it is that which knows; matter, because
without form and quality it cannot be perceived. Yet both are fundamental
conditions of all empirical perception. Thus the knowing subject, merely as
such, which is likewise a presupposition of all experience, stands in opposition,
as its clear counterpart, to crude, formless, quite dead (i.e. will-less) matter.
This matter is not given in any experience, but is presupposed in every
experience. This subject is not in time, for time is only the more direct form of

---

[18] *The Fourfold Root of the Principle of Sufficient Reason*, pp. 76–8.

all its representing. Matter, standing in opposition to the subject, is accordingly eternal, imperishable, endures through all time; but properly speaking it is not extended, since extension gives form, and hence it is not spatial. Everything else is involved in a constant arising and passing away, whereas these two constitute the static poles of the world as representation. We can therefore regard the permanence of matter as the reflex of the timelessness of the pure subject, that is simply taken to be the condition of every object. Both belong to the phenomenon, not to the thing-in-itself; but they are the framework of the phenomenon. Both are discovered only through abstraction; they are not given immediately, pure and by themselves.[19]

In subatomic physics and cosmology it is common for the existence of unobserved, and perhaps even unobservable, entities to be deduced from what is known. That is methodologically legitimate, provided no observational characteristics are then ascribed to them. Schopenhauer regards his deduction of transcendental subject and object as being legitimate in the same sense. But we are left confronting them as two mysteries: the unknowable subject and unknowable matter. (Perhaps they are rather one mystery, for our analysis has already led us to expect them to be different aspects of the same thing.) The transcendental subject, as the sustainer of the world of space and time, cannot itself be in the world of space and time; as sustainer of the realm within which the principle of sufficient reason operates, it can itself be neither object nor agent of that principle. For these reasons it could never be an object of empirical knowledge to anyone — quite apart from the fact that, for other reasons considered separately, it cannot be an object of knowledge to itself. Yet its existence is a necessary presupposition of our having the experience that we do have. Putting this the other way round, this whole world of experience is perfectly real, just as real as it presents itself as being, but it is unconceptualizable in any terms other than such as presuppose the existence of a subject. This is, in a nutshell, what transcendental idealism *means*. 'The whole world of objects is and remains representation, and is for this reason wholly and for ever conditioned by the subject; in other words, it has transcendental ideality. But it is not on that account falsehood or illusion; it presents itself as what it is, as representation, and indeed as a series of representations, whose common bond is the principle of sufficient reason. As such it is intelligible to the healthy understanding, even according to its innermost meaning, and to the understanding it speaks a perfectly clear language. To dispute about its reality can occur only to a mind perverted by over-subtle sophistry . . . The perceived world in space and time, proclaiming itself as nothing but causality, is perfectly real, and is absolutely what it appears to be; it appears wholly and without reserve

[19] *The World as Will and Representation*, ii. 15.

as representation, hanging together according to the law of causality. This is its empirical reality.'[20]

At this point, some readers might begin to feel that we have gone just about as far as this philosophy can take us. And, in a sense, we have. So why not let us stop here? A decision to do so would be supported, after all, by the facts of our historical situation. Our attempts as a species to get to know the real empirical world of which Schopenhauer speaks have been remarkably successful. Even at the modest level of comprehension which we have attained up to now in our natural history we obviously know more or less how to conduct empirical enquiries. Of course, there will always be plenty of room for improvements in method and technique, and there will always be plenty of the world left to discover, for since each discovery raises new questions the exploration of the world is bound to be a permanently open task. Even so, we seem to know roughly how to go about extending both our competence and our knowledge, and the use of the methods we already have is meeting with spectacular success (I am tempted to say with as much success as we know how to cope with). And although, ahead of our present level of comprehension, it is virtually certain that conceptual revolutions of a fundamental character are lying in wait for us in the future, even that is something we already 'know' and are prepared for. So one might ask oneself, Why should we not, as human beings, settle for this — for this empirical world as being all the reality we need concern ourselves with? That, after all, is what most commonsensical people seem to do, including most scientists, and most empiricist philosophers.

Schopenhauer's twofold answer has been given already in Chapter 2. There is first of all our wonder and amazement that the empirical world should exist at all, or we in it, reinforced by the fact that none of our characteristic modes of empirical explanation really do, beyond a certain limited and circular extent, explain it. (To summarize very swiftly what has been said on that point: explanation in science means reduction to scientific laws, forces of nature, chemical reactions, the table of elements, atomic or subatomic structure, and so on, and these things themselves then remain before us as mysteries. If we ask for an explanation of *them*, the scientist or the empiricist philosopher throws up his hands and says: 'That, I'm afraid, just happens to be what there is. These things are the given, the brute facts of our world, the elements out of which all explanation has to be constructed.' Schopenhauer then asks: 'What is the use of explanations that ultimately lead back to something just as unknown as the first problem was?'[21] And, as I

---

[20] *The World as Will and Representation*, i. 15 and 14.
[21] Ibid. i. 125.

remarked earlier, for professional philosophers to rest content with such explanations is an abnegation of philosophy: the true philosopher is one who is at his most perplexed and most interested when confronted with such mysteries, whereupon his questioning becomes more, not less, intense.) Secondly, there is the age-old search for significance in the whole. We are intensely *interested* in the world, fascinated by it, avidly curious about its workings. Its affairs do not unfold before indifferent eyes. And yet — why do they not? Why should we *care* about any of it, beyond the matter of our own survival in it? Yet the fact is that we feel about it as if it had meaning, significance, import. We certainly do not feel about it as if it were a mere parade of shadows. Consequently, one of the things that drives us on to pursue our philosophical investigations beyond the point we have now reached 'is that we are not satisfied with knowing that we have representations, that they are such and such, and that they are connected according to this or that law, whose general expression is always the principle of sufficient reason. We want to know the significance of those representations; we ask whether this world is nothing more than representation. In that case, it would inevitably pass by us like an empty dream, or a ghostly vision not worth our consideration. We ask whether it is something else, something in addition, and if so what that something is.'[22]

Of course, from the fact that some of us feel a profound conviction that there must be a significance attaching to the world of our experience beyond what is contained in the representations it does not follow that there is. The case may merely be one of the wish being father to the thought. Furthermore, such a wish may make us *want* to investigate, but what form could any such investigation take? 'On the path of *objective knowledge*, thus starting from the *representation*, we shall never get beyond the representation, i.e. the phenomenon. We shall therefore remain on the outside of things: we shall never be able to penetrate into their inner nature, and investigate what they are in themselves, in other words, what they may be by themselves. So far I agree with Kant.'[23] Confronted by empirical reality we are like soldiers besieging a castle who have sought endlessly and in vain to find a way of penetrating its walls, and whose only hope, whether they realize it or not, lies in a different mode of entry, a tunnel that will bring them up inside the fortress without penetrating those walls at all.

---

[22] *The World as Will and Representation*, i. 98–9.
[23] Ibid. ii. 195.

Chapter 6

Bodies and Wills

To the Kantian contention that we can have access to material objects only through our sensory and intellectual apparatus, and therefore that we can know them only in the subjectively determined modes of our own perceiving and thinking and not as they are in themselves, there is one apparent exception which has been under our noses all the time, namely our own bodies. These are material objects in time and space, and they present themselves as such in all the usual ways, to our own or anyone else's perceptions; yet in addition to this each one of us has direct knowledge of his own body from inside, and this knowledge is of a radically different order from any of the modes of apprehension discussed so far. 'A subjective and an objective existence, a being for self and a being for others, a consciousness of one's own self and a consciousness of other things, are in truth given to us immediately, and the two are given in such a fundamentally different way that no other difference compares with this. About *himself* everyone knows directly, about everything else only very indirectly. This is the fact and the problem.'[1]

That Kant could have overlooked so elementary a fact in this context, with its radical consequences for his philosophy, is astonishing. He had a great deal to say about inner sense, but the startling implications of the fact that what inner sense is located on the inside of is a material object seem never to have struck him. Perhaps this is to be explained, in spite of his having done more than anyone else to liberate us from the limiting assumptions of the subject–object dichotomy, by his having been unconsciously under the influence of those assumptions, at least to the extent of not noting the materiality of the one physical object of which his knowledge could not be accounted for by his theory of knowledge. Be that as it may, it fell to Schopenhauer to make the observation, and to follow its implications through; and this is really the starting-point of his independent contribution to philosophy — for up to this stage of our discussion he has done little more than ameliorate Kant, albeit in a gifted and distinctive way, whereas from now on he is striking out on his own.

[1] *The World as Will and Representation*, ii. 192.

To the simple observation that constitutes his point of departure people sometimes 'feel' rather than think two objections which can be disposed of straight away. One is that our bodies are, in some strange way, not really material objects in the way other material objects are. The other objection is that, though our bodies may be conceded to be material objects, they are not objects of empirical observation and knowledge in the same way as other material objects are. Both of these objections are, quite simply, false. It is certainly true that we do not *like* to think of ourselves as material objects, and in some peculiar way find it difficult to do so — perhaps this fact has something to do with Kant's oversight in this regard — but of course we *are* material objects. I am not saying we are *only* material objects: but we are at least that. An elephant is not only a material object, it is also an elephant, but to be an elephant it needs to be, among other things, a material object. And we are in the same case. It is essential to our safety and well-being that we never relax an at least subliminal awareness of the fact that we are material objects, for we have at all times to position and navigate our bodies in a potentially dangerous world of other material objects — I am doing this willy-nilly with every movement I make. Furthermore, I treat my body as a physical object not just in my moment-to-moment actions, like stopping a swinging door with my hand, or hanging a pair of spectacles on the front of my head by hooking them over my ears, but in a general yet active concern to keep the whole thing clean and wrapped up, away from naked flames or injurious glares, sharp edges or piercing points, and protected from dangerous impacts with other objects. If, in spite of my efforts, any part of it does get noticeably dirty, scuffed, burned or broken, I carry out cleaning operations and physical repairs as best I can, as I might do on any other material object.

Few, even among the religious, would now doubt that the human race has emerged by a continuous process of evolution from inorganic, inanimate nature, and is at least in that sense one with nature. Our bodies are made of the same stuff as the rest of the world — indeed, they grow and are sustained through a continuous and direct exchange of matter with it: every day we push matter into our bodies from the external world, and pass matter out back into it, the matter we retain turning into part of our personal substance. We can specify what we are made of, just as we can specify what any other object is made of: to put it in the broadest terms, we are some 60% water, plus varying amounts of carbon, hydrogen and nitrogen, plus a further list of ingredients that runs down to such small amounts as 2% calcium and 1.4% phosphorus, and then into the small print of 0.3% potassium, 0.2% sodium, less than 0.008% iron and about 0.003% zinc. All the atoms in the material universe, including those in our bodies, have the same basic internal structure; and the protons, neutrons and electrons in any one atom are the same as those in any other. So the physical world is all of one substance, and each of us is made of the same material as all the rest of it. In this respect we are one not only with animals and plants but with metals and gases, indeed with everything there is: the outermost stars of the cosmos are constructed of the same fundamental elements as our bodies. So the notion that we are in some unnameable way not fully and completely material objects is not sustainable — though, I repeat, this is not the same as to say that these material objects are fully and completely us: that is another matter. The essential point is this: the fact that we have direct knowledge of these material objects from inside is not to be explained in terms of their being made of something different from other material objects. They are not.

Equally, the claim cannot seriously be sustained that our bodies are not perceived or known in all the same ways as other physical bodies are known. Anyone who encounters me in his visual field will see a material object with all the same characteristics as other material objects have: size, shape, colours, textures and the rest — in fact in tricky light, or if I am on the edge of his visual field, he may unsurprisingly mistake me for some such thing as a tree or a pillar or a lamp-post, or a coat hanging from the back of the door. I have weight, mass, extension. People can bump up against me just as they bump up against the furniture. They can pick me up and carry me. I can get in their way, impede their light, fall on them and hurt them, for that matter drop on them and kill them. I emit sounds when struck or moved. I give off a range of smells, even a range of tastes. Everything that was said on p. 65 about the multifarious ways in which an apple is knowable applies to my body. On the anatomist's table my body could be, perhaps one day will be, dissected for the instruction of medical students as in the most technical sense an object of empirical observation. Even my own knowledge of my body is gained to an important degree, as other people's knowledge of my body is gained, through the senses of sight and touch. I am used to the sight of myself in a mirror, and it is only from external reflections and pictures of me that I know what my face looks like. When I look down I see, from my chest downwards, a physical object in external space, and I see it in its relation to immediately surrounding objects. It is only from this, and from its feel to my hands, that I am familiar with its shapes and surfaces and textures. 'A blind man without hands would never get to know his form.'[2] Knowledge of my body as a material object in space — a knowledge gained by me through my external organs of sense — is

---

[2] *The World as Will and Representation*, i. 20.

indispensable to my ability to function as a normal human being. It is not an alternative to, or substitute for, the knowledge I have of it through inner sense.

So it can be thoroughly established that our bodies are material objects in the fullest, unqualified sense, made of the same stuff as other material objects, and knowable by perceiving subjects in all the ways in which other material objects are knowable. Yet in addition to this we know them in an entirely different way, from inside. Each of us has this inner knowledge of only one such body, and it is by virtue of this that we are individuals. This material object here, and this one alone, I can know with a direct, non-sensory, non-intellectual knowledge from within: everything else in the universe I can know only from without, via the representations of sense and intellect, which are themselves functions of physical organs which are parts of this body of mine — which means that my knowledge of all other bodies is gained from the standpoint of this one and its position in time and space. This individuation, and the fact that all knowing is only for an individual (not to mention the fact that there is a dichotomy between knowing and being, such that we do not even know what we are) — these things lie very near the heart of life's mystery. 'Everyone can *be* only one thing, whereas he can *know* everything else, and it is this very limitation that really creates the need for philosophy.'[3]

The fact that each individual can never have direct knowledge of anything other than himself has given rise in many a one to the thought, or a passing fear, that his may be the only real existence, all else being only his representation and literally nothing more. This possibility seems to strike a lot of people during the period of normal development at which the individual is most enclosed in himself and anxious about his own identity, namely adolescence. The name for it — the belief that only I exist — is theoretical egoism, or solipsism. Schopenhauer regarded it as logically irrefutable, but he remained cheerfully untroubled by it. 'Theoretical egoism, of course, can never be refuted by proofs, yet in philosophy it has never been positively used otherwise than as a sceptical sophism, i.e. for the sake of appearance. As a serious conviction, on the other hand, it could be found only in a madhouse; as such it would then need not so much a refutation as a cure. Therefore we . . . shall regard this sceptical argument of theoretical egoism, which here confronts us, as a small frontier fortress. Admittedly the fortress is impregnable, but the garrison can never sally forth from it, and therefore we can pass it by and leave it in our rear without danger.'[4]

---

[3] *The World as Will and Representation*, i. 104.
[4] Ibid.

It has always seemed to me that solipsism is indeed refutable by one of those rare arguments — like the one about code-breaking on p. 37 — which are not logically conclusive yet which it is inconceivable that any rational person would not accept. If I alone exist then I alone have created all the music I have ever heard, all the plays I have ever seen, all the books I have ever read, which means specifically that I have composed, as just a small part of the total, all the plays of Shakespeare, all the symphonies of Beethoven, all the operas of Wagner (not to mention the philosophies of most of the world's greatest philosophers); and of course, for me it remains logically possible that I have, and certainly impossible for me to prove to myself that I have not. But I find it equally impossible to conceive that anyone could believe this of himself who was not as insane as Nietzsche was in the final phase of his life when he prided himself on not having carried his egoism so far as to desist from the creation of the world.

Since I do not believe this, I accept as a fact that other individuals exist besides myself, that they have direct knowledge of their bodies by inner sense as I have of mine, and that their phenomenal world in time and space contains me in it as an empirical object just as my world contains them. In this empirical world, if we did not have interior knowledge of ourselves, our own and each other's physical movements would seem to us just like all the other movements of external physical objects, and would present themselves at first as being equally mysterious, to be understood only from outside. There are forms of brain damage in which it seems to the patient that objects unconnected with him are in arbitrary motion in front of him which are in fact his hands. Something like this is obviously true for all of us in babyhood — it is not until the age of four or five months that the normal human being learns to recognize his feet, those objects with whose close appearance he has long been familiar, as his. (Note the word *learns* — we observe the movements of these physical objects in external space for weeks, and with rapt attention, before it occurs to us that they are ours, indeed that they are us.) If I were *only* a perceiving subject, and other human beings were just as they are, I would perceive their lower jaws flapping and hear sounds coming out; I would observe them erupting into sudden bursts of movement and then equally suddenly stopping; I would see them folding up into chairs and then unfolding out of them again; and the only ways open to me of making sense of any of this would be the same ones as those which are available to me in my observation and understanding of the rest of the material world.[5] What in practice

---

[5] It is in terms such as these that empiricist philosophers formulate one of their standard problems, what they call the problem of Other Minds: how can we know that

makes it otherwise is that I am like those other people, and know from my own experience that all these actions of theirs are acts of will, accompanied by a form of internal self-knowledge which, did I not share it, would be inconceivable to me. What they are engaged in is willed activity. Only as such can what they are doing be understood.

It is essential not to fall into the error of supposing that movements of the body are *caused* by acts of will. 'The act of will and the action of the body are not two different states objectively known, connected by the bond of causality; they do not stand in the relation of cause and effect; but are one and the same thing, though given in two entirely different ways, first quite directly, and then in perception for the understanding. The action of the body is nothing but the act of will objectified, i.e. translated into perception.'[6] If I get up out of this chair I am sitting in and walk into the next room to a bookcase, take down the book I have just realized I am about to quote from, and return with it to my desk, it is not the case that each of the voluntary acts constituting this series is preceded by an invisible act of will which pulls the levers which in turn bring about the physical movements, as if my body were a vehicle being operated from inside by an invisible driver. The voluntary act *is* the act of will. The fact that we use 'will' as a substantive in this context is a misfortune, for it seems to imply that there is a continuing entity which it denotes. There is no such entity: there are only our acts, which we know as and when they occur, connected or unconnected as they may be. This being so, the direct knowledge we have of our own willing is not knowledge of an entity but knowledge of activity: as we encounter it, our willing is activity through and through.

One hundred and thirty-one years after Schopenhauer expounded this doctrine something closely akin to it was the central thesis of Gilbert Ryle's *The Concept of Mind*, published in 1949. 'The clown's trippings and tumblings are the workings of his mind, for they are his jokes . . . Tripping on purpose is both a bodily and a mental process, but it is not two processes, such as one process of purposing to trip and, as an effect, another process of tripping. Yet the old myth dies hard. We are still tempted to argue that if the clown's antics exhibit carefulness, judgement, wit, and appreciation of the moods of his spectators, there

there are minds other than our own if they are permanently unobservable to us, and if all we can observe is bodies and their movements, including of course the sounds made by their movements? Some have tried to solve it by saying that people's bodily movements *are* the workings of their minds. But the initial formulation of the problem incorporates the false assumption that all our knowledge of the world, including of other people, is derived from observation through our organs of external sense and intellect.

[6] *The World as Will and Representation*, i. 100.

must be occurring in the clown's head a counterpart performance to that which is taking place on the sawdust. If he is thinking what he is doing there must be occurring behind his painted face a cogitative shadow-operation which we do not witness, tallying with, and controlling, the bodily contortions which we do witness.'[7] Some four years after *The Concept of Mind*, Wittgenstein's posthumous *Philosophical Investigations* was published, and in that a good deal of space is devoted to showing in a quite different way that our bodily movements are not caused by the acts of will which we associate with them.

Schopenhauer was repeatedly explicit about this. 'I say that between the act of will and the bodily action there is no causal connection whatever; on the contrary, the two are directly one and the same thing perceived in a double way, namely in self-consciousness or the inner sense as an act of will, and simultaneously in external brain-perception as bodily action.'[8] Consistently with this he denied that we could will future actions. 'Resolutions of the will relating to the future are mere deliberations of reason about what will be willed at some time, not real acts of will. Only the carrying out stamps the resolve; till then, it is always a mere intention that can be changed.'[9]

In inner sense I have direct knowledge of a great many things besides my acts of will — feelings, emotions, moods, all sorts of things — and when what we are considering is the inner knowledge we have of ourselves all these will have to be taken into account. But acts of will have a unique importance for the present argument. Those other things need not manifest themselves as physical movement which is observable to outer sense — they commonly do, but they need not — whereas acts of will of the kind we have been considering have to, for they are one with their outward manifestation. This makes them pivotal for Schopenhauer's whole philosophy. They are the sole example of empirically observed movements of physical objects in space and time which are also, of their nature, known simultaneously and directly from within in a way which is not mediated through the senses. Furthermore, they prove that the empirically observable is not all there is to the empirically observable: in the case of at least this one material object which is my body I know that if, following the thought-experiment described on p. 65, I think away every observable feature from its movements, what would remain would be not nothing but acts of will. The sum total of its observable features comprise, therefore, only one aspect of its existence: it is also, at the same time, something else.

The fact that this something else is act of will is destined to be a

[7] Gilbert Ryle, *The Concept of Mind*, pp. 33–4.
[8] *The Fourfold Root of the Principle of Sufficient Reason*, pp. 114–15.
[9] *The World as Will and Representation*, i. 100.

crucial factor in the later discussion. Meanwhile, however, having established these first steps in the argument, Schopenhauer allows himself to make the first of two extensions of the significance of the term 'will'. This extension covers everything directly known to us in self-consciousness except for passionless conceptual thought, if there can be such a thing. 'In observing his own self-consciousness everyone will soon be aware that its object is always his own volitions. By this one must understand, to be sure, not only the deliberate acts of will which are immediately put into effect and the formal decisions together with the actions which follow from them. Whoever is capable of somehow discerning the essential element, even when it is disguised under various modifications of degree and kind, will not hesitate to include among the manifestations of will also all desiring, striving, wishing, demanding, longing, hoping, loving, rejoicing, jubilation, and the like, no less than not willing or resisting, all abhorring, fleeing, fearing, being angry, hating, mourning, suffering pains — in short, all emotions and passions. For these emotions or passions are weaker or stronger, violent and stormy or else quiet impulsions of one's own will, which is either restrained or unleashed, satisfied or unsatisfied. In their many variations they relate to the successful or frustrated attainment of that which is willed, to the endurance or overcoming of that which is abhorred. Consequently, they are explicit affections of the same will which is active in decisions and actions.[10] To this context belongs even that which goes under the name of feelings of pleasure and of displeasure. Of course, these are present in a great variety of degrees and kinds, but still they can always be traced to the affections of desiring or abhorring, that is, to the will itself becoming aware of itself as satisfied or unsatisfied, restrained or unleashed. Indeed, here should be included the bodily emotions, pleasant or painful, and all the innumerable others which lie between these two, since the nature of these emotions consists in this: they enter directly into the self-consciousness as either something which is in accordance with the will or something which opposes it. Even of his own body one is directly conscious, strictly speaking, only as the externally active organ of the will and as the seat of receptivity for pleasant or unpleasant sensations.'[11]

[10] At this point Schopenhauer appends the following footnote. 'It is well worth noting that the church father Augustine recognized this fully, while many modern thinkers, with their alleged "feeling faculty", do not see it. Namely in *The City of God*, Book XIV, chapter 6, he speaks of affections of the soul, which in the previous book he brought under the four categories of desire, fear, joy, sadness, and says, "For the will is in them all; yea, none of them is anything else than will. For what are desire and joy but a volition of consent to the things we wish? And what are fear and sadness but a volition of aversion from the things we do not wish?" '

[11] *Essay on the Freedom of the Will*, pp. 11–12.

We are now confronted with two definitions of the term 'will': that of ordinary usage, and the one just cited. In due course there will be a third, the quite different meaning carried by the word in the title *The World as Will and Representation*. But one of the things we must do before we get to that is to make clear the distinction between willing, in either of the two senses we have encountered so far, and knowing. This can be put baldly by saying that our will is what is known in inner sense, as distinct from the process of that knowing. 'All knowledge inevitably presupposes subject and object; and so even self-consciousness is not absolutely simple, but, like our consciousness of other things (i.e. the faculty of intuitive perception), is divided into a known and a knower. Now here the known appears absolutely and exclusively as will. Accordingly the subject knows itself only as a *willer*, not as a *knower*. For the ego that represents, thus the subject of knowing, can itself never become representation or object, since as the necessary correlative of all representations it is their condition . . . Consequently, there is no *knowledge of knowing*, since this would require that the subject separated itself from knowing and yet knew that knowing: and this is impossible.'[12] Elsewhere Schopenhauer puts it more concisely. 'The knower himself, precisely as such, cannot be known, otherwise he would be the known of another knower.'[13] In a later century the point was spelled out at length in the idiom of linguistic philosophy in that section of Gilbert Ryle's *The Concept of Mind* called 'The Systematic Elusiveness of "I"' (pp. 195–8): e.g. '. . . when a person utters an "I" sentence, his utterance of it may be part of a higher order performance, namely one perhaps of self-reporting, self-exhortation or self-commiseration, and this performance itself is not dealt with in the operation which it itself is. Even if the person is, for special speculative purposes, momentarily concentrating on the Problem of the Self, he has failed and knows that he has failed to catch more than the flying coat-tails of that which he was pursuing. His quarry was the hunter.'

As we have seen, Schopenhauer's second use of the term 'will' covers everything that the subject of knowing (which can never know itself) can know in inner sense, apart from emotionally neutral processes of conceptual thinking. When one considers what is thus embraced in the fullness of its entire range it is as marvellous as what is known to us through our external senses. In this way I know, and with such immediate directness that it is almost as if I *am*, my body's lusts, its hungers and thirsts, its tensions and reliefs of tension, its pains and

---

[12] *On the Fourfold Root of the Principle of Sufficient Reason*, pp. 207–8.
[13] *The World as Will and Representation*, ii. 202.

tirednesses, its nervous and mental disorders, its elations. My immediate cognition of such things ranges all the way from overwhelming emotions that change my life down to the most trivial itches, twitches, twinges, pangs, throbs, qualms, and hankerings. I have direct interior knowledge of the thoughts going on in my brain, and of the perpetual weaving around these of a tapestry of connotations and allusions, anticipations, memories, evocations. Stronger than all these, and saturating them, I am directly aware of interest, involvement, affection, love, excitement, fear, aversion, boredom, grief and a hundred other emotions. Even when I am asleep I have a vivid and immediate awareness of the activity of my brain in dreaming. So powerful and extensive is the direct knowledge available to us of what is going on inside these physical objects which are our bodies — a polyphonic flow, orchestra-like in the multiplicity of its complexities and significance — that no brief verbal description can begin to do it justice. And we know with the utmost directness and indubitability that we are experiencing these things: no knowledge could be more immediate or more certain.

Are we, then, to leap now to a conclusion and say that this amazing knowledge of these physical objects from inside is knowledge of things as they are in themselves, and therefore knowledge of the noumenon? We are not. This is first and most obviously because, although what is known by us in inner sense is not apprehended as existing in the dimensions of space, nor as subject to the principle of causality, it is nevertheless apprehended by us as existing in the dimension of time — indeed, time is its essential and indispensable form — and time can characterize only phenomena; it could not characterize the noumenal. But there are other reasons that go deeper — one of them to do with what must be the nature of the noumenal, another to do with the nature of knowledge.

So far in this book we have seen Kant's conception of the noumenal rejected but not replaced. However, we have seen that the phenomenal is not all there is. On p. 116 it was argued that for the experiences we have to exist at all there must be something transcendental about both subject and object. More concretely and indubitably, willed behaviour is an example of the movement of physical objects in time and space to which there is certainly more than is observable through the organs of sense and intellect: there is an inner reality, known directly from inside the physical objects themselves, and their movements are comprehensible only in terms of the possibility of such knowledge. Even so, if there is anything that is noumenal, this complex inner world that we directly know cannot be it; for what, if anything, was noumenal could not be manifold, since it is only by means of some ultimate reference to space or time that the notion of differentiation can be given any significance. This is because it is impossible to talk of there being more than one anything, or of anything's being different from anything else, without making use of concepts that can be defined only with reference to notions of temporal succession or of space location. (For this reason Schopenhauer often refers to space-time as *principium individuationis*.) But space and time are of subjective origin, and characterize only the world of phenomena, not the world of things as they are in themselves, if indeed there could be such a world. Therefore it is only in the world of phenomena that things can be different from other things. Things as they are in themselves, lying as they would outside all possibility of space and time, would not be differentiable. But this means that we have to give up talking even speculatively about 'things as they are in themselves'. The noumenon, whatever it is, must be undifferentiable, so even the word itself cannot rightly be used in the plural. To suppose that in knowing our bodies from inside we had knowledge of things as they are in themselves would be to slide into Kant's mistake of talking as if phenomena were presented to our senses by noumena which shared their location and were their substrata. The noumenon must be 'free from all plurality, although its phenomena in time and space are innumerable. It is itself one, yet not as an object is one, for the unity of an object is known only in contrast to possible plurality. Again, [it] is one not as a concept is one, for a concept originates only through abstraction from plurality; but it is one as that which lies outside time and space, outside the *principium individuationis*, that is to say, outside the possibility of plurality.'[14] What this means is that the noumenon should not really be spoken of even as one: but we have to use language if we are to talk at all, and the singular form here is clearly preferable to the plural.

The other of our two main points, about the nature of knowledge, is deeply connected with this. All knowledge takes the subject–object form, but only in the world of phenomena can subject and object be differentiated. 'The necessity or need of knowledge in general arises from the plurality and *separate* existence of beings, from individuation. For let us imagine that there exists only a *single* being, then such a being needs no knowledge, because there would not then exist anything different from that being itself — anything whose existence such a being would therefore have to take up into itself only indirectly through knowledge, in other words, through picture and concept. It would already *itself* be all in all; consequently there would remain nothing for it to know, in other words, nothing foreign that could be apprehended

---

[14] *The World as Will and Representation*, i. 113.

as object. On the other hand, with the plurality of beings, every individual finds itself in a state of isolation from all the rest, and from this arises the necessity for knowledge . . . Therefore knowledge and plurality, or individuation, stand and fall together, for they condition each other. It is to be concluded from this that, beyond the phenomenon, in the true being-in-itself of all things, to which time and space, and therefore plurality, must be foreign, there cannot exist any knowledge . . . Accordingly, a "knowledge of things-in-themselves" in the strictest sense of the word, would be impossible, because where the being-in-itself of things begins, knowledge ceases, and all knowledge primarily and essentially concerns phenomena.'[15]

So our direct knowledge of ourselves in inner sense is still knowledge of phenomena, not of the noumenon; and the essential form of this knowledge is one of the indispensable dimensions of anything and everything that has being in the phenomenal world, namely time. Even so, it is significantly different from the knowledge we have of ourselves in other ways, and also different from the knowledge we have of all other objects. Our knowledge of all other objects is mediated through the organs of sense and intellect, and as such it is subject to the categories of space and causality — and we have plentiful knowledge of ourselves of this kind too. But of ourselves we have also, alongside and in addition to this mediated and therefore indirect knowledge, a direct knowledge from within which is unmediated through the organs of sense and intellect and not subject to two of the three categories which shape all other knowledge of phenomena. Clearly, then, this direct knowledge of physical objects from within, even though still not noumenal, is partially liberated from the constraints that shape all other empirical knowledge, and brings us closer to an understanding of the inner nature of things (we ourselves being things). It also shows that there is something special about time as being the only one not just of the dimensions but of the categories which is indispensable to knowledge, indeed to awareness.

For precisely the reason that the category of time is indispensable to awareness, in addition to the reason given by Schopenhauer regarding the nature of knowledge, we have to accept that we are permanently precluded from any direct knowledge (what Bertrand Russell was to call 'knowledge by acquaintance') of the noumenon. Nevertheless we may hope to discover something *about* it (Russell's 'knowledge by description'). We have made one very important discovery already, namely that whatever is noumenal must be undifferentiated. This alone is a substantial advance beyond Kant. With Kant the noumenon

[15] *The World as Will and Representation*, ii. 274–5

remained at best a blank, an x, a totally mysterious something about which nothing could be known beyond the fact that it manifested itself in the world of phenomena as physical objects and their movements in space and time. Now we know that we have direct, unmediated knowledge of at least some of these movements from within, and that what in this direct, unmediated way we know them to be is activity of will. Although this is not knowledge of the noumenal it seems to provide us with a path worth following, and one which might conceivably lead us to a knowledge of the inner nature of objects. For although the movements of only one material object are known from within to each of us, the fact that the noumenon, whatever it is, must be undifferentiated means that any knowledge we might acquire about it would be knowledge concerning its whole nature.

This brings home something that ought to have been evident to us long ago. From the moment the distinction of total reality into phenomena and noumenon was postulated we ought to have realized that, if every object in the world is both, then we ourselves must be both. It would mean, indeed, that each individual person would have to be a complete microcosm, for his sensorium is open to the whole of the world of phenomena ('he can *know* everything else') while at the same time whatever is noumenal must be identical in him as in everything. It follows from this that the likeliest pathway to a knowledge of total reality, including the noumenon, is the path of self-examination, since this alone yields the addition of knowledge by inner sense to knowledge by outer sense. It is obvious, too, that our willing is a vital clue in all this, for although our knowledge of it remains knowledge of phenomenon it is a uniquely significant phenomenon in that it is bound up with direct knowledge of a material object from inside.

It looks, then, as if the next stage in our enquiry should be an investigation of what it is that constitutes our willing. However, when we do launch ourselves into such an investigation we come up against the surprising fact that much if not most of what constitutes our willing is not open to our knowledge. And this turns out to be true whether we take 'willing' in the narrower or the more extended of the two senses we have considered so far. In the narrower sense, the sense of willed action or behaviour, I find myself unable to give any explanation of how I initiate an action at all. For instance, if I hold up the forefinger of my right hand and say, 'I am now going to count to three, and on the word "three" I shall crook my finger', I shall infallibly do it, but *how* I do it is a mystery to me which my studying physiology or neurology will do nothing to dispel. My finger bends, but how do I bend my finger? Motor nerves carry instructions, but how am I able to send such instructions *at will*, as we so significantly say? How, in this sense, do

I decide or do anything at all in the way of willed activity? The mystery is as baffling to us today as it was to the ancients.

Although the second, extended sense of 'willing' is very different, it nevertheless lands us in mysteries which are as deep. For we find on investigation that most of the workings not only of our emotions, which is surprising enough, but of our minds, are as inaccessible to our conscious awareness as are most of the workings of our physical organs. 'We often do not know what we desire or fear. For years we can have a desire without admitting it to ourselves or even letting it come to clear consciousness, because the intellect is not to know anything about it, since the good opinion we have of ourselves would inevitably suffer thereby. But if the wish is fulfilled we get to know from our joy, not without a feeling of shame, that this is what we desired; for example, the death of a near relation whose heir we are. Sometimes we do not know what we really fear, because we lack the courage to bring it to clear consciousness. In fact we are often entirely mistaken as to the real motive from which we do or omit to do something, till finally some accident discloses the secret to us, and we know that our real motive was not what we thought of it as being, but some other that we were unwilling to admit to ourselves, because it was by no means in keeping with our good opinion of ourselves. For example, as we imagine we omit to do something for purely moral reasons; yet we learn subsequently that we were deterred merely by fear, since we do it as soon as all danger is removed. In individual cases this may go so far that a man does not even guess the real motive of his action, in fact does not regard himself as capable of being influenced by such a motive.'[16]

Schopenhauer argued at length, and with a psychological insight which was altogether unprecedented, that empirical evidence points to the conclusion not only that most of our thoughts and feelings are unknown to us but that the reason for this is a process of repression which is itself unconscious; that it is unconscious because our most primitive and powerful emotions and wishes cannot be accommodated by the conception of ourselves which we wish to preserve; and that it is upward from these depths that the emotions, wishes and so on of which we *are* aware emerge into consciousness, suitably cleaned up so as not to offend our self-esteem, but nevertheless pushed from below by hidden, primitive and exceedingly powerful drives in terms of which most of what we think, say and do would have to be fully understood. His handling of the whole subject is full of concrete and detailed perception — for instance, he suggests that if we want to know what we really think of a person we should note our immediate reaction when an unexpected

---

[16] *The World as Will and Representation*, ii. 209–10.

letter from him flops on to our doormat. It is tempting to quote several such passages at length. Instead, however, I shall reproduce one which expounds his doctrine of the unconscious mind in general terms, and clinches it with characteristic concreteness in the final sentence. 'To make the matter clear, let us compare our consciousness to a sheet of water of some depth. Then the distinctly conscious ideas are merely the surface; on the other hand the mass of the water is the indistinct, the feelings, the after-sensation of perceptions and intuitions and what is experienced in general . . . Now this mass of the whole consciousness is more or less, in proportion to intellectual liveliness, in constant motion, and the clear pictures of the imagination, or the distinct, conscious ideas expressed in words, and the resolves of the will are what comes to the surface in consequence of this motion. The whole process of our thinking and resolving seldom lies on the surface, that is to say, seldom consists of a concatenation of clearly conceived judgments; although we aspire to this, in order to be able to give an account of it to ourselves and others. But usually the rumination of material from outside, by which it is recast into ideas, takes place in the obscure depths of the mind. This rumination goes on almost as unconsciously as the conversion of nourishment into the humours and substance of the body. Hence it is that we are often unable to give any account of the origin of our deepest thoughts; they are the offspring of our mysterious inner being. Judgments, sudden flashes of thought, resolves, rise from those depths unexpectedly and to our own astonishment . . . Consciousness is the mere surface of our mind, and of this, as of the globe, we do not know the interior but only the crust.'[17]

There are many ways in which these passages are remarkable, not least in constituting an unmistakably clear and explicit exposition of an idea now generally credited to Freud, who was not yet born. The point they establish which is of most importance to our present argument is that, although willing may be accompanied by consciousness, it need not be, and usually is not. This realization makes possible a wholly new extension of our understanding of the body–will relationship. 'That even those parts of the body whose movements do not proceed from the brain, do not follow upon motives, and are not voluntary, are nevertheless ruled and animated by the will, is shown by their participation in all unusually violent motions of the will, i.e. emotions and passions. We see, for instance, the quickened pulse in joy or alarm, the blush in embarrassment, the cheek's pallor in terror or in suppressed anger, the tears of sorrow, the difficult breathing and increased activity of the intestines in terror, watering of the mouth at the sight of dainties,

[17] *The World as Will and Representation*, ii. 135–6.

nausea occasioned by that of loathesome objects, strongly accelerated circulation of the blood and even altered quality of bile through wrath, and of saliva through violent rage . . . The organism is further deeply undermined by lasting grief, and may be mortally affected by fright as well as by sudden joy.'[18] To the earlier point that what is known to outer sense as a physical movement of my body is known to inner sense as an act of will we can now add the point that what is known to inner sense as an affection of the will is accompanied by purely physical and involuntary changes (and this must always involve movements) in my body. Every feeling or emotion we experience, however slight, has a physical concomitant in some such thing as a minute raising or lowering of muscular tension, or blood pressure, or temperature, or the level of activity of some gland or organ — so stirrings of the will and motions of the body are always correlative.[19] The realization whose threshold we are approaching is that the body *is* the will — that they are the same thing known in two different ways. This, of course, would explain why their voluntary acts, as we have established already and independently, are the same thing known in two different ways.

It could be said that each one of us has always been aware of this, in the vital sense that we have lived our lives in accordance with the knowledge. We take for granted all the time the identity of wants, needs, fears, and the rest, with physical sensations, and we use much of the same vocabulary for both, including the key term 'feeling' (which, significantly, is seldom if ever ambiguous in any confusing sense). We also take it for granted that gratifying or assuaging these wants, needs and fears *consists in* bodily activity, whether of the everyday kind like putting liquids and solids into our mouths, and intertwining our bodies with those of others in the act of love, or of less everyday kinds like heaving our body up a mountainside so that the eyes in it can look at the sunset, or flying it to Australia to be with the body out of which it originally came. Hearing a great live performance of a Beethoven symphony may be a 'spiritual' experience of the profoundest kind, yet hearing it involves me in getting a vehicle to transport all 100 kilos of my meat, bones and offal to a concert hall and finding there a space for it to occupy, preferably a seat to support its weight. The interfusion of

[18] *On the Will in Nature*, pp. 246–7.

[19] Cf. the following exchange from *Men of Ideas* (p. 172):

'MAGEE: What you are saying is that wishes, emotions, feelings, decisions, thoughts, and so on, are all processes which take place in, or are propensities of, certain physical objects, namely people, and that not only are they always accompanied by microphysical changes — changes in our brains and our central nervous systems, and so on — but that they *are* those microphysical changes.

QUINE: Exactly.'

our willing with our physical being is such that we cannot conceive of any other way to be. Similarly with our view of other people: we take it for granted that their bodies — their faces especially, but not only their faces — are the outward forms, the visible histories, of their will, the running total of their willing so far in their lives. And we cannot conceive of any other way of regarding them which would not involve ceasing to see them as persons. Not only does all this go without saying in our everyday living: even at the level of conscious theory it is an old idea. For instance the Old Testament Jews (to whose general way of thinking Schopenhauer was abusively antipathetic) regarded the body as the soul in its outward form.[20] Aristotle regarded the human being as a thing that thinks. In our own day many well-known philosophers, such as Ryle, Quine, and a whole school in Australia, have insisted on the identity of so-called inner activity with bodily activity.

Precisely because the identity of body and will is something immediately and directly known it is not something that can be proved, for there is nothing more directly known to us from which it can be derived. 'The identity of the will and of the body, provisionally explained, can be demonstrated only as is done here, and that for the first time, and as will be done more and more in the further course of discussion. In other words, it can be raised from immediate consciousness, from knowledge in the concrete, to rational knowledge of reason, or be carried over into knowledge in the abstract. On the other hand, by its nature it can never be demonstrated, that is to say, deduced as indirect knowledge from some other more direct knowledge, for the very reason that it is itself the most direct knowledge. If we do not apprehend it and stick to it as such, in vain shall we expect to obtain it again in some indirect way as derived knowledge. It is a knowledge of a quite peculiar nature, whose truth cannot therefore be brought under one of the four headings by which I have divided truth in the essay *On the Principle of Sufficient Reason*, § 29 seqq., namely logical, empirical, transcendental and metalogical. For it is not, like all these, the reference of an abstract representation to another representation, or to the necessary form of intuitive or of abstract representing: it is a reference of the judgement to the relation that a representation of perception, namely the body, has to that which is not a representation at all, but is *toto genere* different therefrom, namely will. I should therefore like to distinguish this truth from every other, and call it *philosophical truth* κατ' ἐξοχήν [*par excellence*]. We can turn the expression of this truth in different ways and say: My body and my will are one; or, What as representation of perception I call my body, I call my will in so far as I

[20] J. Pedersen: *Israel*, i. 170.

am conscious of it in an entirely different way comparable with no other; or, My body is the *objectivity* of my will; or, Apart from the fact that my body is my representation, it is still my will.'[21]

[21] *The World as Will and Representation*, i. 102–3.

Chapter 7

The World as Will

In Chapter 2 great stress was laid on the fact that valid arguments add no information to what is already contained in their premisses, but merely uncover, spell out, make explicit, what is already there. This means that — to put the same thing the other way round — once the requisite premisses have been assembled, what is required to establish a conclusion is not any additional information but a mere pointing out that the conclusion does indeed follow from what has been given. In our search for the identity of the noumenon we are now in an analogous situation. Along the way we have succeeded in establishing a number of important positions; if we now treat these as premisses, and look at them in the appropriate relationship to each other, we will find that the conclusion we are seeking is already contained in them. Let us consider them in the following order:

1. A material object is a space filled with energy. This energy and the matter that constitutes the object are at bottom one and the same.

2. My body, considered as material object, is not made of anything different from other material objects.

3. The movements of the material object which is my body are known to me not only through external sense, as are the movements of other material objects, but also directly, non-sensorily, non-intellectually from within, as acts of will.

4. Thus, in at least this one case, it is possible for an act of will and the movement of a material object to be one and the same thing apprehended in two different ways. This leads us to the realization that it is possible for will and material object to be one and the same thing apprehended in two different ways.

5. Willing need not be accompanied by consciousness, and is not so accompanied for most of the time even in material objects which are nevertheless conscious.

6. If all material objects are in one sense phenomenon and in another sense noumenon then human beings too, as material objects, must have this dual nature, and therefore we must in some sense be noumenal.

7. Such willing as we are conscious of cannot be noumenal but must, despite the unique character of our knowledge of it, be phenomenon of something else.

8. The inner depths within ourselves from which willing rises to the surface remain sealed off from our own direct knowledge.

9. The noumenon, whatever it is, is forever sealed off from any possibility of being known directly.

The conclusion now stares us in the face: the noumenon is of the nature of that willing which is unconscious and inaccessible to consciousness; the willing of which I am conscious is a phenomenal expression of that noumenon; and since the noumenon is one and the same in everything, whatever the noumenon is of which my cognized willing is phenomenon must be the same as the noumenon of which every other phenomenon is phenomenon.

We have seen that our inner world consists largely of the operation of primitive forces unaccompanied by consciousness. So too does the outer world, the physical world in space. Every object attracts every other with a force so powerful that the whole universe consists of matter in motion, for the most part of unimaginably vast physical objects hurtling through space at unimaginably high velocities. Most of the surface of the one we are living on is covered with immeasurable quantities of water which are also, because of this same force, in perpetual motion. What is not covered with water is half covered with plants shooting and vegetating, pushing down roots, turning their leaves or their flowers to the sun. The air above all this is in perpetual motion too, and so are the clouds in the air. Even a pocket of perfectly still air exerts a pressure on everything it touches. In this environment live uncountable billions of automotive insects, fish, birds and animals, all of them in constant motion. And the very atoms that make up everything, whether living or dead, are themselves micro-worlds within which perpetual movements are taking place at speeds approaching the velocity of light. So the whole material world is a welter of movements, pressures, forces, tensions, attractions, repulsions and transformations of every kind — over a range and on a spatial scale so tremendous as to be altogether beyond any human powers of determinate representation, and without any known beginning or end in time — and all of it, except for the tiny animal and human component which has arrived on the scene so lately, unaccompanied by consciousness.

To the question 'How is all this energy generated?' Schopenhauer's reply would be that even so apparently simple a question incorporates a false assumption. It implies that the energy is derivative, that it is not itself ultimate, that there must be something else that produces it (something else that is perhaps ultimate). But in the world of phenomena there is nothing else. We may find it hard to conceptualize energy that just *is*, without being generated, but given the law of the conservation of energy there is no escaping the fact that the energy which imbues the universe as a whole must be of this kind. What Schopenhauer is saying is that this energy is itself what is ultimate in the world of phenomena. (It was not until the twentieth century that the science of physics reached the same conclusion.[1]) He is saying, furthermore, that what is indicated by our knowledge of the one material object in the universe that we know from the inside is that all material objects, in their inner nature, are primitive, blind, unconscious force inaccessible to knowledge. Everything that appears to our organs of sense and intellect as matter in motion is, in its unknowable inner nature, this unconscious force — they and it are the same thing manifested in different ways, just as my physical movement and my act of will are the same thing manifested in different ways. The whole universe is the objectification of this force. It constitutes gravity, which is everywhere, and is everywhere the same; it forms the chicken in the egg, and the child in the womb; it pushes up the plants; it sweeps along the winds and the tides and the currents; it crashes through the cataracts; it is the go in the running animal, the pull of magnetism, the attraction of electricity, the energy of thought. All these are phenomenal manifestations of a single underlying drive which ultimately is undifferentiated.

This is Schopenhauer's central doctrine. He is clear about its logical status. He knows that he has not proved it, but holds that this is because no such doctrine could be proved: the principle of sufficient reason, which is the organon of proof, has its application only within the world of phenomena, and the present doctrine is about the relationship of that world as a whole to something else — so we are now in a realm which proofs cannot reach. That is not to say that the doctrine is unsupported by rational argument: on the contrary, much of the present volume consists of rational arguments which, in Schopenhauer's view, lead us to this conclusion so insistently that no reasonable person who fully understands them is likely to refuse to accept it. It is like, he thinks, the case against solipsism, which equally cannot be proved but can nevertheless be supported by rational arguments which it is impos-

[1] e.g. Werner Heisenberg, *Physics and Philosophy*: 'Energy is in fact the substance from which all elementary particles, all atoms and therefore all things are made, and energy is that which moves. Energy is a substance, since its total amount does not change, and the elementary particles can actually be made from this substance as is seen in many experiments on the creation of elementary particles. Energy can be changed into motion, into heat, into light and into tension. Energy may be called the fundamental cause for all change in the world . . .' (p. 61). 'Since mass and energy are, according to the theory of relativity, essentially the same concepts, we may say that all elementary particles consist of energy. This could be interpreted as defining energy as the primary substance of the world' (p. 67).

sible to resist. He holds, moreover, that when reality is viewed in this light the problems and paradoxes melt away; all the details fall into place, everything makes sense; and in view of that it then becomes incredible that the correct solution has not at last been found, just as it does when a code is effectively broken — though it remains, as in that case, a logical possibility that we have involved ourselves in a mis-understanding. However, given that all this is the case, it is not a valid objection to the doctrine to say that it has not been proved. It would be an objection, and devastatingly so, if proof were a possibility; but only then. Since proof is not a possibility, Schopenhauer claims that, when he has spelled out all its implications, his conclusion has all the support it could possibly have, and therefore that to demand more exhibits a failure to understand the reality of the situation.

Having finally, as he thinks, identified the nature of the noumenon, we are faced with the practical necessity of giving it a name if we wish to talk about it — and we certainly do. The fact that we can never have direct knowledge of it but can know it only through its particular manifestations in individual objects, including ourselves, and in their movements, including our own, makes this a problem. Schopenhauer is aware of the difficulty and discusses it at some length. He considers the word for 'force', and rejects it on the ground of its association with natural science, whose entire significance is confined to the realm of the phenomenal. In the end, to avoid choosing an associationless word which would merely be a longer equivalent of 'x', he decides, albeit with some misgiving, to name the noumenon after that unique one of its phenomena which we know directly from within instead of only in-directly, from without, and our knowledge of which it thus was that gave us the vital clue to the noumenon's identity. 'In the case of every emergence of an act of will from the obscure depths of our inner being into the knowing consciousness, there occurs a direct transition into the phenomenon of the thing-in-itself that lies outside time. Accordingly the act of will is indeed only the nearest and clearest *phenomenon* of the thing-in-itself; yet it follows from this that, if all the other phenomena could be known by us just as immediately and intimately, we should be obliged to regard them precisely as that which the will is in us. There-fore in this sense I teach that the inner nature of everything is *will*, and I call the will the thing-in-itself. In this way Kant's doctrine of the inability to know the thing-in-itself is modified to the extent that the thing-in-itself is merely not absolutely and completely knowable; that nevertheless by far the most immediate of its phenomena, distinguished *toto genere* from all the rest by this immediateness, is its representative for us. Accordingly we have to refer the whole world of phenomena to that one in which the thing-in-itself is manifested under the lightest of all veils, and still remains phenomenon only in so far as my intellect, the only thing capable of knowledge, still always remains distinguished from me as the one who wills, and does not cast off the knowledge-form of *time*, even with *inner* perception.

'Accordingly, even after this last and extreme step, the question may still be raised what that will, which manifests itself in the world and as the world, is ultimately and absolutely in itself; in other words, what it is, quite apart from the fact that it manifests itself as *will*, or in general *appears*, that is to say, *is known* in general. This question can *never* be answered, because, as I have said, being known, of itself, contradicts being-in-itself, and everything that is known is as such only phenomenon. But the possibility of this question shows that the thing-in-itself, which we know most immediately in the will, may have, entirely outside all possible phenomenon, determinations, qualities, and modes of existence which for us are absolutely unknowable and incomprehensible, and which then remain as the inner nature of the thing-in-itself.'[2]

Schopenhauer has now introduced a third meaning for the word 'will', and it differs radically from the first two. He warns the reader that, in appropriating it as a technical term in his philosophy to denote the noumenon, he is not using it in either of his two previous senses, and certainly not in its normal sense. For this he makes the following excuse. 'No word could exist to describe the concept of this genus. I therefore name the genus after its most important species, the direct knowledge of which lies nearest to us, and leads to the indirect knowledge of all the others. But anyone who is incapable of carrying out the required extension of the concept will remain involved in a permanent misunderstanding.'[3] He never said a truer word. His use of the term 'will' in this third sense has proved nothing short of an intellectual catastrophe, in that it has precipitated widespread misunderstanding of his philosophy ever since.

There are at least four common misunderstandings, three of them closely related. First, the very fact — which Schopenhauer by some astonishing lapse or aberration took to be a recommendation — that 'the concept of *will* is of all possible concepts the only one which has its origin *not* in the [observable] phenomenon, *not* in the mere representation of perception, but which comes from within, and proceeds from the most immediate consciousness of everyone'[4] makes it almost impossibly difficult for even a careful and self-disciplined thinker to maintain consistency in associating it with representations of perception without implying some sort of suggestion that they are being credited with some

[2] *The World as Will and Representation*, ii. 197–8.   [3] Ibid. i. 111.   [4] Ibid.

kind of inner sense. Schopenhauer, who elsewhere insisted so strictly that concepts cannot contain anything different from the perceptions from which they are derived, has erred grievously here. Second, for similar reasons, the fact that the concept is wholly derived from personal experience, and from observation of persons and animals, causes any application of it to carry implied overtones of the attribution of personality — so that if, say, one describes in Schopenhauerian terminology the colossal energy put forth by the sun as 'a manifestation of will' an uncomfortable yet inescapable feeling is created that some sort of personality (however dumbly and blindly material) is being insinuated of the sun. The third misunderstanding, again similar, derives from the fact that, even apart from ourselves with our inner sense, the other creatures from the observation of which the concept 'will' is partially derived are all characterized by consciousness. Throughout the history of Western thought, until Schopenhauer, will was assumed to be one of the modes of consciousness, and in ordinary usage it still is; and this again makes it almost impossibly difficult to use the term without seeming to imply the existence of some sort of consciousness, however dim and darkling, in what it is applied to. The fourth misunderstanding is different from the others, and derives from the fact that in the ordinary usage of the word, willing always has an aim, an object, whereas of course the noumenon does not and cannot have any aim or object. It seems strange to use the word 'will' with no indication that it is *directed* towards anything, but Schopenhauer is clear about this too: 'Absence of all aim, of all limits, belongs to the essential nature of the will in itself, which is an endless striving.'[5]

'Will' in Schopenhauer's third sense is not conative at all, unless by coincidence. It has no necessary reference to anything to do with life, personality, consciousness, inner sense or aim. It is his name for the force exemplified in the constitution and motion of everything in the universe from the cosmic wheeling of the galaxies to the perpetual whirl of subatomic particles. He has given it the name 'will' for no other reason than that the nearest we as experiencing subjects can come to a direct apprehension of it is through the manifestation of primal energy that each one of us experiences in inner sense as the ordinary drive of life, the ongoing thrust, however weak, of being alive; or, if you like, simply the will to live, to survive, to keep going. This is the most ordinary, everyday, directly experienced of phenomena for each of us, and Schopenhauer's central doctrine is quite simply that it is noumenally at one with the force that drives everything else in the universe. Understood in this way, what Schopenhauer is saying may be difficult

---

[5] *The World as Will and Representation*, i. 164.

to grasp imaginatively, but it is not intellectually bizarre. He warns his readers over and over again against misunderstanding it. The following quotations are all illustrations of such warnings, and to avoid unfruitful repetition I have chosen and assembled them in an order which constitutes a development of the argument. 'The will, considered purely in itself, is devoid of knowledge, and is only a blind, irresistible urge, as we see it appear in inorganic and vegetable nature, and in their laws, and also in the vegetative part of our own life.'[6] 'An essential point of my teaching is that the phenomenal appearance of a *will* is as little tied to life and organization as it is to knowledge, and that therefore the inorganic also has a will, whose manifestations are all its fundamental qualities that are incapable of further explanation.'[7] 'It appears as a blind urge and as a striving devoid of knowledge in the whole of inorganic nature, in all the original forces. It is the business of physics and chemistry to look for these forces and to become acquainted with their laws.'[8] 'I am the first who has insisted that a *will* must be attributed to all that is lifeless and inorganic. For, with me, the will is not, as has hitherto been assumed, an accident of cognition and therefore of life; but life itself is manifestation of will. Knowledge, on the contrary, is really an accident of life, and life of Matter. But Matter itself is only the perceptibility of the phenomena of the will.'[9] 'With me it is the will-without-knowledge that is the foundation of the reality of things.'[10] 'The will as the thing-in-itself, constitutes the inner, true, and indestructible nature of man; yet in itself it is without consciousness.'[11] 'Without the object, without the representation, I am not knowing subject but mere, blind will; in just the same way, without me as subject of knowledge, the thing known is not object, but mere will, blind impulse. In itself, that is to say outside the representation, this will is one and the same with mine; only in the world as representation, the form of which is always at least subject and object, are we separated out as known and knowing individual. As soon as knowledge, the world as representation, is abolished, nothing in general is left but mere will, blind impulse.'[12]

Schopenhauer could certainly not have been more explicit about this (and, one is tempted to say, more repetitive) yet the damage has been done. He has made inevitable the misunderstandings he is trying to ward off. In choosing the word 'will' to denote a noumenon whose essential nature is not conative at all but is through and through non-human and impersonal, without consciousness, without inner

[6] *The World as Will and Representation*, i. 275.   [7] Ibid. ii. 296–7.
[8] Ibid. i. 149.   [9] *On the Will in Nature*, 309.
[10] *The World as Will and Representation*, ii. 269.
[11] Ibid. ii. 201.   [12] Ibid. i. 180.

sense, without aim and — perhaps the most important point of all — without life, he has brought it about that all his formulations about it carry, hidden somewhere on board, something counter-intuitive in their cargo. The most grievous thing of all is that this was wholly unnecessary. Any innocuous name would have avoided it. The term 'force', rejected by him, would have been vastly preferable. 'Energy' would have been better still. After all, the physical universe simply *does* instantiate unimaginably vast quantities of energy throughout its every detailed particle and motion, energy which is simply *there* inexplicably to us, self-subsistent and not generated 'elsewhere' (there is no else-where); and we know from our science that it actually does constitute everything that exists in the phenomenal world, not only as regards its motion but as regards its material structure. And all Schopenhauer is saying is that what this phenomenon is phenomenon of is what is ultimate in total reality. However, by a disastrous choice as regards the key term in his vocabulary he has ensured that all but close students of his work are bound to take him to be saying something else. People reading brief accounts of his ideas only too naturally, one is forced to say inevitably, misconstrue them because of the nomenclature. Equally naturally, the title of his chief work is misconstrued unless and until the book is read, and even then the misconstruction is likely to be brought to a first reading. Ever since he wrote, Schopenhauer has been widely regarded as saying that the will *in something akin to the ordinary sense of the word* is the noumenon. The quite common idea that there is something semi-occult, perhaps even a bit crackpot about his philosophy is based on this misunderstanding. So is the notion that he is in any way whatever a precursor of Nazi ways of thinking. Unfortunately — as is illustrated by the fact that it has taken us thus far into this book to formulate clearly what his key use of the term 'will' actually does mean — the mistake is one which it is not possible to correct briefly, other than by mere assertion. And, alas, it is not feasible at this time of day to change the vocabulary in which the discussion of Schopenhauer's philosophy is carried on. This is now firmly established not only by his own work but by all references to it in the works of others over the period of more than a century since he wrote. So we have little choice but to accept his use of the term 'will', in this third and most character-istic sense. From now on we shall often refer to the noumenon as 'will', and by this we shall mean no more than a universal, aimless, un-individualized, non-alive force such as manifests itself in, for example, the phenomenon of gravity. ('The will proclaims itself just as directly in the fall of a stone as in the action of a man.'[13]) When the word is being

---

[13] *The World as Will and Representation*, ii. 299.

used in this sense the reader will simply have to exclude from his mind what he normally understands by it if he is not to misconstrue the most central and important doctrines of Schopenhauer's philosophy. This is an unsatisfactory state of affairs, I concede, but I see no practicable way of remedying it.

I say 'when the word is being used in this sense' because Schopenhauer proceeds to use it side by side in all three of his stipulated senses. Quite often he uses it in two of them in the same sentence. To be fair to him, this does not result in ambiguity or confusion, for it is always clear from the context what is being said. Unfortunately, when his work is translated into English, or discussed in English, the accidental misfortune occurs that a fourth sense is added to the other three, for the German language has a separate word, '*Willkür*', for free will, and when this is translated into English a further use of the word 'will' is unavoidable.

With his third definition Schopenhauer has fulfilled the chief aim of his philosophical undertaking, which was to uncover the identity of the noumenon. He believes that only when the world of phenomena is seen as phenomenon of will in his third sense does reality become properly intelligible, and that it then does so as fully as is available to human understanding. When he says, as he does more than once, that what is imparted by his philosophy is a single thought, this is the thought. All his serious philosophical writing is devoted either to trying to persuade the reader of its truth or to exploring its implications.

It will be remembered that *The Will in Nature*, the first book he wrote after *The World as Will and Representation*, was devoted to showing how his central doctrine had been corroborated by subsequent developments in the natural sciences. To us, with our much longer hindsight than he was ever able to have, this is one of the most remarkable things about his work. It is post-dated by the whole of biology since Darwin, the whole of psychology since Freud, and the whole of physics since Einstein, and yet all of these lend massive corroboration to his arguments — indeed, as we are seeing, his arguments anticipated all three with striking precision. Twentieth-century physics in particular has provided the most powerful confirmation that could be imagined on the scientific level to Schopenhauer's central view of the material world. In the fullest scientific sense we now *know* that matter and energy are equivalent; that at the subatomic level the concept of matter dissolves completely into the concept of energy; that every material object is, in its inner constitution, a concatenation of forces and nothing else; and that it is theoretically possible to transform every material object without remainder into the energy that constitutes it. In other words it just is the case that every material object is material object only if regarded in a certain way; and that looked at in another way it is blind force; and that the two are one and the same thing. It is no surprise to learn that the founder of quantum mechanics, Erwin Schrödinger, was consciously and enthusiastically a Schopenhauerian.

It would not have surprised Schopenhauer to learn that mankind's acquisition of the ability to make matter transform itself into the blind force that constitutes it, and this blind force to manifest itself in the place of that matter in the world of phenomena, constitutes a threat to destroy our world. He was possessed by the idea that there is something inherently evil, monstrous, wicked about the ultimate force that consti- tutes the world, though oddly enough this does not reveal itself in his attitude to the inanimate cosmos. When others have glimpsed the material universe in the same light as he did — as a beginningless and endless expenditure of groundless energy on an astronomic scale, utterly without self-awareness or purpose — they have often reacted with either nausea or terror, but Schopenhauer is seized by the point- lessness, the nothingness of it all, rather than by any sense of dread. It is only when he comes to consider the lot of living creatures that the note of horror, of revulsion, creeps into his voice — though even then his preponderant feeling remains a sense of the nullity of things. Of the human world, typically, he writes: 'Many millions, united into nations, strive for the common good, each individual for his own sake; but many thousands fall sacrifice to it. Now senseless delusion, now intriguing politics, incite them to wars with one another; then the sweat and blood of the great multitudes must flow, to carry through the ideas of indi- viduals, or to atone for their shortcomings. In peace industry and trade are active, inventions work miracles, seas are navigated, delicacies are collected from all the ends of the earth, the waves engulf thousands. All push and drive, some plotting and planning, others acting; the tumult is indescribable. But what is the ultimate aim of it all? To sustain ephemeral and harassed individuals through a short span of time, in the most fortunate case with endurable want and comparative painless- ness (though boredom is at once on the lookout for this), and then the propagation of this race and of its activities. With this evident want of proportion between the effort and the reward, the will-to-live, taken objectively, appears to us from this point of view as a folly, or taken subjectively, as a delusion. Seized by this, every living thing works with the utmost exertion of its strength for something that has no value. But on closer consideration, we shall find here also that it is rather a blind urge, an impulse wholly without ground and motive.'[14]

Of animals he writes: 'The futility and fruitlessness of the struggle of

---

[14] *The World as Will and Representation*, ii. 357.

the whole phenomenon are more readily grasped in the simple and easily observable life of animals. The variety and multiplicity of their structural organization, the ingenuity of the means by which each is adapted to its element and to its prey, here contrast clearly with the absence of any lasting final aim. Instead of this, we see only momentary gratification, fleeting pleasure conditioned by wants, much and long suffering, constant struggle, *bellum omnium*, everything a hunter and everything hunted, pressure, want, need and anxiety, shrieking and howling; and this goes on *in saecula saeculorum*, or until once again the crust of the planet breaks.'[15]

In writing about the natural world as a whole, Schopenhauer makes the point that we seem spontaneously to categorize it under four main headings: inanimate matter, plants, animals and humans. In his terminology these are four differentiable grades of the will's objectification, and they form a natural hierarchy because of their relative positions in the evolutionary process. Dumb, insensible matter — which of course is nearly everything, the entire inorganic universe — is the lowest, and is what was first. The next grade up is plant life, which comes next in time, more individualized and more sophisticated, both in its internal organization and in its responsiveness to stimuli, and uniquely differentiated from inorganic nature by its power of self-reproduction. Then came the third grade, animal life, more individualized still, with its purposive movement and its development of a central nervous system and a brain — perhaps even, in some cases, a personality. And humanity of course is the fourth and highest grade of the will's objectification, with its achievement of individual self-consciousness and its unique gift of reason, its powers to investigate and understand and know, which at last provide that which is objectified with the capacity for self-awareness — and thus, in a sense, bring the whole process to some sort of fruition, or perhaps one might say complete some kind of developmental cycle.

The most important distinction within these four grades is not between the fourth and the rest but between the first and the rest, between life and non-life. 'The boundary between the organic and the inorganic is the most sharply drawn in the whole of nature, and is probably the only one admitting of no transitions, so that here the saying *Natura non facit saltus* [*Nature does not make jumps*] seems to meet with an exception. Many crystallizations display an external form resembling the vegetable, yet even between the smallest lichen, the lowest fungus, and everything inorganic there remains a fundamental and essential difference. In the *inorganic* body the essential and perma-

---

[15] *The World as Will and Representation*, ii. 354.

nent element, that on which its identity and integrity rest, is the material, is *matter*; the inessential and changeable, on the other hand, is the *form*. With the organic body the case is the very opposite; for its life, in other words its existence as something organic, consists simply in the constant change of the *material* with persistence of the *form*; thus its essence and identity lie in the form alone. Therefore the inorganic body has its continued existence through *repose* and isolation from external influences; only in this way is its existence preserved; and if this state or condition is perfect, such a body lasts for ever. On the other hand, the *organic* body has its continued existence precisely through incessant *movement* and the constant reception of external influences. As soon as these cease, and movement in it comes to a standstill, it is dead, and thus ceases to be organic, although the trace of the organism that existed still for a while continues.'[16]

To explain the multiplicity of identical, or more or less identical, forms in nature — the top three grades of the will's objectification consist of nothing but genera and species — Schopenhauer summons from the wings the notion of the Platonic Idea. It is a disconcerting thing for him to do at this stage, since in Plato's philosophy the Ideas (in the specialized sense Plato gives to the word) constitute ultimate reality: they, the unchanging forms of which all the objects of our experience are ephemeral images, are alone permanent. However, Schopenhauer is careful to tell us that he does not cast the Ideas in the same role as Plato did — indeed, he tells us that they could not possibly play that role. For reasons which he has now made clear, ultimate reality must be undifferentiated and undifferentiable, and therefore the Ideas, being plural, cannot be ultimate. If the word were to be used as the term for ultimate reality it would have to be used always and only in the singular, as a synonym for 'the one and indivisible will [and thus] the Idea'.[17] Even then it would be a misnomer, because of its inseparable association with the mind or cognition; nothing to do with knowledge, and nothing mental, can be ultimate. Failure to realize this was, in Schopenhauer's view, Plato's most important error, and it was at bottom the same as Kant's, namely a failure to identify the noumenon correctly. Schopenhauer preserves Plato's use of the term 'Ideas' in the plural, but redefines it. Ideas cannot be ultimate but they can be intermediate. Furthermore, if plural, they must be within the phenomenal world, not outside it. With these two changes, Schopenhauer proceeds to put the concept to his own uses. How he does so can perhaps best be explained as follows.

Let us recall for a moment the distinction made earlier between

---

[16] *The World as Will and Representation*, ii. 296.   [17] Ibid. i. 158.

directly and indirectly knowable phenomena of the will. On the one hand my body and its movements are phenomena of the will and are perceivable, like any other object and its movements, via the media of sense and intellect. On the other hand the 'acts of will' (in the first of the three meanings of 'will') which those selfsame movements manifest are also phenomena of will (in the third meaning) and are known by me directly in inner sense. We have, therefore, the will manifesting itself in two different ways simultaneously in the same object, one indirectly, the other directly. So far this is familiar to us. Schopenhauer now goes on to say that the same is true for all physical objects: although it is only in the case of one kind of physical object, namely living bodies, that this direct manifestation of the will is *known*, it nevertheless *occurs* in all phenomenal objects, so that if, *per impossibile*, we could have knowledge of them from inside we should know directly all sorts of things about them which, as matters stand, we can know only indirectly by observing them from outside. The Platonic Ideas, in Schopenhauer's view, are the forms of this *direct* self-manifestation of the noumenon in phenomenal objects. Put in very general terms like this the point may seem bizarre and even unintelligible, but a simple example transforms it into something quite intelligible, and perhaps even credible. Let us consider, as a real example, scientific laws. Like the noumenon whose direct objectification they are, they are always one and the same, in and through everything, utterly irrespective of place and time: yet it is only in the world of phenomena that they can have any existence. (This illustrates to perfection their intermediate status.) To give a particular scientific law as an instance, we know that any object released at any point above the earth's surface will at once move towards its centre with a velocity which, if unimpeded, will accelerate in every second at a rate of 32 feet per second; and this will happen regardless of what the object is, regardless of whether the time at which the event takes place is today or five hundred years ago or a thousand years hence, and regardless of whether the place at which it occurs is over Europe or Africa or the Pacific Ocean. However, it is impossible that humanity should have acquired knowledge directly, in pure abstract form, of the scientific law thus stated, as if it were some Ideal object which we could apprehend in immediate cognition: it can be perceived only at work, and thus indirectly, in its particular manifestations, in the individual movements of individual objects at particular places and times. So, just like my acts of will when considered by any observer except myself, scientific laws are direct manifestations of the noumenon in the world of phenomena which are, however, not knowable as such directly but only indirectly in so far as they manifest themselves in physical movement.

All such direct manifestations of the will in the world of phenomena are called by Schopenhauer 'Ideas'. We have had several examples already — all the forces of nature, such as gravity, and all scientific laws. These function in the same ways as Plato said the Ideas function. They operate in the world like dies that put a uniform stamp on innumerable phenomena which are then, though all different, all the same. Schopenhauer regards the species too as Ideas, stamping out millions of individual plants and animals which are the same now as a thousand years ago, the same here as in China. The reader may say: But if this is so, how are my acts of will, which are direct phenomenon of the will in precisely the sense under consideration, to be fitted in to this explanation? Where does the Platonic Idea come in in me? Schopenhauer's reply is that that which is directly known by each one of us in the knowledge we have of ourselves in inner sense is indeed a Platonic Idea, and it does indeed have the intermediate status between the noumenon and the world of phenomena which he has accounted for. However, in this unique case, the Platonic Idea can be and is directly known by a knowing subject, in addition to being susceptible of indirect knowledge by knowing subjects in general as are all other Platonic Ideas. This has an immediate further significance in that, as we know, wherever there is anything that is object of knowledge there is also a precisely correlative subject of knowledge. In the case of each human individual there is one and only one subject of knowledge, distinct and unique, who has direct knowledge of the Platonic Idea in inner sense — therefore one and only one Platonic Idea, distinct and unique, is thus known. In short, each human being instantiates a unique Platonic Idea. Thus, at the highest grade of the will's objectification, complete and self-aware individuation is achieved. The unique Idea that is each human being also manifests itself in the world of phenomena as the individual's unique character or personality. But again, exactly as with other Ideas, this character cannot be perceived or known directly, but only in its outer manifestations, indirectly, through the successive movements and actions of the physical body in space and time, in other words through behaviour. The truth of this is brought home to us dramatically by the fact that we do not know even our own characters directly, but get to know them (in so far as we ever do get to know them) indirectly, from our behaviour, over long periods of time, and are commonly surprised, not to say disillusioned, by what we discover them to be.

Schopenhauer is insistent that the word 'Idea' is correctly to be used only in this sense, as derived from Plato and corrected by him. Specifically, he is insistent that it should not be used with the sense introduced into English and French philosophy by Locke and his popularizer Voltaire, nor with the sense given to it by Kant. 'That Englishmen and Frenchmen were induced through the poverty of their languages to misuse the word is bad enough, but not important. Kant's misuse of the word *Idea* by the substitution of a new significance, drawn in on the slender thread of not-being-object-of-experience, a significance that it has in common with Plato's Ideas, but also with all possible chimeras, is therefore altogether unjustifiable. Now, as the misuse of a few years is not to be considered against the authority of many centuries, I have used the word always in its old original, Platonic significance.'[18] And he talks elsewhere of Ideas 'in the Platonic sense, the only one which I recognize for the word *Idea*'.[19]

This should arm us against a misunderstanding of the title *Die Welt als Wille und Vorstellung* which was for a long time propagated by the first English translation. It so happens that the word *Vorstellung* was introduced into the vocabulary of German philosophy as a translation of Locke's term 'idea'. Schopenhauer may not have known this; but it is wholly inadmissible, his views being as I have cited them, to translate the title *Die Welt als Wille und Vorstellung* as *The World as Will and Idea*. Furthermore, frequently to translate *Vorstellung* as 'idea' in the book itself is to sow confusion on a profligate scale. Yet this is what its first English translators, Haldane and Kemp, did in their translation published in 1883. This remained the only English translation of the book until the appearance of E. F. J. Payne's in 1958 under the title *The World as Will and Representation*. The earlier translators — their author having already ensured that one of the two key terms in his title would be generally misunderstood — gratuitously made similar provision for the other, and ignored, in doing so, explicit prohibitions contained in the book itself. Admittedly there is no satisfactory translation into English of *Vorstellung*. In this book I have had a lot to say about our knowledge of the external world as construed by us through the representations of sense and intellect, and I have used such formulations in a way that presupposes the Kantian theory of perception. Schopenhauer used the word *Vorstellung* to mean 'representation' in precisely this sense. So the English word 'representation' is the best translation available; but it does have to be understood in this specific and somewhat technical sense. At least it has the advantage of being to some degree international in this context: the standard translations of the book into French, Italian and several other languages use the corresponding word (e.g. *Le Monde comme Volonté et Représentation*). What really matters, however, is the *point* of the title, and of the word as used in the book, and this we are at last in a position to pin down unambiguously.

The title *Die Welt als Wille und Vorstellung* is heavily, almost densely,

---

[18] *The World as Will and Representation*, i. 488.   [19] Ibid. ii. 408.

allusive. It sums up a claim that might be spelled out as follows: 'The central task of philosophy, and therefore the central aim of this book, is to lay bare the true nature of the world. The supreme achievement of Kant was to show that the world is divisible into noumenon and phenomena, but he was wrong about what these are. This book corrects him, and thus completes his task. It shows that in so far as the world is noumenon it is *Will*, in a special sense of the term which is elucidated; and that in so far as the world is phenomena it consists of the *Representations* of sense and intellect, in a way which was more nearly, but still not quite properly, understood by Kant. His chief error here was to regard percepts as a weaker form of concepts, when in fact it is entirely from percepts that empirical concepts are derived. But not only does this book give the correct identification of noumenon and phenomena, it also shows how these are related to each other, and how in the light of this analysis the whole of our experience becomes comprehensible. And this is as far as philosophy can go. So what our title signifies is: "*The World* is noumenon, which is *Will*, and phenomena, which are *Representations*", and beyond these there is nothing, or at least nothing that we can ever have any grounds for postulating. As far as we can ever know, Will and Representation comprise total reality.'

That aspect of my remarks which is concerned with how Schopenhauer saw his central doctrine in relation to Kant's and Plato's can be best elucidated in his own words.

Now if for us the will is the *thing-in-itself*, and the *Idea* is the immediate objectivity of that will at a definite grade, then we find Kant's thing-in-itself and Plato's Idea, for him the only ὄντως ὄν[20] — those two great and obscure paradoxes of the two greatest philosophers of the West — to be, not exactly identical, but yet very closely related, and distinguished by only a single modification. The two great paradoxes, just because, in spite of all inner harmony and relationship, they sound so very different by reason of the extraordinarily different individualities of their authors, are even the best commentary on each other, for they are like two entirely different paths leading to one goal. This can be made clear in a few words. What Kant says is in essence as follows: 'Time, space, and causality are not determinations of the thing-in-itself, but belong only to its phenomenon, since they are nothing but forms of our knowledge. Now as all plurality and all arising and passing away are possible only through time, space, and causality, it follows that they too adhere only to the phenomenon, and by no means to the thing-in-itself. But since our knowledge is conditioned by these forms, the whole of experience is only knowledge of the phenomenon, not of the thing-in-itself; hence also its laws cannot be made valid for the thing-in-itself. What has been said extends even

---

[20] 'Truly being' [Tr.].

to our own ego, and we know it only as phenomenon, not according to what it may be in itself.' This is the meaning and content of Kant's teaching in the important respect we have considered. Now Plato says: 'The things of this world, perceived by our senses, have no true being at all; *they are always becoming, but they never are.* They have only a relative being; they are together only in and through their relation to one another; hence their whole existence can just as well be called a non-being. Consequently, they are likewise not objects of a real knowledge (ἐπιστήμη), for there can be such a knowledge only of what exists in and for itself, and always in the same way. On the contrary, they are only the object of an opinion or way of thinking, brought about by sensation (ζόξα μετ᾽ αἰσθήσεως ἀλόγου).[21] As long as we are confined to their perception, we are like persons sitting in a dark cave, and bound so fast that they cannot even turn their heads. They see nothing but the shadowy outlines of actual things that are led between them and a fire which burns behind them; and by the light of this fire these shadows appear on the wall in front of them. Even of themselves and of one another they see only the shadows on this wall. Their wisdom would consist in predicting the sequence of those shadows learned from experience. On the other hand, only the real archetypes of those shadowy outlines, the eternal Ideas, the original forms of all things, can be described as truly existing (ὄντως ὄν), since they *always are but never become and never pass away.* No plurality belongs to them; for each by its nature is only one, since it is the archetype itself, of which all the particular, transitory things of the same kind and name are copies or shadows. Also *no coming into existence and no passing away* belong to them, for they are truly being or existing, but are never becoming or vanishing like their fleeting copies. (But in these two negative definitions there is necessarily contained the presupposition that time, space, and causality have no significance or validity for these Ideas, and do not exist in them.) Thus only of them can there be a knowledge in the proper sense, for the object of such a knowledge can be only that which always and in every respect (and hence in-itself) is, not that which is and then again is not, according as we look at it.' This is Plato's teaching. It is obvious, and needs no further demonstration, that the inner meaning of both doctrines is wholly the same; that both declare the visible world to be a phenomenon which in itself is void and empty, and which has meaning and borrowed reality only through the thing that expresses itself in it (the thing-in-itself in the one case, the Idea in the other).[22]

Before leaving these comparisons altogether it may be remarked that Schopenhauer's intellectual personality is as different from Kant's and Plato's as theirs is from each other's. His philosophical doctrines have more in common with Kant's, obviously, but he does not have Kant's low-temperatured equability, nor his massive, serene, detached liberalism, nor his optimism, nor his Christian faith. His literary personality is more like Plato's — the artistic genius, the Olympian irony and

---

[21] 'A mere thinking by means of irrational sense perception' [Tr.].
[22] *The World as Will and Representation*, i. 170–2.

anger, the contemptuous distrust of mankind in general, the resultant anti-democratic political and social views. But there is something horror-stricken about Schopenhauer's view of the world which is foreign to Plato. In passages (and there are many of them) like that quoted on p. 146 the tone is one of Swiftean revulsion, half the revulsion being at the global and unending prospect of anguish, the other half at the pointlessness of it all. He loved animals, and his permanent sense of the reality behind the phrase 'nature red in tooth and claw' was like an unhealing wound: he actually *felt* the fact that at every single moment, in all the continents of the world, thousands of screaming animals are in the process of being torn to pieces alive. This alone, he thought, is enough to make the world a terrible place. Towards humans his attitude was a more ambivalent one, in which compassion was qualified by contempt, though both were experienced pungently. So vivid was his sense of the cruelty, violence and aimlessness of both animal and human worlds that it amounted to a horror of life as such. He believed it would have been better for most living creatures never to have been born. He cited with approval Swift's 'custom of celebrating his birthday, not as a time of joy, but of sadness, and of reading on that day the passage from the Bible where Job laments and curses the day on which it was said in the house of his father that a man-child had been born'.[23]

The tone of all this is equally far from ancient Greece and from the Enlightenment. Nor is it akin to Romanticism. The two central notions of Romanticism — the idealization of Nature, and the glorification of self-expression in life and art — are both of them diametrically opposite to Schopenhauer's views. This being so, the not uncommon description of him as a 'romantic German philosopher' could scarcely be more mistaken. The fact is that Schopenhauer's world-view is unmistakably 'modern'. It rejects the Christian cosmology, but does not look to Science as a substitute for it, in spite of the fact that it is so deeply in accord with modern physics, modern biology and modern psychology. It prefigures humanist existentialism in that it sees both the universe and all the life in it as being utterly without aim or purpose, and then seeks to overcome the *Angst* and alienation which, without using those terms, it acknowledges as consequent on that view.

When reading Schopenhauer's numerous descriptive passages about the endless restlessness of matter and the teeming activity of the animal and human worlds, such as were quoted earlier in this chapter, it is important to remember that these are not descriptions of the will as it is in itself but only as it manifests itself in the world of phenomena.

[23] *The World as Will and Representation*, ii. 586.

Nevertheless it is clear that he takes this as telling us something about the essential nature of the will. For one thing, this violent and ceaseless striving creates a situation in which the violent collision and conflict of the will's phenomena *with one another* is bound to occur. In the animal world the war of all against all is a struggle in which one manifestation of the will survives by devouring, by literally eating, another. It is a hungry will, insatiable and unassuageable, and the will's phenomena have only each other to feed on, for there is nothing else in the world. In this sense the will devours, and can devour only, itself. From this situation springs Schopenhauer's view that simply what *is* is inherently terrible — inherently violent and inherently tragic.

Because the will in itself is a sheer, blind striving, Schopenhauer contends that its manifestation in each one of us is devoted above all else to sustaining itself in existence, and hence to survival. This view is confirmed, he thinks, if we try to pin down in ourselves what it is that is irreducible in the phenomenon of the will as we experience it directly in inner sense. In most people, most of the time, we find that what is ultimate in their inner lives is a will to live. They will struggle for this end against anything and anybody to the utmost limits of their powers, and in the last resort all else will be sacrificed to it, including the lives of other people. From this 'it is easy to explain that man loves above everything else an existence which is full of want, misery, trouble, pain, anxiety, and then again full of boredom, and which, were it pondered over and considered purely objectively, he would of necessity abhor; and that he fears above everything else the end of this existence, which is nevertheless for him the one and only thing certain. Accordingly, we often see a miserable figure, deformed and bent with age, want, and disease, appeal to us from the bottom of his heart for help for the prolongation of an existence whose end would necessarily appear as altogether desirable if it was an objective judgment that was the determining factor.'[24]

Schopenhauer writes at great length about how this determination to survive, this will to live, has caused such-and-such plants to develop such-and-such features, and such-and-such animals to develop such-and-such organs or habits. Although he attacks Lamarck, much of what he writes is distinctly Lamarckian. He prefigures many ideas that were later to be spread throughout our culture by evolutionary biology — the development of which has on the whole superseded what he had to say on these topics (most of which is now of historical interest only, for that very reason). But there is one aspect of it all that remains of importance for a consideration of his philosophy, namely his account of

[24] *The World as Will and Representation*, ii. 359.

the development of mind. Well before Darwin, he took an evolutionary view of mind, seeing it essentially as a survival mechanism which was necessitated at a certain stage in the evolution of living organisms.

His view was this. For so long as a living thing can both nourish itself and reproduce itself without moving (it need not accomplish these ends through activity: it may be passive, as when a plant is pollinated by an insect) it has no need of a mind. But as soon as a certain degree of complexity is passed, the right kinds of nourishment at the right intervals in the right quantities cannot be relied on simply to be always on the spot ready and waiting to feed themselves into the organism; and, similarly, increasingly elaborate and vulnerable processes of sexual fertilization reach a stage where they can no longer be reliably accomplished by the vagaries of the winds and the bees. So, beyond this point, further development calls for powers of purposive movement on the part of the organism, so that it can seek out — and accomplish — its own nourishment, or the circumstances of its own reproduction. It was specifically for these tasks, Schopenhauer believed, that mind evolved in nature. Its job of construing for a now-of-necessity-mobile organism the circumstances in which its survival and reproduction were to be achieved involved, among other things, providing the organism with an accurate and reliable picture of its surroundings, and noting where in that picture the necessities of food, reproduction and safety lay, and computing what the organism had to do to seize them. The performance of these evolutionary tasks became the function of physical organs evolved specifically for them — the brain, the central nervous system and the senses — and the fundamental character of these is determined by their *raison d'être*. Their province is the understanding of the environment, in other words empirical knowledge, above all with a view to survival. Thus the mind has been evolved entirely for use within the world of phenomena. This explains why it is able only to apprehend connections between things in space or time, and on the basis of the principle of sufficient reason (plus, in the mind's highest evolutionary development in man, concepts derived from these phenomena, and from man's relationship to them). It explains why, for the mind, the world of its own construing is the one and only world that can be known, outside which it has no purchase, and thus why the primal and fundamental error of realism has such a grip on the human mind, despite that mind's ability to make use of abstract concepts. It thereby makes plain why the human mind is radically unsuited to metaphysical tasks, or to any form of activity in which it tries to detach itself from the phenomenal world, even if its purpose in doing so is to understand that world as a whole, or seek connections between it and whatever else there might be. Hence the almost unmanageable counter-intuitiveness of not only the most important philosophical truths but even the most important truths of science, once these no longer concern themselves with the domain of experience but rather with, say, the astronomic — and, as we might now add, the subatomic — level. It is almost, grumbles Schopenhauer, 'as if our intellect were intentionally designed to lead us into error'.[25]

The mind, created by the will for purposes of survival, exists to serve it, and is subservient to it throughout the life of the organism. This subservience consists not only in that — in Hume's well-known formulation — the ends we pursue are determined by our needs, desires, fears and so on, in other words by our passions, whereas the concern of reason is the relationship of means to the achievement of those ends. It goes further than this. The will keeps most of its operations permanently secret from the conscious mind, as we saw in the last chapter. And it does not allow even the intellect to carry out its task objectively within its own sphere. Throughout our lives our rational thinking is all-pervadingly distorted and corrupted by our willing. '*Love* and *hatred* entirely falsify our judgment; in our enemies we see nothing but shortcomings, in our favourites nothing but merits and good points, and even their defects seem lovable to us. Our *advantage*, of whatever kind it may be, exercises a similar secret power over our judgment; what is in agreement with it at once seems to us fair, just and reasonable; what runs counter to it is presented to us in all seriousness as unjust and outrageous, or inexpedient and absurd. Hence so many prejudices of social position, rank, profession, nationality, sect, and religion. A hypothesis, conceived and formed, makes us lynx-eyed for everything that confirms it, and blind to everything that contradicts it. What is opposed to our party, our plan, our wish or our hope often cannot possibly be grasped and comprehended by us, whereas it is clear to the eyes of everyone else; on the other hand, what is favourable to these leaps to our eyes from afar. What opposes the heart is not admitted by the head. All through life we cling to many errors, and take care never to examine their ground, merely from a fear, of which we ourselves are unconscious, of possibly making the discovery that we have so long and so often believed and maintained what is false. Thus is our intellect daily befooled and corrupted by the deceptions of inclination and liking.'[26]

Schopenhauer sees the human mind and its capacities as pitifully limited, and as inherently both subsidiary and subservient. He points out that 'everything that takes place without it, in other words, without

---

[25] *The World as Will and Representation*, ii. 286.
[26] Ibid. ii. 217–18.

intervention of the representation — such, for example, as generation, procreation, the development and preservation of the organism, the healing of wounds, the restoration or vicarious repair of mutilated parts, the salutary crisis in diseases, the works of animal mechanical skill, and the activity of instinct in general — turn[s] out so infinitely better and more perfect than what takes place with the aid of the mind, namely all the conscious and intended achievements and works of man. Such works and achievements, when compared with those others, are mere botching and bungling.'[27] Consistently with this, Schopenhauer dissociates himself from the entire tradition of Western thought that sees reason as the salient characteristic of man. 'All philosophers before me, from the first to the last, place the true and real inner nature or kernel of man in the *knowing* consciousness. Accordingly they have conceived and explained the I, or in the case of many of them its transcendent hypostasis called soul, as primarily and essentially *knowing*, in fact *thinking*, and only in consequence of this, secondly and derivatively, as *willing* . . . The remarkable phenomenon that in this fundamental and essential point all philosophers have erred, in fact have completely reversed the truth, might be partly explained, especially in the case of the philosophers of the Christian era, from the fact that all of them aimed at presenting man as differing as widely as possible from the animal.'[28]

In Schopenhauer's view what is essential and indestructible in man is the same as what is essential and indestructible in animals, namely noumenal will, while the human intellect is merely a late and comparatively superficial evolutionary differentiation. Nor does he regard man as possessed of a soul, to be his most important possession and to differentiate him from the animals: he regards the concept 'soul' as a muddle. 'Since the concept "soul" supposes knowing and willing to be in inseparable connection, and yet independent of the animal organism, it is not to be justified, and therefore not to be used.'[29] His point here is this. What people tend to think of as the soul is the self as known in inner sense, or else some sort of imagined, underlying, immanent spirit (what Schopenhauer has just called a 'transcendent hypostasis') of this. But the self as known in inner self is not simple. Like everything known, it is a compound of subject and object. And in this case one of

---

[27] *The World as Will and Representation*, ii. 269. Bernard Shaw, who had read Schopenhauer, used this thought in 'The Revolutionist's Handbook' which he appended to the published text of his play *Man and Superman*. 'The unconscious self is the real genius. Your breathing goes wrong the moment your conscious self meddles with it. Except during the nine months before he draws his first breath, no man manages his affairs as well as a tree does.'

[28] Ibid. ii. 198–9.   [29] Ibid. ii. 349.

the two elements in the compound, the subject of knowing, is through and through perishable, whereas the other, will, is not (though of course, without the subject of knowing, will cannot subsist as object, but only knowledgelessly as thing-in-itself and for itself). So the connection of knowing and willing is not only separable, it is doomed to certain and inevitable separation: knowing is the function of a physical organ, the brain, and could no more be disembodied than there could be digestion without a stomach, or circulation of the blood without veins and arteries. When the organism dies, knowing must cease, and so the compound of knowing and willing must cease. So the soul, conceived as the self known in inner sense (or its 'transcendent hypostasis') is not an intelligible concept independently of the animal organism. Nor, for that matter, is consciousness, since consciousness always involves knowing; so there can be no possibility of consciousness surviving death either. But then, there could be no possibility of the individual surviving death in any sense, since individuation is a possibility only in this world, the world of phenomena. What is indestructible in man is the noumenal will; but that is knowledgeless, and therefore without self-awareness or inner sense. It is also unindividualized. So (to anticipate a later discussion) what there is outside life — and therefore, figuratively, 'after' death — is not nothing, yet we cannot say or conceive what it is, for it is inherently unknowable and un-understandable by us. 'Behind our existence lies something else that becomes accessible to us only by our shaking off the world.'[30] 'If a being of a higher order came and took all the trouble to impart it to us, we should quite unable to understand any part of his disclosures.'[31]

We are standing now on the outermost ridge of intelligible ontology: one more step and we shall tumble over into the abyss of non-sense. So there is no further progress to be made along this line. It remains only, before we bring this chapter to an end, to clear up two outstanding problems in epistemology. The first, which we have been holding on stand-by for an unconscionable time, is how it is possible for a transcendental idealist to account for the fact that we as subjects of knowledge inhabit a shared world. The short answer to this is: because the world of phenomena, although immeasurably differentiated, is in its inner nature one, and undifferentiable, and furthermore it is a world with which all of us, in our innermost nature, are also one. More light on this is cast by the answer to the second question. How can a phenomenal world which contains within itself as material objects all the brains there are be accounted for as product of brain? Or, to formulate the same question from the other end of the process, how is it possible for

[30] *The World as Will and Representation*, i. 405.   [31] Ibid. ii. 185.

phenomena to impinge on our senses and thereby trigger off the intellectual process which creates the world in which they themselves exist? The first point to make in answer to this question is that, as we have already established, nothing can ever be both object of knowledge and subject of knowledge at the same time. Therefore the subject of knowledge can never appear in its own world. So there can never actually be an instance of the sort of circularity that is being postulated. Just as my eye can never figure as a physical object in its own field of vision, so my brain can never occur as a material object in the world of its own construction, even though both can perfectly easily be such objects for other subjects. A brain surgeon could look at and handle my brain as a physical object, a grey pulpy mass of material weighing, I suppose, about two kilos; but for me no such experience is ever possible: I can never handle my own brain. I can experience it only from within, and then not as material object but as awareness, thoughts, memories, and all the other amazing things that go on in it. For the surgeon my brain is the substantial thing under his hands, but for me it can only be ideas, imaginings, music, and a thousand other such vivid immediacies. 'All immediate existence is subjective; objective existence is present in the consciousness of another, and hence is only for this other.'[32] It is not only a question of the same phenomenon being experienced in two different ways. The more crucial point is that in the case of the organs of perception it is never possible for the two ways to co-exist in the same experience, and therefore in the same empirical world. So what is being said, literally, is that there can be no empirical world in which both of them are (since the world of experience is always the creation of a subject) and this in spite of the fact that both of them are real. In formulating our problem we illegitimately postulated a single world containing both kinds of entity — indeed, to explain how it could do so was the problem — but there can be no such world, and there is therefore no such problem. The secret presuppositions of realism had once again been smuggled into the formulation of a difficulty which could exist only if they were true.

The nub of any Schopenhauerian explanation of the sharedness of the world of phenomena is that it is not the case that only that world exists. The will, too, exists, and the world of phenomena is its objectification. And since the will is one and the same, undifferentiated in everything there is, it must be one and the same in all subjects of knowledge as well as in all objects of knowledge. Indeed, noumenally these are one and the same too. Ultimately, there *is* only one thing. This brain of mine and my eyeballs are physical components of a material

[32] *The World as Will and Representation*, ii. 281.

object, my body, which is all, including them, self-objectification of will. But everything there is for them to perceive is also self-objectification of will. 'At bottom it is *one* entity that perceives itself and is perceived by itself, but its being-in-itself cannot consist either in perceiving or in being perceived.'[33] . . . 'The whole process is the *self-knowledge of the will*; it starts from and returns to the will.'[34] This circuit of self-knowledge *is* the constitution of the world of phenomena, and explains why that world is, so to speak, free-floating. Without the circular process there would be no world. There would not be nothing, there would be will: but it would be knowledgeless.

We have at last reached a position from which, for the first time, we are able to give a sketch of Schopenhauer's ontology and epistemology in complete outline. Let us, then, swiftly recapitulate it in a single picture before we move on to consider his aesthetics and his ethics. He taught that the entire world of phenomena in time and space, internally connected by causality, was the self-objectification of an impersonal, non-alive, timelessly active energy which he termed 'will'. Phenomena and the will comprise between them everything there is: beyond them there is nothing, or at any rate nothing that we could ever have any grounds for postulating. Where and whence this will came is a question that can not be asked, not because of anything particularly to do with the will itself but because questions about time, space and cause are meaningful only when what they refer to is within the world of phenomena, not outside it. 'The nature of things before or beyond the world, and consequently beyond the will, is open to no investigation.'[35] By the same token the will does not *cause* the world of phenomena, it *is* the world of phenomena, but it is the not-externally-observable inner nature of that world, just as the externally observable acts of my body are, in their not-externally-observable inner nature, acts of will. The phenomenal world consists of four grades of the will's objectification: will has objectified itself in matter; matter has produced plant life; plant life has led to animate organisms; and animal organisms have developed minds and personalities. As all this shows, will is decidedly not a function of mind. On the contrary, mind is a product of will: mind 'is at bottom tertiary, since it presupposes the organism, and the organism presupposes the will'.[36] Similarly, will 'is not, like the mind, a function of the body, but *the body is its function*'.[37] Will, then, in Schopenhauer's sense, is primary, and is more body-like than mind-like, for it objectifies itself first of all in physical substances and bodies, a small number of which then develop minds as a subsidiary by-product.

---

[33] *The World as Will and Representation*, ii. 18.
[34] Ibid. ii. 259.   [35] Ibid. ii. 642.
[36] Ibid. ii. 278.   [37] Ibid. ii. 214.

The chief characteristics of each of the four grades of the will's objectification are determined by Platonic Ideas, which mould their contents and behaviour. What scientists and philosophers call the uniformity of nature, which is at its most evident in the lowest of the four grades, is to be accounted for by the operation of Platonic Ideas in the form of natural forces and scientific laws. The fact that the middle two grades consist entirely of large classes of similar individuals is to be accounted for by the incidence of Platonic Ideas in the form of species. And the fact that the highest grade consists of unique individuals is to be accounted for by the fact that each of them is the manifestation of a separate Platonic Idea.

Platonic Ideas have not, up to this stage in our discussion, been said to be knowable directly, but only indirectly, in so far as they manifest themselves in physical objects and their movements. Knowledge by perception of such physical objects and their movements in space and time is the function of physical sense organs and brains developed for the purpose in the two highest grades of the will's objectification. But since both knower and known, the subject of knowledge and the object of knowledge, are self-objectification of will, knowledge is at bottom a process of self-awareness, the same entity knowing itself. Subject cannot exist without object, nor object without subject. The two are correlative. To say that the subject has such and such modes of apprehension available to it is only the same as to say that the objects it knows have such and such knowable characteristics possible to them. The constitution of phenomena in space and time, and their causal interconnection, are as much proclivities of subjects as characteristics of objects, and can never occur except as activities involving a subject. However, all such activity is ephemeral, since both subject and object exist only in the world of phenomena, and that world consists entirely of things which come into being and pass away. Only outside time can anything be unchanging and permanent. But there can be only one such thing, and therefore nothing else for it to know. This one thing is something we have decided to call will. Everything other than it, including ourselves, is its manifestation. When we cease to exist in the world of phenomena we no longer have any being as individuals, and all possibility of knowledge ceases, but what our phenomenal existence was noumenally grounded in remains unaffected by that. For all we ever were in the world of phenomena was ephemeral manifestation of noumenal will; and the noumenal continues outside time exactly the same as it always 'was' and always 'will be', undifferentiable and knowledgeless.

It will be remembered that the first edition of *The World as Will and*

Representation consisted of four books and an appendix — the four books dealing with, in order, epistemology, ontology, aesthetics, and what I have called metaphysics of the person, and the appendix with the philosophy of Kant. We have now reached the point where our outline of the subject-matter of the appendix and the first two books is complete. The contents of the third book will be dealt with in the next chapter, and those of the fourth book in Chapter 9. In the tenth and final chapter I shall discuss some of the main problems to which Schopenhauer's philosophy gives rise. The ensuing appendices will be devoted to topics which are extrinsic to the philosophy but presuppose a knowledge of it, notably its influence on other people.

Chapter 8

The Flower of Existence

An appropriate point from which to launch a discussion of
Schopenhauer's aesthetics is consideration of one particular form of
direct experience, and one which, I take it, most readers of this book
will have had. There are times when we look at something, whether
new or familiar — it can be anything from a panoramic vista to a small,
mundane object such as an apple or a doorknob — and realize we are
seeing it in a singular way. We seem to be taken out of ourselves. It is as
if time had stopped, and only the object existed, standing before us
unencumbered by any connections with anything else — just simply
there, wholly and peculiarly itself, and weirdly, singularly thingy. And
yet the fact that it is being seen as if *not* enmeshed in time and space, and
as if nothing else existed, seems to imbue it with a universal significance, our sense of which is the most powerfully felt aspect of the
whole experience. Often such a happening takes us by surprise: we can
be walking down our most familiar street when, all of a sudden, we see
the street as if touched by magic and lifted out of time, endowed with a
significance which is universal yet inexpressible except in terms of the
experience itself.

What this is, says Schopenhauer, is the aesthetic experience. It is
what happens when we see something as being beautiful. And he goes
on to use the Kantian term 'the sublime' for a sub-class of 'the beautiful'. The sublime, he says, is what we experience when we view in this
detached, aesthetic, transported way anything which otherwise — if
looked at in more practical terms of what it would mean to us to be
directly up against it or in amongst it — would be lethal, and is
therefore, in such less detached circumstances, mortally terrifying: for
instance an electric storm, or a range of airless and sub-zero mountain
peaks, or simply the night sky (one thinks of Pascal's 'the eternal silence
of those infinite spaces fills me with terror'). In other words, the
sublime is that part of the beautiful whose detached contemplation
involves the suspension of a natural fear. Perhaps this is why the
exhilaration which characteristically accompanies it is so like that
which accompanies adventure, which is also bound up with the mastery of fear, usually in sport, war, hostile natural surroundings, or the
unknown.

Imaginative literature abounds in attempts to describe experiences of the beautiful. Three notions that crop up in the descriptions again and again are that of time standing still, that of the universal being perceived in the particular, and that of the spectator being taken out of himself and forgetting his own existence altogether in the rapt contemplation of what lies before him. Schopenhauer's account of the whole experience is such as to bring out clearly why these things are so. From the previous chapter we know already what are those entities which, according to him, inhabit the world of phenomena and are universal and timeless, yet are instantiated only in individual objects and events. They are the Platonic Ideas, as understood in his special sense of the term: and what he is now saying is that when we see something as beautiful we literally are seeing the universal in the particular, because what is happening in such moments is that we are catching a cognitive glimpse of the Platonic Idea of which the object of our contemplation is an instantiation. We are apprehending in and through the object the timeless reality of which the phenomenal object itself is merely an ephemeral image. We are seeing it, as it were, 'pure': we are seeing *through* the sense-dependent trappings of accidental qualities, and the mind-dependent trappings of location in time and space and causal interconnection, to the universal that all these are manifestations of. And, as always with Schopenhauer, the object's way of being known and the subject's way of knowing are understood as correlative in every particular. The object's being seen as if not in a spatial context corresponds to the subject's seeing it as if 'taken out of himself', in other words as if not *from* a spatial location. The object's being seen as if lifted out of time corresponds to the subject's feeling that time has stopped. The object's being seen as the manifestation of something universal, and in that sense as transcending the customary bounds of its individuality, corresponds to the subject's liberation, in his disinterested perception of it, from any consideration of his own personal well-being or purposes, and thus transcending the customary limitations of *his* individuality. This last point could be put another way by saying that to the object's being seen as independent of the principle of sufficient reason there corresponds the subject's seeing it as independent of anything to do with his willing — not as useful, or protectively enveloping, or obstructive, or dangerous, or in any other way instrumental or mediating, but simply as itself. In sum, to the pure object of knowledge there corresponds the pure subject of knowing: 'the person who is involved in this perception is no longer an individual, for in such perception the individual has lost himself; he is *pure* will-less, painless, timeless *subject of knowledge*'.[1]

[1] *The World as Will and Representation*, i. 179.

It looks as if most members of the human race only fleetingly and seldom have this experience in the face of natural objects, and probably many of them never have it at all. But the more deeply perceptive an individual is, the more frequently and sustainedly he will at least discern the universal in the particular. And at the very top of the scale, according to Schopenhauer, there are people whose mode of perception is of this kind predominantly. These are the people to whom, in ordinary talk, we ascribe genius. 'Always to see the universal in the particular is precisely the fundamental characteristic of genius, whereas the normal man recognizes in the particular only the particular as such; for only as such does it belong to reality, which alone has interest for him, has reference to his *will*. The degree in which everyone not so much conceives as actually perceives in the particular thing only the particular, or something more or less universal up to the most universal of the species, is the measure of his approach to genius. In accordance with this, the real object of genius is only the essential nature of things in general, the universal in them, the totality. The investigation of individual phenomena is the field of the talents. . . .'[2]

Perception for Schopenhauer is always predominantly mental, and so, in the present context, he is led naturally to talk of genius as a superabundant endowment of mind. This makes it all the more important for us to be clear that he is not talking about intellectual ability in the sense of an outstanding capacity for conceptual thought. On the contrary, when we are looking at things aesthetically 'we do not let abstract thought, the concepts of reason, take possession of our consciousness, but, instead of all this, devote the whole power of our mind to perception, sink ourselves completely therein, and let our whole consciousness be filled by the calm contemplation of the natural object actually present, whether it be a landscape, a tree, a rock, a crag, a building, or anything else. We *lose* ourselves entirely in this object, to use a pregnant expression; in other words, we forget our individuality, our will, and continue to exist only as pure subject, as clear mirror of the object, so that it is as though the object alone existed without anyone to perceive it, and thus we are no longer able to separate the perceiver from the perception, but the two have become one, since the entire consciousness is filled and occupied by a single image of perception.'[3]

Schopenhauer is repeatedly insistent that 'knowledge of the Idea is necessarily knowledge through perception, and is not abstract',[4] and therefore that 'the true nature of genius must lie in the completeness

---

[2] *The World as Will and Representation*, ii. 379–80.   [3] Ibid. i. 178–9.
[4] Ibid. i. 186.

and energy of the knowledge of perception'.[5] By contrast, commonsense knowledge is knowledge of the relations between things, or of that relationship in which they stand to states of human willing — their usefulness, workability, value, intrusiveness, or whatever it may be — and is in that sense indirect rather than direct; furthermore it cognizes only the world of phenomena. Scientific knowledge is commonsense knowledge made more critically self-aware and raised to the level of generality, and although it is much more objective and impersonal (if never perfectly so) it remains knowledge of the world of phenomena in terms of the relations between things, and therefore remains indirect in the same sense; and because of its essential generality it can exist only in concepts. What we are now setting against both commonsense knowledge and scientific knowledge, by way of contrast, is a form of knowledge which is direct, a knowledge of the things themselves, and not just of the relations between things, or between them and our will. It exists in terms not of concepts but of direct perceptions and insights, and is thus concrete and specific, not abstract. We have finally reached something the need for which was formulated in Chapter 2 — a way of getting under the outer skin of experience and digging deeper perceptually into what lies before us; and thus a way of acquiring that new knowledge which no amount of reasoning, of conceptual thinking, can give us, because it is experiential and, as such, constitutive of the premisses from which all reasoning has to begin.

But if such knowledge is impossible of communication in concepts, does that mean that only those geniuses who are capable of acquiring it for themselves can possess it? Could there be any other way, some way different from communication in concepts, in which they are able to convey it to the rest of us? Schopenhauer's answer is that there is, and that every human society known to us contains a publicly established and accepted form of communication among its members whose precise function is to convey knowledge of the kind we are considering. 'It is *art*, the work of genius. It repeats the eternal Ideas apprehended through pure contemplation, the essential and abiding element in all the phenomena of the world. According to the material in which it does this, it is sculpture, painting, poetry, or music. Its only source is knowledge of the Ideas; its sole aim is communication of this knowledge.'[6]

Thus art is essentially cognitive. It is not, for instance, expression of emotion. What the artist is attempting to convey is a form of knowledge, an insight into the true nature of things. And as with all other forms of communication it is possible for what is being communicated

<hr>

[5] *The World as Will and Representation*, ii. 376.   [6] Ibid. i. 184–5.

to be understood differently by different people, or to be misunderstood altogether, and it is possible for people to be moved by it, or uninterested in it, or indifferent to it, or excited by it, or insincere in their responses to it, or hostile towards it. But whereas our common everyday perception of objects gives us the commonsense knowledge of appearances which is communicated in everyday speech, and our perceptions of the relations between such things is what develops into rational thought, and this in turn into science — both of which take place and are communicated in concepts — our direct perception of Platonic Ideas gives us knowledge of the timeless, universal realities behind the world's ephemeral surfaces, and this knowledge, not communicable in concepts, is embodied and communicated in works of art. This explains not only the especially penetrating character of the perceptions and insights that art gives us but also why it is that we are unable to say in words what these are, for that would be communication in concepts. As this whole way of putting it makes clear, the commonsense, the scientific and the aesthetic approaches are in no way logically in conflict with each other — on the contrary, they complement each other: as Hume said, no experience can contradict another experience. All three are ways of acquiring knowledge, of extending our understanding of the world, and of communicating truths about it to others. Each has its own realm, and nothing could be further from the truth than to describe Schopenhauer as denying any of the valid claims of rationality. On the contrary, 'the method of consideration that follows the principle of sufficient reason is the rational method, and it alone is valid and useful in practical life and in science'.[7] But the realm of art is still more significant, for it penetrates to the level at which the phenomenal makes contact with something that is not phenomenal. It thus brings us closer than anything we have yet considered to a perception of the inner significance of life. 'If the whole world as representation is only the visibility of the will, then art is the elucidation of this visibility.'[8]

It follows from Schopenhauer's analysis that every genuine work of art must have its origin in direct perception and must communicate direct perception; that is to say, it does not originate in concepts, and concepts are not what it communicates. This is what more than anything else differentiates good art from bad, or, more accurately, authentic from inauthentic art. The latter often originates in a desire on the part of the artist to meet some demand external to himself — to win approval, say, or be in the fashion, or supply a market — or else to put over a message of some sort. Such an artist starts by trying to think

[7] *The World as Will and Representation*, i. 266.   [8] Ibid. i. 185.

what it would be a good idea to do — in other words, the starting-point
of the process for him is something that exists in terms of concepts. The
inevitable result is dead art, of whatever kind, whether imitative,
academic, commercial, didactic or fashion-conscious. It may be successful in its day because it meets the demands of its day, but once that
day is over it has no inner life of its own with which to outlive it. 'It
follows from all that has been said that the concept, useful as it is in life,
serviceable, necessary, and productive as it is in science, is eternally
barren and unproductive in art. The apprehended Idea, on the contrary, is the true and only source of every genuine work of art. In its
powerful originality it is drawn only from life itself, from nature, from
the world, and only by the genuine genius, or by him whose momentary
inspiration reaches the point of genius. Genuine works bearing immortal life arise only from such immediate apprehension. Just because the
Idea is and remains perceptive, the artist is not conscious *in abstractio* of
the intention and aim of his work. Not a concept but an Idea is present
in his mind; hence he cannot give an account of his actions. He works,
as people say, from mere feeling and unconsciously, indeed instinc-
tively. On the other hand, imitators, mannerists, *imitatores, serrum pecus*
in art start from the concept. They note what pleases and affects in
genuine works, make this clear to themselves, fix it in the concept, and
hence in the abstract, and then imitate it, openly or in disguise, with
skill and intention. They suck their nourishment, like parasitic plants,
from the works of others, and like polyps they become the colour of their
food . . . but they can never impart inner life to a work.'[9] 'Therefore a
work of art the conception of which has resulted from mere, distinct
concepts, is always ungenuine. If, when considering a work of plastic
art, or reading a poem, or listening to a piece of music (which aims at
describing something definite), we see the distinct, limited, cold, dispassionate concept glimmer and finally appear through all the rich
resources of art, the concept which was the kernel of this work, the
whole conception of the work having therefore consisted only in thinking clearly this concept, and accordingly being completely exhausted
by its communication, then we feel disgust and indignation, for we see
ourselves deceived and cheated of our interest and attention. We are
entirely satisfied by the impression of a work of art only when it leaves
behind something that, in spite of all our reflection on it, we cannot
bring down to the distinctness of a concept.'[10]

Schopenhauer's theory of art, as I have pointed out already, is not
one that sees art as expression of emotion, or indeed as self-expression
of any kind. This is one of the many reasons why it is uncomprehending

[9] *The World as Will and Representation*, i. 235–6.   [10] Ibid. ii. 409.

to think of him as a romantic philosopher (the notion of art as expression of emotion being central to Romanticism). To make an elementary logical point, the fact that our emotions are deeply moved by something does not mean that the purpose of that something is to move our emotions — no one, I take it, would contend that the beauties of nature are vehicles of emotional expression. Great art is great by virtue of its insight into, and its truthfulness to, something other than the artist: the fact that it moves us *and, incidentally, him* so profoundly does not mean that he creates it in order to express his emotions, nor that he is directing it at ours.

If this is so, why do we care so much about art? Not only the few geniuses who produce it but a vastly greater number, a number many times that of the artists themselves, regard the consumption of art as the most profoundly nourishing activity in life, or at least as something very close to that. Why? Schopenhauer's answer is, because it provides us with a release, if only momentary, from the prison we ordinarily inhabit. We have seen how he regards the normal human condition as that of the enslavement of the individual to his own willing, to his desires, appetites, needs, fears, fantasies and so on, and how he sees this state as incapable of producing any real, genuinely non-illusory satisfaction or peace of mind. Our restlessness and striving never cease in this world, unless perhaps we are saints. Many of our hopes and aims are doomed to permanent disappointment, and that in itself is obviously a cause for perpetual dissatisfaction. But fulfilment of aims brings disappointment too, either because they do not live up to expectation or, if they do, because this very fact encourages further desires — appetite grows by what it feeds on, satisfaction incites demand. In those rare cases when we are able to dispose of our wants altogether this either results in their simply being replaced by other wants, other hopes, other aims, or — and this is the most appalling affliction of all — boredom, emptiness, the sense that we have nothing to aim for, and therefore nothing to hope for, and therefore that nothing has any point or significance. So, whatever happens, the deepest-lying of the many layers of our dissatisfaction is self-perpetuating and inescapable. As with a convict on a treadmill, our effort and motion are unceasing and yet we remain always in the same situation. Nor is there any natural culmination to it: we simply go on going on until death destroys us as individuals. Everyone's life ends in this utter destruction of the individual that is death, and most peoples' contain other catastrophes along the way. Because of all this, and if only subliminally, we feel our lives to be a state of bondage from which we long for some release that is not death. Now according to Schopenhauer, aesthetic experience provides us with just such a release. When we are taken out of ourselves in disinterested contemplation of anything — whether it be a work of art or a natural or man-made object — we are for the duration of that experience released from the tyranny under which we customarily live. 'Then all at once the peace, always sought but always escaping us on that first path of willing, comes to us of its own accord, and all is well with us. It is the painless state, prized by Epicurus as the highest good and as the state of the gods; for that moment we are delivered from the miserable pressure of the will. We celebrate the Sabbath of the penal servitude of willing; the wheel of Ixion stands still.'[11]

Although this sense of a harmony and well-being which go deeper than words may be felt by us in the contemplation of anything, and not only works of art, it is nevertheless likely to well up in fullest measure in the presence of those works of art that have particular appeal for us. Partly this is because the object is then presented to us purely and simply as an aesthetic object and nothing else, and stands before us in isolation, distilled, unsullied, not embedded in the dross of the world; but chiefly it is because works of art give us the privilege of seeing with the eyes, or hearing with the ears, of the geniuses who place them before us, and thus raise us to levels of perception higher than those we would be able to reach by ourselves. The artists who create these works that make such a difference to our lives are people who perceive things differently from the rest of us, either seeing what we do not see or commanding a sustained vision where we, unaided, catch only glimpses. As Schopenhauer once put it, the man of talent is like a marksman who hits a target others cannot hit, but the man of genius is like a marksman who hits a target others cannot see. And I say 'man' here advisedly: Schopenhauer considered that, although women could possess the highest talent, they were incapable of the impersonal objectivity required by genius. It is only fair to add that, of course, he considered nearly all men incapable of it too. But such men of genius as there are are able to transcend the bounds of their personal subjectivity to the point of seeing individual things in all the fullness of their universal significance, and consequently of seeing the world as being made up of the universalities that constitute it. And so, 'whereas to the ordinary man his faculty of knowledge is a lamp that lights his path, to the man of genius it is the sun that reveals the world'.[12]

Schopenhauer freely acknowledges that, according to his own philosophy, there is something counter-natural about art. 'Genius is an intellect that has become unfaithful to its destiny.'[13] This is because mind was called into existence to serve the will, as indeed was percep-

---

[11] *The World as Will and Representation*, i. 196.
[12] Ibid. i. 188.　　　　[13] Ibid. ii. 386.

tion itself. They are survival mechanisms, their built-in structures formed so as to enable them to function effectively in the domain of the principle of sufficient reason. In human beings, as in animals, the amazing driving force of energy that goes into perceiving and knowing flows from the will, with the result that throughout the organism's life its appetites, fears, hopes, desires, anxieties, strivings and the rest determine the uses to which its perceiving and knowing are put — not the other way round. It may look like a truism to say that the perceptions and thoughts of human beings are permanently attuned to what sustains their lives, or causes them anxiety, or interests them, or comforts them, or in one way or another impinges on them personally. How, one might be tempted to ask, could it be otherwise? Yet Schopenhauer is telling us that at one end of the almost unimaginably wide spectrum of human abilities there is a handful of individuals whose intellectual powers are so in excess of what is used in the service of their willing that — not all the time, necessarily, but much or most of the time — they look at things and see them without any relation to their own interests or aims, their own use, profit or harm. If such people are artists they are then able to articulate their perceptions, not in-directly, in an abstract, unspecific, de-individualized medium of con-cepts, but directly in a concrete, specific, unique work of art which will communicate them to the rest of us, that is to say communicate percep-tions that penetrate more deeply into the nature of things than any that have yet been considered in this book. For this to be possible, the capacity for will-less cognition 'must be inherent in all men in a lesser and different degree, as otherwise they would be just as incapable of enjoying works of art as of producing them'.[14] To that extent the description of the relationship between the mind and the will that has been put forward earlier in this book needs to be qualified.

The fact that works of genius can come only from a mind while it is working independently of the will has important consequences both for the artist and for art. For the artist as such, primarily interested in things from a standpoint unconnected with his or anyone else's self-interest, it means that he is often unsuited for practical business or administration, and sometimes even for conducting the ordinary affairs of daily life — it tends to make him an inadequate husband and father, and a poor provider, unless an admiring public or patron beats a path to his door. As Schopenhauer puts it, genius is of about as much use in the mundane affairs of everyday life as an astral telescope is in a theatre. The fact, too, that other people share with one another domi-nating interests and ways of looking at things which are different from

[14] *The World as Will and Representation*, i. 194.

his (as Schopenhauer rather startlingly expresses this, 'they are only moral beings, and have merely personal relations'[15]) tends to isolate him from them; it makes him 'different', and it makes intimate communication, and therefore close companionship, either difficult or impossible — hence a phenomenon which has long been remarked on, the solitariness of genius. A remarkably high proportion of outstandingly creative people have lived alone, and a large number of those who married and had families have complained of lifelong feelings of being cut off from other people. For reasons such as these, genius had better be, if somewhat grimly, considered its own reward: a man of genius is unlikely to live a happy personal life.

As for the work of art itself, the fact that the circumstances of its production are unconnected with anyone's willing or self-interest has the consequence that it serves no useful purpose (unless perhaps incidentally, and then the question of whether or not it is useful has no bearing on the question of whether or not it is beautiful). Unlike the objects of everyday life, the work of art exists simply for its own sake. 'The work of genius may be music, philosophy, painting or poetry; it is nothing for use or profit. To be useless and unprofitable is one of the characteristics of the works of genius; it is their patent of nobility. All other human works exist only for the maintenance or relief of our existence; only those here discussed do not; they alone exist for their own sake, and are to be regarded in this sense as the flower or the net profit of existence.'[16]

The reader will notice that Schopenhauer includes philosophy here together with the arts among the products of genius. This is because the philosopher and the artist are both engaged in truth-seeking activities that go beyond the limits of commonsense knowledge and of science; both activities are attempts to penetrate the surface of things and achieve a deeper understanding of the true nature of the world; both, if they are authentic, are deeply rooted in original perceptions and insights; and both, if their products have any validity, have a validity which is impersonal. 'Not merely philosophy but also the fine arts work at bottom towards the solution of the problem of existence. For in every contemplation of the world, a desire has been awakened, however concealed and unconscious, to comprehend the true nature of things, of life, and of existence. For this alone is of interest to intellect as such, in other words, to the subject of knowing which has become free from the aims of the will and is therefore pure; just as for the subject, knowing as mere individual, only the aims and ends of the will have interest. For this reason the result of every purely objective, and so of every artistic,

---

[15] *The World as Will and Representation*, ii. 390.   [16] Ibid. ii. 388.

apprehension of things is an articulation of more of the true nature of life and of existence, of more of the answer to the question "What is life?" Every genuine and successful work of art answers this question in its own way . . .'.[17] But — he goes on to say — art always gives its answer in the language of perception, and therefore in terms of the uniquely particular; and it is this that differentiates it from philosophy. Philosophy, as was shown in Chapter 2, has to *start* from perceptions, and therefore from the uniquely particular, if it is to have any content, but it then goes on to formulate its conclusions in terms of concepts. The finished product is therefore abstract and general, not concrete, not particular. When put before others it presents itself to them as a subject for reflection, not as an object of perception. It is almost as if philosophy sets before us rules, of which works of art set before us examples. This makes philosophy harder both to understand and to practise than art — and for that reason both its public and its practitioners are less numerous.

In the light of all this, art ought always to have been of central concern to philosophers, and it is one of Schopenhauer's most pointed criticisms of his predecessors that this was not so. Most of them had dealt with art either perfunctorily or not at all. Only two had much of interest or significance to say about it — though these two, admittedly, were the greatest: Plato and Kant. However, what Plato had to say was antagonistic: he was hostile to art. This was because of his mistaken view that works of art are imitations of things and events in the phenomenal world, giving us their appearance without their function; and that since the things themselves are mere transient images, works of art are doubly fraudulent in that they are images of images. The aim of every genuine seeker after truth, thought Plato, should be to pierce the veil of phenomena and enter the eternal, abstract world beyond it; but the degenerate semblances of art, by their very attractiveness and charm, rivet our attention on the ephemera they represent — ephemera of which they are not even genuine instantiations — thereby holding us back from our proper journey. They are like windows on which pictures of such seductiveness have been painted — and painted so thickly — that not only do the windows themselves become the objects of our attention and interest but it is actually impossible to see through them to what is on the other side. Thus art literally puts the immortality of our souls in jeopardy. It would therefore be banned from an ideal state.

Kant's contribution was more positive than this. Most of the philosophers before him who had considered aesthetic questions had done so in some such form as: 'How is it that some objects are beautiful and

---

[17] *The World as Will and Representation*, ii. 406.

others not? What is it about an object that makes it beautiful?' With such questions in mind they proceeded to investigate objects. Thus their mode of enquiry was in fact, if not self-consciously, empirical, for they were examining particular instances in the hope of finding answers to general questions. Kant, in keeping with the rest of his philosophy, turned this procedure round and looked at matters from the subjective end. He asked, in effect: 'Given that the empirical world is one that we to a large extent ourselves structure in the process of perceiving it, how does it come about that we see some of the objects in it as being beautiful and others not? What is the difference in the modifications of the perceiving subject as between the two cases?' This, says Schopenhauer, was an advance of decisive significance. But the making of it almost exhausted Kant's contribution to aesthetics. For what Kant had to say in answer to his own questions was so inadequate that Schopenhauer considers it unnecessary to spend time on a detailed consideration of it. He does point out, though, that just as the cardinal virtue of Kant's aesthetics is something which is characteristic of his philosophy as a whole, so is its chief shortcoming. 'I refer to the method of starting from abstract knowledge in order to investigate knowledge of perception, so that the former serves him, so to speak, as a *camera obscura* in which to gather and survey the latter. Just as in the *Critique of Pure Reason* the forms of judgments were supposed to give him information about the knowledge of our whole world of perception, so in this *Critique of Aesthetic Judgment* he does not start from the beautiful itself, from the direct, beautiful object of perception, but from the *judgment* concerning the beautiful, the so-called, and very badly so-called, judgment of taste. This is the problem for him. His attention is specially aroused by the circumstances that such a judgment is obviously the expression of something occurring in the subject, but is nevertheless as universally valid as if it concerned a quality of the object. It is this that struck him, not the beautiful itself. He always starts only from the statements of others, from the judgment concerning the beautiful, not from the beautiful itself. Therefore it is entirely as if he knew it from hearsay alone, and not immediately. A very intelligent blind person could almost in the same way combine a theory of colours from accurate statements that he heard about them.'[18] Nevertheless Schopenhauer greatly respected Kant for the value of his positive contribution. 'We are bound to wonder how Kant, to whom certainly art remained very foreign, and who in all probability had little susceptibility to the beautiful, in fact probably never had the opportunity to see an important work of art, and who seems finally to have had no

---

[18] *The World as Will and Representation*, i. 530–1.

knowledge even of Goethe, the only man of his century and country fit
to be placed by his side as his brother giant — it is, I say, wonderful
how, in spite of all this, Kant was able to render a great and permanent
service to the philosophical consideration of art and the beautiful.'[19] In
aesthetics, as in all other aspects of philosophy, Schopenhauer regarded himself as having completed the revolution begun by Kant,
correcting his mistakes along the way.

Up to this point in our discussion all our considerations have been
confined to the philosophy of 'art' in general. But Schopenhauer goes
on to offer an explanation of why it is that art is differentiated into a
number of different arts, and to make detailed comments on each of
them. The differentiation is explained in the following way. We are
familiar from earlier chapters with the doctrine that the will's self-
objectification in the world of phenomena comprises four categories or
grades: inorganic matter, plant life, animal life and human life. There is
a progress from the first of these to the last not only in evolutionary
terms but in terms of significance and value, the movement being from
inert and un-self-aware masses of inorganic matter via ever greater and
greater differentiation and autonomy to the emergence of automotive
individuals possessed of self-awareness and other-awareness, moral
and intellectual beings with unique characters and personalities. There
is therefore an intelligible sense in which the earlier grades can be said
to be 'lower' and the later grades 'higher'. Now every object in the
world of phenomena, without exception, has to belong to one or other of
these grades. In the present chapter we have noted that every object,
without exception, can be seen as being beautiful. According to
Schopenhauer, then, the differentiation of art into arts is explained by
the fact that the medium most appropriate for the communication of a
perception of the beautiful differs according to the grade of the will's
objectification to which the object seen as being beautiful belongs.

For instance, the lowest grade of the will's objectification is inorganic
matter, inanimate nature, and the Platonic Ideas characteristically
inherent in this include those of mass, extension, light, water, stone.
The art which is usually most appropriate for communicating insights
into these is the one whose expressive medium itself consists largely of
them, particularly of great masses of inorganic matter, namely
architecture. It needs to be remembered that what is being articulated
is insight into the Ideas *inherent* in matter, and that these include not
only Ideas of the visual but also of such characteristics as weight and
thrust. However, architecture is very little able to communicate
perception of the Ideas inherent in the next grade up, that of plant life.

[19] *The World as Will and Representation*, i. 529.

When such things as flowers and trees are seen as being beautiful, this is usually best conveyed by painting. It may also be conveyed by verbal description, whether in verse or prose, but that is somewhat indirect, the expressive medium being not itself visual in the direct way that painting is. On the other hand, painting finds itself circumscribed in its ability to render perceptions of the beautiful when we move up another grade still, into the animal kingdom. Not only is the physical presence of animals, their size, weight, solidity and mass, more vividly articulated in the three-dimensionality of sculpture than in paint, but so also are such characteristic attributes of automotive creatures as balance and poise, which happen also to be especially productive of aesthetic response. What neither painting nor sculpture can do is give more than momentary indications of our aesthetic responses to beauty in movement. These may be described in words, but once again, because the medium itself is non-visual, the effect is unsatisfactorily indirect. (A ballet lover might say that ballet is the art whose essential character is to articulate insight into beauties of movement, but this is not a point Schopenhauer makes.) When we turn for our subject-matter to the highest grade of the will's objectification, the life of humans in all its fullness, it is the turn of language to come into its own as an aesthetic medium. Painting and sculpture have marvellous contributions to make at this level too, but they are limited in what they can deal with both by their visual nature and by the fact that they are static in time. Because of their visual nature they are circumscribed in their ability to convey insight into inner states: in general they are surpassed in this — in depth, complexity, the power to combine richness and particularization, and perhaps above all the power to convey insight into *movement*, especially the motions of feeling — by lyric poetry. And the fact that they are static in time makes them short-breathed in their rendering of insights not only into movement and action but also into character and destiny, both of which unfold only over time. The supremely appropriate medium for these is drama. (Schopenhauer left in the ink-well the point that poetic drama therefore combines the best of two worlds: the poetry makes it possible for the finest articulation of inner states to accompany the dramatic unfolding of action and character and destiny, thus giving us insight into the internal and the external simultaneously.) So the verbal arts above all, inherently discursive as they are, are in general the best suited for the communication of insights into the highest of all grades of the will's objectification, the human individual with his unique personality and fate. Altogether, then, we have a hierarchy of arts corresponding at each level to the hierarchy of grades of the will's objectification, and thus able to communicate perceptions of anything in the phenomenal world as being beautiful, all the way from the dumbest inorganic mass up to the most complex and individualized human states and activities.

There remains, however, one art which does not fit into this hierarchy, but I shall leave it aside for a moment. It is music. The reason for its being different is that, unlike the others, it is not an art that finds its subject-matter in perceptions of anything in the world of phenomena. From this it follows that it does not communicate knowledge of Platonic Ideas. And from this it follows that it has an explanation inherently different from that of all the other arts. What this explanation is we shall come to shortly. Before we do, it is worth examining some of the things Schopenhauer has to say about the verbal art that he places at the top of his hierarchy. He has a section dealing with each of the verbal arts in turn, and makes a number of detailed observations on them, often on individual works. These remarks of his, as on the other arts, by no means consist simply in applications of his general theory. He was a passionate lover of the arts all his life: he read works of imaginative literature every day, played music every day on the flute, went to the theatre almost every evening to attend an opera or concert or play. During his extensive travels up to the age of forty-five he visited many of the most beautiful cities of Europe, and always took a special interest in their art galleries and their buildings. For no other of the great philosophers was an active involvement with the arts so integral to daily life. And this is reflected in his work. His writings throughout are rich in literary quotation and artistic allusion; and when it comes to his observations on particular arts, and indeed on particular works of art, these are studded with insights which are obviously rooted in lived experience, in personal aesthetic response, and have the ring of authenticity about them. I will pass most of them by, for the same reason as I have passed most of his essays by: although they are directly related to his philosophy a consideration of them is not necessary for an understanding of it, and to pursue him into that degree of detail would be digressive.

He thought, conventionally enough, that the highest form of literature was poetry. At this level he considered that the lyric carried the lightest cargo ('even the man who is on the whole not very eminent can produce a beautiful song'[20]) while 'the most objective, and in more than one respect the most complete, and also the most difficult, form of poetry'[21] was poetic drama. This makes it important to remember that almost the whole of classic drama up to Schopenhauer's time had been written in verse, for whenever he refers to 'poetry' what he has in mind, unless he specifically says otherwise, is drama. In effect, then, it is *the*

---

[20] *The World as Will and Representation*, i. 249.   [21] Ibid. i. 249.

theatre that is at the top of his hierarchy of the arts. He knew and loved most of the plays that constitute the central tradition of European drama, from the ancient Greeks to Goethe. The supreme artist in this Pantheon was, in his view, Shakespeare. When his references to 'poetry' are understood in this sense, such statements as 'more is achieved for knowledge of the true nature of mankind by poetry than by history'[22] are not as far-fetched as they might otherwise seem, and are probably not even controversial.

He regarded, again conventionally, tragedy as the highest form of poetic drama, but for a surprising reason. In the light of his philosophy as a whole one might have expected him to hold that tragedy moves us uniquely because it acts out in front of our eyes the 'total, inevitable and irremediable shipwreck' which is the destined end of each one of us. But that is not so. The reason, he says, why it gets at us in such a profound way is that it awakens in us an awareness of the possibility of coming to terms with the prospect of our own non-being. That is to say, we glimpse through it the possibility of our liberation, outside the realm of aesthetic response, from enslavement to the will to live. 'In the tragedy the terrible side of life is presented to us, the wailing and lamentation of mankind, the dominion of chance and error, the fall of the righteous, the triumph of the wicked; and so that aspect of the world is brought before our eyes which directly opposes our will. At this sight we feel ourselves urged to turn our will away from life, to give up willing and loving life. But precisely in this way we become aware that there is still left in us something different that we cannot possibly know positively, but only negatively, as that which does *not* will life . . . So every tragedy presupposes an existence of an entirely different kind, a different world, the knowledge of which can always be given to us only indirectly, as here by just such a presupposition . . . What gives to everything tragic, whatever the form in which it appears, the characteristic tendency to the sublime, is the dawning of the knowledge that the world and life can afford us no true satisfaction, and are therefore not worth our attachment to them. In this the tragic spirit consists; accordingly it leads to resignation.'[23]

With the greatest of tragedies this is not only an effect which the play has on the audience: the central character goes through this process in the play itself, and the most searingly affecting moment in such a play is the dawn of this resignation *within* the drama. An example which Schopenhauer was certainly conscious of as such, and quoted in other contexts, occurs in *Hamlet*. Hamlet's 'there's a special providence in the fall of a sparrow — if it be now, 'tis not to come; if it be not to come, it

[22] *The World as Will and Representation*, ii. 439.   [23] Ibid. ii. 433–4.

will be now; if it be not now, yet it will come: the readiness is all' is the most metaphysically deep moment in the play, the moment of utter stillness, the moment of acceptance, the cessation of the striving of the will. In every great tragedy there is such a nodal point at which the will to live is negated. And in every effective performance it is the moment of most profound raptness in the audience, a magic hush which is unlike any other crowd phenomenon. The resignation of the will to live on the part of real and not fictional characters — insight into the possibility of which is so penetratingly conveyed in these supreme moments — is in practical terms the destination of Schopenhauer's philosophy. What this means we shall come to in the next chapter.

One thing about Schopenhauer's treatment of literature which may surprise some twentieth-century readers is that, although he puts the verbal arts at the top of the hierarchy of the arts, he pays so little attention to the novel. It may seem all the odder to those readers who remember that he himself read novels a great deal, and that his mother became in the course of his lifetime an internationally successful novelist. It is easily explained by the fact that all but a handful of what are now considered the greatest novels did not exist when Schopenhauer was working out his philosophy. At that time, novels were nearly all romances of one sort or another, diversions aiming no higher than to provide a little light entertainment; and he read most of them in much the same spirit as an intelligent man nowadays might read detective stories or relax in front of a television set. But he seems to have been familiar with such great novels as there were, and to have taken them as seriously as they deserved. He refers to many of them in his writings. But he was bound to see their combined bulk and significance as small when compared to that of the greatest European drama over more than two thousand years. His view of what serious novels should aim to do is revealed in the following passage, which also indicates some of his favourite works. 'The task of the novelist is not to narrate great events but to make interesting those that are trifling. A *novel* will be of a loftier and nobler nature, the more of *inner* and the less of *outer* life it portrays; and this relation will, as a characteristic sign, accompany all gradations of the novel from *Tristram Shandy* down to the crudest and most eventful knight or robber romance. *Tristram Shandy* has, in fact, practically no action at all. And how little there is in *La Nouvelle Héloïse* and *Wilhelm Meister*! Even *Don Quixote* has relatively little; it is insignificant, and tends to be absurd. And these four novels are at the top of their class. Consider further the wonderful novels of Jean Paul, and see how much inner life they set in motion on the narrowest foundation of outer. Even the novels of Sir Walter Scott have a considerable preponderance of inner over outer life, and indeed the latter always appears only for the purpose of setting the former in motion; whereas in inferior novels it is there for its own sake.'[24]

Another objection that could possibly occur to a twentieth-century reader would arise at the point where Schopenhauer makes the transition from his treatment of the hierarchy of the arts to that of music. He prepares this by saying that all works of art that are not music either represent objects or doings in the phenomenal world or are themselves objects of decorative or practical usefulness in that world. A twentieth-century reader might demur that this was written before the advent of abstract art, which demonstrates it to be false. However, a deeper analysis reaffirms the distinction. As Iris Murdoch has put it so succinctly: 'Abstract painting is not just wilful fantasy or provocation, it is connected with the nature of space and colour. The abstract painter lives, and his pictures are seen, in a world where colours are taken to be surfaces of objects, and his consciousness of this is part of his problem. Such tensions between aesthetic vision and "ordinary" reality may give rise to very refined and difficult judgments.'[25] Schopenhauer's point survives re-examination. It certainly retains the credence of many sophisticated artists in the twentieth century who are familiar with abstract art: for instance W. H. Auden, whose poem addressed to *The Composer* begins

> All others translate: the painter sketches
> A visible world to love or reject;
> Rummaging into his living the poet fetches
> The images out that hurt and connect
> From Life to Art by painstaking adaption,
> Relying on us to cover the rift;
> Only your notes are pure contraption,
> Only your song is an absolute gift.

The notion that music is in some radical way different from the other arts, and superior to them, is old, and has been reiterated down the ages — surprisingly, by poets as much as by anyone, despite the fact that they are artists in a rival medium. And the distinction has persistently been associated with the fact that music does not depict anything in the phenomenal world. This also long ago gave rise to the idea that it must speak of another world. In religious contexts this was usually thought to be Paradise. Although I do not think anyone ever supposed there were sculptures or plays in heaven, it came to be taken for granted that there was music. The underlying sense of this ancient wisdom was

[24] *Parerga and Paralipomena*, ii. 440–1.
[25] *Men of Ideas* (ed. Bryan Magee), pp. 283–4.

endorsed by Schopenhauer, who provided what he believed to be the true explanation of it.

According to him, all the arts except music communicate knowledge of something which is *intermediate* between the noumenon and phenomena, namely Platonic Ideas. This is made possible by the fact that Platonic Ideas are instantiated in all phenomena, and that the arts in question represent those phenomena in ways that unveil the instantiation. To put the same point in another way: in so far as these arts give us glimpses of the noumenal it is indirectly, via what is intermediate, and their capacity to do even this rests on their ability to represent things which instantiate the intermediate. Music, by contrast, does not represent anything in the phenomenal world, or have anything at all to do with it so far as its content goes.[26] Therefore it has nothing to say about the Platonic Ideas, which are instantiated in the phenomenal world alone and have no existence separately from it. This means that music by-passes the Platonic Ideas; so whereas all the other arts speak of the noumenal indirectly, via them, music speaks of it directly. That is its essential nature: music is the direct articulation of the noumenon. Hence the age-old notion that it comes to us from another world. But since the noumenon is one and undifferentiable, any manifestation of it must be a manifestation of the whole of it. 'Thus music is as *immediate* an objectification and copy of the whole *will* as the world itself is, indeed as the Ideas are.'[27] So the reason why music does not communicate knowledge of the Ideas is that it is itself an *alternative* to the Ideas: like them, it is the direct manifestation of the noumenon in the world of phenomena. In this sense music is indeed an alternative to the world, and as such 'could, to a certain extent, still exist even if there were no world at all, which cannot be said of the other arts'.[28] (This statement looks highly peculiar at first, yet it is nothing but the conventional and familiar assumption, referred to just now, that there is music in Heaven but not novels or paintings.) Music is a manifestation of that of which the phenomenal world is also a manifestation, namely the noumenon. Therefore what it articulates is that which is also the inner nature of the phenomenal world, 'as it were the innermost soul of the phenomenon without the body'.[29] If it is to be spoken of as 'representing'

[26] Schopenhauer was aware, of course, that natural sounds are sometimes imitated in music (he himself instances Haydn's oratorios *The Seasons* and *The Creation*) as are also man-made sounds, like those in the battle pieces which were so popular in his day. He regarded such onomatopoeic music as crude, 'effects', essentially non-musical at bottom. His theory of music is to be taken as applying to music that is autonomously expressive, to what has since come to be called 'absolute' music — though he also sees it as applying *mutatis mutandis* to song and opera, as will appear.

[27] *The World as Will and Representation*, i. 257.

[28] Ibid. i. 257.   [29] Ibid. ii. 262.

anything at all, then what it represents is the noumenon, but in the rather peculiar sense in which the phenomenal world also 'represents' the noumenon. 'Music expresses, in a exceedingly universal language, in a homogeneous material, that is to say, in nothing but tones, and with the greatest distinctness and truth, the inner being, the in-itself, of the world.'[30] It 'expresses the metaphysical to everything physical in the world, the thing-in-itself to every phenomenon. Accordingly we could just as well call the world embodied music as embodied will.'[31]

Schopenhauer could not have known the now celebrated remark of Moses Mendelssohn's grandson, the composer Felix, that 'the thoughts which are expressed to me by music that I love are not too indefinite to be put into words, but, on the contrary, too definite',[32] but I think he would have applauded it if he had. For it follows from what he has to say that the standard notion that music goes deeper than words is correct, and that the reason why words cannot dig down to the same level lies in their excessive generality. This is due to a fact which we have considered already, that language cannot but make use of concepts which are formed by a process of generalization, and this means that it can never communicate insight into the unique in-itself-ness of anything. Music, however, does. And in doing so it is 'completely and profoundly understood by [man] in his innermost being as an entirely universal language whose distinctness surpasses even that of the world of perception itself'.[33] Now since what a philosopher like Schopenhauer is trying to do is to formulate an 'expression of the inner nature of the world in very general concepts', it follows that the composer is already doing *in concreto* what the philosopher is attempting to do *in abstractio*. Therefore if, *per impossibile*, we could succeed in giving a 'perfectly accurate and complete explanation of music which goes into detail, and thus a detailed rehearsal in concepts of what music expresses, this would also be at the same time an adequate rehearsal and explanation of the world in concepts, or one wholly corresponding thereto, and hence the true philosophy'.[34] Leibniz had described music as an unconscious exercise in arithmetic in which the mind does not know it is counting: he would have been nearer the mark if he had called it an unconscious exercise in metaphysics in which the mind does not know it is philosophizing. 'The composer reveals the innermost nature of the world, and expresses the profoundest wisdom, in a language that his reasoning faculty does not understand.'[35] His is therefore the purest, the

[30] *The World as Will and Representation*, ii. 264.   [31] Ibid. i. 262.
[32] In a letter to Marc-André Souchay, 1842.
[33] *The World as Will and Representation*, i. 256.
[34] Ibid. i. 264.   [35] Ibid. i. 260.

most undiluted form of genius of all, because it is the least contaminated by conceptual thought or conscious intention.

By this time it goes without saying that the inmost nature of the world is as much to be found in our noumenal selves as anywhere. I have already quoted Schopenhauer as saying that the point at which we are closest to a direct awareness of the noumenon is the point at which we apprehend the first light cast by a decision, or other act of the will, on its dawning emergence from the inaccessible depths of our unconscious selves. It can therefore be said that it is from these inscrutable regions that music speaks. In this sense what it articulates is insight into, and in *that* sense knowledge of, the hidden, inner nature of our own willing, 'the secret history of our will and of all its stirrings and strivings with their many different delays, postponements, hindrances and afflictions'.[36] It is important to grasp a distinction here. Music does not express the phenomena of emotion: it 'does not express this or that particular and definite pleasure, this or that affliction, pain, sorrow, horror, gaiety, merriment, or peace of mind, but joy, pain, sorrow, horror, merriment, peace of mind *as such*, to a certain extent in the abstract, yet their essential nature, without any accessories, and so also without the motives for them'.[37] This last point is of crucial importance for explaining our enjoyment of music. 'The inexpressible depth of all music, by virtue of which it floats past us like a paradise quite familiar and yet eternally remote, and is so easy to understand and yet so inexplicable, is due to the fact that it reproduces all the emotions of our innermost being, but entirely without reality, and remote from its pain . . . .'[38] In other words music, because it is the only art that articulates the noumenal will directly, without the mediation of anything in the phenomenal world, is also the only art that impinges directly on the will of the receiver, without any superficial, diversionary clutter from that 'real' world. This is why for so many of us, even many who themselves are creative artists in other media, 'the effect of music is so very much more powerful and penetrating than is that of the other arts; for these others speak only of the shadow, but music of the essence'.[39]

The ability of music to give us insight into the inner nature of emotions and moods in a way that eludes concepts is what makes songs so beautiful and moving — they integrate poetry with something that no words can express. The same is true of opera, but in a vastly expanded and enriched way that takes in character, situation, and indeed the full unfolding of all that is possible in a drama. The statement has often appeared in print that Schopenhauer disliked opera,

[36] *The World as Will and Representation*, ii. 451.
[37] Ibid. i. 261.   [38] Ibid. i. 264.   [39] Ibid. i. 257.

but that is false: he loved it and was an enthusiastic opera-goer all his life. The mistake has resulted from a confusion about terms. In the English-speaking world, at least, it has long been generally supposed among that great majority of the public which is not particularly musical that the term 'grand opera' is a synonym for 'opera', its point being to distinguish the full-scale thing from 'comic opera', 'light opera' and 'operetta'. This is not so. 'Grand opera' is the special term for a form of opera which developed in Paris in the nineteenth century — nearly always in five acts, nearly always containing a ballet — whose *raison d'être* was the mounting of popular and grandiose stage spectacle. Wagner wrote blistering attacks on it for its dramatic nullity, which he hit off in the biting phrase 'effects without causes'. Schopenhauer was equally rude about it for much the same reasons, regarding it as vulgar, inflated, empty and, in the last analysis, silly. Unfortunately, generations of readers who have encountered these insulting references to 'grand opera' have taken them as referring to opera as such. The truth is that Schopenhauer regarded opera as an art-form of the weightiest calibre and most penetrating power, which it derived from the capacity of music to articulate the inner nature of everything. 'This close relation that music has to the true nature of all things can also explain the fact that, when music suitable to any scene, action, event, or environment is played, it seems to disclose to us its most secret meaning, and appears to be the most accurate and distinct commentary on it.'[40] . . . 'It gives the most profound, ultimate, and secret information on the feeling expressed in the words, or the action presented in the opera. It expresses their real and true nature, and makes us acquainted with the innermost soul of the events and occurrences, the mere cloak and body of which are presented on the stage.'[41] As far as my knowledge goes, Schopenhauer was the first person to see and state clearly that the essence of opera was that it was a form of drama in which the *inwardness* of emotion, character, relationships, actions, situations, and so on, was articulated by music, which has a unique capacity for doing so. Wagner arrived at much the same theory independently, and published it before he — or many other people, for that matter[42] — had heard of Schopenhauer, but Schopenhauer published it first. It was a frivolous unconcern for the utilization of its powers that seemed to Schopenhauer and Wagner alike the most contemptible of the many contemptible things about 'grand opera'. But Schopenhauer loved the

[40] *The World as Will and Representation*, i. 262.
[41] Ibid. ii. 448.
[42] This is an important point, because it virtually rules out the possibility of indirect influence: the disregard of Schopenhauer up to and beyond the time when Wagner wrote was almost total.

operas of Mozart, Rossini and Bellini, and he mentions them all in *The World as Will and Representation*, where Mozart's *Don Giovanni* is set beside Shakespeare's *Hamlet* and Goethe's *Faust* as one of 'the most perfect masterpieces of the very greatest masters'.[43] Of Bellini's *Norma* Schopenhauer writes: 'Quite aside from its excellent music, and from the verbal idiom that can be only that of a libretto, and judged solely on the basis of motivation and inner economy, this piece is, on the whole, a tragedy of extreme perfection.'[44]

As something of a postscript to our discussion of Schopenhauer's theory of music it is worth remarking that among the inner refinements of the doctrine that music is an *equivalent* of the world, and one which articulates its inner nature, is the view that, like the world, although being capable of limitless internal differentiation it falls into four broad divisions which comprise the whole. These are the basic elements of the four-part harmony which is fundamental to Western music — the division into soprano, alto, tenor and bass, or its equivalents in orchestral and instrumental writing. The parallels between this and the four grades of the will's objectification in the world of phenomena are pursued in some detail. 'The ground-bass is in harmony what inorganic nature, the crudest mass on which everything rests and from which everything originates and develops, is in the world. Further, in the whole range of notes that produce the harmony between the bass and the leading voice singing the melody, I recognized the whole gradation of the Ideas in which the will objectifies itself . . .' — and so on and so forth, until 'finally, in the *melody*, in the high, singing, principal voice, leading the whole and progressing with unrestrained freedom, in the uninterrupted significant connection of *one* thought from beginning to end, and expressing a whole, I recognize the highest grade of the will's objectification, the intellectual life and endeavours of man.'[45]

Before this is dismissed as fanciful nonsense, serious attention must be paid to the fact that it is remarkably similar to something written by the young Wagner — again, years before he had even heard of Schopenhauer, let alone read his work — in the course of an attempt to characterize the complex expressive medium which is constituted by voice and orchestra taken together. 'Instruments represent the primal organs of Creation and Nature; their expression can never be clearly defined and formulated since they convey the primal feelings as they first issued forth from the chaos of the Creation; perhaps even before there was any human heart to hear and feel. The genius of the voice is

[43] *The World as Will and Representation*, ii. 410.
[44] Ibid. ii. 436.   [45] Ibid. i. 258–9.

completely different: this represents the human heart, the separate individual sensibility, limited, but clear and definite . . .' and so on.[46] When two of the most insightful of all theorists of music[47] bring forward such obviously related formulations independently of each other it cannot be assumed without the most searching consideration that there is nothing to what they say.

I suspect that a more richly explanatory theory of music than any that has yet been produced could be partially derived from the fact of the physical integration of diatonic harmony with inorganic nature. Pythagoras was the first to show that the basic intervals on which Western (and in fact not only Western) music is constructed inhere in the world, independently of man. In his most famous demonstration he plucked a string to sound a note, then halved the length of the string and showed that plucking it produced the same note an octave higher. He then showed that two-thirds of the original length yielded the interval of a fifth above the first note, and three-quarters that of a fourth. Not only by plucking strings, but equally by striking various lengths of any reverberant material, or tapping hollow objects, one can show that the intervals that constitute the foundations of Western harmony are built into the world, and what is more, that the decisive measurements of whatever objects are producing the sounds stand in simple arithmetic relations to one another — as, in the examples I have given, 1:2, 2:3, and 3:4. None of this is man's doing. The significance of it seems to me incalculable. For it means that music is not arbitrary in the sense that language is. Language is entirely a human creation; but music is rooted in the nature of things. The fundamental harmonic intervals permeate independently, and always have permeated, the material environment within which man has come into existence, and out of which he is formed (and, among other things, in response to which the biological mechanisms of hearing were evolved). What all this indicates, I think, is that some of our structures of response involving music are programmed into us at much earlier and 'lower' evolutionary levels than anything to do with language — levels which are by countless ages pre-human. And it seems obvious that this fact has a connection with our feeling that music goes deeper than words. It

[46] From Wagner's short story *A Pilgrimage to Beethoven*. For the above translation and the continuation of the passage see page 80 of *Wagner Writes from Paris . . .*, edited and translated by Robert Jacobs and Geoffrey Skelton.

[47] At least one great composer has regarded them as *the* two most insightful. Mahler, who was well read in aesthetics and in philosophy generally, 'thought that Schopenhauer's book contained the most profound analysis of music that had ever been made, comparable to Wagner's article on Beethoven' (Henry-Louis de la Grange: *Mahler*, i. 853). The Wagnerian reference here is not to the short story quoted in this chapter but to Wagner's essay on Beethoven published in 1870.

could also help to explain why it is that atonal music, after nearly a hundred years, still seems to most music lovers, including most professional musicians, to be 'not music'. More to the point of our present considerations, it relates music at a very deep level with the emergence of man — and hence of consciousness — out of inorganic nature, and thus provides solid substance to the overblown passages I have quoted to this effect from Wagner and Schopenhauer. Finally, I suspect it has something to do with what it is that Schopenhauer is trying to express when he says that music articulates the inner nature of things.

As usual, Schopenhauer is clearly aware of the logical status of what it is he is saying, and anxious to keep his readers clear about it too. Of his theory of music taken as a whole he writes: 'I recognize that it is essentially impossible to demonstrate this explanation, for it assumes and establishes a relation of music as a representation to that which of its essence can never be representation, and claims to regard music as the copy of an original that can itself never be represented . . . I must leave the acceptance or denial of my view to the effect that both music and the whole thought communicated in this work have on each reader.'[48]

[48] *The World as Will and Representation*, i. 257.

Chapter 9

Metaphysics of the Person

We have had a lot to say about Schopenhauer's uses of the term 'will', yet we have managed to get this far in our consideration of his philosophy with scarcely a reference to the most notorious philosophical problem in connection with which the term is normally used, namely that of the freedom of the will. On the face of it, this ought to constitute an especially difficult problem for Schopenhauer, for his insistence that all phenomenal objects and their movements are governed by the principle of sufficient reason must inescapably extend to human beings in so far as they are phenomenal objects. 'Man, like all objects of experience, is a phenomenon in time and space, and since the law of causality holds for all such *a priori*, and consequently without exception, he too must be subject to it.'[1] This doctrine raises no problems in so far as the movements of our bodies are unwilled: as when, for example, we are carried about by a vehicle, or struck by a moving object, or dropped from a height. What happens to us in such circumstances is straightforwardly explicable in terms of the laws of physics. But what about what happens when our behaviour is willed behaviour — when I consider what to do and then do it, perhaps choosing between alternatives: how is what I do then to be explained in terms of physical causality?

Schopenhauer does indeed so explain it, and the key to his explanation is this: in willed behaviour the movements of our bodies are determined by our motives, and motives are causes experienced from within. We encountered this idea briefly in Chapter 2, but are only now in a position to see it in full context. The medium of motives is the mind. That is to say, the presence of danger, food, a mating partner, or any of the innumerable situations that could conceivably precipitate action does so only in so far as it impinges on the potential agent via his organs of perception, and arouses conscious or unconscious feelings of desire, fear, hunger, lust, or whatever it may be, which in turn motivate the appropriate bodily movements. I am not supposing for one moment that in the case of humans the range of possibilities is anything like so small and simple as my range of examples, which are chosen to cover

[1] *Essay on the Freedom of the Will*, p. 46.

animals as well: in the case of humans the possibilities of subtlety and sophistication are endless. But however complex, numerous and conflicting the motives may be in any given situation, whatever emerges on balance as the strongest holds sway. And Schopenhauer's main point is that we cannot freely decide for ourselves what that shall be. The prevalence — or, if that is not conceded, the undeniably considerable extent — of unconscious motivation is in itself enough to demonstrate this. But it is a truth that holds also at the level of conscious choice. This can be demonstrated by a simple example. If I am ordering a meal in a restaurant I may be free to choose whatever I like from among the alternatives on the menu. But I am not free to choose what *what I like* shall be. I cannot say to myself: 'Up to this point in my life I have always detested spinach, but just for today I am going to like it.' Nor am I in a position to ask myself: 'Shall I decide that I am in the mood for fish, or shall I decide that I am in the mood for chicken?' What I am in the mood for, and what I like or detest, are not at my command. It is not they that are matters of choice for me: they are given to me as accomplished facts, and *it is on the basis of them* that I make my choice. I can choose whatever it is I wish to choose, but I cannot will what it is that I shall wish to choose. As it has often been put, I can choose what I will but I cannot will what I will.

The validity of this example is not dependent on the presence in it of the element of taste, and it will be found to remain valid however complicated the choice-situation becomes. It is quite often the case that what I order in a restaurant is not decided by what I most feel like eating. I may be trying to lose weight, or I may be anxious to fit in with what my companions are having, or with the fact that one of them has only a limited time, or I may be influenced by the relative prices of the dishes. I may even be swayed by the potential reactions of someone who is not present (for instance the thought, if I am a timid husband, that my wife will nag me when I get home if I have spent too much money, or ordered something fattening, or failed to squeeze some errand into my lunch-hour). It could only too easily be that every one of these motives is operative at the same time — the complex of motivation in even so trivial a matter can be intricate. Yet whatever these conflicting motives balance themselves out at, *that* will decide what I shall order. And *it is not open to me to choose how they will balance out*. If I am anxious about the reactions of my companions or of my wife, I can pretend to be indifferent, but I cannot *be* indifferent. I cannot decide that the amount of money in my pocket shall be twice what it is; and if I have an appointment in half an hour I cannot decide to spend a further hour over lunch without being late for my appointment. But that is what a genuinely 'free' choice would be like. It would be a choice untrammelled by the principle of sufficient reason. My wishes would determine reality. In other words it would be magic, the magic of wish-fulfilment. And of course we simply do not have free choice, and therefore free will, in that sense (though it is illuminating that the notion has such profound appeal to us that it is a central element in many perennial human creations, such as myth, fairy story, personal daydreams, magic, ritual, and others). All the factors I have given in my example are what they are, independent of my wishes, and they will all impinge on what I decide. In short, we will what we are most strongly motivated to will by factors which we do not determine, and we *then* choose accordingly.

The full point of what this means is brought out if we consider what the alternative would be like. If I were to say to the waiter: 'Taking everything into consideration my preference today is for lamb chops, but please bring me a Dover sole,' both he and my companions would think I had taken leave of my senses. And they would be right: rationality in such situations consists in acting in accordance with the balance of actual considerations. Not to do so is arbitrary, eccentric, mad — 'free', certainly, (if you like) but not in any desirable sense. It is more like being insane. And if we were to start being 'free' in this way in all our behaviour we should very quickly find it impossible to conduct our dealings with other people, or to cope with our environment at all, and before long we should have to be taken into care, if we had not already destroyed ourselves by sitting in the fire, or strolling into the path of an oncoming vehicle, or taken some other such action as disregarded the principle of sufficient reason with disastrous consequences.

In the sense which these examples make clear, Schopenhauer denied that we possess free will. That is not to say that everyone in the same circumstances behaves in the same way — they do not, of course, and the reason why they do not is that their characters and personalities are different. Any one of my restaurant companions may like spinach, have been advised by his doctor to put on weight, be equally indifferent to the convenience of the rest of us and the cost of the meal, be unafraid of his wife, and notoriously late for appointments, so all the relevant considerations will motivate him to behave differently from me in the same situation. We each have the character and temperament and personality we have, with all their intricacies and foibles, and each of us, given what he is, can react in any given set of circumstances to any given set of motives in only one way. In the remarkable fourth chapter of his *Essay on the Freedom of the Will*, headed 'Predecessors', Schopenhauer demonstrates by means of extensive quotation that this view of the matter, or something obviously very similar to it, has been held by most of the great philosophers who went before him. It has

certainly been held by many philosophers since. Today it is something
of an orthodoxy in the philosophy of the English-speaking world,
where, for example, it is one of the arguments set out in standard
textbooks.

Some philosophers who accept the argument are inclined to say:
'What is meant in ordinary usage by "acting freely" is acting in
accordance with our personal motivations without being subjected to
external constraints, so in the ordinary sense of the term we do indeed
have, or can have, free will.' To determine, therefore, whether a philosopher is in accord with Schopenhauer on this issue one has to look not
at the terms in which he states his conclusion — that we do, or do not,
have free will — but at the arguments with which he supports it. A case
in point is Quine, who asserts that we have free will yet is in full
agreement with Schopenhauer (whom, he tells me, he has never read).
'Clearly we have free will. The supposed problem comes of a confusion,
indeed a confusing turn of phrase. Freedom of the will means that *we*
are free to *do* as we will; not that our will is free to will as it will, which
would be nonsense. We *are* free to do as we will, unless someone holds
us back, or unless we will something beyond our strength or talent. Our
actions count as free insofar as our will is a cause of them. Certainly the
will has its causes in turn; no one could wish otherwise. If we thought
wills could not be caused, we would not try to train our children; you
would not try to win votes; we would not try to sell things, or to deter
criminals.'[2]

Because Schopenhauer denies that we have free will he thinks that
questions like 'How ought we to live? or 'What ought I to aim at?' are
mistaken, and do not have answers of the kind which the people who
ask them are looking for. What we choose to do is not itself a matter of
choice for us. Since 'ought' logically entails 'can' it is false to say that I
ought to do something if I cannot do it, and therefore, if I cannot choose
what motives are to determine my actions, it is false to say that I 'ought'
to do one thing rather than another. By the same token, it is false to say
that I ought to have done something which I have not done, for the fact
that I have not done it shows that it was not open to me to do it. People's
mistaken assumptions on this score derive from complex sources. First:
because the ultimate springs of our own decisions and actions are
hidden from us we do not know what they are going to be on future
occasions. We make resolutions well enough, but we frequently break
them, and are not infrequently astonished by some of the things we find
ourselves deciding and doing. This ignorance and uncertainty helps to
create the illusion that our future is an 'open' one, and this in turn

[2] Quine in *Men of Ideas* (ed. Bryan Magee), p. 173.

nourishes the illusion of freedom. Second: most of us have grown up in cultures which from time immemorial have presented ethics as if they were bound up with religion. All religions have their moral laws, their 'thou shalt's and 'thou shalt not's, their multiple 'ought's; and precisely because *ought* does imply *can* this has indoctrinated us from childhood in the illusion of free will. Furthermore, the religious idea of moral laws encourages us to make a false analogy between them and natural laws, and to suppose — just as it was taken for granted in Schopenhauer's day that there were objectively valid scientific laws which describe what happens in nature, regardless of what anyone might think or want — that there are objectively valid moral laws which describe what we 'ought' to do and which are independent of what anyone actually does. Schopenhauer finds this a deeply confused and, at bottom, incoherent idea. How could laws of such a kind be validated? And what would their content be, if not anything that is actually the case?

To these questions moral philosophers might reply: 'The point of moral statements is not to tell you what is the case but to tell you what you ought to do or approve. You ask how such statements can be validated. That is itself the central question of moral philosophy, to which our activities are addressed, just as the central question of epistemology is "How can our knowledge claims be validated?" No wholly satisfactory answer has yet been found to either question. You yourself prefaced your essay *On the Basis of Morality* with the motto "It is easy to preach morality but difficult to establish any basis for it." One might say that all our analyses of moral concepts and moral arguments are, in their different ways, parts of the search for such a basis, or at least attempts to increase our understanding of what such a basis might be.' To this Schopenhauer in turn might reply: 'I'm afraid it is you who have missed my point. You insist on starting out from concepts and forms of utterance which no one knows how to validate and then setting yourself the problem of how to validate them. Would it not be better to start from the world in which you actually find yourself, and to examine what is the case, and see if you encounter any problems which can significantly be labelled "moral" in a sense which you understand? If you don't, then there's no reason to believe such problems exist. If you do, the context in which they present themselves to you will define them, and you can carry on from there. What you *cannot* do, however, is "know" in advance of any enquiry that there are such problems, and what their nature is — which is what you and your predecessors have always done.' Let me clinch this fictional dialogue with a real quotation from Schopenhauer. 'Who tells you that there are laws to which our conduct *ought* to be liable? Who tells you that *what never happens ought to happen*? What justification have you for making this assumption at the outset, and accordingly at once forcing on us, as the only possible one, a system of ethics framed in the legislative imperative form? In opposition to Kant I say that the student of ethics as well as the philosopher generally must be content with the explanation and interpretation of what is given, and thus of what actually is or happens, in order to arrive at a *comprehension* of it; and I say also that here he has plenty to do, much more than has been done hitherto, after the lapse of thousands of years.'[3]

The point of this last dig is that just as moralists generally, who for two thousand years have almost all been religious, have started from false assumptions about the available forms of moral utterance, so these false assumptions have been transmitted to, and accepted by, moral philosophers whose task it is to examine them. The mistake is historically rooted in the association of ethics with religion. 'Putting ethics in an *imperative* form as a *doctrine of duties*, and thinking of the moral worth or worthlessness of human actions as the fulfilment or violation of *duties*, undeniably spring, together with *obligation*, solely from theological morals . . . Consequently, it rests essentially on the assumption of man's dependence on another will that commands him and announces reward or punishment, and is not to be separated from this. The more the assumption of such a will is a settled affair in theology, the less it should be tacitly drawn from there into philosophical morals. We cannot assume in advance that in philosophical morals the *imperative form*, the drawing up of commands, laws and duties, is a matter of course.'[4]

Here, as throughout the rest of his philosophy, Schopenhauer is insistent on taking as his starting-point the facts of experience, not abstract ideas. He sets about trying to investigate human behaviour without any preconceptions of what people 'ought' to do, by looking instead at what they do in fact do, and in particular what sort of motives function as the motives of their actions. His investigation leads him to the conclusion that the springs of most of what has traditionally been considered 'moral' behaviour turn out on a careful analysis to be self-interested, and therefore cannot be regarded as moral in any approving sense, nor indeed in any other significant or useful sense. The chief motives for obedience to the laws of religion and the secular authorities do not, on a serious examination, very obviously include moral sentiments, but they do most obviously include fear of punishment and hope of reward, whether in this world or the next; conformism; social politeness; early conditioning; and desire for the security conferred by acceptance of authority. The fact that these become

[3] *On the Basis of Morality*, p. 52.   [4] Ibid., pp. 56–7.

internalized as what we call *conscience* does nothing to raise their status. The most frivolous or bloodthirsty codes of conduct — for instance knightly chivalry (for which Schopenhauer had a special contempt), the code of military honour, or the vendetta moralities to be found in parts of the Mediterranean — can be and are internalized to every bit as powerful and binding a degree, with the result that many a man has murdered his pregnant sister or blown his own brains out because he thought his code of conduct required him to. 'Many a man would be astonished if he saw how his conscience, which seems to him such an imposing affair, is really made up. It probably consists of one-fifth fear of men, one-fifth fear of the gods, one-fifth prejudice, one-fifth vanity, and one-fifth habit; so that he is essentially no better than the English-man who said quite frankly, "I cannot afford to keep a conscience". Religious people of every faith frequently understand by *conscience* nothing but the dogmas and commandments of their religion, and the self-scrutiny undertaken with reference to them.'[5] Schopenhauer is especially insistent that those motives for action most approvingly regarded as moral in the Judaeo–Christian tradition, namely fear of God and hope of reward in an afterlife, are straightforwardly self-interested — and the more secure the religious faith on which they rest, the more self-interested they are. It is as if a man were to be admired for investing a thousand pounds in an apparently benevolent but risky venture when in fact he was doing it because he believed his investment would be returned to him a thousandfold.

Schopenhauer looks at the sorts of ends towards which motives do in fact direct actions, and finds that, talking in the most general terms, there are three, which of course can be mixed in varying degrees with each other. Far and away the commonest is the desire of the agent to promote his own first-order purposes, or secure his own welfare in some way, and this is what Schopenhauer not unreasonably labels 'egoism'. It is, in one obvious sense of the word, the most 'natural' motivation of all. Animals behave like this for most of the time with complete unself-consciousness. It is the form of motivation on which we place the greatest reliance in our dealings with each other: in most circumstances we regard it as unreasonable to expect people to act against their own self-interest, and if we want to get someone to do something we usually try to persuade him that it is in his interests to do it, or we try to *make* it in his interests to do it. For most of the time we do not adopt any moral attitudes towards this form of motivation — in ordinary circumstances we neither praise nor blame people for acting in their own interests. We merely expect them to do so, so long as they do no significant harm to

[5] *On the Basis of Morality*, p. 127.

others. But then there is another, radically different sort of motivation, and that is the desire to harm others, sometimes for its own sake. This Schopenhauer labels 'malice'. It operates in all of us, and it takes many forms: aggressiveness, competitiveness, envy, spite, the desire to lord it over others, or to be deferred to by others. It often contains an ingredient of cruelty, and in its most extreme and sadistic forms it can rise to the greatest heights of wickedness of which humans are capable. Finally, there is a third form of motivation, which is the desire to promote the welfare of others, sometimes in disregard of our own. Does this ever *really* occur as a motive? Schopenhauer asserts as an ascertainable fact that it does, and gives many examples from both history and literature. He justifies citing literature with the argument that the greatest of creative writers were also great psychologists, and had a profound understanding of the realities of human motivation. It seems to me an obvious mistake to cite fictional examples when the question at issue is whether actual examples exist; but since so many actual examples do exist, and Schopenhauer cites some, his argument is not invalidated.

So here we come up against a problem. What can it be that causes a human being to put himself out to do something which he knows will bring him no benefit, and may perhaps put him in danger or do him harm, even put his life at risk? Putting it personally, how can it come about that the safety or well-being of *another* can constitute a motive for *my* actions? In other words, wherein lies the connection between his well-being and my motivation? The connection, says Schopenhauer, is fellow feeling, compassion, and this in turn rests on self-identification. 'To a certain extent I have identified myself with the other man, and in consequence the barrier between the ego and non-ego is for the moment abolished; only then do the other man's affairs, his need, distress, and suffering, directly become my own. I no longer look at him as if he were something given to me by empirical intuitive perception, as something strange and foreign, as a matter of indifference, as something entirely different from me. On the contrary, I share the suffering *in him*, in spite of the fact that his skin does not enclose my nerves. Only in this way can *his* woe, *his* distress, become a motive *for me*; otherwise it could be absolutely only my own. I repeat that this *occurrence is mysterious*, for it is something our faculty of reason can give no direct account of, and its grounds cannot be discovered on the path of experience. And yet it happens every day; everyone has often experienced it within himself; even to the most hardhearted and selfish it is not unknown. Every day it comes before our eyes, in single acts on a small scale . . .'.[6]

---

[6] *On the Basis of Morality*, p. 166.

In addition to the three general forms of motivation which we have now considered — the desire for our own welfare, the desire for the detriment of others, and the desire for the welfare of others — there would seem to be logically a fourth possibility, namely the desire for our own detriment. But this is never in practice a motive for action except with the neurotic or otherwise mentally ill, or in so far as such pathological elements as masochism enter into the motivation of the normal person. We often willingly accept harm to ourselves in our pursuit of the welfare of others, but we do not want the harm for its own sake. If we want to demonstrate a point, then that is self-interested. Even the man who commits suicide does so (unless the balance of his mind is disturbed) because he sees it as the lesser of two evils — for instance as the only escape from an intolerable state of consciousness, or from the most frightening stages of a terminal illness, or from some ignominious public disgrace — and therefore as his self-interested preference in the circumstances. So in the most general terms there are only three kinds of motive that move sane men. And of these the desire for their own well-being and the desire for the detriment of others are obviously not moral in any sense that calls for congratulation. But Schopenhauer's conclusion is that the third motive, the non-self-interested one, which he labels 'compassion', is.

We must remember that Schopenhauer is still, up to this point, pursuing a descriptive task. He is asking himself: 'In the real world, what sorts of things motivate actions? Do any actions or motivations actually occur which even after careful analysis we still want to describe as moral in any approving sense? If they do, what sorts of actions or motivations are they?' And his conclusion is that even after the most sceptical analysis we still persist in regarding actions approvingly as 'moral' in so far as they rest on motives which are not self-interested but are concerned with the well-being of others; and the greater the degree to which they disregard self-interest — perhaps even bringing serious risk or actual harm to the doer — the greater the moral worth which we ascribe to them, and the more highly we approve them. This, he asserts, is a fact attested to not merely by philosophical analysis but by the most common observation and experience. In support of this view he puts forward no fewer than nine numbered demonstrations, of which the first two are the most persuasive and are worth quoting in full.

(1) . . . Let us suppose that two young men, Caius and Titus, are passionately in love each with a different girl, and that, on account of external circumstances, each is thwarted absolutely by a specially favoured rival. They have both decided to put their rivals out of the way, and are perfectly secure from all detection, even from all suspicion. When, however, each comes to

make more detailed arrangements for the murder, he desists after an inward struggle. They are now to give us a sincere and clear account of the reasons for abandoning their decision. Now, that given by Caius is to be left entirely to the reader's choice. He may have been prevented through religious reasons, such as the will of God, the retribution to come, the Day of Judgment, and so on. Or he may say: 'I consider that the maxim for my proceeding in this case would not have been calculated to give a universally valid rule for all possible rational beings, since I should have treated my rival only as a means and not at the same time as an end.'[7] Or he may say with Fichte: 'Every human life is a means to the realization of the moral law; hence I cannot, without being indifferent to that realization, destroy one who is destined to contribute to it' (*Moral Philosophy*, page 373). (Incidentally, he could get over this scruple by hoping, when once in possession of his beloved, to produce soon a new instrument of the moral law.) Or he may say in accordance with Wollaston: 'I considered that this action would be the expression of a false proposition.' Or like Hutcheson he may say: 'The moral sense whose feelings, like those of any other, are incapable of further explanation, prevailed on me not to do it.' Or like Adam Smith: 'I foresaw that my action would not excite any sympathy at all for me in those who witnessed it.' Or in the words of Christian Wolff: 'I recognized that I should thus work against my own perfection and not help that of another.' Or he may use the words of Spinoza: *Homini nihil utilius homine: ergo hominem interimere nolui.*[8] In short he may say what he likes. But Titus, whose account I reserve for myself, may say: 'When it came to making the arrangements, and so for the moment I had to concern myself not with my passion but with that rival, I clearly saw for the first time what would really happen to him. But I was then seized with compassion and pity; I felt sorry for him; I had not the heart to do it, and could not.' Now I ask any honest and unbiased reader: Which of the two is the better man? To which of them would he prefer to entrust his own destiny? Which of them has been restrained by the purer motive? Accordingly, where does the foundation of morality lie?

(2) Nothing shocks our moral feelings so deeply as cruelty does. We can forgive every other crime, but not cruelty. The reason for this is that it is the very opposite of compassion. When we obtain information of a very cruel deed, as, for example, the case, recently reported in the papers, of a mother who murdered her five-year-old son by pouring boiling oil down his throat and her younger child by burying it alive; or the case, just reported from Algiers, where, after a casual dispute and fight between a Spaniard and an Algerian, the latter, as the stronger, tore away the whole of the lower jawbone of the former, and carried it off as a trophy, leaving the other man still alive; when we hear of such things, we are seized with horror and exclaim: 'How is it possible to do such a thing?' What is the meaning of this question? Is it: How is it possible to have so little fear for the punishments of the future life? Hardly. Or: How is it possible to act according to a maxim that is so absolutely unfitted to

[7] Kant, *Foundations of the Metaphysics of Morals*, Academy 429. A.S.]
[8] 'To man nothing is more useful than man; I was therefore unwilling to kill the man.' *Ethics*, IV, prop. 18, schol. Tr.]

become a general law for all rational beings? Certainly not. Or: How is it possible so utterly to neglect one's own perfection and that of another? Again, certainly not. The sense of that question is certainly only this: How is it possible to be so utterly bereft of compassion? Thus it is the greatest lack of compassion that stamps a deed with the deepest moral depravity and atrocity. Consequently, compassion is the real moral incentive.'[9]

Having now, after establishing that there is such a thing as moral behaviour, established that what it consists in is practical compassion, Schopenhauer addresses himself to the mystery of how the occurrence of compassion is possible. His answer is all of a piece with his metaphysics. Empathy and compassion are made possible, he tells us, by the fact that each of us is, in his inmost nature, at one with the noumenal, and the noumenal is one and undifferentiable; therefore all of us in our deepest nature are one with each other, are undifferentiable from each other. Thus, in my innermost recesses I am not merely *similar* to other human beings — it is merely on the surface that similarity appears: at the very bottom they and I are literally one and the same thing. 'Only as phenomenon is the individual different from the other things of the world; as noumenon he is the will that appears in everything.'[10] To the good man 'others are not mere masks, whose inner nature is quite different from his. On the contrary, he shows by his way of acting that he *recognizes* his own inner being, namely the will-to-live as thing-in-itself, in the phenomenon of another given to him as mere representation. Thus he finds himself again in that phenomenon . . .'.[11] The man who thus acts compassionately is behaving in accordance with the metaphysical realities of the human situation. Morality is practical metaphysics.

It is never suggested by Schopenhauer that people behave morally because they possess a correct theoretical understanding of what is involved. On the contrary, because we cannot decide what we are going to will (he several times quotes Seneca's phrase *velle non discitur* — 'the will cannot be taught'), and because it is the will that governs our behaviour, conceptual knowledge can no more generate valid moral activity than it can generate valid artistic activity: both can spring only from direct intuition, the kind of perception and experience from which concepts themselves are derived. 'Virtue does indeed result from knowledge, but not from abstract knowledge communicable through words. If this were so, virtue could be taught, and by expressing here in the abstract its real nature and the knowledge at its foundation, we should have ethically improved everyone who comprehended this. But this is by no means the case. On the contrary, we are as little able to produce a

---

[9] *On the Basis of Morality*, pp. 168–70.
[10] *The World as Will and Representation*, i. 282.   [11] Ibid. i. 370.

200 Metaphysics of the Person

virtuous person by ethical discourses or sermons as all the systems of aesthetics from Aristotle's downwards have ever been able to produce a poet. For the concept is unfruitful for the real inner nature of virtue, just as it is for art; and only in a wholly subordinate position can it serve as an instrument in elaborating and preserving what has been ascertained and inferred in other ways. *Velle non discitur.* In fact, abstract dogmas are without influence on virtue, i.e. on goodness of disposition; false dogmas do not disturb it, and true ones scarcely strengthen it.'[12]

Schopenhauer goes on to say that the moral insight which gives rise to ethical behaviour, 'just because it is not abstract, cannot be communicated, but must dawn on each of us. It therefore finds its real and adequate expression not in words but simply and solely in deeds, in conduct, in the course of a man's life.'[13] The moral man is engaged in a radically different kind of activity from the moral philosopher with his analyses and expositions in terms of concepts. 'It is therefore just as little necessary for the saint to be a philosopher as for the philosopher to be a saint; just as it is not necessary for a perfectly beautiful person to be a great sculptor, or for a great sculptor to be himself a beautiful person. In general, it is a strange demand on a moralist that he should commend no other virtue than that which he himself possesses.'[14] Although this latter remark is obviously defensive it is also true, and it is the answer to some shallow yet not uncommon criticisms of Schopenhauer.

Just as compassionate behaviour is to be explained in terms of the nature of the noumenon and our intuitions of it, so egoistical behaviour is to be explained in terms of the nature of the phenomenal world, and of our knowledge of that. The egoism of humans 'is due ultimately to the fact that everyone is given to himself *directly*, but the rest are given to him *indirectly* through the representation of them in his head; and the directness asserts its right. Thus in consequence of the subjectivity essential to every consciousness, everyone is himself the whole world, for everything objective exists only indirectly, as mere representation of the subject, so that everything is always closely associated with self-consciousness. The only world everyone is actually acquainted with and knows is carried about by him in his head as his representation, and he is thus the centre of the world. Accordingly, everyone is all in all to himself; he finds himself to be the holder and possessor of all reality, and nothing can be more important to him than his own self. Now while in his own subjective view a man's own self assumes these colossal proportions, in the objective view it shrinks to almost nothing, to a thousand millionth part of the present human race. Now he knows with absolute certainty that this supremely important self, this microcosm,

<hr>

[12] *The World as Will and Representation*, i. 368.   [13] Ibid. i. 370.   [14] Ibid. i. 383.

whose mere modification or accident appears as the macrocosm — thus the entire world of this self — must disappear in death, which for him is equivalent to the end of the world. These, then, are the elements out of which, on the basis of the will-to-live, egoism grows, and always lies like a broad trench between one man and another. If anyone actually jumps over to help another, it is like a miracle that excites astonishment and wins approval.'[15]

It might be said that in so far as our behaviour is moral we are intuiting a reality which, expressed in terms of concepts, is some form of transcendental idealism, whereas in so far as our behaviour is egoistical we are acting on the presuppositions of transcendental realism. In the latter case we are behaving as if this world and this life are all there is, and as if the gap between us and other people is fundamental and permanent — indeed, as if the whole distinction between 'I' and 'everything that is not I' is fundamental and permanent. We live as if detached from the noumenal, enclosed completely in the world of phenomena, and thus we live wholly in the world of the fleeting and the illusory. To the person with no sense of the noumenal at all, and therefore no compassion, other people are nothing but objects in his world. He regards them as obstacles, or disregards them, or makes use of them, or rides roughshod over them, without any intuition that in their inmost being they and he are one. What is thus exhibited in morally bad behaviour is the will at war with itself. 'We see this everywhere before our eyes, in small things as in great. At one time we see it from its dreadful side in the lives of great tyrants and evildoers, and in world-devastating wars. On another occasion we see its ludicrous side, where it is the theme of comedy, and shows itself particularly in self-conceit and vanity. La Rochefoucauld understood this better than anyone else, and presented it in the abstract. We see it in the history of the world and in our own experience. But it appears most distinctly as soon as any mob is released from all law and order; we then see at once in the most distinct form the *bellum omnium contra omnes* which Hobbes admirably described in the first chapter of his *De Cive*. We see not only how everyone tries to snatch from another what he himself wants, but how one often even destroys another's whole happiness or life in order to increase by an insignificant amount his own well-being. This is the highest expression of egoism, the phenomena of which in this respect are surpassed only by those of real wickedness that seeks, quite disinterestedly, the pain and injury of others without any advantage to itself.'[16]

[15] *On the Basis of Morality*, pp. 132–3.
[16] *The World as Will and Representation*, i. 333.

What Schopenhauer here calls 'real wickedness' is explained by him in the following way. We have seen how willing is inherently bound to cause unhappiness because, being without any ultimate aim or goal, it is unsatisfiable — furthermore it expresses itself in longings and yearnings, thirsts, hungers, lusts, needs, and so on whose objects are of necessity ephemeral, and therefore not permanently satisfying — and how, in any case, as soon as an object of desire is actually attained, it is replaced immediately by another. The result of all this can only be an increasing sense of impotence or failure, with a concomitant build-up of such tensions as frustration, disappointment and disillusionment. The really bad man, being full of self-will, is on the rack with all this. Now all of us, even the good, find that the sight of others' misfortunes — whether we view them with pity or satisfaction, or any reaction in between — lessens our awareness of our own, unless we meet it with a literally psychopathic indifference. Indeed, the sight of somebody greatly worse off than ourselves makes us feel easier with our own lot *however bad that may be*. So the bad man injures others in order, literally, to make himself feel better. It may be simply *to make himself felt*, and thus lessen his sense of his own unimportance; but he may also inflict terrible torments on another in order to enable himself to forget his own, or to escape from his own emptiness, in which case the pain of the other, because it uplifts him, becomes an end which he seeks.

Having completed our description of Schopenhauer's three general forms of motivation, I think this is probably the best point at which to give an outline of his political philosophy, so as to exhibit most clearly its connection with his moral philosophy. It has to be said that although his outline of a political philosophy is complete and coherent, it is brief, and he seldom refers to it again. Thus it sits almost separately in his work, and for that reason it may also seem to do so in this chapter. However, there was nothing in the least detached about Schopenhauer's personal relationship to his political views: he held them with passionate conviction, and acted on them whenever it was appropriate to do so.

Schopenhauer's analysis of the use of the basic moral terms 'good' and 'bad' makes it clear throughout why, whether they are applied to actions or to people, what they describe is *motivation*. Therefore it is to the agent that we always look for the criteria governing their use. In the case of the secondary terms 'right' and 'wrong', however, matters are otherwise. The criteria governing the use of the term 'wrong' are found on examination to be located not in the agent but at the receiving end of his action. Since there is no evident reason why a person should not behave as he wishes provided he does no harm to anyone else, I do him a wrong if I force my will on him when he would otherwise follow his own. I may do this by *force majeure* or by misleading him: in either case it is wrong. Further analysis leads us to the conclusion that 'right' is to be defined in terms of 'wrong': I have a right to do anything that is not wrong. This is in the logic of the situation, and therefore such right could be said to be 'natural right' in that it is not defined in terms of any man-made set of arrangements, still less conferred on me by any social agency. However, social institutions will quite certainly be necessary to preserve it against people or groups who are stronger than I. This is why governments and laws come into existence, or at least it is how their existence is to be justified. They do not confer rights: they are evolved to defend already existing rights. So, in sum, we have on the one hand private morality, whose chief concern is with motives, whose basic categories are 'good' and 'bad', and whose ideal aim is that everyone shall do good, which is to say behave compassionately; and on the other hand we have public or social morality, embodied above all in the law, whose chief concern is not with the motives of an action but with its public consequences, whose basic categories are 'rights' and 'wrongs', and whose ideal aim is that no one should suffer wrong.

The chief wrongs that can be done to an individual are interference with his person, interference with his property, and the breaking of agreements with him. Accordingly, the most important rights for governments and laws to uphold are those involving the safety and liberty of the person, the protection of property, and the keeping of contracts. Schopenhauer sees the rights of property as deriving ultimately from labour: if a man applies his labour to something not stolen from another he has the right to the undisturbed use of the result, provided he does not use it to do wrong. If he then wishes to give what is his to another, whether as an outright gift or in exchange for something else, he must be free to do so provided the other person is willing to accept the gift or supply the exchange. Thus if in a primitive society a man fences off land which is not taken from anyone else, and cultivates it, others do him a wrong if they even so much as trample over it. But if he catches fish or hunts wild animals on land belonging to no one, then although he has a right to everything he catches he has no rights over the land itself, since he has applied no labour to its improvement. If he builds a house on land and with materials which are not stolen he has a right to live in it unmolested; and if he then wants to exchange it for another that has been acquired in a similar way he should be free to do so. Similarly, he should be free to give his house away or sell it. Obviously, up to a certain primitive stage in the development of a society most of the property will have been acquired directly by labour, but, after that, most of it will have been acquired by gift — inheritance in most cases — or purchase, or agreements of one kind or another between individuals and groups. Schopenhauer therefore attaches especial importance to the sanctity of contracts, because any form of civilized social life is possible only if agreements are kept. To put the same point in another way: in the last resort, social questions can be settled in one of only two ways, either by force or by agreement; so if agreements are not kept, this compels their settlement by force. Thus the breaking of agreements is the worst, because the most disruptive, of crimes against society.

This brings us naturally to the question of the criminal code. The purpose of the law, as we have seen, is to protect people's rights, and this is equivalent to the prevention of wrongdoing. But from Schopenhauer's doctrines about the freedom of the will it follows that citizens do not choose whether or not to choose to obey the law, any more than they choose whether or not to choose to do anything else — in this as in every other matter they choose whatever they are most strongly motivated to choose. The purpose of the criminal code, therefore, is to see to it, as far as is possible, that they are more strongly motivated to keep the law than to break it. This is achieved by unfailingly meting out unpleasant punishments to whoever is caught breaking the law. 'A criminal code is nothing but a list of counter-motives to criminal actions.'[17] Seen in this light, punishment is essential, and the State must not only have the power to punish but must use it. However, since the *raison d'être* of punishment is deterrence and not retribution the most effective punishments are those which appear worse in prospect than they are in experience (by contrast with, say, solitary confinement, which is much more terrible than people who have not experienced it suppose, and is therefore defective as a punishment, because uneconomical as a deterrent).

Altogether, Schopenhauer sees the State as possessing three functions: first, protection directed outwards, that is to say protection of the society as a whole, not only against other societies but against natural catastrophes and the ravages of nature; second, protection directed inwards, that is to say protection of the individual citizens against the infringement of their rights by each other; and third, protection against the protectors, inasmuch as the very conferring of enough power on any selection of citizens to accomplish the first two of these aims automatically makes them a potential danger to the other citizens. This last threat is best contained, thinks Schopenhauer, by a division of powers, such that the executive, the legislature and the judiciary operate independently of each other. But presiding over all, as a kind of unifying figurehead, there should be a hereditary monarch. Some such parent-

---

[17] *Essay on the Freedom of the Will*, p. 101.

figure is required because human beings are so constituted that they want a leader whom they can identify as an individual; and there are special advantages to making him a hereditary monarch. He is scarcely likely to be motivated by the pursuit of wealth, status or power if he has a superabundance of all three. He will want to secure the well-being of his family, and an honourable succession for his heirs, but the only way he will be able to do this will be to preserve the welfare of the Sate. In such circumstances the interests of a country and of its ruling family become identical. So in Schopenhauer's view the ideal form of government is a constitutional monarchy that governs with the consent of the citizens and whose aim is the protection of their rights and freedoms. For a State to attempt more than this is wrong, for by definition any State activity in excess of this will infringe the citizens' own rights. Schopenhauer is particularly opposed to any idea of a moralizing State which lays down the life-path of its citizens. Above all he is against the personification of the State. 'Nations are in reality mere abstractions; only individuals actually exist.'[18] (These last two perversions were being publicly propounded with great *éclat* by Fichte and Hegel during Schopenhauer's young manhood, and this is among his many reasons for regarding those two philosophers as serious dangers to the public.)

If, having completed our sketch of Schopenhauer's political philosophy, we now return to his moral philosophy, we are reminded that one of its most remarkable features, which comes out all the more strongly by way of contrast to the political philosophy, is that it is so insistently descriptive. It describes, at a high level of generality, how people do in fact behave, and why they behave in the different ways they do, and how those ways are appraised in language. It does not itself appraise very much, commend or condemn, command or forbid. It has no room for 'ought'. (A clear distinction must be kept in mind between approval and any implication of 'ought': in the view of most of us, many an action is highly commendable which the agent was under no obligation to perform, and indeed the very fact that there was no obligation increases the praiseworthiness.) Many readers might be tempted to say that in that case it is not moral in the normal sense of the word — to which Schopenhauer would no doubt reply that indeed it is not, for the normal sense of the word rests on presuppositions whose erroneousness he has exposed, and it needs to be abandoned. He believes there is no place for commendation, blame or 'ought' because we do not exercise significant freedom of moral choice in our behaviour. There are two great reasons why this is so. One has been mentioned repeatedly — that in so far as our actions are not due to the functions of

---

[18] *The World as Will and Representation*, ii. 591.

our autonomic nervous system, to which no one would dream of attaching moral labels, they are motivated; we cannot choose which motives will weigh with us or how they will weigh, yet we are bound to act in accordance with what emerges on balance as the strongest motive. The other has not yet been touched on.

It is based on the Kantian insight that what is possible for us is determined by the way we are constructed. This must be true of everything from a pebble to an elephant — a pebble cannot learn to filch buns from my pocket, nor can a child play ducks and drakes with an elephant. The possibilities of activity or use which are open to anything are exceedingly constricted, and, in the case of everything from an atom to a galaxy, what these are is determined by what it *is*. In the Latin terminology beloved of Schopenhauer, our *posse* is determined by our *esse*. Now it is impossible for anything to be at all without being *something* — yet what that something is at once predetermines the complete range of possibilities open to it. This is why Schopenhauer mocks with such scorn the Judaeo–Christian idea that a God made us and gave us free will. It is, he says, self-contradictory. If human beings are entirely, through and through, the creation of some other personal will, then their scope and limits and all their proclivities and propensities, indeed their every possibility, have been shaped by that Other in ways that determine their entire nature and world. So tightly and narrowly is our range pre-set that each individual human being is not free even to choose what sort of a human being he is to be. I cannot choose to be a great composer or a safe driver or even a passable sprinter; I cannot choose to be an African Negro or a Victorian Englishman; I cannot even choose to be two inches taller than I am, or freckled. I am what I am in a way that rules out nearly all human possibilities from the beginning and leaves to me only a tiny remainder; indeed, in Schopenhauer's view it leaves me no remainder at all.

If we could choose what to *be*, there would be a freedom worth the having. Schopenhauer toys with this idea — which is not, of course, unique to him: variants of it are to be found in a number of Eastern religions. The basic notion is that in the emergence of each of us from the purely noumenal into the world of phenomena we take our present identity on ourselves. It fits flush with Schopenhauer's philosophy on all sides at once. First, it goes hand in hand with his philosophy's requirement of a totally uncaused and inexplicable — and, therefore, in the fullest sense of the word, 'free' — incursion of the noumenon into the phenomenon; indeed, it is that incursion. Second, by locating a free act of the will at that juncture he allows himself after all to admit the vocabulary of praise and blame — but applied to what people are, not to what they do. He argues persuasively that in real life this is mostly how we do in fact use these terms: our commendations or condemnations are largely of people and their characters — a loyal friend, a reliable colleague, a generous opponent, an open-hearted benefactor, an entertaining companion, a brave soldier, an honest business man, a devoted husband, a long-suffering wife, an attentive son, and all the rest of it. We praise or blame them for what they *are*, and when we refer our adjectives to their actions or motives this is usually just a shorthand way of praising people and making it clear why we are doing so. In fact we often transfer the evaluation of an act to that of the person straight away: 'I didn't know you were so generous'; 'I always said she was shrewd'; 'I had no idea he was such a coward'; and so on, the assumption being always that a person's moral character just is whatever it is, and that his individual actions do no more than uncover this, so that moral evaluation applies properly to the person rather than to the action.

Schopenhauer enjoys ringing the changes on the Judaeo–Christian view that our *esse* is determined while our *posse* is free: no, he says, on the contrary, it is our *esse* that is free and our *posse* that is determined. And according to his whole philosophy this must be so, as for him it is only in this sense that there could be free will. If what we *are* is embodiment of will, then any question about freedom of the will must be ultimately a question about the antecedents of the self. He is also, I think, half aware that to have outlawed altogether the vocabulary of commendation and blame would have been strained and implausible, descriptively false, and impossible to adhere to in practice; so I suspect that he is relieved to be let off that hook. Third, it admits universal justice into the order of things, since everything that happens to everybody does so as a consequence of his own choice. Fourth, like his explanation of moral behaviour in terms of empathy, it embraces the fundamental Kantian insight that the moral is located at what one might call the interface between the phenomenal and the noumenal. In sum, the notion that we have in some intelligible sense chosen to be what we are would meet all the main requirements of Schopenhauer's philosophy. Unfortunately it cannot be coherently formulated, or so it seems to me.

Outside the phenomenal world, as Schopenhauer elsewhere always insists, we have no grounds for believing that there is anything other than the noumenon, one and undifferentiated, existing equally in everything independently of time and space. What is it, then, that can be said to have chosen to be me? Not I, certainly. It could only possibly be the noumenon, for there *is* nothing else apart from it and that phenomenal world as which it manifests itself. So even if we pass over the unintelligibility of the notion of the noumenon's 'choosing', we are presumably now in the position of having to apply our adjectives of praise and blame to the noumenon. And leaving aside the unintelligibility of *that*, it is certainly not the same thing as applying them to *me*, and thus holding me responsible for myself. As John Hospers has put it in an argument which was advanced without reference to Schopenhauer: 'What would it be like to be the cause of my own character? To cause my original make-up, I must first have existed, and to exist I must already *have* some "original make-up". I can't cause myself unless I'm already there to do the causing. And if I already existed, then it wouldn't be my original make-up I was creating or choosing, and then where did I get the features or make-up which led me to choose the make-up which I chose? To choose a character, we must already *have* a character. Being the cause of our own original make-up is, we see, a self-contradictory notion.'[19]

Schopenhauer must have realized that this argument could not be driven home, for at this point in his philosophy he begins to toy with incompatible ideas. Alongside the one we have just considered he entertains metempsychosis, and in two or three passages he actually writes as if he believes in the Hindu version of it, according to which in each of our lives we expiate the misdeeds of our previous life. But then, suddenly, he disclaims it. I fear it could no more be coherently formulated within the framework of his philosophy than could the notion that we choose our own characters. What certainly *does* follow from his general philosophy, however, and indeed is necessitated by it — above all by his view that the principle of sufficient reason, the all-unifying connecting tissue of the phenomenal world, can have no purchase outside it — is the view that the entry of the noumenon into phenomena must be uncaused and of its nature inexplicable. Why the noumenal, rather than nothing, exists; why, existing, it manifests itself also in non-noumenal forms; why, being undifferentiated, it manifests itself in a world of almost infinitely differentiated phenomena; and why it manifests itself in *these* phenomena — these are all questions which it is impossible to ask, in the sense that nothing whatever could be an answer to them. Therefore why the world is as it is is unsusceptible of explanation. And this must apply to the existence of human beings along with all other phenomena. Our incursion into the phenomenal world must be uncaused. It must therefore be a 'free', in the sense of spontaneous, act of the will, an inherently unexplainable manifestation of the noumenon. With us, therefore, as with the world in general, although the question 'Where did we come from?' can be answered by saying 'We are manifestations of the noumenon in the world of phenomena', and the question 'What then is the noumenon?' by saying 'It

[19] John Hospers: *Human Conduct: an Introduction to the Problems of Ethics*, p. 516.

is "will" in the third of Schopenhauer's three senses', the question 'Why are we here?' is not one that has an answer.

All we can say is that when we are conceived the noumenal enters into the phenomenon that is us, and the phenomenon that is us ceases to exist when we die. This makes conception and death, which are the temporal poles of our phenomenal existence, the twin points of our emergence from, and return to, the purely noumenal. As such they cry out for the most searching philosophical consideration. It has been common for philosophers to discuss death but not conception — though, as Schopenhauer points out, the latter is every bit as mysterious and, to say the least of it, important to us as the former. His enquiry into it leads him into a discussion of sex. It is astonishing that he is the only one of the great philosophers to see clearly the metaphysical centrality of sex as the means whereby individuals come into existence, and to discuss it from that point of view. In the period when he was writing, it was exceedingly difficult to talk about sex publicly in a candid, unaffected manner, yet somehow he managed to do it. As he says in his own defence, 'we should be surprised that a matter that generally plays so important a part in the life of man has hitherto been almost entirely ignored by philosophers, and lies before us as a raw and untreated material. It is Plato who has been most concerned with it, especially in the *Symposium* and *Phaedrus*; yet what he says about it is confined to the sphere of myths, fables, and jokes, and for the most part concerns only the Greek love of boys. The little that Rousseau says about our theme in the *Discours sur l'inégalité* (p. 96, ed. Bip.) is false and inadequate. Kant's discussion of the subject in the third section of the essay *On the Feeling of the Beautiful and the Sublime* (pp. 435 *seq.* of Rosenkranz's edition) is very superficial and without specific knowledge, and in consequence also partly incorrect. Finally, Platner's treatment of the subject in his *Anthropologie*, §§ 1347 *seq.*, will be found dull and shallow by everyone. Spinoza's definition, on the other hand, deserves to be mentioned for the sake of amusement, on account of its excessive naïvety: "Love is a titillation accompanied by the notion of an external cause" (*Ethics, iv, Prop. 44, dem*). Accordingly, I have no predecessors either to make use of or to refute; the subject has forced itself on me objectively, and has become connected of its own accord with my consideration of the world.'[20] Our discussion of Schopenhauer's treatment of sex will fall most clearly into place if we position it after our treatment of the two more familiar topics of the relationship to the world of an individual who is already in it, and what happens to such a person when he dies.

[20] *The World as Will and Representation*, ii. 532–3.

Two hundred years ago most of the natural world must have been very much as it is now — the two great polar ice caps and all the land and water in between, the jungles teeming with life, the oceans brimming with fish, the vast deserts, the lakes and rivers, the mountains, hills and valleys, the meadows, the prairies, the bush, the forests with their numberless species of plant, animal, insect and bird, the same species as now, all living in minutest detail through the same life cycles as they now pass through. Yet scarcely a single plant or creature that was alive then is alive today, and scarcely a plant or creature that is alive today will be alive two hundred years from now. At each of these points in time there is the same picture, yet all the actual elements that go to make up the picture are different — thousands of them cease to exist in every moment, and in every moment thousands of others are coming into being. The relative stability of the world is like the rainbow that arches a waterfall. The rainbow is made up of numberless drops of water, none of which are in it for more than a fraction of a second; the water is tumbling, roaring, foaming, splashing, spraying in endless and unceasing turmoil, while the rainbow stands there in clear-cut immobility and silence like something of a different order. Yet it is made up *only* of the flashing and flying drops, and nothing else. Schopenhauer sees the entire world of ephemeral phenomena as being sustained before us in this way: real, yet with something of the character of a mirage, though in this case we who behold it are also among the elements that compose it. He thinks, too, that something analogous to this is true of human societies: the literature and history of the world make it as clear as can be that below the surface differences that exist between societies, or between different periods of the same society, much the same varieties of people are living out their lives, and much the same varieties of situation are endlessly being re-enacted, whether it be in the affairs of individuals and families, or in the affairs of whole societies, or in conflicts between societies. In the words of the speaker in Ecclesiastes (one of the few books of the Old Testament for which Schopenhauer did not feel contempt): 'What has happened will happen again, and what has been done will be done again, and there is nothing new under the sun.'

However, it is not the case that this fleeting passage of ours through a phenomenal world that we constitute and sustain comprises the whole of our existence. We are noumenal as well as phenomenal. So, trying not to go beyond what can be justified by the arguments supporting his earlier philosophical analysis, Schopenhauer assesses what can be deduced or inferred about the noumenal and our relations to it. We have seen already how it follows from the whole of his philosophy that the part of us that is noumenal, and therefore outside time, is unconscious and impersonal, since the noumenon is undifferentiated, while the personality is bound up with this particular body — its genetic inheritance and its detailed history in place and time — and could therefore not exist as it is independently of this body. Individuality is likewise bound up with this particular consciousness and this particular mind, and they too, as functions of the brain, are bodily functions, and must cease when the body ceases. Of all the things that 'I' am a unique combination of — consciousness, intellect, body, personality, character, will — the will alone in its inner nature is indestructible. All the rest is bound to perish with the body in death.

At bottom the reason why the entire world of experience is felt by us to be in some inherent and essential way superficial is that it is a construction of the understanding, which is itself a function of our ephemeral and highly perishable sensory and intellectual apparatus. In other words it is not the product of what is essential or permanent about *us*, and we have a deep-lying and correct intuition that in our inmost nature we are more permanent than it. The root error that has vitiated the entire tradition of Western philosophical and religious thinking has been the association of the essential kernel of the human being — the soul, or whatever we think of it as — with some aspect of consciousness, with the result that self-awareness of some kind is seen as being what is indestructible about us, if indeed anything is. One very odd thing about this view is that loss of consciousness is already, within this life, a thoroughly familiar experience — in deep, dreamless sleep, or in comas, or nowadays, to a degree unparalleled by anything possible in Schopenhauer's time, in anaesthesia — yet it does not occur to us to regard the continuity of the personality as destroyed by it. Nor, in the case of sleep, do we dread the loss of consciousness involved, in the way we dread death — quite the contrary: when we go to bed we are perhaps afraid of *not* sleeping, but not of sleeping. We know perfectly well that our essential self will persist through sleep as it does through all other intermittent losses of self-awareness. In this practical way, at least, we take it for granted that our essential self is something different from our consciousness. And we are right to do so. For all the reasons given earlier, what is noumenal about us, and therefore what is indestructible about us, is unconscious.

Whatever the indestructible element is, it must be knowledgeless, both because it is unconscious and because knowledge is inherently of the subject–object form — and no such differentiation as that between subject and object, or indeed any other, can obtain in the noumenal. Lying as it does outside time, outside space, outside all possibility of knowledge, it is of a different order of being from anything in the phenomenal world — and therefore it is unconceptualizable by us, since all our concepts either derive from experience or are constitutive of it, and the noumenal is outside all possibility of experience. But although there are no determinate concepts in which it can be spoken about, or thought about, it is nevertheless not nothing. The fact that it cannot be accommodated by any of those phenomena which we call forms of consciousness may mean that for us as phenomenal beings, and in this phenomenal world generally, it can never appear, and is in that sense nothing; but by the same token the fleeting, ephemeral, doomed-to-disintegration things that constitute this space-filled, time-saturated, causally-interconnected world of phenomena can never impinge on a noumenon lying outside time and space, and outside any possibility of connection with anything according to the principle of sufficient reason, and they are therefore to it also nothing. In this contraposition of two relative nothings, the phenomenal world comes off worse, for *everything* in it is ephemeral, whereas the noumenal is timeless and changeless. If only one of the two worlds is to be regarded as '*really* real', it must be the noumenal.

When we as phenomenal beings confront the prospect of death we rightly see it as the inevitable end of what we are, and it therefore presents itself to us as annihilation. And since what we are is embodiment of the very will to live itself, the prospect of annihilation is terrifying and uncomeable-to-terms-with. It is not determinately conceptualizable by us, and yet even the indeterminate apprehension of it strikes dread to the very centre of our nature. This reaction is the costliest to us of all the consequences of the primal error of transcendental realism in which it is rooted. Anyone who really absorbs Kant's doctrine of the ideality of time in all its fullness and depth will be liberated thereby from the fear of death. For if time and space are of subjective origin there cannot be such a thing as a time without a 'now' in it, or a space without a 'here'. Such things can be constructed in concepts — they can be *thought* — but they cannot *be*. Yet the fear of death rests on the assumption that they can — that there can be a world without a subject; that an individual subject can cease and yet his world continue to exist without him, e.g. that the world as I know it will continue to exist after my death but without me in it or beholding it. When the individual tries to relate it to himself, this continuance of his world without a supporting subject presents itself to his mind as a mystery not determinately imaginable, something located on the other side of an unfathomable abyss. This is due partly to the fact that, for all the reasons given in Chapter 5, it cannot occur. But it is also due to the fact that what he is trying to relate to the presence or absence of a subject is the notion of a time which is objective, and yet constructed (and constructable solely) in terms of concepts — and that is a self-contradiction. Of course, one's mistaken realistic assumptions cause one to interpret the ungraspability of the notion of one's world continuing after one's death as being due to one's own egoism and dread. But all the arguments set forth earlier in this book about the mutual indispensability of subject and object entail the quite different conclusion that, so far as anything that is intelligible to us is concerned, the cessation of our awareness of the world is correlative with the cessation of the world of which we are aware. Indeed, the two are the same thing described in different language. 'It is all one whether we say "Sensibility and understanding are no more" or "The world is at an end".'[21]

The fact that there cannot be a time without a 'now' in it means that wherever there is a time there must always be a now, and this must mean that wherever there is a time it always *is* now. In other words, there is a continuous present, and this is the only time that ever actually exists.[22] This accords with the familiar fact that past and future exist

[21] *The Fourfold Root of the Principle of Sufficient Reason*, p. 210.

[22] Given this view, plus his doctrine on the freedom of the will, Schopenhauer is called immediately to mind by the opening lines of T. S. Eliot's *Burnt Norton*:

> Time present and time past
> Are both perhaps present in time future
> And time future contained in time past.
> If all time is eternally present
> All time is unredeemable.
> What might have been is an abstraction
> Remaining a perpetual possibility
> Only in a world of speculation.
> What might have been and what has been
> Point to one end, which is always present.

Schopenhauer is also called to mind by later passages, for instance:

> Words move, music moves
> Only in time; but that which is only living
> Can only die. Words, after speech, reach
> Into the silence. Only by the form, the pattern,
> Can words or music reach
> The stillness, as a Chinese jar still
> Moves perpetually in its stillness.
> Not the stillness of the violin, while the note lasts,
> Not that only, but the co-existence,
> Or say that the end precedes the beginning,
> And the beginning and the end were always there
> Before the beginning and after the end.
> And all is always now.

Documentary evidence that Eliot had studied Schopenhauer is contained in the book *Josiah Royce's Seminar, 1913–1914* by Harry T. Costello, Rutgers University Press, 1963. The seminar in question was a post-graduate seminar in philosophy at Harvard, and Eliot was one of the hard core of 9 regular attenders. Royce's whole thought was 'strongly influenced by the critical philosophy of Kant as well as by the post-Kantian

always only in concepts and never actually are, whereas the experiences from which those or any other concepts are derived can have their being only in a present. From this it follows — and it is essential that this point be clearly grasped — that the present is the form of all existence. The noumenal will, or the will to live, manifests itself in the world of phenomena not as free-floating abstract concepts but as material objects and active forces, and these are perceptual only: abstract concepts can be formed from them by human minds and then related to the future or to the past, but the phenomena themselves, being not abstract, can exist in a present only. The lack of a present to anything actually existing is impossible. So reality, as such, exists always and only in a now: *actually* there never is anything else. Schopenhauer drives this point home with the phrase 'only in the present are there real objects'.[23] Our language, with tenses built into its most elementary structure, and adverbs and prepositions with temporal implications among its simplest, most common words, is so time-imbued that it is difficult to express this thought without its sounding mystical or paradoxical or (paradoxically) tautologous, but it is none of these things. It is, I believe, significantly true, but it is difficult to convey. It is not original to Schopenhauer. He quotes St. Augustine and the medieval schoolmen as being familiar with it. The latter dubbed the continuous present the *nunc stans*, and asserted that we share the same *nunc stans* with Adam.

This means that we cannot fall out of time, as the realist supposes us to do when we die. The idea that we can is likened by Schopenhauer to childish misapprehensions about space. When a European child first learns that the world is a giant ball, and that Australia is on the other side of it, he commonly imagines the Australians to be walking about upside-down, hanging from the world by their feet like flies from a ceiling, and is puzzled that they do not drop off into space. If he is imaginative he may also wonder why he himself, if he is perched on top of a giant ball, does not slide down the side of it. His puzzlement can be partly removed by gravity's being explained to him, but only partly: such a young child will almost certainly be unable to grasp the point that it has no meaning to talk of an 'up' or a 'down' which is not relative to a subject, so that in a universe thought of as being without an observer there could be no 'up' or 'down' at all. His puzzlement about

philosophy of will in its development by Fichte and Schopenhauer' (p. xiii). Schopenhauer was given to the seminar as a reading assignment (p. 118) and discussed by it (p. 120). However, Eliot later studied similar doctrines about time from other sources, and Schopenhauer's influence was much diluted, but it did not vanish. See p. 389.

[23] *The World as Will and Representation*, i. 279.

space, like an adult's bafflement about time, would spring from regarding a particular state of affairs as objectively existing when in fact it can have being and significance only for a subject. Our minds seem to be constructed in such a way that in both cases it borders on the inconceivable not just that the states of affairs in question should not *be able* to exist independently of us but that they do not *in fact* exist independently of us. Yet so it is. The top of the giant ball is quite simply wherever one is, and separately from that there can be no 'top'. Similarly, 'now' is whenever one is, and separately from that there can be no 'now'.

What happens, then, when we die? 'With death consciousness is certainly lost, but not what produced and maintained consciousness.'[24] I shall cease, but not everything constitutive of my being will cease. The only phenomenal world I know will cease with me, but not everything constitutive of it will cease with my phenomenal self. I might be tempted to say that after I am dead I shall be again what I was before I was born, and that this is not nothing, although no concepts can exist to say what it is. But here the 'again' is misleading, though the rest, according to Schopenhauer, must be true. For if what is noumenal about me is outside time and space, and therefore outside any possibility of change, the reality of it must be as actual 'now' as 'at any other time'. The indestructible part of me must be, changelessly, the same at this moment as I sit here writing this sentence as it will be after my death, and as it was before I was born. It is true that I entered the phenomenal world only when I was conceived, and will fall out of it (or it will fall out of me) when I die, but it cannot be the case that only after I die do I become one with the rest of noumenal reality: I must be one with it now — and it must be impossible for me *ever* to fall out of *that* situation. 'On the other hand, the condition into which death returns us is our original state, that is, the one peculiar to our true nature whose primary force manifests itself in the production and maintenance of the life that is now ceasing. Thus it is the condition or state of the thing-in-itself in contrast to the phenomenon. Now in this original state, such an expedient as cerebral knowledge, as being extremely mediate and therefore furnishing mere phenomena, is without doubt entirely superfluous; and so we lose it. Its disappearance is identical with the cessation for us of the phenomenal world, whose mere medium it was, and it can serve no other purpose. If in this original state of ours the retention of that animal consciousness were even offered to us, we should reject it, just as a lame man who had been cured would scorn to use crutches. Therefore whoever deplores the impending loss of this cerebral consciousness that is merely phenomenal and adapted to the phenomenal

[24] *The World as Will and Representation*, ii. 496.

is comparable to the converted Greenlanders who did not want to go to heaven when they heard that there were no seals there.'[25]

Immediately after this passage Schopenhauer goes on to tout the possibility that some kind of awareness might be possible which is not individual — some kind of self-awareness on the part of the undifferentiated noumenon, which would therefore have to be not a brain function but something transcending the subject–object distinction along with everything else to do with the phenomenal world. This is in accordance with his earlier conclusion, quoted on p. 141, 'that the thing-in-itself . . . may have, entirely outside all possible phenomenon, determinations, qualities, and modes of existence which for us are absolutely unknowable and incomprehensible'. However, since on his own clearly-stated admission any further speculation about it would transgress the bounds of intelligibility, he does not pursue it.

Against this background, let us now turn to Schopenhauer's discussion of procreation. In each of the two highest grades of the will's objectification in the world of phenomena, individuals are brought into existence by acts of sexual intercourse. Since this is the very process whereby the will to live achieves life, it is only to be expected that the urge towards it is the most powerful of the will's demands, next only to the brute survival of what already exists. 'The sexual impulse is proved to be the most decided and the strongest affirmation of life by the fact that for man in the natural state, as for the animal, it is his life's final end and highest goal. Self-preservation and maintenance are his first aim, and as soon as he has provided for that, he aims only at the propagation of the race.'[26] . . . 'Sexual desire bears a character very different from that of any other; it is not only the strongest of desires, but is even specifically of a more powerful kind than all the others are. It is everywhere tacitly assumed as necessary and inevitable, and is not, like other desires, a matter of taste and caprice. For it is the desire that constitutes even the very nature of man. In conflict with it, no motive is so strong as to be certain of victory. It is so very much the chief thing that no other pleasures make up for the deprivation of its satisfaction; for its sake, moreover, animal and man undertake every peril and conflict.'[27] The remark there about sexual desire constituting the very nature of man is unpacked in the paragraph following. 'Indeed, it may be said that man is concrete sexual impulse, for his origin is an act of copulation, and the desire of his desires is an act of copulation, and this impulse alone perpetuates . . . his phenomenal appearance.'[28]

Schopenhauer anticipated Freud as clearly about the omnipresence

[25] *Parerga and Paralipomena*, ii. 274.
[26] *The World as Will and Representation*, i. 329.
[27] Ibid. ii. 514.   [28] Ibid.

of sexual motivation as he did about the existence and character of the unconscious. In addition to the three passages just cited there are, for instance, the following. 'The role played by the sex-relation in the world of mankind . . . is really the invisible central point of all action and conduct, and peeps up everywhere, in spite of all the veils thrown over it . . . This, however, is the piquant element and the jest of the world, that the principal concern of all men is pursued secretly, and ostensibly ignored as much as possible.'[29] 'It is the great Unspeakable, the public secret which must never be distinctly mentioned anywhere, but is always and everywhere understood to be the main thing as a matter of course, and is therefore always present in the minds of all. For this reason, even the slightest allusion to it is instantly understood. The principal role played in the world by this act and by what is connected with it — because everywhere love intrigues are pursued on the one hand and assumed on the other — is quite in keeping with the importance of this *punctum saliens* of the world-egg.'[30]

The reason why Schopenhauer does not believe that this almost universal preoccupation with sex is disproportionate is that what is at stake is nothing less than the constitution of the entire human race throughout all future time — and in the most concrete and particular terms, namely the determination of the individuals who shall comprise it. For the fact is that any given individual can be the offspring of two given parents only, and not of any other couple. So the couplings of parents determine not just that the world shall be peopled but specifically by whom it shall be peopled. This is far and away the most important thing that most of them do in the course of their lives. So the intensity and liveliness of the interest they take in it is no more than proportionate to what is involved. This is not to say that the sexual acts of individuals are motivated by a concern for future generations: that would be an absurd proposition. The medium for such conscious motivation, as for any other, would be the mind, and mind, as we have seen, is tertiary, whereas in sexual matters more than any others people are driven by the will, which is primary and unconscious.

In this context it becomes easy for Schopenhauer to explain the phenomenon of falling in love — or rather, it becomes a straightforward matter for him to give an explanation of why it cannot be explained. Human beings have always been struck by the blindness and irrationality of it. Words like 'madness', 'folly', and so on have always been attached to it. Freud called it 'the psychosis of normal people'. The explanation, says Schopenhauer, is that sexual love is the agency whereby the noumenal enters the world of phenomena, and this

[29] *The World as Will and Representation*, ii. 513.   [30] Ibid. ii. 571.

incursion, as has already been shown, cannot, of its nature, be susceptible of explanation; that is to say, it is not and cannot be subject to the
principle of sufficient reason. Why the will manifests itself in the form of
the particular phenomena it does, and not others, is, as we have seen,
not a question to which there can be an answer. So — given that, with
each and every one of those phenomena which are human beings, it is
the case that for this particular individual to exist, those and only those
two other individuals must have copulated — the inexplicability of a
particular couple's copulation is part and parcel of the inexplicability
of the incursion into the world of any given individual. 'It is the future
generation in the whole of its individual definiteness which is pressing
into existence by means of these efforts and exertions. In fact, it is itself
already astir in that far-sighted, definite, and capricious selection for
the satisfaction of the sexual impulse which is called love. The growing
attachment of two lovers is in itself in reality the will-to-live of the new
individual . . . The quite special and individual passion of two lovers is
just as inexplicable as is the quite special individuality of any person,
which is exclusively peculiar to him; indeed at bottom the two are one
and the same.'[31]

In his speculative attempts to push investigation further back still,
beyond this point, Schopenhauer throws out various incompatible
ideas, but we have already touched on these: the idea that we chose —
pre-phenomenally, as it were — to be who we are, and are therefore
metaphysically responsible for whatever that is; and the idea of
metempsychosis, sometimes in its Hindu version and sometimes not;
and the idea that an unfathomable abyss which is uncrossable in this
life stands between us and any possible understanding of it all, so that
this side of death we can neither form nor comprehend any accurate
account of it; and the quite different idea that it is genuinely random
and inexplicable to the very bottom, *free* in the fullest imaginable sense
of that word, and therefore inherently, through-and-through un-
understandable in any life. Altogether, then, he follows the same procedure in his discussion of procreation as he does in his discussion of
death: he first of all pursues his enquiry by means of argument up to
what he regards as the limits of what can be rationally inferred; then,
stating clearly at that point that what, if anything, lies beyond it is
unknowable by us, he throws out a few speculations about what it
might nevertheless be; and then changes the subject. It does him the
crudest possible injustice, I think, to treat these speculations of his as
being offered to us on the same footing as his serious arguments.

Having said what can be said in explanation of procreation and

<hr>

[31] *The World as Will and Representation*, ii. 536.

death, what of the life whose beginning and end they are? The central feature of it can perhaps be characterized as follows. The human individual is the embodiment of the will to live; this will is a blind, aimless, unassuageable striving; therefore the individual is predestined by his nature to dissatisfaction, disappointment, frustration — not to mention pain and, in the end, the destruction of the very life that is willed. Therefore an essentially tragic course is programmed into us from the beginning; it is in the nature of what we are. 'Suffering is essential to life, and therefore does not flow in upon us from outside, but everyone carries around within himself its perennial source.'[32] Another reason why we are doomed by our nature to suffering is that our pleasures are not positive, but are merely relief from something else that is itself unpleasant, and it is only the unpleasant that is positive. 'The reason for this is that pain, suffering that includes all want, privation, need, in fact every wish or desire, is *that which is positive and directly felt and experienced*. On the other hand, the nature of satisfaction, enjoyment, and happiness consists solely in the removal of a privation, the stilling of a pain; and so these have a *negative* effect. Therefore, need and desire are the condition of every pleasure or enjoyment. Plato recognized this . . . Voltaire also says: "There are no true pleasures without true needs." Thus pain is something *positive* that automatically makes itself known; satisfaction and pleasures are something *negative*, the mere elimination of the former.'[33] Schopenhauer thinks that his reader may be less inclined to doubt this if he reflects in specific terms that what all gratifications are, across their whole range from a sip of cold water to the contemplation of the Sistine Chapel, is either the reduction of willing or its suspension. And willing is like an unquenchable thirst: we may attain some brief satisfactions, some momentary reliefs, but in the nature of things these can never be more than temporary, and then we are on the rack once more. So unhappiness, or at least dissatisfaction, is our normal state of affairs.

There is a further and devilish twist to this in that if, as so rarely happens anyway, an individual does achieve sustained satisfaction of his wants, the fact that the very essence of his nature is a restless striving means that his only way of being dissolves therewith, and he finds himself confronting an inner emptiness brought about by the absence of the only mode in which he can exist. This state is what Schopenhauer calls 'boredom', and he regards it as very terrible — uncountable numbers of human beings have been destroyed by it in one way or another. It is obvious from the frequency and the feeling,

---

[32] *The World as Will and Representation*, i. 318.
[33] *On the Basis of Morality*, 146.

not to mention the insight, with which he writes of it that he has substantial experience of it himself. This deadly state — 'anomie', 'accidie', 'noia': it has many names — is yet another of the characteristically twentieth-century preoccupations of which Schopenhauer not only writes with prescience but of which he also gives an illuminating explanation. It follows from his view of it that human beings are caught between the Scylla of willing and the Charybdis of boredom — hence, perhaps, the classic formula for keeping the mass of mankind in a state of perpetual appeasement: 'bread and circuses', the former to assuage hunger and the latter to stave off boredom. Most people manage shufflingly to zigzag a life-course between the two only in that 'they will, they know what they will, and they strive after this with enough success to protect them from despair, and enough failure to preserve them from boredom and its consequences'.[34]

As much as we can, we avoid confronting the fact that 'life is deeply steeped in suffering, and cannot escape from it; our entrance to it takes place amid tears, at bottom its course is always tragic, and its end is even more so'.[35] It is only too obvious why we do not wish to face this, but the result of our not facing it is alienation from the realities of our own existence. Most people sleep-walk their way through life without *allowing* themselves to meet, or even in any sustained way to think about, the existential challenges posed by the nature of our existence. A facile, evasive, low-key, unreflecting optimism which is quite at odds with the reality of our situation pervades most human attitudes, and finds its expression in every sphere of activity from domestic life to philosophy. Schopenhauer is incensed by the lie at the centre of this, and by the fact that it gets between us and the living of our lives — and above all by the indifference it displays to human suffering. '*Optimism*, where it is not merely the thoughtless talk of those who harbour nothing but words under their shallow foreheads, seems to me to be not merely an absurd, but also a really *wicked*, way of thinking.'[36] '. . . If we were to conduct the most hardened and callous optimist through hospitals, infirmaries, operating theatres, through prisons, torture chambers, and slave-hovels, over battlefields and to places of execution; if we were to open to him all the dark abodes of misery, where it shuns the gaze of cold curiosity, and finally were to allow him to glance into the dungeon of Ugolino where prisoners starved to death, he too would certainly see in the end what kind of a world is this *meilleur des mondes possibles*. For whence did Dante get the material for his hell, if not from this actual world of ours?'[37]

[34] *The World as Will and Representation*, i. 327.   [35] Ibid. ii. 635–6.
[36] Ibid. i. 526.   [37] Ibid. i. 525.

The *actuality* of human suffering on a global scale was something of which Schopenhauer had a very sharp sense. It was real for him that in every moment millions of human beings were in sore distress. And he had an equally sharp realization that the causes of most of it were man-made.

The chief source of the most serious evils affecting man is man himself; *homo homini lupus*.[38] He who keeps this last fact clearly in view beholds the world as a hell, surpassing that of Dante by the fact that one man must be the devil of another. For this purpose, of course, one is more fitted than another, indeed an archfiend is more fitted than all the rest, and appears in the form of a conqueror; he sets several hundred thousand men facing one another, and exclaims to them: 'To suffer and die is your destiny; now shoot one another with musket and cannon!' and they do so. In general, however, the conduct of men towards one another is characterized as a rule by injustice, extreme unfairness, hardness, and even cruelty; an opposite course of conduct appears only by way of exception. The necessity for the State and for legislation rests on this fact, and not on your shifts and evasions. But in all cases not lying within the reach of the law, we see at once a lack of consideration for his like which is peculiar to man, and springs from his boundless egoism, and sometimes even from wickedness. How man deals with man is seen, for example, in Negro slavery, the ultimate object of which is sugar and coffee. However, we need not go so far; to enter at the age of five a cotton-spinning or other factory, and from then on to sit there every day first ten, then twelve, and finally fourteen hours, and perform the same mechanical work, is to purchase dearly the pleasure of drawing breath. But this is the fate of millions, and many more millions have an analogous fate.

We others, however, can be made perfectly miserable by trifling incidents, but perfectly happy by nothing in the world. Whatever we may say, the happiest moment of the happy man is that of his falling asleep, just as the unhappiest moment of the unhappy man is that of his awakening.[39]

Finding himself, willy-nilly, in a world of which these are a few of the realities, what is the individual to do? Schopenhauer contends that anyone who has *really* absorbed his philosophy, not just intellectually but with his whole personality, will be undeceived thereby about the true nature of the world, and will also understand that his own being in this world of phenomena is no different from that of all the other empty ephemera that constitute it. He will understand the essential nullity and nothingness of his own life. This insight, if grasped really deep down, will liberate him from thraldom to that will to live of which this whole world of illusion is manifestation. By this, Schopenhauer means not that he will commit suicide but that he will achieve a condition in

[38] 'Man is a wolf for man.' (Tr.)
[39] *The World as Will and Representation*, ii. 577–8.

which he is unseduced by willing, undiverted by it, unconcerned, uncorrupted, in other words just simply independent of it. We have encountered this condition already as the one in which great works of art are produced or contemplated. But neither the artist nor his audience can be in this state for more than part of the time, and usually a quite small part of the time. What we are considering now is the possibility of such a state as a permanent condition. As soon as we begin to think about this we realize that we are already familiar with the existence of individuals for whom this is so — for instance, some of the well-known saints and mystics. Whether Christian, Hindu, Buddhist or secular, some of these have lived a life which denied to their own will the most imperious of its demands, for example the demands for food, drink, bodily and mental comfort, sex, worldly goods, and the approbation of others. They have done this and yet been renowned for their indifference to the resultant hardship and misfortune, their serene readiness to accept and suffer all, with malice toward none. These are people who have conquered the self-will in themselves, and achieved in consequence the most enviable of all states of consciousness. It is contended by Schopenhauer that a proper understanding of his philosophy makes what is being done by such people fully comprehensible, and perhaps even attainable.

Suicide, in his view, is not an effective denial of the will to live. On the contrary — anticipating Freud — he sees it as a form of aggression and quite specifically an assertion of self-will. 'Just because the suicide cannot cease willing, he ceases to live.'[40] For the suicide does not reject life as such but only the terms on which it is being offered to him: he is turning away from the pain of it, or the disgrace, or the terror, or the depression, or the boredom — but whatever it is, in most instances it is obvious that if he were given the option of continuing his life without the cause of his distress he would take it. On the other hand the ascetic, the saint, the mystic, is turning away from the 'good' things of life, from its pleasures, and that is something altogether different. Suicide is above all a *mistake*, on at least two counts. First, Schopenhauer believed passionately that the only overriding aim of human life that possesses validity is the achievement of insight (he certainly lived his own life in accordance with that judgement) and furthermore he believed that life has to be lived forwards yet can be understood only backwards. This being so, the suicide, by refusing to go on, abjures the possibility of insight. Most sharply pointed of all, he forgoes the extra possibility of deepening his insight which his very tribulations offer him through their mortification of his will. So suicide is a form of evasion — evasion

[40] *The World as Will and Representation*, i. 399.

of a challenge which is greater than life itself. Second, although the suicide is trying to annihilate himself, the fact is that his true nature is indestructible. So he neither gains what he hopes to gain nor loses what he wants to lose: what is phenomenal about him would have died anyway, and what is noumenal about him cannot cease to exist. To adapt one of Schopenhauer's earlier metaphors, he is like a man who tries to remove the rainbow from a waterfall by scooping out the water with a bucket. However, although suicide is a tragic mistake, Schopenhauer took the view that it was very wrong to treat it, and to treat attempts at it, as a crime (as was generally done in his day). 'The only valid moral reason against suicide . . . lies in the fact that suicide is opposed to the attainment of the highest moral goal, since it substitutes for the real salvation from this world of woe and misery one that is merely apparent. But it is still a very long way from this mistake to a crime . . .'.[41]

Salvation is to be achieved not by the annihilation of our own phenomenon but by the denial of, so to speak, 'our separate noumenon', of our own will. This, as we have seen, is a condition achieved by true mystics, of all religions and of none. Although they may reach it by different paths — in different religions, different societies and different centuries — the things they do on the way have an extraordinary amount in common: the same, or similar, practices of self-isolation and fasting and chastity, the mortification of the flesh; similar meditations based usually on a close study of the most metaphysical doctrines of whatever is their particular religion. The aim of all this, too, is in nearly all cases to grasp the ephemeral and illusory nature, and hence the essential nothingness, of this phenomenal world, and to free the self from its bondage, and the will from its service, and to gain some apprehension of the nature of the noumenal (which in many cases they call 'God'). They even say very similar things about the noumenal: for instance that it is not knowable; that it is one and undifferentiated, and yet exists in and through all apparently separate things; that it lies outside space and time, and yet that the human individual nevertheless is, or can be, 'at one' with it in some ultimate way; that when this state is achieved of a oneness with the noumenal unobscured by the phenomenal, the boundaries of the self disappear altogether; and that this unqualified union with the noumenal is the most desirable of all conditions, notwithstanding the fact that it involves the dissolution of the self. And having said these things, they usually add that there are no further concepts in which anything else about it can be apprehended or expressed. This long list of specific similarities puts it beyond doubt

[41] *Parerga and Paralipomena*, ii. 309.

that what we are considering here are much the same experiences and much the same insights in different people and traditions.

So Schopenhauer is far from believing that it is only his philosophy that can bring people to the desired condition: they can journey towards it through great art, or through one of the major religions, or through a life of natural goodness. He sees it as an obvious fact of experience, for example, that when confronted by their own death, large numbers of perfectly ordinary people achieve a calm suspension of willing that they would not previously have thought possible or even have understood. This does not usually consist of a sudden religious conversion. Indeed, religion is only incidental in all this — even the religion which Schopenhauer admired most of all, Buddhism, which does not postulate the existence of a god at all. Schopenhauer himself did not believe in God. At no point in his philosophy has any need for the hypothesis arisen. Furthermore, the concept itself, in his view, is incoherent. If what is meant is a personal God, he points out that most of the elements that go to make up our concept of personality are derived from attributes which theists specifically say God does not have; and if this is so God cannot be personal in any sense of 'personal' which is intelligible to us. What is clearly at work here, he thinks, is a form of anthropomorphism, the projection by human beings of their own characteristics on to the unknown. But if, on the other hand, what is meant is an *im*personal God, then the term is being used to mislead, for it is being used merely as a substitute for 'X', the unknown, or for 'the noumenon', or 'energy', or 'the world', and yet it smuggles in all sorts of irrelevant and inappropriate religious connotations. (No one could deny that the word 'God' has religious connotations!) In truth, as Schopenhauer says of Spinoza's pantheistic use of it, 'to call the world "God" is not to explain it, but only to enrich the language with a superfluous synonym for the word "world" '.[42] In Schopenhauer's view, it is quite clear that what the profoundest of the mystics meant by 'God' was the noumenal, which they were struggling to understand with a conceptual equipment less adequate than his philosophy provides, though with a personal equipment more impressive and admirable than he had; and, unlike him, they were trying to reach this understanding through living, through moral action, as well as conceptually.

What Schopenhauer regards as his own special contribution is to have developed the central tradition of Western philosophy to the point where it too encompasses these ultimate insights, and does so in a manner proper to philosophy — that is to say, without any reference to

[42] *Parerga and Paralipomena*, ii. 99.

God, or any appeal to religious faith, or to revelation, or any claim to unique personal insight, or to any other form of authority, but expressed throughout in terms of concepts whose formulation has been achieved by rational argument, argument which displays its credentials at every point along the way — and which receives manifold support from, without ever being in contradiction with, the great corpus of our scientific and other knowledge. This has been achieved by carrying forward by one more crucial step the great tradition that runs through Descartes, Locke, Berkeley, Hume and Kant. The giant stride in this progress is not the step between Kant and Schopenhauer but the step between Hume and Kant. This is what makes Kant the greatest single figure in modern philosophy.

Schopenhauer sees his completion of the Kantian–Schopenhauerian philosophy as the apotheosis not merely of his own work but of philosophy as such, for beyond this there is nowhere left to go. He realizes that he has left behind him, as it were, a few problems in his rear, which others after him may come along and clear up. But there is no forward goal left for philosophy to progress towards. This is not because all reality has been filled with explanation, but because the limits of intelligibility have been reached — and in ways, and for reasons, which are themselves understood by us. We keep running up against the necessity of there being something more to things than we know, but what it is we can never apprehend. 'It is indeed an insoluble problem, since even the most perfect philosophy will always contain an unexplained element, like an insoluble precipitate or the remainder that is always left behind by the irrational proportion of two quantities. Therefore, if anyone ventures to raise the question why there is not nothing at all rather than this world, then the world cannot be justified from itself; no ground, no final cause of its existence can be found in itself; it cannot be demonstrated that it exists for its own sake . . .'.[43] In the end the totality of everything, whatever that may be, must be free-floating, inexplicable. It could not be explained by the existence of a God, because if there were a God then he would be part (or all) of that totality, and therefore part (or all) of what it was that required to be explained. Schopenhauer believes that he has explained the world in the only way possible, by unlocking the code that reveals how everything has significance in relation to everything else, and what that significance is. But how the *totality* of it comes to exist — why there is anything at all rather than nothing — is something an explanation of which is inherently and for ever impossible.

[43] *The World as Will and Representation*, ii. 579.

Chapter 10

Some Criticisms and Problems

In the exposition I have given of Schopenhauer's philosophy I have dwelt only on those aspects of it which are required for an understanding of it *as a system*. This may have involved a sacrifice not only of incidental riches but even, beyond a certain point, of the elaboration of some of the main arguments. But my book is intended to be an introduction to Schopenhauer's work, after all, not a substitute for it, and I hope that when the reader has finished with me he will turn to Schopenhauer's own writings. If he does, he will find that they are extensively rich in a way that my book has not indicated, and that whole doctrines of considerable interest have been omitted from my treatment. For instance, I have not so far mentioned Schopenhauer's theory of mental illness. He believed that people became mentally ill because of experiences that are too painful to be faced, so that the sufferer withdraws himself from reality, or blots out certain memories, with the incidental result that the continuity of his sense of self is disrupted. This view of insanity as a defence-mechanism, a form of self-protection, an internal flight from the intolerable — and, as such, something which the sufferer himself actively though unconsciously *does* — was extraordinarily prescient, given subsequent developments in psychology that still lay far in the future.[1] There are many equally striking passages in his works which I have passed over. There are also many passages in which he expresses a clear view on one side, to my mind often the right side, of a controversial issue which is still current: for instance, he argued that language was not constitutive of thought at the most fundamental of all levels, but that thought was in some immediate sense pre-verbal, and that its essential forms must therefore be embodied in the structures of all intelligible languages.[2] Besides omitting mention of most such incidental arguments, I have also failed to give him credit for being correctly dismissive of a number of ortho-

---

[1] See p. 283. In spite of Freud's comment quoted there, it is characteristic of Schopenhauer that his theory was *not* spun out of first principles, but was based on detailed observation. He was a frequent visitor to insane asylums, where he would hold long conversations with the inmates, and go back again and again to talk to those who particularly interested him.

[2] *The World as Will and Representation*, i. 478–80.

doxies in the natural sciences of his day, often long before scientists themselves followed his example: for instance, he was always confident that there was no such thing as aether.

On the other hand, he was wrong about a lot of things which I have also not mentioned. For instance, he was confident that atoms were as fictitious as aether — though, to do him justice, the atomic theory which he rejected was to the effect that any given piece of matter was made up of an infinitely large number of infinitely small — and therefore, because infinitely small, indivisible — particles. He persisted in upholding Goethe's theory of light against Newton's. He firmly believed that we inherit our characters from our fathers and our intellects from our mothers, and he had a good deal to say about the implications of this, though I find on consulting geneticists that there is not a scrap of evidence for any of it. In the case of the first of these examples, the one concerning the existence of atoms, it has to be admitted that the theory he rejected was not the same as the one which modern science has established, and the truth has in fact turned out to be supportive of his philosophy in a way surpassing anything he himself could have imagined. But on many other matters, what he had to say is now indefensible, and there seems to me to be no point as far as this book is concerned in rehearsing views of his which no one nowadays would dream of holding or wanting to hold, and then setting forth the evidence that they are mistaken. It is difficult to imagine what help this could be to anyone, or whom it would interest. But it does mean that I have omitted many criticisms to which he is vulnerable.

The most important shortcoming of Schopenhauer's philosophy, to my mind, has to do with the fundamental epistemological analysis which he took over from, and shares with, Kant. The roots of the mistake reach down into the very foundations, to Kant's formulation of the basic problem it was he was trying to solve — though one has to say, paradoxically, that had Kant not made the false assumption in question it is unlikely that he would have achieved his revelatory insights either, insights whose validity and significance transcend the problem in response to which they were reached, and therefore survive the exposure of error in the formulation of that problem. Like everyone of his time, and for long after, Kant took it as an indisputable fact that Newtonian physics had unveiled the laws of nature, and that these scientific laws were certainties, incorrigible truths, cast-iron facts about the workings of the world: they were 'knowledge' of an utterly safe and sure kind, the safest which mankind had ever possessed. What left no room for doubt about this was the unqualified reliability of their predictive powers. With any measurable physical system whatsoever, from the solar system to a pocket watch, we had only to observe the state of the system at any given time t_1 and then, by means of Newton's laws, we could predict with total accuracy what the state of the system would be at any subsequent time t_2. This being so, the world *must* be as physics described it, and must work as physical laws said it did.

It should be remembered in this context that Kant was genuinely expert in mathematical physics, a subject which he taught at university and in which he had produced important original writings. His supreme insight, into which he was shaken by reading Hume, was that the world as presented to us by science is not only not the world of direct experience but cannot be derived from direct experience by logical deduction. From the position we have now reached in this book, what is at stake can be expressed in more significant terms than were used in an earlier chapter, when what was being described was the derivation of Kant's forward move from the philosophy that had gone before him. Put crudely, it is the realization that science cannot be constructed only out of facts and logic — that there must be something else to it as well.

Kant was undoubtedly correct in this realization. But in fact, had he paid sharp phenomenological attention to experience (something which he seems not to have been in the habit of doing) he would have realized that the gulf between our scientific knowledge and the content of our experience is even wider than he had supposed. For instance, the time-content of our actual experience is scarcely at all like the uniform, mathematically measured time of Newtonian physics, and there is no way of *deducing* the latter from the former. Furthermore, it is impossible that a time sequence extending to infinity both forwards and backwards, as postulated by classical physics, could either be given in experience or deduced from experience. Inescapably, there is something *constructed* about such a time. And similarly with space: the aesthetic space of our subjective experience is not uniformly ordered in three dimensions according to the principles of Euclidean geometry, as is the mathematically measured space of Newtonian physics; and even if it were, the infinite extension of such a space in all directions could neither be experienced nor guaranteed by experience. Again, there is something created, or at least postulated, about such a space. Yet again with both material objects and causality: the fact that the position of material objects at time t_2 conforms with the predictions we made for them at time t_1, when they were at different locations, may leave us subjectively in no doubt that they have been in continuous existence between our two observations, and also that their causal connections with each other have functioned during that time according to physical laws; and since this is true between any pair of observations whatsoever we may be convinced that material objects must exist, and interact causally with each other, independently of anyone's observing them.

But Berkeley had shown that direct experience cannot entail the existence of anything which is independent of experience, and therefore does not warrant even so much as the notion of a material object; and Hume had shown that causal connection between entities of any kind, objects or otherwise, can never be given in experience. In sum, every one of the basic features of the world as presented to us by Newtonian science — a world of independently existing physical objects, causally connected with each other and persisting through a uniform, mathematically determined time sequence which is infinitely extendable in two directions, and in a framework of Euclidean space which is infinitely extendable in three dimensions — is not given to us in experience, and is not deducible from experience.

Kant's perception of this, if not fully complete, was nevertheless decisive, in that it led him to formulate the seminal question of his critical philosophy. If our scientific knowledge cannot be accounted for by experience-plus-the-application-of-logic-to-experience, how is it possible for us to have it? That was his central problem. Clearly there must be at least a third component in our knowledge: the question was, what was it? He came to the conclusion, as we have seen, that all those features of scientific (and commonsense) knowledge that could not be validated by experience or logic were furnished by the knower in advance, that is to say in advance of the experiences that supplied the empirical content of the statements to which logical procedures could then be applied. They were, so to speak, the frameworks into which we were pre-programmed to gather whatever we might encounter. On this view, the forms of our sensibility *are* the spatio-temporal framework, and the pre-existing categories of our understanding include such categories as 'material object' and 'causal connection'. The reason why we all impose the same forms and categories on the world is that we all share the same human nature, by virtue of which it is that we are human beings in the first place; and we must also all be dealing with the same 'given', whatsoever that may be; and so it comes about that the world as publicly revealed by science is a shared and stable one which we inhabit in common — unlike the immeasurably variegated worlds of subjective experience, which are indescribably different for each one of us.

The mistake at the root of this view, a mistake which has been fully revealed only by scientific development in the twentieth century, is the assumption that Newtonian physics is a permanently and incorrigibly true body of fact. It is not. But because Kant believed that it was, he was bound to assume that everything about the a-priori forms and categories with which human sensibility and understanding were to be credited, *whatever they were*, must be such as would yield, and would yield only — and therefore must *necessarily* yield — a world which conformed to the laws of Newtonian science. All other possibilities must be ruled out. He was right to perceive that Berkeley and Hume had revealed the question of the nature and source of common sense and scientific knowledge as an unsolved philosophical problem whose implications went to the heart of man's conception of the world and of himself, and of the relationship between the two. Where he went wrong was in formulating the problem as that of explaining the provenance of a view of the world which was already in our possession and known to be incorrigibly and unchangingly true. It led him to produce an explanation not just of why something which is not the case is, but of why it *necessarily* is; and this explanatory theory can only be false as it stands. Schopenhauer took it over from Kant, and improved it, but left its central defect untouched. Not only did he retain necessity in the role of a universal and seamless causality governing the entire ongoing history of the natural world, he extended its sway throughout the realm of human choice. In doing this he argued that he was making Kantianism more consistent. I would say that in doing that he was making it more defective. The deterministic feature of Kantian–Schopenhauerian philosophy is one of its main shortcomings.

The nature of what requires to be explained is different from what Kant and Schopenhauer thought it was, and therefore a theory different from theirs is required to explain it. We see now not just that Newtonian science proved to be corrigible in fundamental respects, and was superseded, but also that the whole history of science consists of the criticism and replacement of theories in a process that never ends. So the problem of relating our scientific knowledge to the world is not that of explaining how it is possible for theories known to be correct to *be* correct when they are not derivable from observation of the events which they explain: it is the problem of deciding which of alternative theories to prefer until we find a better one, and how we shall know of any new one that it is better, given indeed the fact that none of them can be derived from observation of the events they explain, and none of them can be deduced from any such observations. Similar things can be said about commonsense knowledge, with which philosophers are also deeply concerned. For instance, what is self-evident to 'everyone' changes. For thousands of years it was self-evident to human beings that the sun went round the earth. Nothing could be more obvious: you directly saw it doing so every day of your life. Yet now everyone knows that it does not. At one time everyone knew that the earth was flat: now we all know it is not. The fact is that what we think of today as commonsense knowledge is historically recent. Primitive peoples, with their all-pervading animism, have almost none of it, and until as late as the seventeenth century the majority of Europeans were still explaining natural phenomena to themselves and each other in terms of saints and devils and spirits of all sorts, superstitions, ritual practices, incantations, curses, witchcraft, magic, and the rest. Common sense as we conceive it has held sway for 300 years at the most. And already the advance of science is exposing it as defective. Clearly, then, it is, like scientific knowledge itself, both ephemeral and replaceable, and involved likewise in an unending process of historical change.

This must mean, by the way, that Schopenhauer's strongly held and frequently expressed belief in the unimportance of history was mistaken. It may be that in politics, administration, government and war — and also in individual careers, and the passions and conflicts of private life — the same situations perpetually recur, so that *plus ça change, plus c'est la même chose*; but Schopenhauer failed to appreciate the importance of the development of some kinds of social and political institutions as against others. One wonders, for instance, how he himself would have managed in a society in which anyone who questioned the established religion was killed, and no writings incompatible with it were allowed to be circulated — which was largely the case throughout Europe during the Middle Ages. When it comes to the intellectual and cultural matters which were closest to his heart, historical differences are if anything even more important than they are in institutional arrangements. For instance, on his own submission (see the quotations on p. 7) it made all the difference to his life and work that he came on the scene after Kant and not before. But he only just made it. He was born after *The Critique of Pure Reason* was published but in the selfsame year as *The Critique of Practical Reason* appeared; he was two when *The Critique of Judgment* came out, and sixteen when Kant died. Had he been born eighty years earlier his life's work would have been impossible, and so he himself believed. But the truth is that all intellectual and cultural activity is subject to considerations of this kind. A historical dimension is inherent and constitutive both in ideas and in works of art. This is not to say that ideas and art necessarily improve or progress, but merely that they are subject to change, and that the processes of change are at least in part organic, not entirely random or mechanical. There clearly are, at least sometimes, influences and developments out of which living traditions arise — one has only to consider, for instance, the relationship between Haydn and Mozart, Mozart and Beethoven, Beethoven and Wagner, Wagner and Mahler, and Mahler and so-called 'modern' music. As we saw in Chapter 3, the great tradition of modern philosophy to which Schopenhauer regarded himself as belonging was such a line of direct descent, from Descartes through Locke, Berkeley and Hume to Kant, each of them taking up the central problems of philosophy at the point where they had been left by his immediate predecessor and developing them to the point at which they were taken up by his immediate successor. Ironically but significantly, the first modern thinker to familiarize the world with the notion that thought and art are inherently developmental was the one Schopenhauer most hated, and in whose work he could see no merit: Hegel. In my view Hegel was right not only about this but also — though for reasons different from those he put forward — about the character of the developmental movement, which he saw as being dialectical. The real reason, I think, why it often does have some sort of a dialectical character is that what are perhaps the two chief activities which motivate change are, first, problem-solving, and, second, reaction against such things as tradition, authority, established convention or parental restraint.

The assumption, which Schopenhauer shared with Kant, that the validity and applicability of Newtonian science were historically unchanging — or, to put it better, were *not historical* — is no longer even entertainable. But in rejecting this important error it is important not to throw out the baby with the bath-water. In his new and revolutionary formulation of the problem of validating human knowledge, Kant had been correct, and he was even partially correct about the solution: we really do, in a way no one before him had realized, bring to bear, in advance of experience, categorial frameworks in terms of which our transactions with the world are rendered intelligible. And this really does have as a consequence that our knowledge of the world will never be accountable for in terms of empirical facts plus logic. For philosophy there can be no going back on either of these two discoveries. Admittedly there remains a neo-Humean tradition, still extant, whose adherents have never acknowledged them, but for precisely that reason they have never got beyond Hume. Where Kant went wrong was only in assuming that there is one inescapable set of such frameworks, common to us all and unchanging through time, which provide us with the public and permanent world of Newtonian physics. The fact is that these sets of frameworks differ as between one historical period and another, and also as between one culture and another. They — our categorial schemes, our commonsense and scientific presuppositions, our mental sets, describe them how one will — are vulnerable to critical appraisal, revision, and replacement, and thus to change over time. The exposure of Kant's error in this respect has left us ever since with the problem of what their nature is. Such questions as the extent to which they are 'free' creations of individual geniuses such as Newton, or are socially, historically and culturally evolved, or are pre-programmed into us biologically, are at the centre of current philosophical enquiry, as are questions about how they are communicated, how they become institutionalized, and how and why they change.

The attempt to extend our understanding of experience and its structure, and hence of the world and its structure, through a close investigation into the workings of language — and this has been the dominant feature of twentieth-century philosophy in the English-speaking world — is obviously an enterprise which is deeply rooted in these considerations, and is therefore profoundly Kantian in character, even when not self-consciously so. It is not mere happenstance that the outstanding figure in the history of linguistic philosophy, Wittgenstein, was more influenced by Schopenhauer than by any other philosopher (see Appendix 3). The deep-lying Kantianism that pervades his work was derived directly from Schopenhauer. 'From Spinoza, Hume and Kant he said that he could get only occasional glimpses of understanding.'[3] The various frameworks, linguistic and otherwise, in terms of which humans interpret the world and conduct their transactions with it have become central to other forms of enquiry too: those of linguists, obviously, and also those of psychologists, sociologists and anthropologists. One way and another, this way of thinking can be said to be among the chief intellectual preoccupations of our age. And the fact that there is now no longer believed to be one single view of reality whose validation is even in principle possible raises the deepest philosophical problems of all.

Fruitful contributions to these enquiries have been made in recent decades by philosophers of many different kinds, some of them at odds with each other. The sheer bulk of linguistic philosophy speaks for itself in this context. Among non-linguistic philosophers, Ernst Cassirer — and some of his followers, such as Suzanne K. Langer — have incomparably deepened and enriched our insight into the extent to which not only the world as presented in language as such but also the world as presented in myths, the world as presented in all the many religions, and the world as presented in all the various arts and sciences are man-made worlds — and, as such, cultural phenomena. Specifically, they are symbolic structures whose function is to represent, and help us to come to terms with, and make sense of, and communicate, the various aspects of our experience. Cassirer came to see man as being essentially an animal that makes and uses symbols, this — not just his use of those particular symbols that we call language — being his defining characteristic. Collingwood impatiently drew our attention to the historical character of our presuppositions, and hence to the extent

---

[3] G. H. von Wright, 'Biographical Sketch' in *Ludwig Wittgenstein, a Memoir* by Norman Malcolm, p. 21.

to which they need to be understood historically as well as scientifically and philosophically. Karl Popper began by stressing almost solely what it was that had made the displacement of Newton possible, namely the contribution of the bold, imaginative creativity of the innovating scientist to the growth of our knowledge; but he then moved on to see parallels between this activity and what goes on in all other fields, and was eventually led to draw up a general theory of problem-solving as an overall explanatory framework covering man's transactions with his environment. Much of his later writing is devoted to tracing the emergence of this in the processes of biological evolution. However, in most recent years it is Chomsky who has stressed more than anyone else the extent to which we as biological organisms have the categories in terms of which we apprehend the world pre-programmed into our physical apparatus — and he acknowledges that this is a fundamentally Kantian conception.[4] I pick out these names by way of example only: others also have valuable insights to offer. The Preface to one of the more recent books from the seam that was opened by Cassirer, *Ways of Worldmaking* by Nelson Goodman (1978), ends with a concise piece of self-orientation which illuminates admirably the perspective now being advanced. 'I think of this book as belonging in that mainstream of modern philosophy that began when Kant exchanged the structure of the world for the structure of the mind, continued when C. I. Lewis exchanged the structure of the mind for the structure of concepts, and that now proceeds to exchange the structure of concepts for the structure of the several symbol systems of the sciences, philosophy, the arts, perception, and everyday discourses. The movement is from unique truth and a world fixed and found to a diversity of right and even conflicting versions or worlds in the making.'

Note that Goodman writes here of a mainstream that *began* with Kant. There is a crucial sense in which he is right to do so. Most of the central problems in philosophy remain to this day those towards which Kant pointed us. Above all, Kant was the great discoverer of the true nature of the problem of experience. His formulation of that problem appears inescapable, but neither he nor anyone else has yet succeeded in providing a satisfactory solution to it. Consequently, one thing which nearly all major figures in contemporary philosophy have in common — though they may be as far apart in other respects as

---

[4] See, for instance, Bryan Magee: *Men of Ideas*, p. 221:

'MAGEE: . . . your work always puts me in mind of Kant; in fact you seem to me almost to be redoing, in terms of modern linguistics, what Kant was doing. Do you accept any element of truth in that?

CHOMSKY: I not only accept the truth in it, I've even tried to bring it out, in a certain way . . .'.

Wittgenstein and Heidegger — is that either the problems they confront or the methods they use in confronting them are in some recognizable sense Kantian.[5] The one strand in contemporary philosophy that has not absorbed the achievements of Kant is also the most notoriously desiccated one, namely the persistent tradition of would-be pure empiricism. One and a half centuries after Kant the chief representatives of this tradition, the Logical Positivists, were still clinging to the pre-Kantian error of believing that scientific and commonsense knowledge could be accounted for in terms of statements of observed fact plus what could be logically derived from them. Indeed, they proclaimed as their central doctrine that only the two corresponding kinds of statement — statements of fact verifiable by observation, and statements in logic or mathematics — were meaningful.

I remarked earlier that one of the chief defects of the Kantian–Schopenhauerian philosophy was its deterministic character, and that this was imposed on it by its false assumption of the incorrigibility of Newtonian science. Determinism is still a live issue in philosophy. This is not the place for me to plunge into a current controversy, but there are one or two observations I should like to make on it. First, it was classical physics that raised the issue of determinism in the form in which it has plagued philosophy since the seventeenth century, and yet physics itself has now developed to a point where it dispenses with the notion of 'cause'. (Among the terms with which quantum mechanics has most familiarized us are indeterminacy principle' and 'uncertainty relations'.) So physics can be said first to have landed philosophy with the problem and then ceased to entertain it as such. I believe it can be effectively shown that in most of the forms in which it is still current (e.g. in Marxism) determinism rests on an erroneous conception of science, and that in so far as the philosophical problem was science-

---

[5] Even, by the end, Russell. His last philosophical book, with its Kantian title *Human Knowledge: its Scope and Limits*, comes to a distinctly Kantian conclusion in its final chapter headed 'The Limits of Empiricism'. He shows that it is impossible for us to acquire knowledge of the world without the use of what he calls 'causal principles' or 'postulates', and then begins his final paragraph: 'But although our postulates can, in this way, be fitted into a framework which has what we may call an empiricist "flavour", it remains undeniable that our knowledge of them, in so far as we do know them, cannot be based upon experience, though all their verifiable consequences are such as experience will confirm. In this sense, it must be admitted, empiricism as a theory of knowledge has proved inadequate . . .'. Of course, in Kant's critical work the recognition of precisely this is the point of departure, not the destination. This fact epitomizes for me the tragedy of Russell's intellectual career. Frege, likewise, took most of a long and productive life to arrive at an essentially Kantian view which, until he reached it, he repudiated. Today's heirs of the empiricists tend to take the view that these philosophers — and others too, such as Whitehead — softened with age after having done their serious work.

based it has now dissolved. Second, determinism seems to me to be refutable by one of those arguments which, though not logically hermetic, is in practice irresistible, like those we considered with respect to solipsism and code-breaking. If determinism is true, every last feature of both the natural and the man-made worlds must have been materially and irreversibly specified in the protozoic slime. More than that: if the Big Bang theory is correct, in the very opening fractions of a second of that cosmic explosion all the necessary and sufficient conditions were present for everything that has ever existed or happened since: the exact specifications and movements of every physical object that has ever existed, including every flick of every wrist and every flicker of every eyebrow, plus the precise character of every abstract entity that has ever been evolved within this world (every idea; every symphony; even, say, every television programme . . .), not to mention every word that every person has ever uttered. Logically, of course, it is possible that this was so. But I do not see how anyone could believe it.

In the Introduction to his *Four Essays on Liberty* Isaiah Berlin has argued, convincingly to my mind, that regardless of whether determinism is correct or incorrect (and although he does not mention Schopenhauer, his formulation on p. xiii of the doctrine he is discussing is precisely that employed by Schopenhauer) its consistent adoption would require us to expunge from our minds, and from our language, all such existing concepts as moral responsibility and choice, praise, blame, encouragement, fairness, justice, equity, merit and the like; and moreover to expunge from all our public relationships and institutions, as well as from our private behaviour, all activities which rest on the use of any of these concepts. Berlin goes on to assert that no advocate of determinism has ever faced up to what this involves. It is clear that he doubts that the task is even determinately conceivable, let alone practically possible. He also seems to doubt whether, if it could be carried out, such a programme would be compatible with our remaining human. 'Of course,' he writes, 'the fact that there have been, and no doubt may still be, plenty of thinkers, even in our own culture, who at one and the same time profess belief in determinism, and yet do not feel in the least inhibited from dispensing . . . moral praise and blame freely, and pointing out to others how they should have chosen, shows only, if I am right, that some normally lucid and self-critical thinkers are at times liable to confusion. My case, in other words, amounts to making explicit what most men do not doubt — namely that it is not rational both to believe that choices are caused, and to consider men as deserving of reproach or indignation (or their opposites) for choosing to act or refrain as they do' (p. xxii).

In this respect Schopenhauer is guilty in the highest degree. In fact he exemplifies Berlin's criticism almost to perfection. His writings are carbuncled with attacks and denunciations and vilifications — and also, be it said, commendations — which can simply have no application or significance if his doctrine about the freedom of the will is correct. If human beings cannot choose what they choose to do, they are not to be blamed for what they choose, nor will they be brought to choose differently by exhortation. Nor can Schopenhauer's position be salvaged by locating moral choice at the point of entry of the noumenon into the human phenomenon, for, as I showed in the last chapter, that is not a doctrine that can be formulated coherently. The fact is that on Schopenhauer's assumptions there is no point at which moral responsibility can be ascribed — and therefore there can be no morality. This being so, it is even more difficult than it would otherwise be (and that would be difficult enough) to see what meaning could attach to his assertion that the world *as a whole* has a moral significance.[6] It would also seem to make criticism of individual doctrines within Schopenhauer's moral philosophy superfluous.

Several of these, quite separately, are open to fairly obvious criticisms. For instance the doctrine (which earlier I deliberately refrained from discussing) that there is nothing wrong in my doing anything I have a right to do has the curious consequence that there is nothing wrong in my withholding help from the desperate — nothing wrong, for instance, in my denying bread to a starving family, or standing on the canal bank and looking idly on while somebody drowns. Another criticism would be this: in the light of Schopenhauer's various doctrines, taken together, that the noumenon cannot be causally impinged on, that the world of phenomena is a world of evanescent images, and that the individual must cease to exist with death, it is difficult to see how it can make any difference *to me* how I live, and therefore why I should not, for instance, live along the line of least resistance. Leaving aside any question of injuring others, how could it make any difference to me in the long run whether I devoted my life to playing cards (an activity which Schopenhauer despised especially) or indulging in promiscuous sexual activity, or grubbing for money, or any other form of loafing or base self-seeking? In each case it would all come to nothing in the end, of course, but so would whatever else I did. Yet clearly Schopenhauer does not believe this, in fact he passionately rejects it; but it is difficult to see what consistent grounds he could offer for doing so.

His treatment of the noumenal will is likewise self-contradictory. For instance, whenever discussing its nature directly he insists on its blind

---

[6] e.g. 'That the world has only a physical and not a moral significance is a fundamental error.' *Parerga and Paralipomena*, ii. 201.

aimlessness. The reader will recall all the quotations to this effect on p. 143. But in other contexts he persistently attributes unconscious directionality and purpose to it. A typical example of this is: 'The one-year-old bird has no notion of the eggs for which it builds a nest; the young spider has no idea of the prey for which it spins a web; the ant-lion has no notion of the ant for which it digs a cavity for the first time. The lava of the stag-beetle gnaws the hole in the wood where it will undergo its metamorphosis twice as large if it is to become a male beetle as if it is to become a female, in order in the former case to have room for the horns, though as yet it has no idea of these. In the actions of such animals the will is obviously at work . . .'.[7] Schopenhauer never addresses himself to the question of how it comes about that a blind, aimless drive objectifies itself in a world full of purposeful activity — a world, furthermore, in which every particle and motion obey the laws of Newtonian physics. To push the question one stage further back, he never asks himself how it comes about that a blind urge manifests itself directly in Platonic Ideas (such as Newton's laws). He goes no further than to say that the self-objectification of the noumenon in the phenomenon is inexplicable. But, surely, a through-and-through blind and aimless will would manifest itself in, if anything, a chaos?

Further difficulties present themselves regarding the nature of this world as which the noumenal will manifests itself. We need do no more than touch on one or two of them. If, for instance, the perceiving subject constructs the phenomenal world in the process of perceiving it, and if, as Schopenhauer insists, that world is just what it appears to be and nothing else, what is the ontological status of, shall we say, the entities of subatomic physics? In other words, how is it possible for such a world to contain non-perceptible material components or attributes — elements which are, what is more, non-perceptible *in principle*, because their dimensions are smaller than any wavelength? There are many features of this world for which we now have explanations which were not available to Schopenhauer but which are clearly better than those he advanced. For instance, as the quotation in the forgoing paragraph illustrates, he explained in terms of unconscious activity of the will behaviour in animals which serves purposes of which the animals themselves cannot have any conception: however, such behaviour is more convincingly explained in terms of genetic pre-programming. Similarly, he adduced Platonic Ideas to explain how it is that three of the four grades of the will's objectification consist of classes of similar objects: this is now more satisfactorily explained in terms of evolutionary biology. I am not sure that the apparent naturalness of our dividing

---

[7] *The World as Will and Representation*, i. 114.

the phenomenal world into the four categories of dead matter, plants, animals and human beings is more than culture-relative. And I am not convinced that the Platonic Ideas — adduced primarily to explain the existence of genera and species — are necessary to Schopenhauer's philosophy at all. A careful shave with Occam's razor could, I suspect, succeed in removing these without trace.

In the first edition of *The World as Will and Representation* Platonic Ideas are not introduced until three-quarters of the way through Schopenhauer's exposition of his epistemology and ontology — whereupon they suddenly, disconcertingly, claim a pivotal function in the entire explanatory framework. I cannot help suspecting that they were introduced *ad hoc* at this point and then got out of hand. I suspect that the reason for their introduction was that — without having at his disposal any of the conceptual apparatus since made available to us by Darwin and the subsequent development of biology — Schopenhauer could not see how else to explain the fact that everything is like something else: every sparrow is like every other sparrow, every blade of grass like every other blade of grass, every star like every other star, and so on, throughout the whole of the known universe, regardless of the evident unconnectedness of individual things with each other in time as well as in space. Why are not all things different from each other? Plato's explanation was classic in philosophy, and it did not appear to have been superseded. However, allowing it suddenly to enter Schopenhauer's system had the unthought-out consequence of making Platonic Ideas an indispensable feed-pipe between the noumenon and the world of phenomena. As such they became a third constituent of total reality. They were not phenomena, being purely abstract, and not observed or experienced by ordinary processes of perception, not subject to causal change, and independent of space and time; but on the other hand they were not aspects of the noumenon, for they had their being only within the phenomenal world, in and through specific phenomena, and no other existence at all. So whereas Schopenhauer's philosophy makes so much of presenting itself to us as an account of reality in terms of two irreducible categories — the noumenon and phenomena — it actually makes use of three; what he shows us is not a two-decker reality consisting of will and representations but a three-decker reality consisting of will, Platonic Ideas and representations. But it is clear from the way in which this comes about that it is not what he intended. I think that what he meant to convey in the title of his main work is nearer both to his intentions and to the requirements of his system.

The only other part of that system in which Platonic Ideas have any function is the theory of art — and there Schopenhauer himself says that they play no role in the most important art of all, namely music. That being so, what he is putting forward is not one aesthetic theory but two — one for music, another for the rest of the arts. And it seems to me clear that the second of these could be reformulated in a way that dispenses with Platonic Ideas. It would be out of place for me to attempt that here at any self-sustaining length, but I suspect that such a theory would proceed along the following lines. We have just seen how Schopenhauer usually speaks of the phenomenal world as a direct, unmediated manifestation of the noumenal, yet sometimes, inconsistently, speaks of it as being mediated through Platonic Ideas, which are then seen as being themselves the direct manifestations of the noumenal, and every actual thing in the world as being an instantiation of *them*. I see no reason why Schopenhauer's existing arguments about the representational arts as giving us a special sort of knowledge of Platonic Ideas *which are direct manifestations of the noumenal* should not be transferred, *mutatis mutandis*, to the representational arts as giving us a special sort of knowledge of the empirical world *which is a direct manifestation of the noumenal*. Such a theory would still attribute to the arts other than music the same metaphysical function as before, so Schopenhauer's various subsidiary theories about them could still apply; their representational character would be conceded, indeed accounted for; and the nature of the distinction between them and music would be preserved, in that their contact with the noumenal would still be seen as being at one remove, while music is seen as a direct manifestation of the noumenal.

Schopenhauer's theory of music contains one glaring inconsistency. It asserts the following sets of propositions:

1. Music and the phenomenal world are both direct, unmediated manifestations of the metaphysical will. Therefore they do not stand to each other as *representation* to *represented* but as *equivalents*.
2. The metaphysical will is inherently evil, and the phenomenal world, as its embodiment, is an appalling place, a hell.
3. Music is marvellous, uniquely so, and to be showered endlessly with laudatory adjectives — 'such a great and exceedingly fine art', 'this wonderful art', 'the inexpressible depth of all music, by virtue of which it floats past us as a paradise . . .' and so on.

To make 3 compatible with 1 and 2 Schopenhauer would have had to contend that there is something uniquely *terrible* about music, something infernal, something nightmarish. Interestingly enough, there have been people who subscribed seriously to the view that music was inherently bad — and they include no less a philosopher than Plato — but Schopenhauer was not one of them. As it is, his theory is so starkly self-contradictory that one is at a loss to understand how he could have failed to notice. Only wilful blindness could account for it. This takes us back to the point I made in my opening chapter about his pessimism being rooted in his psychological development and logically separable from his philosophy. I believe that any desired reconciliation of the above arguments is to be sought along the lines of repudiating 2, not repudiating 3.

This brings us to a shortcoming of Schopenhauer's theory of the arts in general which derives from his pessimism. He asserts that the appeal of art as such resides in the fact that art provides a temporary escape from the otherwise almost intolerable unhappiness of life. But it seems to me an obvious empirical fact that we are not as unhappy as all that, most of us, for most of the time. Here, as in the case of music, we are confronted with an instance of Schopenhauer's personality disorder distorting the contents of his philosophy. If anything — and there are places in his writings where he says as much — what is typical of human beings is to drift through life in a somewhat neutral, equable mood which for much of the time tends to look hopefully, if also uncertainly, on the bright side. This weak, tentative optimism may be unjustified by the realities of our situation, and may therefore be facile, but it is a wholly different state of mind from the frustrated misery which Schopenhauer attributes to us as our normal condition. Likewise, his purely negative definition of happiness as the absence of suffering, or boredom, or anxiety, or unsatisfied longing — and his related definition of pleasure as the absence of pain — run counter to direct experience. We are indeed exhilarated by relief from pain or danger, and it can be a marvellous feeling, but in the enjoyment of great art, or love, or friendship, there is something altogether more outgoing than this. These things involve us in a relationship with something or someone outside ourselves, a gratified extension of ourselves which is self-enhancing, and thus life-enhancing, and in that specific sense positive. Something of the sort is true of even our purely physical pleasures. When confronted with good food and drink we do not usually push them aside the moment our hunger and thirst are assuaged, but carry on eating and drinking for the sheer enjoyment of it. And this is *normal* behaviour. Addictions provide examples of pleasure in Schopenhauer's sense, but they also illuminate the difference between that and something more positive. A compulsive smoker (I have been one) rarely feels '*My God, I am enjoying this cigarette!*' For most of the time that he is smoking he is only subliminally aware of the fact. It is when he is *not* smoking that smoking fills his consciousness, in the form of an almost intolerable craving to smoke. He smokes in order not to suffer this craving — the reason why he keeps lighting cigarettes is

242 Some Criticisms and Problems

not that he enjoys them so much but that he cannot bear *not* smoking. Thus far, then, the analysis confirms Schopenhauer: the so-called 'pleasure' of smoking is the perpetual staving-off of an intolerable craving. But the fact is that, in addition to this, there are times — after a good meal, very often, or with the first cigarette of the day — when the compulsive smoker *does* feel '*My God, I am enjoying this cigarette!*' And that is an altogether different kind of experience, as anyone who has had both will testify. Among other things, it is an unmistakably positive pleasure. But the Schopenhauerian analysis rules out the possibility of it. And this is an inadequacy of the Schopenhauerian analysis across the whole range of pleasure in activity, happiness in life, and apprecia-tion of the arts.

The last criticisms I want to make in this chapter concern Schopenhauer's doctrine of the renunciation of the will. Given the rest of his philosophy, there is no way in which this could happen. First, his denial that any of our actions or choices are free means that it is not an option for us. Second, he is insistent throughout that for all motivated action the medium of motives is the mind, whether conscious or un-conscious, and that mind is the creature of will in the literal sense that it was brought into being by the will and exists to serve it. Admittedly, in his theory of art he asserts that there are brief periods when the mind frees itself from this servitude; but that is a far cry from any talk of the mind *directing* the will. That would run counter to his whole system. But, this being so, how can insight lead to renunciation — for that would be a case of willing being directed to the very point of elimination by an activity of mind? When discussing the activity of the knowing subject in aesthetic situations Schopenhauer is insistent that willing cannot be eliminated even by act of *will* (which would be far more powerful than mere act of mind) *and therefore that its elimination is not up to us.* 'The change in the subject required for this, just because it consists in the elimination of all willing, cannot proceed from the will, and hence cannot be an arbitrary act of will, in other words, cannot rest with us.'[8] Given all this, there is simply no way in which we can be the decisive agents in the denial of our own willing. In addition, there is a quite separate point to be made in support of the same conclusion, to the effect that it is inconceivable that a will which is inherently evil would choose, in the light of insight, to suppress itself. The upshot, I think, is that either Schopenhauer has to give up this notion of renun-ciation of the will altogether or see it as something that happens to people without its being any of their doing (in which case he requires a different explanation for it) — or else he needs to make changes elsewhere in his system to make their doing it possible.

[8] *The World as Will and Representation*, ii. 367.

I think, personally, the notion has to be given up. Otherwise, as they stand, Schopenhauer's most characteristic ethical doctrines are incompatible with each other. On the one hand he tells us that all morality is based on compassion: on the other he says that the most ethically desirable state for an individual to attain is the renunciation of all willing. But clearly, it is impossible to be compassionately concerned for another without activity of will. Putting this point the other way round, if I have renounced all willing then I must be as indifferent to the good or harm of another as I am to my own. If it really is true that all morality is based on compassion, then the cessation of willing must be accompanied by an indifference to moral considerations. So it is not possible for both of Schopenhauer's two most important ethical doctrines to be valid. If the one that says all morality is based on compassion were to be renounced, then his entire ethics would be swept away in disregard of the powerful arguments in its favour and the absence of decisive arguments against it. But if the other is given up, in acknowledgement of the independent existence of already decisive arguments against it, an adequate explanatory theory of ethics remains which is both consistent and persuasive.

The shortcomings I have listed in this chapter are severe, and of course there are other faults, large and small, in Schopenhauer's work. But the work of every great philosopher has severe shortcomings. What makes such work great is not the absence of great faults but the presence of great insights. In view of that, no words could be more fitting for this concluding paragraph of our main text than the quotation from Voltaire with which Schopenhauer prefaced the self-contained critique of Kant (over a hundred pages in length, and some of it radical) with which he concluded the first edition of *The World as Will and Representation*. 'It is the privilege of the real genius, especially one who opens up a new path, to make great mistakes with impunity.' Speaking for myself, I am more indebted to Schopenhauer for the insights I have gained through his philosophy than words can express.

APPENDICES

These appendices deal with matters which are not necessary for an understanding of Schopenhauer's philosophy but for which an understanding of Schopenhauer's philosophy is necessary. Their chief concerns are the relationships between it and other bodies of thought, and its influence on creative artists. In drawing these connections, one side, the Schopenhauer side, is taken for granted as having been presented already, so there is little repetition of material, however germane. This means that the appendices are not self-contained essays (and should not be treated as such) but form part of the book as a whole, and presuppose that the rest of the book has been read.

Appendix 1

Schopenhauer and the Neo-Kantians

There are walks of life of which we have no difficulty in believing that an individual in one of them may be a showman and part-charlatan and at the same time possessed of genuine talent, perhaps even greatness. Politics is an obvious example. Other fields that spring to mind are acting, orchestral conducting, indeed the performing arts generally. I refrain from offering instances because the real abilities of individuals of this kind tend to be unusually contentious, some people hailing them as obviously great, others dismissing them as frauds. What makes such arguments difficult to resolve is that important assertions on both sides may be true. The same combination of contradictory attributes can crop up also in less likely places — for instance in imaginative literature. The truth, as many novelists and playwrights have illustrated perceptively in their works, is that it can crop up anywhere. It is my opinion that Fichte, Schelling and Hegel were persons of this type, and that Schopenhauer saw their vices accurately but underrated their abilities 'Fichte, Schelling and Hegel are in my opinion not philosophers, for they lack the first requirement of a philosopher, namely a seriousness and honesty of enquiry. They are merely sophists who wanted to appear to be, rather than to be, something. They sought not truth but their own interest and advancement in the world. Appointments from governments, fees and royalties from students and publishers — and, as a means to that end, the greatest possible show and sensation in their sham philosophy — such were the guiding stars and inspiring genii of those disciples of wisdom. And so they have not passed the entrance examination, and cannot be admitted into the venerable company of thinkers for the human race. Nevertheless they have excelled in one thing, in the art of beguiling the public and of passing themselves off for what they are not; and this undoubtedly requires talent, yet not philosophical.'[1]

Because Schopenhauer took this view of the neo-Kantians there is scarcely any serious discussion of their work to be found in his writings, other than comparatively brief and passing references, usually on specific points. The contempt in which he held them is evinced by his

---

[1] *Parerga and Paralipomena*, i. 21.

remark that he would as soon think of taking part in their so-called philosophical disputes as of joining a scuffle in the street. He saw them as time-servers merely, men whose reputation and livelihood depended on success in academic careers at universities whose professorships were in the gift of government officials, and in which political interference and intrigue were perennial; and who therefore taught on morals, religion and politics whatever the authorities wanted taught, and made it all super-normally imposing by cloaking it in mystifying and oracular language. However, not only were they, in his eyes, contemptible toadies: he saw them also as actively injurious — as cheating the public, addling the brains of their students (and thereby debauching the intellect of a whole generation), and, worst of all, vandalizing the legacy of Kant. The relation of their work to Kant's, he said, put him in mind of the ancient Greeks' custom of enacting farces over the graves of the great. Two things about their methods set him specially in a rage. One was their fraudulent misuse of language. The other was their deliberate use of pseudo-demonstrations, that is to say their habitual attempts, by rhetorical means, to sweep their readers into taking one thing as following from another when, on calm examination, it does not. Both practices were in extreme contrast to his own methods: he used the German language with a clarity which has never been surpassed, and his integrity in argument was such that whenever he was aware that something of which he hoped to persuade his readers was not actually proved by the arguments he was offering in its support he would himself point this out. The wilful obscurity of the neo-Kantians seemed to him a calculated exploitation of the fact that Kant's thought had been so profound that almost no one was capable of grasping it at a first reading, with the consequence that the educated public had been newly conditioned to associate incomprehensibility with profundity. 'What was senseless and without meaning at once took refuge in obscure exposition and language. Fichte was the first to grasp and make use of this privilege; Schelling at least equalled him in this, and a host of hungry scribblers without intellect or honesty soon surpassed them both. But the greatest effrontery in serving up sheer nonsense, in scrabbling together senseless and maddening webs of words, such as had previously been heard only in madhouses, finally appeared in Hegel. It became the instrument of the most ponderous and general mystification that has ever existed, with a result that will seem incredible to posterity, and be a lasting monument of German stupidity.'[2]

Schopenhauer's writings are characterized throughout by violent

---

[2] *The World as Will and Representation*, i. 429.

eruptions of personal insult against the same three men: in the middle
of an argument on almost any subject the reader may suddenly find the
molten lava of his wrath against them gushing out of the page. In
intensity and amount this highly personal abuse of named contemporaries or near-contemporaries has no equal in the history of philosophy.
Here are a few examples:

'I protest against all association with this man Fichte, just as Kant did
publicly and expressly . . . Hegelians and like ignoramuses may continue to talk of a Kantian–Fichtean philosophy: there is Kantian
philosophy, and there is Fichtean humbug.'³

'. . . the bickering and abusive tone which everywhere pervades
Schelling's writings [is] an obligato accompaniment. Now if all this
were not the case, and if Schelling had gone to work with honesty
instead of with bluff and humbug, then, as being decidedly the most
gifted of the three, he might at least have occupied in philosophy the
subordinate position of an eclectic, useful for the time being.'⁴

'First Fichte and then Schelling, both of whom were not without talent,
but finally Hegel, that clumsy and nauseating charlatan, that pernicious person, who completely disorganized and ruined the minds of a
whole generation . . .'.⁵

'Schelling was followed by a philosophical ministerial creature, to wit
Hegel, who for political and indeed mistaken purposes was from above
dubbed a great philosopher — a commonplace, inane, loathsome,
repulsive and ignorant charlatan, who with unparalleled effrontery
compiled a system of crazy nonsense that was trumpeted abroad as
immortal wisdom by his mercenary followers, and was actually regarded as such by blockheads . . .'.⁶

When Schopenhauer insisted on making a distinction between Fichte's
'windbaggery' and Hegel's 'charlatanry' it was not only a joke: he saw
Fichte as primarily a rhetorician, and Hegel as primarily a swindler.
The neo-Kantian philosophy as a whole he likened to 'a prostitute who
for shameful remuneration sold herself yesterday to one man, today to
another'.⁷

This vituperation, so repetitive as to be partially obsessional in
character, has often since been ascribed to professional jealousy. But to
anyone familiar with Schopenhauer's work the charge is too im-

³ *The Fourfold Root of the Principle of Sufficient Reason*, p. 120.
⁴ *Parerga and Paralipomena*, i. 24.
⁵ Ibid. i. 168.   ⁶ Ibid. i. 96.
⁷ *The Fourfold Root of the Principle of Sufficient Reason*, p. xxviii.

plausible to entertain. If he had one salient characteristic it was intellectual integrity, and he never for a moment hesitated to take his hat off in public to anyone whose achievement he respected; not only Kant and Goethe but a host of minor and often now forgotten contemporaries and near-contemporaries are saluted in his pages. Besides, against Fichte the charges of fraudulence begin to appear in the student notebooks, before Schopenhauer had formed any conception of what his own work was to be, let alone any expectation (which he never entertained — quite the contrary) that it would be disregarded. The fact is that Schopenhauer really did feel and think the things he said about Fichte, Schelling and Hegel; and he expressed them so intemperately because of the ferocity with which he felt them, and also because of his view that bad thinking queers the pitch for good thinking, so that getting a hearing for the good involves driving out the bad. It is true, and not surprisingly, that his wrath became heightened to the point of apoplexy when he found his own work passed over in favour of the intellectual forgeries of these despicable counterfeiters; but that did not shape his view of them. Perhaps the genuineness of his opinions will be more readily credited if it is realized that other perceptive people shared them, both at the time and since. With regard to Fichte, 'Schiller arrived at a similar opinion, and so did Goethe; and Nicolovius called Fichte a "sycophant and a deceiver".'[8] As for Hegel, it is ironical in this context to note that even Schelling, during the years following the publication of Hegel's *Phenomenology of Spirit*, 'became obsessed by the thought that his former friend had foisted on a gullible public an inferior system of philosophy'.[9] In our own century there have been outstanding philosophers who were almost as insulting about Hegel as Schopenhauer had been — Bertrand Russell, for instance: 'To anyone who still cherishes the hope that man is a more or less rational animal, the success of this farago of nonsense must be astonishing.'[10] Karl Popper takes a similar view, and his criticism of Hegel draws extensively on quotations from Schopenhauer.

On the other hand the intemperateness of Schopenhauer's anger against the neo-Kantians has always done him harm, not least during his own lifetime. In 1840 the Royal Danish Society gave as one of its reasons for not awarding a prize to his essay 'On the Basis of Morality' (his entry was anonymous, and the only one): 'we cannot pass over in silence the fact that several distinguished philosophers of recent times are mentioned in a manner so unseemly as to cause just and grave

---

[8] Karl Popper, *The Open Society and its Enemies*, ii. 313.

[9] Frederick Copleston, *A History of Philosophy*, vol. vii, part 1, p. 124.

[10] Bertrand Russell, *Philosophy and Politics*, published separately and also included as the first essay in the volume *Unpopular Essays*.

offence.' Characteristically, Schopenhauer then published this essay with the epigraph '*Not* awarded a prize by the Royal Danish Society of Scientific Studies at Copenhagen on 30 January 1840'. Between the lines of his Preface to the revised edition of *The Fourfold Root of the Principle of Sufficient Reason*, dated September 1847, indications can be descried that he had resisted suggestions from friends that he should tone down some of the newly interpolated insult ('. . . if the old man sometimes boils with indignation, the fair and sympathetic reader will not censure him . . .'). Since his death the fact that, contrary to his confident expectations, posterity has not only taken Hegel seriously but continued by and large to pay more attention to him than to Schopenhauer has caused Schopenhauer's lack of respect for Hegel to be seen as something to be explained in terms of Schopenhauer's, not Hegel's, shortcomings. And the fact that Hegel is someone whose intellectual influence has since been so great that it has to be taken seriously makes Schopenhauer's noisy dismissal of him look irresponsible in intellectual terms, a failure of intellectual seriousness, and therefore unbalanced as well as ungenerous. Finally, the suspicion of jealousy has led, among people who have not read Schopenhauer, to the false assumption that he felt himself to be in intellectual rivalry with Hegel, and therefore that he was trying to do much the same thing as Hegel — that they were similar sorts of philosopher, only that Hegel was the more successful.

My view is that Schopenhauer's main charges against the neo-Kantians were true as far as they went, but that there was another side to the story. Fichte, Schelling and Hegel were indeed exploited by the political authorities, and did indeed lend themselves to this in order to advance themselves in the world and make themselves heard. They also tried to render what they had to say as magisterial as they could by clothing it in a prolix verbal grandiosity, with the result that there is nearly always less to it than appears, and many passages are preposterously inflated ways of saying something very simple (often something simply false), or even of saying nothing at all. But at the same time all three of them did have worthwhile things to say. And because they closely preceded Schopenhauer in time, in the same country, and thus shared with him the same language and the same immediate cultural environment and traditions — in particular, they too had taken Kant as their point of departure — they had more in common with him than he discerned.

Although in the world of Anglo-Saxon philosophy there has recently been a revival of interest in Hegel, Schelling is scarcely read at all, and Fichte very little: in so far as English-speaking philosophers have any mental image of these two it seems to be not unlike Schopenhauer's, though of course much more dim and distant. It remains an unfair view. This being so, although it is not feasible for me to embark on systematic expositions of the respective philosophies of Fichte and Schelling, I would like to say just enough about each of them to show that their work has a genuine content which is not negligible, and also that it foreshadowed Schopenhauer's (and for that matter twentieth-century philosophy) in important and interesting ways.

Because it is what they themselves did, we had best take our starting-point from Kant. *The Critique of Pure Reason* is primarily a work in epistemology and the philosophy of science. The central question to which it addresses itself is: how do we come to have the knowledge of the world that we do have? And because that is its concern, it attempts to account for man as a knowing subject but has little to say about him as a moral agent. However, the epistemological analysis which Kant put forward did itself give rise to serious problems about man as a moral agent, which he then went on to confront in the next stage of his work. The chief of these can be expressed in the following three points considered together. 1. It is a plain empirical fact, experienced as immediately by most of us as any other, that nearly all of us have deeply held moral convictions which we are unable to disregard even if we wish to. 2. These moral convictions presuppose freedom of choice, for how could *right* and *wrong, ought, duty, integrity* and all the rest of our moral concepts have any significance if human beings were never at liberty to refrain from the courses of action they pursue? 3. How, though, can any such free action be possible in a universe in which the motions of all bodies are governed by Newtonian laws — indeed what, in such a world, could the notion of freedom even so much as mean? For our immediate purposes the answers at which Kant arrived might be summarized as follows. What freedom means is independence of causal law (scientific law, the laws of Nature). *Within* the world of phenomena there is no such freedom, since everything in it is causally determined. However, human beings are not phenomenal only, they are also noumenal; they are material objects in the empirical world, but in addition to that they are also things-in-themselves. Now causality has no purchase outside the world of phenomena. Therefore in so far as human beings are noumenal beings they are not subject to causal laws. Therefore no contradiction or conflict is involved in saying that human individuals do exercise freedom, make decisions and choices, and have moral attributes: they do so in their capacity as noumenal beings. The thought can be put differently in the following way. Every movement or event in the world of phenomena is determined by what came before it, and determines what comes after it, and these causal chains cannot be arbitrarily altered or interfered with. (Belief in magic or miracles is based on the contrary notion that they can.) Human beings, however, being part noumenal and part phenomenal, contain within themselves the interface between the noumenal and the phenomenal. Or, to change the metaphor to a Euclidean one, the two contiguous spheres of existence can be thought of as touching at a dimensionless point. Kant, like Schopenhauer after him, saw that point as the nodal point of total reality, the ultimate focus of the mystery of existence, which must be there even though it did not, and never could, come *within* the world of our knowledge. At that point of contact between the phenomenal and the noumenal, and at that point alone, the two worlds impinge on each other: thus the free decisions of the noumenal self can and do make contact with the phenomenal world, and initiate causally connected chains of events, from a point on the outer limit of that world, which then ramify into the rest of its sphere. Now precisely because these causal series, once inaugurated, cannot be altered or interfered with, responsibility for them and for their naturally foreseeable consequences lies at the point of their inauguration. However, because that point is not *within* the phenomenal sphere, what 'happens' 'there' is not susceptible of causal (commonsense, physical, scientific) explanation. In other words, although we know perfectly well from our most immediate and direct experience that in our inner, noumenal being we are perpetually making choices and decisions which precipitate motions of matter in space outside us, which are then subject to natural law, we do not *and never can* know how we do it. Indeed, there is no *how* about it, in the sense that, like everything from the realm of the noumenal, such things must be, of their nature, inexplicable.

Kant believed, and so have many people since, that this account is not only coherent and persuasive on a theoretical level but accords with the reality of life as each one of us lives and experiences it; and that it is unclear or mysterious only at those points at which our most direct experience is itself unclear or mysterious. It is an account of the world of causality and the world of morality as being each autonomous, and not overlapping or in conflict with each other, and yet in touch with each other. Both are, or can be, internally consistent, and both are fields of cognition, though from no amount of knowledge in the one is it possible to deduce any knowledge in the other: you cannot derive an 'ought' from an 'is', or an 'is' from an 'ought'; you cannot construct moral concepts from empirical data, nor can you deduce the existence of any factual states of affairs from moral premises. It is true that the dimensionless point at which the two spheres touch, and the nature of the transmissions that take place at that point, baffle elucidation or description within this explanatory framework — but then, so do they in real life.

Fichte's most original and important insight consisted in seeing that the empirical and moral spheres, as thus apprehended, possessed, unperceived by Kant, a certain fundamental characteristic in common, and that this had far-reaching implications. Let us look first at the sphere of natural knowledge. We have seen how no amount of factual knowledge can guarantee the truth of a scientific law: the laws simply do not follow deductively from factual observations, and no number of such observations can bridge the gap. Fichte learnt this from Kant; but in doing so he was struck by the fact that there is a valid deductive relationship which runs in the opposite direction. Although scientific theories are not logically deducible from facts, facts are logically deducible from scientific theories, and must occur if the theories are correct. Now if one takes it for granted — as Fichte and Kant both did, and as everybody had done since Newton — that the laws of classical physics are objectively and timelessly true, then it is inescapably the case that the way things are follows with absolute logical necessity from an ordered conception of the world which we carry within us, namely our scientific conception of the world. This suggests a solution to what had been the fundamental problem of philosophy since Descartes, the problem of the relationship between our conceptions of the world and the world itself. Philosophers had always taken it for granted that the former must derive from the latter, and had become increasingly baffled by their inability to explain how it could do so. The answer, however, said Fichte, is that the latter derives from the former. In putting forward this doctrine he was pushing Kant's Copernican revolution to its limit. He saw the whole empirical world as deriving from the subject and taking the precise and detailed form it does out of logical necessity. However, since the world derives from our conception of it, and not the other way about, our conception of the world must itself be a free creation on our part — 'free' in this context meaning precisely that it has no empirical derivation. This doctrine was astonishingly prescient, foreshadowing as it does the logico-deductive scientific method, belief in some form of which has become an orthodoxy in the twentieth century. Thus it comes about that there are significant philosophers of science in our own day, for instance C. I. Lewis, who have consciously learned from Fichte — while others who have not, such as Popper and Chomsky, have something very obviously in common with him.[11] Unfortunately for Fichte himself, some of the

---

[11] Cf. my formulation of a view of Popper's which has been endorsed by him as accurate: 'If Newton's theory is not a body of truth inherent in the world, and derived by man from the observation of reality, where did it come from? The answer is it came from Newton.' (Bryan Magee: *Popper*, pp. 29–30.) Or: 'At every level, then, our knowledge can consist only of our theories. And our theories are the products of our

most fruitful implications of his original insight are visible only to people who are in a position to realize that scientific laws do not provide a rock-solid and unchanging basis for our knowledge of the world, but are corrigible and replaceable; and this realization was not reached until the twentieth century. The thing that struck *him* most forcibly about it was the identity of provenance which it revealed between the physical universe and the moral universe: for it meant that *both worlds derive from 'free' activity on the part of the noumenal self.* This self, the same self (what he called the *ego*) can thus be said to 'create' both worlds: and this, he thought, provides us with the key to the nature of total reality. This is so for the following reason. For morality to be possible there must be choice, and for choice to be a possibility for me it is necessary that something should exist other than my self. Similarly, for moral action to be a possibility for me there needs to be some challenge, something that exists in opposition to my self, or at least something that is a potential obstruction to my activity. So if I am to be a moral being at all it is necessary that there should be a world which is not me, a world of objects which can obstruct me. On the basis of this central argument Fichte evolved a philosophy according to which what is primal and original is the noumenal moral will, and this will brings into existence the phenomenal world as the requisite field for the self-objectification of moral activity. Thus the two worlds of the moral and the empirical are not logically unconnected in the way Kant presented them: the one presupposes the other, and their creation is interlinked.

Without going into the matter any further it can be noted at once that such a philosophy has the following features in common with Schopenhauer's. 1. What is primary and fundamental in the world is described as will — though of course the two philosophers use the word in different senses. 2. The entire world of phenomena is seen as being the creation of this will. 3. The act of creation involved is a 'free' act on the part of the will in the sense of being outside the domain of the principle of sufficient reason. 4. Since this domain of natural causality is co-extensive with the domain of natural knowledge, of understanding and reason, and hence of intellect, then intellect is a creation of will, and is brought into being to serve its purposes. 5. Man is not primarily

minds.' (Ibid., p. 34.) Cf. also Chomsky's: 'I assume that one of our faculties — one of our mental organs, if you like — is what we might term a science forming capacity, a capacity to create intelligible explanatory theories in certain domains. If we look at the history of science we discover that, time after time when particular questions were posed at a particular level of understanding, it was possible to make innovative leaps of the imagination to rich explanatory theories that presented an intelligible picture of that sub-domain of the universe. . . . Where it's possible, and we develop intelligible theories, we actually gain some comprehension of an aspect of the world.' (*Men of Ideas*, ed. by Bryan Magee, p. 216.)

a rational creature; what is primary in man is not reason but will. 6. It is inherent in the very nature of the phenomenal world, constitutive of its being, that it obstructs, if not opposes, the willed activity of individuals. 7. Morals and ontology are seen as two sides of the same coin, not unconnected as in Kant: the moral unity of the world, and the onto-logical and epistemological unity of the world, derive from the same source in such a way that the very existence itself of the world has a moral significance. 8. The whole philosophy thus outlined is seen as being the natural next step after Kant's, and thus the fulfilment of Kant's work: it develops implications of his thought which he himself did not perceive; and where it differs from him it is more accurately seen as a correction of his errors than as a rejection of him.

Even if the reader takes fully into account the difference in the two uses of the word 'will', and also the fact that I have ignored all those things that differentiate the two philosophies — and therefore artifici-ally highlighted the features which they have in common — he is still bound, I think, to be struck by the similarities. I cannot help suspecting that during the two years in which the student Schopenhauer attended Fichte's lectures a good deal more of what was said penetrated his mind and lodged in it than he subsequently appreciated. All thinkers are affected unconsciously by intellectual influences, and in this case their operation would have been facilitated by the extreme obscurity of Fichte's mode of utterance; for — given that what he was saying, though obscure, was not empty — someone of Schopenhauer's speci-fically philosophical genius would be likely to absorb more of so obfus-cated a content than he consciously realized.

Schelling came in for less abuse from Schopenhauer than did Fichte: patronization rather than direct insult was his portion. But, like Fichte, he had things of genuine originality, value and abiding influence to convey. In the course of a long and prolific life he developed his thought through a number of distinguishable and sometimes incompatible phases. The most famous and, until the twentieth century, the most influential of these was the so-called Philosophy of Nature, which he was propounding at about the turn of the century. Schopenhauer himself spoke grudgingly of 'the undeniable merit of Schelling in his *Naturphilosophie*, which is also the best of his many different attempts and new departures'.[12] In this philosophy Schelling depicted the total-ity of what exists as something which is perpetually evolving, and is therefore to be understood only in terms of the direction which its evolution takes. And the direction is towards an ever-increasing self-awareness. Since it is the totality of what exists that is involved in this

[12] *Parerga and Paralipomena*, i. 24.

process, the whole of reality can be viewed as one single developing organism. The most significant steps in this progress have been, first, the emergence of organic out of inorganic nature, and then, within organic nature, the emergence of man. The point to be stressed here is that it is *within* the natural world that man has come into existence, and developed, and he remains inextricably interwoven with it; he is of one stuff with it. He is, literally, spiritualized matter. So the human spirit, having emerged by imperceptible degrees within the material world, can be regarded as the inner essence of that world rendered conscious: Spirit is invisible Nature. Therefore Nature must be visible Spirit. The two are, in the depths of their being, one. Any view of reality which polarizes them is mistaken. Furthermore, both are essentially creative. We see nature being creative all around us all the time, *natura naturans*, bringing each day millions of new plants and animals of every kind into existence with a simply incredible profusion. But it is likewise the character of the human spirit to be perpetually creative, and in multiple ways, the highest of these being art. The only difference between the two creative processes is that in Nature the process is unselfconscious whereas in man it is self-conscious. In man's case it is the self-consciousness of his creative activity that reveals to him the innermost depths of his own being. But this can only mean that in the creation of the greatest art the ultimate purpose of the world's existence is accomplished, for the self-awareness of Spirit must include awareness of its identity with Nature, and the achievement of self-awareness on the part of total reality is the purpose of all existence.

Like Fichte's, this philosophy of Schelling's has a number of striking features in common with Schopenhauer's. To say that Nature is visible Spirit looks to me suspiciously like saying that the phenomenal world is the perceptible manifestation of the noumenal. Schelling and Schopenhauer both see the character of this phenomenal world as essentially evolutionary; both see the fundamental driving force of this evolutionary process as something which is not rational or mental; both see the goal of the process as being the achievement of self-awareness on the part of what exists; both see man as having been produced in the course of this process in order to serve the ends of the process; both assert an identity of inner nature between man and the natural world; both see creative art as the highest, or among the highest, of human activities, one that lets us look into the ultimate nature of what is (though in Schopenhauer's case music was thought of as being the only art that did this). One can say that Schelling and Schopenhauer are in a class apart from all other well-known philosophers in the importance they attribute to art in the total scheme of things. By Schopenhauer's lights, Schelling's whole philosophy is superficial in that its application

is largely within the world of phenomena — as indeed its label 'the
Philosophy of Nature' implies — but, nevertheless, what the two
philosophers have to say about this phenomenal world is, in all the
many points I have just listed, similar.

I do not think there can be much doubt that Schelling had a greater
influence on the German romantic movement than any other philosopher. This was chiefly because his insistence on the identity of man
with Nature, and on the quasi-religious importance of art, accorded
with already-existing fundamental features of romanticism, as did also
his anti-rationalism, and his view of creative geniuses as the embodi-
ments of the world's *raison d'être*. Many of the leading romantics regarded him as having organized into a conceptual system the ultimate
truths which were expressed individually in works of great art. His
influence on them was enhanced by personal acquaintance: many of
the best-known German romantic artists were friends of his, including
Goethe, Weber, Hölderlin and Novalis, and his wife had been formerly
the wife of August Schlegel. However, it was not only the romantics of
Germany who came under his influence: Coleridge was deeply in his
debt intellectually, and through Coleridge he had an important influence on English romanticism.

Schelling's thought, partly because it was so chameleon-like and
changeable, was rich in suggestion, and some of the leads he threw out
were not to be fully taken up and worked on until the twentieth century.
For example, it is now claimed for him that he anticipated Gestalt
psychology (see Macmillan's *Encyclopaedia of Philosophy*, volume vii, p.
307). Ernst Cassirer regarded Schelling as his only significant fore-
runner in paying serious philosophical attention to myth (see the many
references to Schelling in Cassirer's *The Philosophy of Symbolic Forms*,
volume 2, *Mythical Thought*). And in the final phase of the development
of Schelling's philosophy (when incidentally his lecture audience in
Berlin included Kierkegaard, Burckhardt, Engels and Bakunin)
Schelling addressed himself directly to what many people nowadays
would think of as the ultimate question of modern existentialism — in
his own words, 'the final desperate question: why is there anything at
all? Why not nothing?' We have seen earlier that this question had been
posed previously by Leibniz and reiterated by Schopenhauer;[13] but
Schelling had written already in 1785, before Schopenhauer was even
born, that 'the main function of all philosophy is the solution of the
problem of the existence of the world'. Kierkegaard did not like Schelling's lectures, and stopped going to them, but the fact remains that they

---

[13] See also Wittgenstein: 'It is not *how* things are in the world that is mystical, but *that*
it exists.' (*Tractatus Logico-Philosophicus*, 6. 44.)

are of active interest to the post-Heideggerian existentialists of today, and are often referred to in their writings. Altogether, then, it can securely be claimed for Schelling that his thought had real content, that it has exercised a substantial influence on gifted people, and that he published before Schopenhauer did a good many of the thoughts which Schopenhauer considered worth publishing.

The relationship of Schopenhauer's thought to Hegel's was, in one sense, the opposite of what it was to Fichte's and Schelling's. As I have shown, the work of these last two bore widespread similarities to Schopenhauer's which his rage at their fraudulent misuses of language and of argument blinded him to. When others pointed them out he dismissed them contemptuously: 'My works had scarcely excited the attention of a few when the dispute as to priority arose with regard to my fundamental idea, and it was stated that Schelling had once said "willing is original and primary being" — and anything else of this kind that could be adduced. With regard to the matter itself, it may be observed that the root of my philosophy is to be found already in the Kantian, especially in Kant's doctrine of the empirical and intelligible characters, but generally in the fact that, whenever Kant brings the thing-in-itself somewhat nearer to the light, it always appears through its veil as *will*. I have expressly drawn attention to this in my "Criticism of the Kantian Philosophy", and accordingly have said that my philosophy is only his, thought out to the end. Therefore we need not wonder if the philosophemes of Fichte and Schelling, which also start from Kant, show traces of the same fundamental idea, although they there appear without sequence, continuity, or development, and accordingly may be regarded as a mere foreshadowing of my doctrine. In general, however, it may be said on this point that, before every great truth has been discovered, a previous feeling, a presentiment, a faint outline thereof, as in a fog, is made manifest, and there is a vain attempt to grasp it just because the progress of the times prepares the way for it. Accordingly, it is preluded by isolated utterances; but he alone is the author of a truth who has recognized it from its grounds and has thought it out to its consequents; who has developed its whole content and has surveyed the extent of its domain; and who, fully aware of its value and importance, has therefore expounded it clearly and coherently . . . Columbus is the discoverer of America, not the first shipwrecked sailor who was cast up there by the waves.'[14]

In the case of Hegel, by contrast, what he had to say that is of real value is radically different from anything Schopenhauer had to say.

---

[14] *Parerga and Paralipomena*, i. 132–3.

Indeed, some of Hegel's most significant contributions to thought correspond directly to shortcomings in Schopenhauer's philosophy. This obviously helps to explain why Schopenhauer was so blind to their substance. I have instanced already Hegel's grasp of the fact that the history of ideas is constitutive of all ideas, and the history of art of all art, an insight which Schopenhauer — passionate scholar though he was, and with a special reverence for the classics — surprisingly failed to absorb, despite the fact that he was lucidly aware not only that, but also how, the history of philosophy was constitutive of his own philosophy. (He even went so far as to cite the essentially historical character of Hegel's philosophy as an illustration of its valuelessness.) Another important example of complementarity between the two philosophers is Hegel's understanding that, precisely because all aspects of culture and civilization are constituted by their own histories, they are all essentially social phenomena; and that one of the consequences of this is that the classical liberal conception of independent individuals coming together to form a society and to decide on its terms is profoundly uncomprehending. For the individuals are themselves largely constituted by society. Its language provides them with the very categories in terms of which they think, and everything about their outlook and values is historically and socially influenced. This means that the relationship of the individual to his own society is organic, not mechanical, and it means also that he has a special relationship to other members of the same society — he is like them on the inside, as it were; they are tissue of the same social organism — which is fundamentally different in kind from his relationships to members of other societies. All these valid and important insights are such as Schopenhauer — with his essentially Humean political outlook, his rampant individualism and his militant misanthropy — was incapable of sharing. Significantly, it has continued to be philosophers who, so far as politics goes, are in the direct line of descent from classical liberalism, such as Russell and Popper, who fail to see the point of what Hegel is saying. But despite the calibre of these sceptics I find myself unable to regard the existence of genuinely weighty and intelligible content in the philosophy of Hegel as being in doubt.

As for Hegel's influence, it is difficult to gainsay Walter Kaufmann's characterization of him as 'one of the most influential philosophers of all time: indeed, the history of philosophy since his death could be represented as a series of revolts against him and his followers. A little more than a century after his death, few followers were left, but much of his thought had been absorbed by his opponents, and to gain some historical perspective on Kierkegaard and Marx, on Marxism and existentialism, on pragmatism and analytic philosophy, on neo-orthodoxy and the so-called new criticism, Hegel's influence must be taken into account as one of the key factors.'[15] This is indeed so, and if only for that reason I look on any refusal to take Hegel seriously as indefensible. What makes it so seductively easy in our day to sympathize with hostility to Hegel is the fact that he was the common philosophical forebear of the two most destructive forms of totalitarianism that have afflicted the world since his death — Nazism, through his shaping influence on the development of German nationalism, and Communism, through his decisive influence on Marx. However, to deny his ability on these grounds seems to me as absurd as it would be to deny the genius of Karl Marx. It is true that the ideas of both men played an important role in the formation of states which then murdered a great many millions of their own citizens; but it is true also that both men made contributions of lasting value to human thought.

[15] *The Concise Encyclopaedia of Western Philosophy and Philosophers*, edited by J. O. Urmson, p. 157.

Appendix 2

Schopenhauer and Later Thinkers

Towards the end of Chapter 1 I mentioned some of the reasons why, and some of the ways in which, Schopenhauer's reputation began to grow in the middle and late 1850s. That sudden and unprecedented rash of articles, lectures and references did not fade after the first flush, as intellectual fashions normally do, but took hold, and spread, so that most people with an awareness of movements in contemporary thought began to encounter Schopenhauer's name either then or at some point during the subsequent decade. By the end of the century he had come to be regarded generally as one of the 'great' philosophers. The period of highest estimation and influence ran from somewhere around 1880 to about the First World War. After that, although his name has ever since remained known to educated people, acquaintance with his work declined to the point where even most professional philosophers ceased to study it. Only in the last few years has that movement gone into reverse — indeed now, at last, there are unmistakable signs of a serious revival of interest.

This is due to many things. There is an increasing disenchantment with positivism and the empiricist tradition generally, and in consequence of this a turning towards Kant and the traditions of thought inaugurated by him. And of the philosophers in that tradition, the most congenial to readers reared in empiricism is likely to be Schopenhauer — whose work was long ago described as 'Kant seen through the eyes of a British empiricist'. It will be remembered that he made a conscious attempt to write like Hume. His vigorous commitment to rationality, argument, clarity, and scientific criteria of validation in empirical matters is profoundly congenial to many Anglo-Saxon readers, and is in almost comic contrast to philosophy produced in traditions that derive from Hegel or Marx. Furthermore, a lot of what are characteristically thought of as 'modern' ideas concerning science, religion, psychology, sex and other central concerns of life were put forward for the first time by Schopenhauer, sometimes surprisingly vividly. Professional philosophers have belatedly come to realize that his influence on Wittgenstein was so great that Wittgenstein's work cannot be understood without substantial reference to it. In other quarters he is seen as one of the forerunners of humanist existentialism. It is for these among other reasons that he is becoming once more a focus of interest for philosophers, some of them philosophers of incompatible kinds.

However, when his fame was new the aspects of Schopenhauer's thought which caught people's attention and were liable to attract or influence them were not the same as they are now. Without trying to marshal these into an order of importance, there was first his atheism: Schopenhauer was, perhaps surprisingly, the first major Western philosopher to make a point of atheism. (Hobbes and Hume, both of whom may well have been atheists in fact, went out of their way to dissociate themselves from atheism; and all the other great philosophers since the fall of the Roman Empire had been Christians.) By the middle of the nineteenth century a substantial proportion of intelligent and educated people had ceased to believe in God, yet they saw no large-scale thought-system available to them which dispensed with the concept of God, except for the one implicit in science. Added to that, and no doubt related to it in giving Schopenhauer his appeal, there was his tragic view of life. This was in startling contrast to the optimism of alternative currents of thought, whether religious, scientistic, neo-Kantian, Anglo-Saxon liberal, Continental liberal, socialistic, or nationalistic. Then there was his evolutionism, which, after Darwin, became one of the most prominent characteristics of 'advanced' thinking in the second half of the nineteenth century. Schopenhauer was the first great philosopher to see the mind in biological terms, to see it first and foremost as a physical organ at work, a survival mechanism whose operations are to be understood only in terms of the functions for which it has been evolved; and to see in this light that man is not a rational animal, since mind is not a spectator but an instrument, constructed not for the detached observation of the world or the impersonal acquisition of knowledge but to light the field for action, and is therefore not sovereign but subordinate to the purposes of the will. This was as influential as any of his doctrines, and was embraced by many people who came to feel that the standard Enlightenment view of the place of intellect in human life was indefensible. In addition, Schopenhauer had shown more insight than anyone else into the role of the unconscious at a time when educated people were beginning to encounter that concept for the first time. The newness of this whole range of ideas was what most struck the majority of his readers in the decades following his death — a newness which, to state the obvious, is lost to us now and can never return. To these attractions are to be added yet others. The spectacular achievements of the seventeenth century in science and mathematics, which so tyrannized over philosophy for two hundred years, began to slip from their position of exclusive dominance after the Enlightenment, with the result that during the nineteenth century thoughtful people put more and more emphasis on alternative ways of exploring human experience — for instance the romantic movement elevated the arts into something approaching a religion, and this so suffused the general mental climate that in the remainder of the century most cultivated Europeans, and not only romantics, attributed an unprecedented importance to art in the total scheme of things. To all of these historically important developments in thought, perceptions and attitudes during the middle and late nineteenth century, Schopenhauer's contribution was as great as anyone's.

By the turn of the century, then, Schopenhauer was an all-pervading cultural influence. In some places this influence was almost inescapably strong.[1] This being so, the thread of it cannot be neatly unravelled from the fabric of the times and laid before the reader by itself. At some points it is merely a suggestion, a tinge, a colour; sometimes its presence is disclosed in an unexpected quarter by the unattributed use of one of Schopenhauer's memorable phrases or images. Because of the sharp aphoristic quality of his prose he came to be widely quoted, but as an index of influence that can be misleading — for instance Darwin quoted Schopenhauer approvingly in *The Descent of Man* (Chapter 20, second paragraph) but it looks as if Darwin never himself actually read Schopenhauer but got the quotation from an article which had appeared in the *Journal of Anthropology* for January 1871 under the title 'Schopenhauer and Darwinism', which he had naturally read with interest. However, there have been some thinkers since Schopenhauer on whom his influence was so great that their work cannot be understood without reference to it. These include two major philosophers, Nietzsche and Wittgenstein. The rest of this appendix will concern itself with Nietzsche and other important figures up to the early years of the twentieth century, and the next with Wittgenstein. Without wishing to suggest in any way that creative artists are not thinkers I shall, if only for the sake of clarity, hold over until later appendices the discussion of their response to Schopenhauer's influence.

According to Nietzsche it was Schopenhauer who enabled him to become a philosopher at all. This was done, not by any process of conversion or external revelation but by helping him to find his true self. For he had started by aiming at academic distinction, and achieving it with unparalleled precocity. His student university, Leipzig, awarded him his doctorate without requiring him to submit a thesis or undergo examination, so as to enable him to take up, at the age of twenty-four, an Associate Professorship in Classical Philology at the

[1] For instance in Vienna. See *Wittgenstein's Vienna* by Allan Janik and Stephen Toulmin.

University of Basel — where he was made a full professor in the following year. As his mentor Friedrich Ritschl wrote, 'in Germany that sort of thing happens absolutely never'. By the age of twenty-five Nietzsche was already half-way towards becoming a classical scholar of international reputation (which is what the closest friend of his youth, Erwin Rohde, subsequently did). But instead, under the influence of Schopenhauer's example, he put all this behind him and embraced Schopenhauer's pattern of life, a life of complete independence from universities and all other institutions and authorities, throughout which he expressed a loud contempt for academe in general and university philosophers in particular; a life of extreme personal isolation and loneliness, during which the world disregarded his work almost totally until after he had stopped producing any — by which time he was unable to relish his vindication, having lost his reason. The two men had a remarkable number of personal attributes in common: both were psychologists of genius, deeply musical, superb prose stylists, despisers of the generality of mankind and the world in which they found themselves, venerators of antiquity, atheists, unbalanced haters of women, animal lovers, racists, anti-socialists, despisers of Germany and Germans in spite of being themselves German — one could continue a good deal further the list of their similarities in character and outlook. There is no surprise at all in the fact that when Nietzsche came across Schopenhauer's work for the first time he felt as if he had discovered a philosopher who was writing for him personally.

The discovery happened in a second-hand bookshop in Leipzig in the autumn of 1865, when Nietzsche was a twenty-one-year-old student. He picked up a copy of *The World as Will and Representation* knowing little or nothing about it, bought it on impulse, took it home, and started to read it. The impact was immediate. 'I belong to those readers of Schopenhauer who know quite definitely after reading the first page that they will read every page, and will listen to every word he had to say. My confidence in him was instantaneous, and remains the same today as it was nine years ago. To express myself intelligibly, if arrogantly and foolishly: I understood him as if he had written especially for me.'[2] This quotation is from an account of the experience which Nietzsche published in 1874 under the title *Schopenhauer as Educator*, the third of his four *Untimely Meditations* (*Unzeitgemässe Betrachtungen*, translated also as *Thoughts out of Season*). As he himself was to remark later still, in *Ecce Homo* (1888): although *Schopenhauer as Educator* presents itself as an account of Nietzsche's discovery of Schopenhauer it is really an account of Nietzsche's discovery of himself. It tells how, at the time

---

[2] Nietzsche: *Schopenhauer as Educator*, Chapter 2.

when he encountered Schopenhauer, he was already half-consciously looking for someone who could show him how to be a philosopher in the unpropitious circumstances of the age. Schopenhauer showed him how to do it by insisting on three things: first, an intellectual independence of everything outside himself, and an integrity that followed the truth wheresoever it might lead with as much disregard for self as for others; second, the very special sort of consistency that this confers on the resultant work; and third, pursuing this whole vocation with gusto, zest, exuberance, the exhilaration of adventure and conquest.

The first of these three insistences involves daring to think what one really does think, and this in turn involves penetrating into the depths of oneself. 'How can man know himself? He is a dark and hidden thing; whereas the hare is said to have seven skins, man can take off seven times seventy skins and still not be able to say: "That is you as you really are, that is no longer mere external appearance." Besides, it is a painful and dangerous undertaking to dig down into oneself in this way and to descend violently and directly into the shaft of one's being. How easily a man could injure himself doing this, so that no doctor could cure him.'[3] It was precisely because Schopenhauer had enabled him to do this that Nietzsche regarded him as his chief liberator, and therefore his chief educator. 'Your real educators and shapers disclose the true original meaning and the basic material of your being, which is something quite incapable of being educated or shaped, and to which access is in any case difficult since it is fettered and chained as it is. Your educators can be nothing more than your liberators. And that is the secret of all education . . .'.[4] In this context it is revealing to learn that, according to Freud's biographer Ernest Jones, Freud 'several times said of Nietzsche that he had a more penetrating knowledge of himself than any other man who ever lived or was ever likely to live'.

Within a short time of discovering Schopenhauer, Nietzsche was describing himself to his friends as a Schopenhauerian, and he continued to regard himself as such for several years. However, shortly before he left Leipzig another idol was to step up on to the highest pedestal alongside Schopenhauer, and that was Wagner. On 28 October 1868 Nietzsche heard the preludes to *Tristan* and *The Mastersingers* and was swept off his feet. 'For the life of me I cannot preserve an attitude of cool criticism in listening to this music; every nerve in my being is set tingling . . . .'[5] Eleven days later he met the composer. 'He is an astoundingly vivacious and high-spirited man, speaks very rapidly,

---

[3] *Schopenhauer as Educator*, Chapter 1.
[4] Ibid., Chapter 1.
[5] Letter to Erwin Rohde, reprinted in *The Nietzsche–Wagner Correspondence* (translated by Caroline V. Kerr), p. 4.

is extremely witty, and is very animated when in the company of intimate friends. During the course of the evening we had a long conversation about Schopenhauer, and you can imagine my unbounded joy at hearing him say, with indescribable enthusiasm, how much he owed to Schopenhauer, and to hear Schopenhauer described as the only philosopher who had recognized the true nature of music.'[6] The veneration shared by these two for Schopenhauer was unquestionably one of the things that caused their friendship to develop from those beginnings. And as it did so Nietzsche retained an awareness that, for him at least, Schopenhauer was bound up with it in some deep-lying way. The following summer he wrote to Erwin Rohde: 'Wagner embodies all the qualities one could possibly desire. The world has not the faintest conception of his greatness as a man and of his exceptional nature. I have learned an enormous amount from my association with him: it is like taking a practical course in Schopenhauerian philosophy.'[7] At about the same time he wrote to Wagner: 'The highest and most inspiring moments of my life are closely associated with your name, and I know of only one other man, and that man your twin brother of intellect, Arthur Schopenhauer, whom I regard with the same veneration — yea, even more, as *religione quadam*.'[8] It is clear that by this time Wagner and Schopenhauer had become so associated with each other in Nietzsche's mind that in some ways he thought of them as a sort of composite personality. As one of his English biographers, R. J. Hollingdale, has put it (obviously echoing Nietzsche's phrase just quoted): 'Wagner and Schopenhauer now combine to become what is emotionally Nietzsche's new religion.'[9] When Nietzsche spent the following Christmas as a guest of the Wagner family his Christmas present to the composer was a portrait of Schopenhauer with Wagner's coat of arms on the frame.

Nietzsche and Wagner, themselves geniuses of the front rank, and in different fields, each regarded his reading of Schopenhauer as having changed the course of both his life and his work. The two of them discussed Schopenhauer incessantly. Their friendship, one of the most remarkable in the history of European culture, is the subject of a small literature, and there is no need for me to go here into the story of its ripening and disintegration.[10] Suffice it to say that to the twilight of his

---

[6] Letter to Rohde, 9 November 1868 (ibid., pp. 8–9).

[7] *The Nietzsche–Wagner Correspondence*, p. 15.

[8] Ibid., p. 12.

[9] From page 22 of the volume containing Hollingdale's translation of Nietzsche's *Ecce Homo*, published by Penguin Books, 1979.

[10] Probably the best version of this is the one embedded in the fourth volume of Ernest Newman's *Life of Richard Wagner*.

days, through and beyond all the subsequent hostilities between himself and Wagner, Nietzsche treasured the memory of their conversations as the most enriching experience of his life. Needless to say, their talk about Schopenhauer inhabited a wider context of conversation about other things. Several decades later, in 1914, Nietzsche's sister Elizabeth recalled one occasion when they had all been out walking together. 'Wagner, Frau Cosima and my brother began to speak of the tragedy of human life, of the Greeks, of the Germans, and of their mutual plans and wishes. Never in my whole life, either before or since, have I heard such marvellous harmony in the conversation of three persons so fundamentally different. Each one had his own strong personal note, his own theme which was sharply emphasized, yet the whole was like some wondrously beautiful symphony. Each one of these three rare natures was at its best, each shone with its own brilliance, and yet no one of the three was overshadowed by the others.'[11] In his own later life, Nietzsche looked back on this period as his lost Eden. In *Ecce Homo*, written only weeks before his final collapse, he wrote: 'I need to say a word to express my gratitude for that which of all things has refreshed me by far the most profoundly and cordially. That was without any doubt my intimate association with Richard Wagner. I offer all my other human relationships cheap; but at no price would I relinquish from my life the Tribschen days, those days of mutual confidences, of cheerfulness, of sublime incidents — of *profound* moments ... I do not know what others may have experienced with Wagner: over *our* sky no cloud ever passed ... My first contact with Wagner was also the first time in my life I ever drew a deep breath ... I declare Wagner to have been the greatest benefactor of my life.'

Nietzsche's rebellion against both Wagner and Schopenhauer was more or less inevitable. His idolization of both was such that outgrowing it was a necessity for the achievement of his own maturity and independence. The need was given additional edge by the fact that the overriding tendency of Schopenhauer's influence on him was its encouragement of him to dare to be himself. And it was sharpened still further by the fact that the special nature of Nietzsche's genius lay in the audacity with which he rejected assumptions of a fundamental character and looked the consequences of doing so in the eye. But at the same time there was something undeniably adolescent about the particular character of his rebellion, for his attitude to both Schopenhauer and Wagner had been in some obvious way filial. He regarded Schopenhauer, as we have seen, as his chief educator. Wagner had been born in the same year as Nietzsche's father, was thirty-one years older than him, and was already internationally famous when the young student Nietzsche met him. It is notoriously often the case with adolescent revolt that the rebel is obsessed, and in that sense still dominated, by what he rebels against; and thus it was to prove for Nietzsche. His obsession with Wagner was lifelong: to quote Hollingdale again, Wagner was 'an influence which, despite all his efforts, Nietzsche could not shake off until his dying day'. In the last year before he went mad he published *The Wagner Case* and wrote *Nietzsche Contra Wagner* (his very last book). As for the influence of Schopenhauer, Nietzsche's philosophy developed in such a way as to retain Schopenhauer's insistence on the primacy of the will as its cardinal point, but to adopt an attitude towards the will which was the diametrical opposite of Schopenhauer's. He regarded this as constituting a fundamental rejection of Schopenhauer's teaching — and then wrote of him:

> What he *taught* is put aside;
> What he *lived*, that will abide —
> Behold a man!
> Subject he was to none.

Nietzsche's thought was always highly personalized, and it was part of his strategy as a polemicist to say deliberately shocking things about whoever he was criticizing; so it is easy in his later writings to find remarks about Schopenhauer and Wagner which, if looked at by themselves, seem to express contempt. But when all the evidence is gathered in, no doubt is left whatever that he went into the dark with his underlying veneration for both of them intact. When Wagner died he remarked to a friend: 'It was hard to be for six years the enemy of the man one most reveres.'[12]

For most of his working life Nietzsche made no attempt to create a systematic philosophy of the kind Schopenhauer and Kant had each produced. He wrote chiefly (not entirely) in two forms: long essays and aphorisms. The best of the latter incorporate lightning flashes and thunderbolts of insight which it is impossible to imagine being seamlessly integrated into any interlocking philosophical system — indeed, for a long time Nietzsche consciously believed that to systematize was to adapt and therefore to bend and falsify. But in his last four working years he began to plan a book which was to be the summation of his life's work, a book which would at last bring his manifold insights together and exhibit them in their relations to each other. It was to be called *The Will to Power*. He prepared hundreds of pages of material for

[12] J. P. Stern, *Nietzsche*, p. 35 of the Fontana edition.

it, but never wrote it. (Various assemblages of this material have been published by different editors with the same title, which makes for a somewhat confused situation.) He abandoned *The Will to Power* during the year before his madness, and decided instead to draw the elements of his philosophy together in a four-part work under the title *The Revaluation of all Values*. Only the first part was written. However, by this time the outlines of a coherent approach were clear in his work, as he himself had obviously come to realize, and it is possible to give a sketch of that approach which derives support from his writings at every point.

Nietzsche came to believe that the world of actual and possible experience, what Schopenhauer had referred to as the world of phenomena, is the only world there is — that there is no noumenal world, no ideal realm, no God, no autonomous domain of values or of morals, all these being human inventions. So if we want to think straight, and see things as they really are, we have to extricate and extirpate from our thinking everything that to any degree at all incorporates these illusions. This, easy to say, is almost impossibly difficult to do, for it means getting underneath the deepest-lying presuppositions of most of our important beliefs and assumptions, and proceeding from that level to create new ones. The independence of mind with which Nietzsche embarks on this task is frightening for almost anyone who makes a serious attempt to follow him in it. As the familiar props and stays of our world are exultantly ripped out and tossed behind us our accustomed orientation dissolves. Our guide out there in front may be showing every sign of exhilaration, but in us, more mundanely liable to vertigo, anxiety begins to rise as the light brightens but the landmarks disappear; the air dazzles, becomes difficult to breathe; agoraphobia sets in. 'Philosophy, as I have hitherto understood and lived it, is a voluntary living in ice and high mountains . . . How much truth can a spirit *bear*, how much truth can a spirit *dare*? that became for me more and more the measure of real value.'[13]

Nietzsche always remained in agreement with Schopenhauer that what is ultimate in this world of ours is energy, the force that constitutes it all and drives it; and he went along with Schopenhauer in giving that energy the name 'will', applying this, as Schopenhauer did, to inorganic as well as organic Nature. But he held that in equating this will with the will to live (or, in the case of inorganic nature, some sort of not-further-explicable will to exist) Schopenhauer had made what may seem at first sight to be a small but is in fact a highly significant error. For it should be equated with the will to *survive*, and this introduces the

---

[13] Nietzsche, Foreword to *Ecce Homo*.

all-important notion of struggle. The only way anything that exists can be, and can continue, is by imposing itself on its environment, and in one sense or other conquering, subjugating, absorbing, displacing or repelling other things in it. Plants, animals and men all live off each other in the literal sense that they devour each other and transubstantiate what they have devoured into their own physical substance: they survive, and can survive only, by destroying each other. As for human beings, in addition to devouring animals and plants wholesale they destroy other human beings on almost as profligate a scale, and in even more multifarious ways. No one has described all this more vividly, indeed unforgettably, than Schopenhauer. But whereas Schopenhauer recoiled from it as from a nightmare, exclaiming that it would have been better for nothing to exist at all than for existence to sustain itself on these terms, Nietzsche — and here comes the pivot of his diametrical opposition — embraced it with the insistence that life is the supreme and ultimately the only value, so that if one loves life, asserts life — says *Yes* to life, as he puts it — and if life obtains only on these terms, then one embraces these terms. One cannot revel in life, exult in life, and at the same time reject the pre-conditions of life. Indeed, the more one loves life *as it is* (and there is no other) the more one rejoices in the pre-conditions that enable it to be as it is.

In Nietzsche's eyes it was simply a fact of biology that the evolution of mankind from the beginnings of life itself via a continuous process of development through higher and higher species was an endlessly internecine affair whose central principle was the survival of the fittest (he was much influenced by Darwin[14]), the perpetual elimination of the 'lower' by the 'higher'. In human history, similarly, civilization and culture in all its forms have developed out of bestiality and barbarism only because the stronger or the cleverer, or the more ingenious, or the more creative, or the braver, or the more persistent, or the more energetic, or the more enterprising, are for ever displacing the less. If it were not so there would be no civilization, indeed no humanity. So people who regard the elimination of the weak by the strong as a barbarism are standing reality on its head. And here we come to Nietzsche's root-and-branch opposition to the moralities of the Greek and Christian traditions. His most simple, central point was that the processes which have produced the evolution of ever higher and higher species, and which in the highest species of all have produced civilization, ought to be encouraged and not obstructed, approved and not denounced; and that the recognition of this constitutes true values, and

[14] 'There can be no doubt that even though Nietzsche's conception of life as a warlike process owes something to Heraclitus, it owes a good deal more to Darwin and his followers.' J. P. Stern, *Nietzsche*, p. 73.

the denial of it constitutes false values. In following up this point it seemed to him obvious that the creation, preservation and transmission of all the things that go to make up civilization are the work of a gifted few, and that the rest of mankind is a sort of rabble; so he considered it both morally and culturally desirable that the creative activities of the former should not be hamstrung by any undue consideration for the latter. However, the latter, being the vast majority, have imposed moralities and values that favour themselves — to the effect that people with the power to settle conflicts in their own favour should not do so, but should submit instead to processes of law; that the strong should defer to the weak, the minority to the majority; that everyone should count as equal, regardless of ability or intelligence; that the feeble, the sickly, the defective and the unproductive should not be eliminated but, on the contrary, nurtured and preserved by the strong and healthy at their own expense and risk; and so on. These moralities, put forward in the name of 'humanity' as being a necessary foundation for civilized life, are in reality the precise opposite: they run counter to everything that has made the evolution of mankind — and then, after that, the development of civilization — possible. In other words, during the last two thousand years or so (Nietzsche dates the decline from Socrates) the principles on which the whole evolution before that from the amoeba up to civilized man had been based have been put into reverse, and opposite principles are now universally propagated which can only have the effect of preventing further advance and corrupting what has been already achieved.

This is 'morality' as it actually is. Gifted individuals, like all others, are now born into societies which inculcate it from birth, so that it becomes constitutive of each developing personality at such a deep level that it is almost impossible for the individual to uncover and expose it within himself. Thus the natural development of his personality, as it would have occurred without such a deformation, is denied him — he is, as Nietzsche puts it, un-selfed. '*Anti-nature* itself has received the highest honours as morality, and has hung over mankind as law, as categorical imperative! . . . That contempt has been taught for the primary instinct of life; that a "soul", a "spirit" has been *lyingly invented* in order to destroy the body; that one teaches that there is something unclean in the precondition of life, sexuality; that the principle of evil is sought in that which is most profoundly necessary for prosperity, in *strict* selfishness (— the very word is slanderous!); on the other hand that one sees in the typical signs of decline and contradictoriness of instinct, in the "selfless", in loss of centre of gravity, in "depersonalization", in "love of one's neighbour", the *higher* value! . . . The sole morality which has hitherto been taught, the morality of unselfing, betrays a will to the end, it *denies* the very foundations of life.'[15]

So Nietzsche declares himself implacably hostile to the whole of morality as it has historically existed, and his programme is to sweep it away and replace it with the opposite, true values of nature and life-assertion. 'This is my formula for a supreme coming-to-oneself on the part of mankind.' It is the most important part of his programme for 'the revaluation of all values'. He believes he has achieved it in himself by what one might now see as a process of self-analysis in a near-Freudian sense — the reader will remember both his words about it being 'a painful and dangerous undertaking to dig down into oneself in this way' and my quotation of Freud's tribute to his unique self-knowledge. If Freud's judgement is accepted then Nietzsche's claim 'It is my fate to have been the first . . . to know myself in opposition to the mendaciousness of millennia' is not without foundation. Nietzsche believed that as the pioneer showing the way he would be the first of many, and that this would reactivate the now moribund processes of evolution and lead to the development of a new and superior kind of human being, what he called an *Übermensch*. This concept has been much misrepresented. What Nietzsche meant by it was primarily someone being his full natural self, living out his instinct and impulses and drives and desires, *being* to the top of his bent, authentic and whole, and exulting in the spontaneity and pleasure of it. In Freudian terms the *Übermensch* is an unrepressed human being, someone uncrippled and untrammelled by inhibitions, whether of morality or any other sort; someone who has been without a Super-ego from the beginning, and is all Ego and Id. Of course, between individuals living in this unrestrained way there would be conflict without compromise, and those who came off worst would suffer or die, but that is as it should be, and as creative evolution always has been (and that of course is why it is creative) — and it is therefore to be welcomed. 'To regard *states of distress* in general as an objection, as something that must be *abolished*, is the *niaiserie par excellence*, in a general sense a real disaster in its conse-quences, a fatality of stupidity — almost as stupid as would be the will to abolish bad weather — perhaps from pity to the poor.'[16]

Serious consideration of whether and how anything that could be called a society could function in these circumstances is notably absent from Nietzsche's thought. It is clear from his writings that he envisaged the society he was advocating as consisting of the masses led by an élite; but all the serious problems of how the individual members of the élite

---

[15] *Ecce Homo*, 'Why I am a Destiny', §7.
[16] Ibid., §4.

274 Schopenhauer and Later Thinkers

could relate to each other on Nietzschean principles, how any large-scale organization that required co-operation between leaders would be possible, and what the nature of such a society's institutions would have to be, are passed over in silence. There is, astonishingly, no social or political (and, consequently, no historical) dimension to Nietzsche's thought at all: he writes only in terms of the individual and the anonymous mass, and as if the self-realization and self-becoming of the individual were all in all. I suspect, indeed I believe, that the questions to which he failed to address himself are insoluble in terms of his approach.

An even more striking gap in Nietzsche's philosophy, and one that bears much more closely on our present concerns, is his disregard — astonishing in so self-aware and profoundly courageous a thinker — of the fundamental problems of ontology and epistemology. As J. P. Stern writes: 'Nothing is so characteristic of his way of thinking as his lack of interest in the classical problems of epistemology and his habit of converting every epistemological problem into a moral and existential one . . . It is not knowledge and the pursuit of it that are absolute, but "life" and the personal being of those who heed its demands.'[17] This led him to rest on 'solutions' to what some of us regard as the most fundamental problems of all which can only be regarded as frivolous in so audacious a thinker. In particular, his way with the two most intractable problems that must confront every transcendental realist is preposterously short. The first, the antinomies of time and space, he solves by simply asserting a doctrine of eternal recurrence: everything that happens has happened before and will happen again. In an infinite number of earlier epicycles I have sat here at this desk with this pen in my hand writing these words, and I shall do so again in an infinite number of future epicycles. Of necessity, this is a doctrine of the eternal recurrence of space as well as of time, and it enables him to posit both time and space as being endless yet not unbounded, and thus to 'answer' the questions which are posed on both sides of each antinomy. The second fundamental problem, the problem of our knowledge of objects, he 'solves' by a simple concession of defeat. It is perfectly true, he says, that our consciousness of objects must be something categorially different from the objects themselves, and that direct access to objects as they are in themselves, independent of the forms of our experience of them, is something we can never have, so that the difference between the world as it is and the conception we have of it is to its very bottom un-understandable by us. But this merely means that we must recognize that consciousness *as such* is made up of illusions. Truths about the world are simply not available to us, nor can we form

[17] J. P. Stern: *Nietzsche*, p. 66.

any conception of what they would be like. At this, the deepest of all epistemological levels, 'error and delusion are the conditions of life — I mean the most profound errors. To know them is not to be rid of them.'[18] So with these ultimate errors which we cannot extirpate we must live as best we can, and not let our ignorance hinder our being.

Although I agree that every consistent realist must acknowledge a radical, categorial difference between the world and any possible knowledge we can have of it, for him to do so is to bring forward a problem, not a solution. Nietzsche's way with the implications of this is at each stage the cavalier one of putting forward solutions which are really problems. A typical example is the following. 'How then (Nietzsche asks), if we have no positive contact with "the real world", can we sustain life? How is it that the world works? It works with the help of an illusion, on an "as if —" principle. We act in the world as if we were in touch with a benevolent reality, as if we were capable of comprehending its cosmic purpose, as if there were a divinity whose decrees we fulfil and who gives meaning to our individual lives. Between words and things there is no direct relationship . . . words are said to be the distant and distorted "echoes of nervous impulses". These "echoes" or rudimentary elements are "poeticized" and given coherence according to rules entirely invented by man: the relationship that obtains between words and "the real world" is a metaphorical or aesthetic one.'[19]

Since our purpose here is not to develop a critique of Nietzsche's thought but to point out some of the relationships between it and Schopenhauer's I shall simply let that stand — with the observation, however, that if it is true it is not a possible resting-place, for on the basis of that alone it would be impossible to account for man's physical mastery of his environment. Our proven ability to build aeroplanes that do in fact fly, bridges that stay up and carry heavy loads, and all the rest of the achievements of human engineering, prove that the relationship of our knowledge to the world cannot be only metaphorical and aesthetic (though there may be considerable amounts of both those elements in it). But without pursuing any of these considerations further, enough has been said to make it plain why Nietzsche regarded his repudiation of Schopenhauer's denial of the will as the starting-point of his own distinctive contribution to philosophy, and to suggest that he may have been right to do so. He ringingly *asserted* the will, and advocated its untrammelled assertion. To the end of his creative life he retained a sense that his philosophy had been developed *against*

[18] Quoted by J. P. Stern: *Nietzsche*, p. 72.
[19] Ibid., p. 134. It is perhaps worth reminding the reader that the first clear statement of the indispensable role of 'as if' in our transactions with the world had been put forward already, and long before, by Kant.

Schopenhauer's. The first part of what was intended as nothing less than the apotheosis of his life's work was given a title whose point was not just to affirm what Schopenhauer denied but to emphasize that it asserted what Schopenhauer had pronounced to be the most monstrous error possible to the human mind. In *Parerga and Paralipomena* Schopenhauer had written: 'That the world has only a physical and not a moral significance is a fundamental error, one that is the greatest and most pernicious, the real perversity of the mind. At bottom, it is also that which faith has personified as Antichrist.'[20] To the first book, the only part he completed, of *The Revaluation of all Values*, Nietzsche gave the title *The Antichrist*.

When Nietzsche was at the University of Basel a professorial colleague for whom he had profound respect, and whose lectures he attended, was the historian Jacob Burckhardt (1818–1897), author of the now classic *The Civilization of the Renaissance in Italy*. Burckhardt's most characteristic contribution to the development of historical method consisted in embracing the then new scientific approach while at the same time insisting that it was not in itself enough, at least not as it was at first being generally understood. Painstaking research, meticulous documentation, a systematically critical use of sources, all these were certainly necessary for any accurate reconstruction of the past, and the new kind of historian was right to insist on them; but all these activities, if understood in a deep way, involved taking source materials not just as creations of the past that happened to have survived into the present but as things which in their time were *freshly* created for a contemporary purpose; and in order not to misuse them it was necessary to understand what that purpose was. This meant arriving — through an interaction with the materials, since this is the only way in which any knowledge of the past can be arrived at — at an understanding of how things looked and felt to the people of the time: the possibilities of a situation, the mood of an assembly, the flavour of a place, and in aggregate a view of the world, a whole vision of life. The historian's relationship to his materials is thus, in a profound sense, akin to the artist's: the key difference is that the historian cannot freely choose what those materials shall be, still less invent them himself or create them, and he must never allow himself to be seduced into trying to do this. Nevertheless, it is a fact that every piece of historical evidence was in its origins a *creation* on somebody's part, and it is important for the historian to remember that. With the right kind of talent and insight he

[20] *Parerga and Paralipomena*, ii. 201.

can then take the most mundane morsel of evidence — a laundry list, a snatch of popular song, an everyday utensil or piece of furniture — and draw from it real illumination of the way of life in which it was embedded, above all the inwardness of that life, what it was like for the people who lived it. In this way Burckhardt both widened the view of what constituted evidence for the serious historian and deepened the imaginative conception of what could be done with it. His work, while remaining scrupulous as history, has also many of the qualities of a great novelist's — which no doubt helps to explain why it is read as much now as it was in its own time.

Because of the indispensability of intuition, imagination, empathy and psychological insight to the historian, plus the ability to make artistic use of given materials, Buckhardt insisted that his task could not be systematized into any so-called 'philosophy of history'. But as Erich Heller says in *The Disinherited Mind* (pp. 66–7), 'in spite of his disclaiming it, Burckhardt has, of course, a philosophy; that is, he thinks philosophically about history. He has, however, no system which could be expounded apart from, and beyond, his historical and philosophical thinking. His metaphysical beliefs and fundamental thoughts, therefore, have to be perceived through his reflexions about things. Yet there is one philosopher in whom he finds the dispersed elements of his own thought crystallized into a definite system. It is Schopenhauer, whom Burckhardt in conversations with Nietzsche called "our philosopher". The introduction to his *Reflections on World History* is in part a précis of what Schopenhauer has to say about the subject . . .'. The truth is, as Heller goes on to say (p. 68), that 'Schopenhauer's philosophy pervades the whole work of Jacob Burckhardt.' That is partly because the man himself, apart from his work, was so deeply imbued with its spirit. This is revealed in his private letters, in contexts that have nothing to do with history or historiography. To a friend called Riggenbach he wrote on 12 December 1838: 'At every moment I would be prepared to exchange my life for a never-having-been.' Many years after that remark, in a letter to one Brenner dated 16 March 1856, he wrote a sentence which Schopenhauer himself might have envied. 'What beggars we mortals are at the gates of happiness!'

It will be remembered that Nietzsche had drawn attention to an inescapable element of 'as if' in our transactions with the world. The philosopher most notable for his expansion and illumination of this insight is Hans Vaihinger (1852–1933). Vaihinger wrote a number of books, including one on Nietzsche's philosophy, and he also founded the journal *Kant-Studien*; but his most important work was *The Philosophy of 'As If'*. He laboured on this for thirty-five years, starting in 1876 and publishing it in 1911. In his own words, it is 'only a special application and a more serious development of what can already be found in Kant, Herbart, Fichte and Schopenhauer'.[21] It went through many editions, and achieved both fame and influence, for some time occupying the highest point of intellectual fashion in parts of the philosophical world, and spawning a small literature of its own. It is still in print, in English as well as in German. By way of introduction, the English edition contains an intellectual autobiography in which Vaihinger recalls, among other things, Schopenhauer's influence on him. He had, he tells us, 'studied Schopenhauer very thoroughly. Schopenhauer's teaching gave me much that was new and great and lasting, pessimism, irrationalism and voluntarism. The impression which he made upon me was, although not extensively, yet certainly intensively greater than that of Kant . . . Now for the first time I came across a man who recognized irrationality openly and honourably, and who attempted to explain it in his system of philosophy. Schopenhauer's love of truth was a revelation to me. I did not follow his metaphysical constructions, because since I had studied Kant the impossibility of all metaphysics had seemed to me to be obvious. But that part of Schopenhauer's teaching which can be established empirically became my lasting possession and a source of fruitful inspiration.'[22]

Like most serious thinkers since Berkeley, Vaihinger felt compelled to accept the demonstration that nothing in our experience can guarantee the independent existence of physical objects. He saw the notion 'physical object' — denoting something which exists independently of our experience of it but possesses perceptible attributes — as one of the categories which we bring to experience, in terms of which we then render that experience intelligible to ourselves. 'Thought creates an object to which it attaches its own sensations as attributes and then, by means of this fiction, disengages itself from the mass of sensations that rush in from all sides.'[23] Similarly, he accepted Hume's demonstration that causal connection can never be guaranteed by observation; and again he took the Kantian view that causal connection is one of those categories of subjective origin in terms of which experience is ordered. Such notions, he said, are 'simple representational constructions for the

---

[21] H. Vaihinger: *The Philosophy of 'As If'*, p. 102.

[22] Ibid., p. xxix. To the word 'pessimism' in this quotation Vaihinger appends a long footnote which begins: 'Schopenhauer's pessimism became in me a fundamental and lasting state of consciousness. . . .'

[23] Ibid., p. 169.

purpose of apperceiving what is given. Objects possessing attributes, causes that work, are all mythical.'[24] However, instead of going on to say — as Berkeley and Hume did, at least by implication — that if objects and causes are mythical then we should attempt to construct a view of reality that dispenses with them, Vaihinger asserted the opposite. It is quite impossible, he said, for us to dispense with such concepts in our view of reality, and therefore impossible for us not to live, indeed to think, *as if* there are objects and causes. His reasons for this, put in general terms and with some of their wider implications, were as follows. All that is given to us in experience, and therefore all that is guaranteed to us by experience, are the direct perceptions of sense — individual shapes, colours, pressures, sounds, and all the rest of it. These, by themselves, do not constitute a world in which we can live. We secure a world only by ordering our experiences in intelligible forms — but when we do that it is we ourselves who are doing the ordering and providing the forms. These forms, categories, structures, are not part of what is given to us, and in that sense are not part of objective reality; but Vaihinger's central point is that we have no choice but to proceed *as if* they were, because we cannot live at all (because we cannot have a world at all) unless we do. And his point applies not just to objects and causes but to everything whatsoever that is not direct experience: everything that constitutes our world, except for the immediate perceptions of sense, is construct, deduction, framework, inference, hypothesis, assumption, presupposition, speculation, fiction, or something else that is contributed by us and is therefore not part of reality as it is in itself. Vaihinger distinguishes between all these things, and in particular he distinguishes between fictions and hypotheses. A hypothesis, he says, may be true, and is usually hoped or believed to be true by its users. A fiction, on the other hand, is known to be false, but is used nevertheless, either because it is useful or because it is indispensable.

According to Vaihinger, all the most fundamental categories of our epistemology are fictions, as we have seen already in the case of *physical object* and *cause*. 'The strongest proof of the subjectivity of space and time lies in their being infinite, and the ordinary concepts of space and time are thus unmasked as fictional, as mere auxiliary ideas, helpful pictures, developed by the logical function to bring order into reality and to understand it . . . Only a subjective operation can be constantly thought of as if it were without end and were yet complete.'[25] We make use of fictions not only in our direct apprehension of the world but also in our theoretical activities. Adam Smith knew perfectly well that in

[24] H. Vaihinger: *The Philosophy of 'As If'*, p. 31.   [25] Ibid., pp. 62–3.

their economic activities individuals do not pursue solely their own economic advantage, but he discovered that by calculating *as if they did* he was able to make the biggest advances ever made in the history of economics. Historians and political theorists know equally well that there was never an occasion when the as-yet ungoverned people of any modern democracy came together and instituted government voluntarily on the basis of a social contract, but to look at things *as if they had* casts the most helpful illumination on matters to do with government by consent, and individual rights. Mathematicians were always well aware that a circle is not a polygon with an infinitely large number of infinitely short sides, but by treating it *as if it were* they vastly extended their knowledge of the properties of the circle. Furthermore, on fictions closely related to this one are based the whole of co-ordinate geometry and differential calculus. 'Mathematics itself is really the most ingenious method for determining reality and assists in the development of that scale of measurement to which we refer the whole world — space, and motion in space . . . That this system of motion in space together with all its subsidiary concepts is only a fictional conceptual construct follows both from the contradiction in the concept of motion itself and from those in the concept of space, upon which it is based. We are dealing here with a closely woven net, a fine tissue of subjective and fictional concepts in which we envelop reality. We achieve a passable success; but that does not mean that the content must necessarily take the form of the net woven round it.'[26]

Vaihinger pursues these investigations, and the problems they raise, with considerable brilliance. The most important of the problems is: How can our thought or behaviour start out from assumptions which we know to be false and yet still reach conclusions which are valid? His answer to this derives from a view of mental activity which he got directly, he tells us, from Schopenhauer — the view that mind is a biological phenomenon evolved for purposes of the organism, primarily a survival mechanism functioning in the service of the will to survive. Biologically, the end and aim of mental activity is not knowledge but action: our minds work in such a way as not to give us pictures of reality but to enable us to handle it and cope with it. 'This conceptual world is not a *picture* of the actual world but an *instrument* for grasping and subjectively understanding that world.'[27] . . . 'Not even elementary sensations are copies of reality; they are rather mere gauges for measuring the changes in reality.'[28] The most important error we characteristically make about the nature of reality is that we mistake the instru-

[26] H. Vaihinger: *The Philosophy of 'As If'*, p. 73.
[27] Ibid., p. 63.   [28] Ibid., p. 16.

ments we have for coping with it for pictures of it: this is in fact how most of our fictions are born. (This is, of course, precisely the mistake which, subsequently, the older Wittgenstein considered that his younger self had most crucially made: the chief difference between the earlier and the later philosophies of Wittgenstein centres on his shift from a view of meaning as a picturing relationship to a view of meaning as the putting-to-work of a tool. I do not know whether Wittgenstein had read Vaihinger, but there are many deep-lying parallels between the two. However, Wittgenstein was concerned with the problem in logic, whereas Vaihinger was concerned with it in epistemology.) The tools we make and use in our attempts to manipulate reality become more and more numerous, and more and more finely tuned, and we ourselves become more and more sophisticated in our use of them, but to the very end it all remains an activity on our part: reality as it is in itself, independently of all this, remains unknown and unknowable, and therefore the nature of the interface between reality and the mind must also remain a permanent mystery. However, precisely because the only contact we can ever have with reality is through the experience of our own transactions with it we have no other way of conceiving it than in terms of those transactions, and therefore we come inevitably to think of it in those terms: we think of the transactions *as if* they were the reality with which we are dealing. Vaihinger has what he considers a knock-down argument that our conceptual world cannot be the same as the real world: it is that minds were developed by the natural world and within the natural world, and of course it is only in minds that there can be conceptual worlds, so any conceptual world is merely one among numberless elements within the natural world; therefore the two cannot be the same. 'It is because our conceptual world is itself a *product* of the real world that it cannot be a reflection of reality.'[29]

From such an epistemology the criterion of truth that most naturally emerges is a pragmatic one: we regard that as true which works. If we then find another approach that works better we change. 'The boundary between truth and error is not a rigid one, and we were able ultimately to demonstrate that what we generally call truth, namely a conceptual world coinciding with the external world, *is merely the most expedient error*.'[30]

Among Vaihinger's other books was one called *Hartmann, Dühring and Lange* (1876). The first of these names was that of Eduard von Hartmann (1842–1906), a philosopher who, like Vaihinger after him,

---

[29] H. Vaihinger: *The Philosophy of 'As If'*, p. 65.   [30] Ibid., p. 108.

enjoyed the utmost celebrity in his day and is now almost forgotten. As Frederick Copleston has written, 'the influence of Schopenhauer upon his thought is obvious, and von Hartmann was never so foolish as to attempt to deny it, though he protested against being regarded as a mere continuator of Schopenhauer.'[31] Hartmann was struck by the fact that if ultimate reality were the blind, aimless, irrational force that Schopenhauer said it was it would not have manifested itself in an intelligible world but in a chaos. Still less would it have manifested itself in an intelligible world *process*, which is what we do in fact find ourselves involved in. Ultimate reality must therefore have a dual nature: it must *both* provide for the sheer contingency of the world's existence, the irrational fact that anything exists at all, and the not-further-explainable force that constitutes and drives it, *and* provide for the intelligibility of the resultant world process, the conformity of everything in the phenomenal world to scientific laws, the uniformity of Nature. The former Hartmann explained in terms of Schopenhauer's metaphysical Will. The latter he explained in terms of Schelling's and Hegel's notion of a teleological process inherent in the world, some sort of intelligible Idea evolving through and with the world over time. He agreed with Schelling and Hegel that this teleological principle could not *itself* be self-aware — which meant that the Idea shared with the Will the characteristic of being unconscious. Through arguments such as these Hartmann arrived at the conclusion that ultimate reality must be some sort of metaphysical Unconscious whose dual nature is unconscious Will and unconscious Idea, which together constitute the world.

His most famous book, which he called *The Philosophy of the Unconscious*, was published in 1869. It went through eight editions in ten years, and was the most widely read philosophical book of its time — in fact I think one can say that its popularity was unprecedented for a serious philosophical work (not to mention a work of such proportions — it was in three volumes). It has since fallen into almost complete neglect; but historically it is important for three reasons. First, its universal celebrity saw to it that in the course of the 1870s some of the central ideas of Schopenhauer's philosophy became known to every serious student of philosophy who had not encountered them already. Second, it was the first large-scale attempt — of which there were subsequently many — to integrate Schopenhauer's ideas with those of his execrated arch-enemies, the neo-Kantians. Third, it did more than any other single book to familiarize educated people with the notion of the primacy of the unconscious, and was thus important in paving the

[31] Frederick Copleston: *Arthur Schopenhauer: Philosopher of Pessimism*, p. 197.

way for Freud. Freud himself read Hartmann, and quoted from him frequently.

We have seen how many of the ideas that constitute the core of Freudianism were set out fully and clearly by Schopenhauer — the idea that our actions, responses and thoughts are for the most part unconsciously motivated; that most of what is unconscious is unconscious because it is repressed; that it is repressed because we would find it too disturbing to keep it available to consciousness; and that sexual motivation, whether conscious or unconscious, is omnipresent. Freud acknowledged that these intellectual discoveries had appeared for the first time in Schopenhauer, but claimed that he had made them independently. A typical example of both assertions is the following: 'The theory of repression I certainly worked out independently. I knew of no influence that directed me in any way to it, and I long considered this idea to be original until O. Rank showed us the passage in Schopenhauer's *The World as Will and Representation* where the philosopher is struggling for an explanation for insanity. What he states there concerning the striving against the acceptance of a painful piece of reality agrees so completely with the content of my theory of repression that once again I must be grateful for the possibility of making a discovery to my not being well read. To be sure, others have read this passage and overlooked it without making this discovery, and perhaps the same would have happened to me if, in former years, I had taken more pleasure in reading philosophical authors. In later years I denied myself the great pleasure of reading Nietzsche's works with the conscious motive of not wishing to be hindered in the working out of my psychoanalytic impressions by any preconceived ideas. I have, therefore, to be prepared — and am so gladly — to renounce all claim to priority in those many cases in which the laborious psychoanalytic investigations can only confirm the insights intuitively won by the philosophers. The theory of repression is the pillar upon which the edifice of psychoanalysis rests. It is really the most essential part of it . . .'.[32]

Elsewhere (*Collected Papers*, IV. 355) Freud concedes that what Schopenhauer had to say about the noumenal will in individual human beings is an adumbration in other terms of his own doctrine of mental instincts. And, of course — as one of Freud's more rigorous commentators has put it — 'his theory of cognition in service to the emotions, the egoistic self, the will, completes the psychologizing of philosophy initi-

---

[32] Sigmund Freud: *The History of the Psychoanalytic Movement*, section I.

ated by Schopenhauer and Nietzsche. Freud begins with the proposition toward which the psychologizing philosophers worked: that mental activity must be explained by a motivation outside itself.'[33] Thomas Mann asserts the connection more baldly. 'Freud's description of the id and the ego — is it not to a hair Schopenhauer's description of the Will and the Intellect, a translation of the latter's metaphysics into psychology?'[34] Mann has no hesitation in saying that 'Schopenhauer, as psychologist of the will, is the father of all modern psychology. From him the line runs, by way of the psychological radicalism of Nietzsche, straight to Freud and the men who built up his psychology of the unconscious and applied it to the mental sciences.'[35]

Freud may, as he claimed, not have read *The World as Will and Representation*, but it is impossible to believe that he had read none of Schopenhauer's writings. It has been observed,[36] for instance, that the dialogue in *The Future of an Illusion* is simply too close to Schopenhauer's *Dialogue on Religion* to be credibly explained in independence of it. And there are so many other centrally important subjects, beside those already mentioned, on which Schopenhauer's distinctive and trenchantly expressed views were reiterated by Freud: women, for instance, or the decisive significance of early childhood for the development of the personality. And, pervading all their specific attitudes, a whole outlook on life, a sort of stoic pessimism, is common to both men. In 1924 one of Freud's contemporary biographers wrote (and do I detect a note of mischief in the tone?): 'Years ago, Freud used to say, quizzically, that he did not read the philosophers, for unfortunately he could not understand them. But, now that he is getting on in years, he slips a volume of Schopenhauer into his pocket when he goes for a holiday.'[37]

Whatever the truth about when Freud read Schopenhauer, there is no doubt whatever that from the beginning he had imbibed some of Schopenhauer's fundamental ideas via the writings of others. This is most conspicuously true on the subject of sex. 'In his analysis of the importance of sex in human life, Schopenhauer was an intrepid pioneer who held ideas far ahead of his time. Jung was directly influenced by him, and two outstanding authorities on sex — Ellis and Bloch — admired him greatly and cited him frequently. Partly due to the efforts of his disciple von Hartmann, Schopenhauer's ideas on sex had gained currency in Europe before Freud began to write. Freud was familiar with these ideas and considered them of great value. "The incompar-

[33] Philip Rieff: *Freud: the Mind of the Moralist*, p. 51.
[34] Thomas Mann: *Essays of Three Decades*, p. 417.
[35] Ibid., p. 408.
[36] e.g. by Philip Rieff: *Freud: the Mind of the Moralist*, p. 295.
[37] Fritz Wittels: *Sigmund Freud: His Personality, His Teaching and His School*, p. 53.

able significance of sexual life had been proclaimed by the philosopher Schopenhauer in an intensely impressive passage", Freud tells us.'[38]

To do Freud justice he never, in his maturity, equivocated over the fact that Schopenhauer had preceded him with his most fundamental ideas, but only over the directness or indirectness of his debt. And as his greatest biographer, Ernest Jones, tells us, he openly regarded Schopenhauer as one of the half-dozen or so greatest men who had ever lived.[39]

[38] R. K. Gupta: 'Freud and Schopenhauer', *Journal of the History of Ideas*, 36, No. 4 (Oct.–Dec. 1975), 721–8. The quotation from Freud comes from *Collected Papers*, V, 169.

[39] Ernest Jones: *Sigmund Freud: Life and Work*, vol. ii, p. 461.

Appendix 3

Schopenhauer's Influence on Wittgenstein

In 1957 the *Philosophical Review* published a review by Professor P. T. Geach of an Italian translation of, and commentary on, Wittgenstein's *Tractatus*. It was favourable on the whole, but took the book's editor to task for a number of things, and then went on: 'I feel sure that Colombo would have been a more sympathetic critic here if he had had a familiar knowledge of *The World as Will and Idea*. As it is, he does not even hint at any influence of Schopenhauer on Wittgenstein. This influence can be asserted with absolute certainty; it is clear in the notebooks, and Wittgenstein himself stated in conversation that when he was young he believed Schopenhauer to have been fundamentally right (though, not surprisingly, he could make nothing of the "objectification of the Will"). But even apart from this, the *Tractatus* is full of Schopenhauerian theses and ideas: the account of what is right and wrong about solipsism (5. 62–5. 641); the distinction between the psychological phenomenon of will, which is a matter for science, and the ethical will, which rewards or punishes itself in its very action (6. 422); the worthlessness of the world (6. 41); the timelessness or eternity of the present moment of life and the consequent folly of fearing death (6. 4311); and the power of the will to change the world as a whole without changing any facts (6. 43). The silence with which Wittgenstein ends recalls how Schopenhauer refused to give any appearance of positive description to that which is chosen when the Will turns round on its tracks; for us who are full of will, it is *nothing*; but, for those who chose it, "this so real world of ours, with all its suns and galaxies — is nothing".'[1]

Two years later Geach's wife, Professor G. E. M. Anscombe — who had been a pupil and friend of Wittgenstein's and was now one of his literary executors and English translators — published a book called *An Introduction to Wittgenstein's Tractatus*, on the opening page of which she wrote: 'As a boy Wittgenstein had read Schopenhauer and had been greatly impressed by Schopenhauer's theory of the "world as idea" (though not of the "world as will"); Schopenhauer then struck him as fundamentally right, if only a few adjustments and clarifications were made. It is very much a popular notion of Wittgenstein that he

[1] *Philosophical Review*, lxvi (1957), 558.

was a latter-day Hume; but any connections between them are in-direct, and he never read more than a few pages of Hume. If we look for Wittgenstein's philosophical ancestry, we should rather look to Schopenhauer . . .'. Then, after a little more about Schopenhauer she goes on: 'For the rest, Wittgenstein's philosophical influences are pretty well confined to Frege and to Russell . . .'.

These quotations refer to facts which are attested to by evidence from other sources and which are of the greatest significance for any serious consideration of the philosophy of Wittgenstein, especially that of the young Wittgenstein. Schopenhauer was the first philosopher whose work he read. He read it at a highly impressionable age, and he accepted its account of the world of experience, the empirical world, as being 'fundamentally right' (a phrase used by both Geach and Anscombe). We have evidence that he then re-read Schopenhauer in his mid-twenties, during the period when he was writing the material that has since been published under the title *Notebooks 1914–1916*. The latter part of this volume, after a gap of ten months in the entries (all of which are dated), is dominated by agonizingly fresh struggles with some of Schopenhauer's ideas, and the natural inference to draw is that he had been reading Schopenhauer during the gap. (There is quite a bit of evidence that he had also been re-reading Schopenhauer before.) A typical example of what I have in mind appears under the date 29. 7. 16:

'Is it possible to will good, to will evil, and not to will?

Or is only he happy who does *not* will?

"To love one's neighbour" would mean to will!

But can one want and yet not be unhappy if the want does not attain fulfilment? (And this possibility always exists.)

Is it, according to common conceptions, good to want *nothing* for one's neighbour, neither good nor evil?

And yet in a certain sense it seems that not wanting is the only good.

Here I am still making crude mistakes! No doubt of that!'

Here, plainly, is a man struggling with the incompatibility between, on the one hand, Schopenhauer's doctrine that the most ethically desirable condition is one in which the will is denied, and therefore nothing is wanted; and on the other the Schopenhauerian doctrine that compassion is the basis of morality — or the familiar ethical requirement to love one's neighbour.

No one disputes that Wittgenstein was soaked in Schopenhauer. The point is, though, that he was not soaked in anyone else: there was no other philosopher of the past whose work he knew even passably well. Perhaps the most surprising aspect of this is that he never studied Kant seriously — surprising, both because of the all-pervading Kantianism of his own work and because one would have thought that understanding Kant was a pre-condition of understanding Schopenhauer (Schopenhauer himself certainly thought so). But evidence on this point comes from many sources. Typical is Georg Henrik von Wright, in his *Biographical Sketch* (pp. 20–1): 'Wittgenstein had done no systematic reading in the classics of philosophy. He could read only what he could wholeheartedly assimilate. We have seen that as a young man he read Schopenhauer. From Spinoza, Hume and Kant he said that he could get only occasional glimpses of understanding . . .'. It was from Schopenhauer, not from Kant, that Wittgenstein got his Kantianism. As for other philosophers, he was exhaustively familiar with the work of his near-contemporaries Frege and Russell, both of whom he knew personally; but all sources agree that he had read scarcely any of the great dead. He dipped into Plato, and he greatly admired Saint Augustine; but that, astonishingly, was about all — unless one adds the ethical-religious writings of Tolstoy, Dostoevsky, Kierkegaard and Pascal, which had an influence not only on his views but on his life. Furthermore, Wittgenstein had a profound affinity with Schopenhauer as regards his general outlook, and the affinity was of a kind which was bound to increase the extent to which he was open, especially in extreme youth, to influence from Schopenhauer's writings. As Norman Malcolm puts it: 'It was Wittgenstein's character to be deeply pessimistic, both about his own prospects and those of humanity in general. Anyone who was on an intimate footing with Wittgenstein must have been aware of the feeling in him that our lives are ugly and our minds in the dark — a feeling that was often close to despair.'[2]

In the light of all this there is nothing surprising about the fact that the philosophy of the young Wittgenstein was to an important degree an attempt to revise and correct Schopenhauer. But Wittgenstein's mode of writing is notoriously enigmatic — the most enigmatic, probably, of any serious philosopher there has ever been — and it is typical of him that he never says that this is what he is doing. He just does it — that is to say, he presupposes, or comments on, or argues with, or revises, or rejects, utterances of Schopenhauer's which he does not mention. We had an example just now with the denial of the will. To take another, in the *Notebook* entry under the date 13. 5. 15 an isolated sentence occurs which runs: 'Just don't pull the knot tight before being

---

[2] Norman Malcolm: *Ludwig Wittgenstein: A Memoir*, p. 72.

certain that you have got hold of the right end.' This bears no evident relationship to anything that comes before or after it. What it is, quite simply, is a response to the following observation of Schopenhauer's in the *Fragments for the History of Philosophy*: 'The phenomena of the world which have to be explained present countless ends to us, of which one only can be the right one; they resemble an intricate tangle of thread, with many false end-threads hanging from it. He who finds out the right one can disentangle the whole.'[3] To anyone familiar with Schopenhauer, but only to such a person, the allusion is immediately obvious. The *Notebooks* and the *Tractatus* abound in instances of this kind. For purposes of illustration I have chosen examples whose obviousness places them above dispute, and in the second of my examples it is easy to guess Wittgenstein's meaning in isolation anyway. But in the first of my examples, how could anyone not acquainted with Schopenhauer's doctrine of the denial of the will, and unaware that it is this doctrine that is here being wrestled with, possibly understand what is being said, at least in any intellectually serious sense of 'understand'? Furthermore, many of Wittgenstein's allusions to Schopenhauer are, characteristically, more oblique than this. In yet other passages, where there is no question of obscurity, it happens over and again that only a key word or image in the delineation of a thought discloses its Schopenhauerian origin. For instance when Wittgenstein says in *Philosophical Investigations* (339) that 'an unsuitable type of expression is a sure means of remaining in a state of confusion. It as it were bars the way out', the Schopenhauer scholar will instantly recall Schopenhauer's observation that mistaken theories 'bar the way to future knowledge'. Allusions of this kind also are profuse throughout Wittgenstein's work. With regard to those many passages which are not independently meaningful, it is, to say the least of it, a peculiar way to write. In the *Notebooks*, which were purely for his own use and not intended for publication, it needs no explanation or excuse, but the *Tractatus*, assembled from the *Notebooks* expressly for publication, is a different matter. In the Preface to the *Tractatus* Wittgenstein writes: 'I do not wish to judge how far my efforts coincide with those of other philosophers. Indeed, what I have written here makes no claim to novelty in detail, and the reason why I give no sources is that it is a

---

[3] This translation is by Ernest Belfort Bax and occurs on p. 79 of his edition of *Selected Essays of Schopenhauer*, published by G. Bell and Sons, London, 1924. The corresponding passage in the E. F. J. Payne translation comes in *Parerga and Paralipomena*, i. 68. As is so often the case, Wittgenstein's comment on Schopenhauer does no more here than repeat Schopenhauer, for the latter's words which immediately lead into the passage just quoted were: 'For it is with philosophy as with very many things; everything depends on whether it is tackled at the right end.' (Payne translation.)

matter of indifference to me whether the thoughts that I have had have been anticipated by someone else.'

A great many of the thoughts that he had had had been anticipated by someone else — one is tempted to say most of them: if one were to remove from the *Tractatus* everything that derives from Schopenhauer, Frege and Russell, I doubt if much would remain, though it has to be said that the mix itself is highly original, and the thought-processes vertiginously intelligent. And to do Wittgenstein justice, he knew that as a thinker he lacked fundamental creativity. In a note now published in the volume entitled *Culture and Value* (pp. 18–19) he wrote: 'I think there is some truth in my idea that I really only think reproductively. I don't believe I have ever *invented* a line of thinking, I have always taken one over from someone else. I have simply straightaway seized on it with enthusiasm for my work of clarification. That is how Boltzmann, Hertz, Schopenhauer, Frege, Russell, Kraus, Loos, Weininger, Spengler, Sraffa have influenced me.' Our concern here, however, is with only one, though perhaps the most important of these influences.

In addition to the uncountable allusions and references to him of the various kinds already cited, dozens of individual statements in the *Notebooks* and the *Tractatus* are simply *restatements* of Schopenhauer. Take for instance one *Notebook* entry which might almost be regarded as a master key to the work of both philosophers:

As my idea is the world, in the same way my will is the world-will.   (Notebooks 17. 10. 16. The German is: '*Wie meine Vorstellung die Welt ist, so ist mein Wille der Welt-wille.*')

There are many much more extended examples than this, such as the following, which occurs in the *Notebooks* under the date 15. 10. 16:

Only remember that the spirit of the snake, of the lion, is *your* spirit. For it is only from yourself that you are acquainted with spirit at all.

Now of course the question is why I have given a snake just this spirit.

And the answer to this can only lie in the psycho-physical parallelism: If I were to look like the snake and to do what he does then I should be such-and-such.

The same with the elephant, with the fly, with the wasp.

But the question arises whether even here, my body is not on the same level with that of the wasp and of the snake (and surely it is so), so that I have neither inferred from that of the wasp to mine nor from mine to that of the wasp.

Is this the solution of the puzzle why men have always believed that there was *one* spirit common to the whole world?

And in that case it would, of course, also be common to lifeless things too.

Or, quite differently, this, under the date 4. 11. 16:

This is clear: it is impossible to will without already performing the act of the will.

The act of the will is not the cause of the action but is the action itself.

One cannot will without acting.

If the will has to have an object in the world, the object can be the intended action itself . . .

The fact that I will an action consists in my performing the action, not in my doing something else which causes the action.

Or the following, under the date 11. 6. 16:

I know that this world exists.
That I am placed in it like my eye in its visual field.
That something about it is problematic, which we call its meaning.
That this meaning does not lie in it but outside it.
That life is the world.
That my will is good or evil.
That therefore good and evil are somehow connected with the meaning of the world.

Or from the *Tractatus* (6. 371 and 6. 52):

The whole modern conception of the world is founded on the illusion that the so-called laws of nature are the explanations of natural phenomena.

We feel that when *all possible* scientific questions have been answered, the problems of life remain completely untouched.

Or (6. 431 and 6. 4311):

. . . at death the world does not alter, but comes to an end.
Death is not an event in life: we do not live to experience death.
If we take eternity to mean not infinite temporal duration but timelessness, then eternal life belongs to those who live in the present.

Our life has no end in just the way in which our visual field has no limits.

Every word of all this, even to the metaphors and images, is from Schopenhauer. A complete list of the Schopenhauerian restatements, echoes and allusions in the *Notebooks* and the *Tractatus* would occupy many pages. But even this is not the most significant connection. As regards the *Tractatus*, what makes the most important Schopenhaue-

rian reference of all is not this or that passage within the book but the
book itself, taken as a whole. Everyone who reads it perceives that an
unarticulated framework of ideas is tacitly presupposed by it: that
framework is derived almost entirely from Schopenhauer — though,
characteristically, his name is never mentioned. It is the framework
which Wittgenstein had absorbed and assented to in his teens and
reinforced in his twenties, a framework with any alternative to which he
never fully acquainted himself; and a framework which, incidentally,
he was never, later, wholly to reject or replace. (One remembers von
Wright's phrase 'wholeheartedly assimilate'.) In his earliest work Wittgenstein sought to enrich it in one importantly new respect which we
shall come to in a moment; but for the rest, he accepted not only his own
epistemology and ontology as fitting into it but also things that mat-
tered a great deal more to him than those, namely morals, aesthetics,
and considerations of the religious or quasi-religious kind indicated a
moment back.

Accepted, first of all, is what Schopenhauer regarded as Kant's most
important contribution to philosophy, namely the distinction between
the noumenal and the phenomenal. 'Both men see the world of science
as phenomenal. For both, the will corresponds to the noumenal.'[4]
Wittgenstein also agrees that the ultimate significance of life is in the
realm of the noumenal ('The sense of the world must lie outside the
world' *Tractatus* 6. 41). For that reason he regards it as radically
unknowable by us. And he insists that what cannot be known cannot
even be asked about. Because his approach is predominantly logical —
by contrast with Schopenhauer's, which is predominantly epistemological — he is the more draconian of the two in his ban on what cannot
be talked about.[5] He insists that *everything to do with* those matters which
have the greatest import for us — the fact that the world (including us)
exists at all; the relationship of the willing subject to the phenomenal
world; our apprehension of the limits of our actual and possible experience; the nature of our death; the possibility of any existence for us
outside this world of phenomena; the nature of morality; the nature of
art; all those things, in short, that are so often subsumed under some
such phrase as 'the significance of life' — have their roots in a knowledgeless realm where language can have no purchase or meaning.
Properly understood, they are not even problems. 'For an answer
which cannot be expressed the question too cannot be expressed. *The*

[4] Allan S. Janik: 'Schopenhauer and the Early Wittgenstein', *Philosophical Studies* (Ireland), (1966), 91.
[5] He says in the Preface that the 'whole sense of the book might be summed up in the following words: what can be said at all can be said clearly, and what we cannot talk about we must pass over in silence'.

riddle does not exist.' (*Tractatus* 6. 5) Any attempt to talk about them, however tentative, lands us straight into nonsense. Of course, all these things must have what one might call an interface with the world of phenomena: if they did not, they could have no import for us whatsoever. But even their manifestations in this phenomenal world — moral actions, for instance, or works of art — baffle any attempt on our part to give a satisfactory description, still less explanation, of them in language. The only things we can get a clear conceptual grasp of, and therefore the only things we can think or talk about clearly in the conceptual medium which is language, are those that fall entirely within this phenomenal world of ours. This means that the nearest we can get to giving even so much at the sketchiest indication of what is most important to us is to establish the limits of what can be said clearly, since this will simultaneously delineate the frontier — and therefore the 'shape', as it were — of what cannot be talked about. As Wittgenstein put it, referring to the *Tractatus* in a private letter: 'My work consists of two parts: the one presented here plus all that I have *not* written. And it is precisely this second part that is the important one. My book draws limits to the sphere of the ethical from the inside as it were, and I am convinced that this is the ONLY *rigorous* way of drawing those limits. In short, I believe that where *many* others today are just *gassing*, I have managed in my book to put everything firmly into place by being silent about it.'[6] In the book itself he says that philosophy 'must set limits to what cannot be thought by working outwards through what can be thought. It will signify what cannot be said, by presenting clearly what can be said' (4. 114 and 4. 115). This, then, is the utmost that philosophy can do in its attempts to probe 'the real meaning of life'. In any other sense, first-order philosophy simply cannot be done, because all meaningful questions, and therefore all authentic philosophical questions (if there are any) must inhabit the phenomenal world. And this must mean that there are no first-order philosophical questions, for within this world of phenomena everything must be open to the examinations and investigations of sense, and therefore everything that can meaningfully be said about anything is verifiable, and thus factual (whether true or false). So all there is for the philosopher to do is to clear up the confusions that are caused by a failure to appreciate this or put it into linguistic practice. Confronted with a meaningless question, his task is not the impossible one of answering it but the unglamorous one of showing it to be meaningless. Philosophy is talk about talk: it is the second-order tasks of clarifying utterance, of

---

[6] Wittgenstein in a letter to Ficker quoted in Paul Engelmann's *Letters from Ludwig Wittgenstein*, p. 143.

developing logic, and of making perspicuous the unclarity of that which is irretrievably unclear. Yet how little has been done when this has been done! The mysteries of life remain untouched, and its significance untouched on.

All this is almost pure Schopenhauer. It has been genuinely rethought and repossessed, inwardly absorbed at a most impressively profound level — I know of no other writing which displays the same sheer depth of insight into the implications of Schopenhauer's thought as does the *Tractatus* — but although it unpacks the implications of the Schopenhauerian framework with unparalleled perception it does not add to it. The chief point of difference between the two philosophers up to this stage of our comparison is in the view they take of philosophy itself. Schopenhauer, like Kant before him, believed that philosophy does have a positive task, namely the discovery and exploration and clarification and exposition of — plus the critical discussion of the implications of, and any views about, not to mention the doing of detailed work within — precisely such a structure as we are now discussing; and that this constitutes the most fundamental, and therefore the most valuable and important, level of conceptual thought accessible to human beings. In a sense, of course, Wittgenstein's practice concedes this, but his words deny it. There can have been few philosophers who pursued the calling of philosopher with such a passionate existential commitment as the young Wittgenstein, and few who so relentlessly pursued and agonized over the significance and implications of a great philosophical system as he did over Schopenhauer's. What he *said* was philosophy's task was not what he was actually doing. But this very disparity was made possible by the relationship of his thought to Schopenhauer's — the fact that he had not himself produced the framework, and neither presented it nor explicitly discussed it, but took it unspokenly for granted as his point of departure (which in turn may be due partly to the fact that he had absorbed it so thoroughly when still scarcely more than a child). If this is done, then of course it can be argued that there is little left for philosophy to do but unravel conceptual puzzles. The point of such a doctrine becomes clear when one realizes that it already presupposes a certain systematic intellectual orientation as being 'fundamentally right, if only a few adjustments and clarifications were made'. This makes it self-contradictory, of course, and Wittgenstein himself acknowledges this at the end of the book, in a famous passage: 'My propositions serve as elucidations in the following way: anyone who understands me eventually recognizes them as nonsensical, when he has used them — as steps — to climb up beyond them. (He must, so to speak, throw away the ladder after he has climbed up it.) He must transcend these propositions, and then he will see the world aright.'[7]

It has often been mockingly remarked of Wittgenstein and Schopenhauer, separately, that each manages to say a great deal about what he is insistent cannot be talked about. But in a sense the joke is on the joker: each philosopher knew what he was doing in this respect — as is shown, in the case of Wittgenstein, by the passage just quoted — and had a deeper understanding of the situation than his critics. Each made much use of the Kantian point that what we know has implications that go beyond itself: for what we know to be the case, other things, not themselves directly knowable, must also be the case. This means that it is legitimate to make certain kinds of assertion about what cannot be directly observed or experienced; though of course *what* assertions can be made is subject to the most stringent criteria. This principle is effortlessly accepted in contemporary science: the elementary particles of subatomic physics are unobservable even in principle, because they are smaller than any wavelength, but they are highly differentiated, they all have names, and we possess a great deal of important knowledge about them. Proceeding in this way, Wittgenstein asserts, following Schopenhauer, that willing or perceiving subjects are not to be found in the world, and are therefore not entities or objects or substances of any kind: they are constitutive of the world, bearers or sustainers of the world, and as such are to be associated rather with its *limits*. ('The subject does not belong to the world: rather, it is a limit of the world.' 5. 632.) This means that we cannot identify the subject or self even in thought, for to do so 'we should have to find both sides of the limit thinkable (i.e. we should have to be able to think what cannot be thought)'. (From the Preface to the *Tractatus*.) The same considerations apply to morality and to values of every kind, including aesthetic values: they are not *in* the world, for if they were they would be matters of fact, which they are not — indeed, if they were that they could not have *value*. 'If there is any value which does have value, it must lie outside the whole sphere of what happens and is the case . . . It must lie outside the world. And so it is impossible for there to be propositions of ethics . . . It is clear that ethics cannot be put into words. Ethics is transcendental' (6. 41–6. 421). Wittgenstein arrives at the conclusion, as had Schopenhauer, that good and bad characterize the exercise of the will. But 'it is impossible to speak about the will in so far as it is the subject of ethical attributes . . . If the good or bad exercise

---

[7] *Tractatus Logico-Philosophicus*, 6. 54. It will be remembered that this metaphor of steps which raise one to higher levels of insight but are then put behind one after one has climbed them, and are not clung to, was itself taken by Wittgenstein from Schopenhauer. See p. 47.

of the will does alter the world, it can alter only the limits of the world, not the facts — not what can be expressed by means of language' (6. 423–6. 43). This, of course, looks very like a restatement of Kant's doctrine that the moral and the factual are two spheres which touch at a limiting point but are separate and autonomous. (See p. 253.)

What has just been said illustrates a point which is of general interest about Wittgenstein. There are several respects in which the closest affinity of his thought is with Kant rather than Schopenhauer, but the fact that it was from Schopenhauer that he acquired the entire Kantian corpus of ideas and insights leads this to show itself in the form of departures from Schopenhauer, or dissatisfied struggles with Schopenhauer, over precisely some of those issues on which (unknown, I am sure, to Wittgenstein) Schopenhauer differed significantly from Kant. However, to return to our line of argument: Wittgenstein joined company with Schopenhauer once more in that he believed that significance of any kind, not only moral significance, exists in relation to the will, and does not characterize facts as they are in themselves. ('Things acquire "significance" only through their relation to my will.' *Notebooks* 15. 10. 16.) As we experience them, then, the world of fact is constituted by the perceiving subject and the world of value by the willing subject. The relationship between these two subjects is inexplicable, just as the relationship of fact to significance is inexplicable. Schopenhauer had regarded it as the ultimate mystery. 'Now the identity of the subject of willing with that of knowing, by virtue of which (and indeed necessarily) the word "I" embraces and denotes both, is the nodal point of the world, and hence inexplicable . . . whoever really grasps the inexplicable nature of this identity will call it, as I do, the miracle *par excellence*.'[8] Correspondingly Wittgenstein, who in some of his writings has a tendency to identify ultimate reality with God, sees the two selves as manifestations in us of what must therefore be an essentially dual godhead. (See, for instance, the entry in the *Notebooks* under 8. 7. 16.)

In view of an almost unbroken parallelism so far between Schopenhauer's philosophy and that of the early Wittgenstein the reader may be beginning to wonder what can have been meant by the assertions of Professors Geach and Anscombe that Wittgenstein was not greatly impressed by Schopenhauer's doctrine of the world as will, or could make nothing of it. At least one commentator has taken up this point and argued that Wittgenstein cannot have meant what he might superficially be taken to have meant, since he largely reproduced Schopenhauer's doctrine of the will and must therefore have understood it. (Allan S. Janik: 'Schopenhauer and the early Wittgenstein',

---

[8] *On the Fourfold Root of the Principle of Sufficient Reason*, 211–12.

Philosophical Studies (Ireland), (1966), 90.) I agree with this, and I have asked Professor Anscombe on what the assertions of her husband and herself were based. She replied that Wittgenstein had told her that he 'did not understand' the doctrine. Now Wittgenstein's use of the phrase 'I don't understand' was notoriously idiosyncratic: what he most commonly meant by it was that he understood perfectly well in the ordinary sense of 'understand' but that he did not see how difficulties which he perceived in the way of acceptance could be overcome. (For some of his imitators the degree of clarity of what they were thus unable to understand became a measure of depth of mind, for it meant that they were perceiving contradictions or difficulties which the unperplexed were missing.) I have already illustrated by quotation Wittgenstein's wrestlings in the *Notebooks* and the *Tractatus* with some of Schopenhauer's ideas about the will, and I have illustrated how in some respects his view of it was nearer Kant's than Schopenhauer's: I think that in this context he was using 'I don't understand' in his customary sense.

In addition to showing how close Wittgenstein's doctrine of the will is to Schopenhauer's, Janik also shows that there are substantial parallels between the two philosophers' views on logic, mathematics, and the natural sciences. With respect to mathematics this is confirmed by Robert J. Fogelin in his book *Wittgenstein*, where he says (p. 198): 'an inspection of [*On the Fourfold Root of the Principle of Sufficient Reason* and *The World as Will and Representation*] will leave little doubt that many of Wittgenstein's central thoughts on mathematics were derived from this source.' In logic, Wittgenstein got what was probably his most influential idea from Schopenhauer, namely the idea that analytically true propositions are tautologies (see pp. 38–40. When I refer to the special influence of this idea I have in mind such examples as its influence on Bertrand Russell, who wrote in *My Philosophical Development*, p. 119: 'Wittgenstein maintains that logic consists wholly of tautologies. I think he is right in this, although I did not think so until I read what he had to say on the subject.') At this stage one might find oneself beginning to recall, uncomfortably, Goethe's remark that if all the ideas he had got from other people were taken out of his writings there would be nothing left — and it is indeed true that if all that the young Wittgenstein had had to offer were what we have considered thus far he would have been in every way an unoriginal philosopher — marvellously intelligent, but in no way whatsoever creative. However, this is not quite the case: he did have the independence of mind to enrich the Schopenhauerian framework with something from outside the range of Schopenhauer's philosophy, and it is quite rightly this that has always been regarded as the *Tractatus*'s most characteristic contribution. Wittgenstein himself was clearly aware that this was so, and devoted most of his book to adumbrating it. It is the account he gives of the nature of representation in 'the world as representation'.

When Schopenhauer said, as he did, that 'all knowing is a making of representations'[9] he was taking it for granted that the making of representations is an epistemological affair. So, indeed, had all philosophers since Descartes, and so they continued to do until Frege. Frege, however, saw representing as primarily a matter of logic. This dethroning of epistemology — what Frege and his successors saw as the depsychologizing of philosophy — is now regarded by many as the revolution which inaugurated distinctively contemporary philosophy. And it was this whole new approach which the young Wittgenstein, who was the first of Frege's significant disciples, brought to Schopenhauer's doctrine of the world as representation. He does not combat, still less reject, Schopenhauer's epistemological account of the world as representation, but goes what he regards as an entire level deeper, and gives an account of it in terms of logic, which he sees as prior, indeed primal. His criticism of Schopenhauer's doctrine would therefore be not that it is wrong but that it is too shallow. He once remarked that 'in Schopenhauer I seem to see the bottom very quickly'.[10] And in *Culture and Value* (p. 36) he writes of Schopenhauer: 'Where real depth starts, his comes to an end.'

Wittgenstein's contribution in this respect will be clarified by a quotation from Michael Dummett's famous article on Frege in Macmillan's *Encyclopaedia of Philosophy*. 'From the time of Descartes until very recently the first question for philosophy was what we can know and how we can justify our claims to this knowledge, and the fundamental philosophical problem was how far skepticism can be refuted and how far it must be admitted. Frege was the first philosopher after Descartes totally to reject this perspective, and in this respect he looked beyond Descartes to Aristotle and the Scholastics. For Frege, as for them, logic was the beginning of philosophy; if we do not get logic right, we shall get nothing else right. Epistemology, on the other hand, is not prior to any other branch of philosophy; we can get on with philosophy of mathematics, philosophy of science, metaphysics, or whatever interests us without first having undertaken any epistemological enquiry at all. It is this shift of perspective, more than anything else, which constitutes the principal contrast between contemporary philosophy and its forebears, and from this point of view Frege was the first modern philosopher. The change of perspective was not yet to be found in Frege's junior, Russell; the first work after Frege's to display it was Wittgenstein's *Tractatus Logico-Philosophicus*.'

---

[9] *The World as Will and Representation*, ii. 194.
[10] *Ludwig Wittgenstein: Personal Recollections*, ed. Rush Rhees, p. 95.

Russell did subsequently make the transition, however, with the result that his work taken together with that of the young Wittgenstein can to an important degree be understood as going over again, in terms of logic, the ground covered in terms of epistemology by the philosophers in the great tradition from Locke to Schopenhauer, with Russell complementing the empiricists and Wittgenstein the Kantians. Russell was fully aware of this relationship between himself and the earlier empiricists, and he acknowledged it frequently — for instance: 'Modern analytical empiricism, of which I have been giving an outline, differs from that of Locke, Berkeley, and Hume by its incorporation of mathematics and its development of a powerful logical technique.'[11] Wittgenstein's early work has the corresponding relationship to the philosophy of Kant and Schopenhauer. Accepting, by and large, a Kantian account of empirical reality, the young Wittgenstein believed that the fact that we can represent it in language must mean that empirical reality and language have something fundamentally in common; and he thought that what this was was a matter of structure, which in the case of language was its 'logical structure'. This doctrine is in a fairly obvious sense the logical counterpart of the epistemological doctrine of the correlativity of subject and object. A further Kantian feature of it was that Wittgenstein saw our logical representations as being just as much created by us as Kant had seen our epistemological representations. 'We make to ourselves pictures of facts' . . . 'The picture is a model of reality'. (*Tractatus* 2. 1 and 2. 12.) The implication here of things in themselves as existing independently of being represented is of course specifically Kantian rather than Schopenhauerian. This shift was directly due to the impact on Wittgenstein of Frege. As von Wright reports it: 'If I remember rightly, Wittgenstein told me that he had read Schopenhauer's *Die Welt als Wille und Vorstellung* in his youth and that his first philosophy was a Schopenhauerian epistemological idealism. Of how this interest was related to his interest in logic and the philosophy of mathematics I know nothing, except that I remember his saying it was Frege's conceptual realism which made him abandon his earlier idealistic views.'[12] Kant's doctrine in this respect was abandoned by his successors: Wittgenstein's was abandoned by himself. In his later philosophy he became radically construc-

---

[11] Bertrand Russell: *History of Western Philosophy*, p. 862. Russell is specifically referring here to a philosophical approach which he himself endorses, and he finishes the paragraph by saying: 'I have no doubt that, in so far as philosophical knowledge is possible, it is by such methods that it must be sought; I have also no doubt that, by these methods, many ancient problems are completely soluble.'

[12] von Wright: *Biographical Sketch*, p. 5, to be found in *Ludwig Wittgenstein: A Memoir* by Norman Malcolm.

tivist, and ceased to postulate any empirical reality apart from the representations we create. (It is for this reason that the structuralists now claim the later Wittgenstein for their own.)

In the present context there is little need for me to say much about what the young Wittgenstein's logical theory of representation actually was, for the very reason that it was not derived from Schopenhauer: there is a substantial literature about it, and I have discussed it in print at an introductory level elsewhere.[13] In any case, Wittgenstein abandoned it in mid-career for a different theory. His earlier philosophy had argued that meaningful propositions about the world derive their meaning from the fact that they picture a possible state of affairs, and that this picturing relationship consists in a community of structure; his later philosophy argued that utterances have meaning only in so far as they have uses, and that the meaning of an utterance is therefore the aggregate of its possible uses. These two theories have different ontological implications. The former postulates that meaning consists in a relationship of utterance to a world consisting of states of affairs which exist independently of being talked about — indeed, it is part of the point of the *Tractatus* that empirical reality must be of a certain character for us to be able to talk about it as we do; and the character ascribed to it is Kantian. The later theory explains meaning in terms of human actions, intentions and purposes, and through them in terms of patterns of interest and behaviour, and thus, ultimately, in terms of ways of life. The former, then, postulates the existence of an independent empirical reality in the odd sense that Kant did: the latter does not. As I pointed out earlier, this parallels a fundamental shift in ideas between Kant and his heirs, including Schopenhauer. Thus the *ontological* implications of Wittgenstein's later philosophy are closer to Schopenhauer's beliefs than are those of the earlier philosophy, and significantly closer to Schopenhauer than they are to Kant — though I do not believe that Schopenhauer had anything to do with the shift, still less that Wittgenstein, by that time, was consciously thinking in terms of those two philosophers. However, just as Schopenhauer and others effected such a change without abandoning the overall Kantian framework, so did Wittgenstein. As David Pears has said: 'He took much of the framework of the *Tractatus* from Kant through Schopenhauer, whom he had read and admired, and, though he modified this framework in his second period, he never destroyed it.'[14] This provides the explanation, and the possibility of reconciliation, of the

---

[13] In my dialogue with Anthony Quinton on 'The Two Philosophies of Wittgenstein' in *Men of Ideas* (pp. 98 ff.). See also my conversation with David Pears on the same subject in *Modern British Philosophy* (pp. 31 ff.).

[14] David Pears: *Wittgenstein*, pp. 45–6.

conflict between those philosophical scholars who insist on the difference between the earlier and the later Wittgenstein and those who insist on the continuity: there are radical differences in the view taken of the nature of our knowledge of empirical reality, and also of meaning, but the wider Kantian–Schopenhauerian framework within which these views are seen as having their place remains much the same.

It is not only a built-over, and in that sense buried, Kantian–Schopenhauerian ground-plan that the later philosophy of Wittgenstein retains in common with Schopenhauer. The ideas most characteristic of that philosophy concern functions of language, and Schopenhauer foreshadowed some of the most important of these. A good exposition of the parallels is to be found in S. Morris Engel's 'Schopenhauer's Impact on Wittgenstein', *Journal of the History of Philosophy*, 1969, 285–302 — also reprinted in the volume *Schopenhauer: His Philosophical Achievement*, edited by Michael Fox. The nature of these parallels is such that it is difficult to illustrate them briefly, but some quotations from Engel will serve to specify their character. After bringing together from different sources in Schopenhauer's writings a number of the things he has to say on the importance of language for philosophy, Engel writes: 'By supporting each other in the way they do, [Schopenhauer's] several works seem to constitute a unified theory regarding the way in which our minds are deceived and held captive by language — a theory which both in outline and in execution is remarkably similar to what can be found on the same theme in the later writings of Wittgenstein' (p. 294). After more quotations from Schopenhauer he claims that 'we have here in undeveloped form some of the key ideas of Wittgenstein's later philosophy. There is, of course, much that is still missing. But on the other hand, well-known theses — such as, for example, the views that philosophic confusion has its source in language; that such confusions can be avoided or resolved by attending to particular usage; that although our craving for generality tends to work against our doing so, usage is and must be, nevertheless, the final arbiter — cannot but remind us of their familiar counterparts in Wittgenstein's later philosophy' (p. 299). At another point Engel says: 'To summarize: we have observed thus far how according to both philosophers, conceptual confusion is something we are almost unavoidably led into; that this is so because of something either in our own nature or because our concepts, being ambiguous and lacking clear boundaries, give rise to superficial resemblances; that these resemblances have far-reaching consequences not only for ordinary discourse but for both science and philosophy, etc. But although this account of the way our language plays havoc with our thoughts is certainly strikingly similar to what can be found on this subject in Wittgenstein, it still leaves a number of rather important questions unanswered. What, more precisely, for example, is it either about ourselves or language that makes us so prone to be thus deceived? And what, if anything, furthermore, can we do to guard ourselves against these dangers and deceptions? And so on.

'Schopenhauer is not silent on these questions. What he has to say about them, and others like them, have again their parallels in Wittgenstein' (p. 294).

The influence of Schopenhauer on the later philosophy of Wittgenstein is not restricted to the tacit framework plus these doctrines about language. As Engel reminds us (p. 287, footnote): 'Occasionally it is as specific and determinate as the direct borrowing of a key term — "family resemblance" (*Familienähnlichkeiten*), for example, which plays such a significant role in Wittgenstein's philosophy and which he took directly, I believe, from Schopenhauer who uses the term (and in a sense not unlike that later given to it by Wittgenstein) a number of times in his work.' Engel might have added 'forms of life' (*Lebensformen*), which Schopenhauer in his turn had taken from Kant, and which Goethe also had used when talking about Kantian philosophy.[15] As for the key term 'paradigm', it is used by Wittgenstein in a sense taken straight from Schopenhauer's much-loved and much-quoted Lichtenberg. Altogether, in his *Companion to Wittgenstein's Philosophical Investigations*' Gareth Hallett points to some thirty passages in that book which call Schopenhauer to mind, and supplies the relevant quotations from Schopenhauer, which often reveal an obvious allusion and sometimes an immediate parallel. Taking all this into account, I think Allan Janik and Stephen Toulmin were justified in saying of Wittgenstein, as they did in their book *Wittgenstein's Vienna* (p. 224): 'The deeper preoccupation of his later years remained the same as that of his youth: to complete the logical and ethical tasks begun by Kant and Schopenhauer.'

I have quoted many sources in support of the view that there is a uniquely important relationship between Wittgenstein's work and the Kantian–Schopenhauerian philosophy. I could have cited more. For instance Erik Stenius, in his book *Wittgenstein's Tractatus: A Critical*

---

[15] See *Goethes Gespräche*, iv, 468. *Lebensformen* was also the title of a book by Eduard Spranger which, being serious and also a best-seller, was known of by all educated people in the Vienna of the 1920s, and must therefore have been known of by Wittgenstein: its central argument was that people with different outlooks have different conceptual schemes which may nevertheless be equally coherent and have equal claims to rationality — the 'contemplative mind', the 'artistic–creative mind', the 'military mind', and so on. There is an obvious affinity between this and the way Wittgenstein uses the term.

Exposition of its Main Lines of Thought, wrote: 'In so far as Wittgenstein adhered to "logical atomism" he could be characterized as a metaphysician of a rather Anglo-Saxon type. But I believe this sort of metaphysics to be in fact of only secondary importance in his philosophical system, which is, on the whole, more related to German metaphysics, and in particular to the metaphysics of Kant . . . Unlike the logical positivists Wittgenstein was in essential respects a Kantian philosopher.' Reviewing Stenius's book in *Mind* (April 1963, 288) David Schwayder wrote: 'The final chapter is a revealing, and in my view correct attempt to place Wittgenstein as a kind of Kantian philosopher.' Alexander Maslow, in his *Study of Wittgenstein's Tractatus*, wrote (pp. xiii–xiv): 'In my interpretation of the *Tractatus* the basic philosophy underlying it has become some kind of a Kantian phenomenalism, with the forms of language playing a role similar to Kant's transcendental apparatus.' Eva Schaper has said baldly: 'I do, of course, consider Wittgenstein a Kantian with a vengeance.'[16] The failure of most of these writers (not Stenius) to indicate that it was from Schopenhauer that Wittgenstein got his Kantianism suggests that they themselves were unfamiliar with Schopenhauer; but they are nevertheless correct about the sort of philosopher Wittgenstein was. Allan Janik makes the point with more understanding when he says that 'the writings of the early Wittgenstein are steeped in a Kantianism which is traceable to his reading of Schopenhauer'; and, later on the same page, 'there can be no doubt that Wittgenstein was a Schopenhauerian of sorts during the period when he wrote the *Tractatus*'.[17] In Patrick Gardiner's book *Schopenhauer* there is a passage of some five pages, too long to reproduce here but well worth reading in full, which begins (p. 278): 'It is indeed arguable that, considered as a whole, the form of the *Tractatus* exhibits markedly Schopenhauerian characteristics, the general structure and limitations which Schopenhauer (following Kant) ascribed both to everyday and to scientific thinking and knowledge reappearing in Wittgenstein's work as necessary restrictions upon what is linguistically expressible . . .'.

In spite of all this, it is only since about 1960 that such a view of Wittgenstein has been at all commonly expressed. Before then an entirely different, and radically uncomprehending, view of his work seems to have been generally held: his early philosophy came to be regarded as a form of logical positivism, and his later philosophy as being similar in aim to (albeit different in approach from) the linguistic

---

[16] Eva Schaper: 'Kant's Schematism Reconsidered', *Review of Metaphysics*, xviii (December 1964), 292.
[17] Allan S. Janik: 'Schopenhauer and the Early Wittgenstein', *Philosophical Studies* (Ireland), xv (1966), 79.

analysis of J. L. Austin. A whole literature was built up on these illusory foundations, and to this day many of the people who were brought up on that literature go on adding to it, thereby perpetuating the false perspectives it incorporates. The history of the *misunderstanding* of Wittgenstein would be an illuminating chapter in a history of twentieth-century philosophy. It began with Bertrand Russell, who was Wittgenstein's teacher, and who wrote the Introduction to the first English translation of the *Tractatus*. This appeared in 1922, when Russell had not as yet properly absorbed the implications of Frege's work and was still taking it for granted that the philosopher's attempt to account for our knowledge of the world was essentially an epistemological task. This led him to see the *Tractatus* as providing the logical framework for an epistemological structure. Later in the twenties the Vienna Circle of logical positivists came into existence, regarding Russell as a sort of intellectual godfather to their movement and the *Tractatus* as its most important philosophical text. The story of these successive misunderstandings is told so well by Stephen Toulmin in one of the chapters contributed by him to *Wittgenstein's Vienna* that it is worth quoting this source at length. 'Wittgenstein's failure to explain publicly at the time, the reasons why he rejected Russell's interpretation of his book helped only to encourage the development of the rival, positivist interpretation. Russell himself was quite content to see his own "propositional logic" expanded, to provide the core of a new epistemology. After all, he himself had interpreted the idea of "atomic facts" in this epistemological way in his own 1914 Harvard lectures, *Our Knowledge of the External World*. So, for some five years from 1922 on, professional mathematicians, philosophers and physical scientists at the University of Vienna, many of them strongly influenced by Mach and Russell, were holding seminars to discuss the *Tractatus* and its wider implications, without Wittgenstein's participation. Wittgenstein, meanwhile, acquired the reputation of being a kind of mystery man, lurking in the background . . . Almost from the moment of its publication, the nature and purpose of Wittgenstein's *Tractatus* gave rise to misunderstandings among his Viennese contemporaries, and his own disappearance from the philosophical scene did nothing to help the situation. If one only sets aside those last five pages (Proposition 6. 3 on), the intellectual techniques developed in the rest of the book lend themselves to quite different uses, both in mathematics and in philosophy, and can be quoted in support of intellectual attitudes quite antagonistic to Wittgenstein's own. As a result, both in England and in Vienna itself, the *Tractatus* became the foundation stone of a new positivism or empiricism; and this developed into a thoroughgoing antimetaphysical movement, which held out scientific knowledge as the model of what rational men should believe

— aiming to put the more loosely expressed positivism of Comte and his nineteenth-century followers on a new and more rigorous basis, by the proper application of Russell and Frege's propositional logic . . . During the crucial years in the middle 1920s, when the logical positivism of the Vienna Circle was taking shape, the philosophers and scientists involved deeply respected the authority of Wittgenstein and his *Tractatus*. Yet he himself remained an onlooker, and an increasingly skeptical one, so that by the early 1930s he had dissociated himself entirely from ideas and doctrines that others continued to regard as *his* brain children . . . Once Wittgenstein had thus been labelled as a positivist, men found it hard to see him in any other light. So when, from 1929 on, he returned to philosophy and moved gradually into his second, contrasted phase of philosophizing, his new style was not regarded as a *rejection* of positivism. Rather, it was seen as a reconstruction of his earlier positivistic position on new and deeper foundations . . . Far from being a positivist, however, Wittgenstein had meant the *Tractatus* to be interpreted in exactly the opposite sense. Where the Vienna positivists had equated the "important" with the "verifiable" and dismissed all unverifiable propositions as "unimportant *because unsayable*", the concluding section of the *Tractatus* had insisted — though to deaf ears — that *the unsayable alone has genuine value*. We can, it tells us, recognise "the higher" only in that which the propositions of our language are *unfitted* to capture; since no "fact", such as can be "pictured" by a "proposition" has any intrinsic claim either on our moral submission, or on our aesthetic approval. Wittgenstein's silence in the face of the "unutterable" was not a mocking silence like that of the positivists, but rather a respectful one. Having decided that "value-neutral" facts alone can be expressed in regular propositional form, he exhorted his readers to turn their eyes away from factual propositions to the things of true value — which cannot be *gesagt* but only *gezeigt*. No wonder Wittgenstein saw the completion of his *Tractatus* as a moment to give up doing philosophy and set out to devote himself to humanly important activities! Paul Engelmann puts the point:

A whole generation of disciples was able to take Wittgenstein as a positivist, because he has something of enormous importance in common with the positivists: he draws the line between what we can speak about and what we must be silent about just as they do. The difference is only that they have nothing to be silent about. Positivism holds — and this is its essence — that what we can speak about is all that matters in life. *Whereas Wittgenstein passionately believes that all that really matters in human life is precisely what, in his view, we must be silent about.*[18]

[18] Allan Janik and Stephen Toulmin: *Wittgenstein's Vienna*, pp. 214, 208, 215–16, 219

From the beginning, the radical misunderstanders of Wittgenstein
have largely been people who take the dismissive view of transcendental idealism which I discussed and illustrated in Chapter 4. The
distinction between what they might and might not be disposed to look
on seriously in the Kantian–Schopenhauerian philosophy has been
drawn most skilfully and clearly by Strawson, with specific reference to
Kant. 'There is in [*The Critique of Pure Reason*] a body of doctrine about
the necessary general structure of experience; and this really means, as
I said before, a body of doctrine about the limits of what we can make
truly intelligible to ourselves as a possible structure for our own experience. Now this body of doctrine, though not acceptable in all
respects, is in its general outline and in many substantial points, I
think, correct. But it's surrounded by, and in Kant's own view it's
dependent on, another, second body of doctrine, probably that by
which he's best known. And this is the doctrine that the nature of things
as they really are, or as they are in themselves, is necessarily completely
unknown to us — that the world as we know it, including our ordinary
selves, is mere appearance, and that experience as we enjoy it has a
certain necessary structure indeed, but only because that structure is
imposed by us on the matter of experience which reaches us from this
necessarily unknown source of things as they are in themselves. Now all
this . . . I take to be a kind of nonsense, though it has a certain
appealingly dramatic and exciting quality, like most metaphysical
nonsense.'[19] In my view one of the clearest ways to indicate where most
logical positivists and, since them, most analytic and linguistic philosophers have gone wrong about Wittgenstein is to say, adopting the
terms of this Strawson quotation, that they took the young Wittgenstein to be meeting the challenge posed by the first of the two bodies of
doctrine, and his originality to lie in the fact that he was the first to
answer it in terms of logic when everyone before him had answered it in
terms of epistemology (thus far they would be correct), but that they
failed to perceive not only that he at the same time accepted something
of the kind expressed by the second body of doctrine but that he
regarded it as of immeasurably greater import than the first — and
furthermore, like Kant, he regarded the first body of doctrine as fitting
into, and filling out a minor part of, a framework constituted by the
fully worked out implications of the second.

The logical positivists in particular tended to be people who believed
that the world of actual and possible experience is the only world there

and 219–20. The indented quotation is from Paul Engelmann: *Letters from Wittgenstein*,
p. 97; the italics in the quotation are Engelmann's.

[19] Peter Strawson in *Modern British Philosophy* (ed. Bryan Magee), p. 124.

is, or at any rate the only world there is any point in our concerning ourselves with.[20] They took the most important constituent of that world to be its logical structure, somewhat like the steel structure within a ferro-concrete building. For them, therefore, the exposure and investigation of this structure was the central task of philosophy. And it was this that really led them to misunderstand Wittgenstein. For they found themselves at one with him on the need for a primarily logical theory of the world as representation, and also at one with him regarding the provision of a correct theory of this kind as the most valuable thing a philosopher could do. And most of the *Tractatus* was devoted to setting forward such a theory. I do not think it ever occurred to most of them that as far as Wittgenstein was concerned what he was doing was filling in the smallest and least important space in a very much larger framework (which is why he stressed how little had been done when that had been done). The reason why he regarded it nevertheless as the most important task for philosophy was merely that it could be carried out, whereas the content of the other, larger spaces in the framework of total reality must remain for ever unconceptualizable, and therefore inaccessible to linguistic expression or conceptual thought. For the logical positivists there could *be* no larger framework, and therefore Wittgenstein was seen by them as providing us with the most important constituent element for a philosophical explanation of total reality. Hence, among so many other distorted consequences, the tendency towards adulation of Wittgenstein on their side accompanied by a concern on his not to be too closely associated with them, and above all not to have their view of his work accepted by anyone else as adequate.

With the benefit of hindsight, but still somewhat uncomprehendingly, this was at least partially confirmed in the intellectual autobiography of the ablest of the logical positivists, Rudolf Carnap. The following quotations are filleted from a much fuller and more rewarding narrative, and contain by no means all the relevant passages. 'Thus there was a striking difference between Wittgenstein's attitude towards philosophical problems and that of Schlick and myself. Our attitude towards philosophical problems was not very different from that which scientists have toward their problems. For us the discussion of doubts and objections of others seemed the best way of testing a new idea in the

---

[20] By contrast, several of the leading analytic philosophers of the generation after the logical positivists were religious believers. The first two philosophers quoted in this Appendix, Geach and Anscombe, are Roman Catholics, and I do not think it at all coincidental that as such they were among the first to perceive something of the real significance of Schopenhauer for Wittgenstein: they had no difficulty in seeing that Wittgenstein's primary concern was with the noumenal.

field of philosophy just as much as in the fields of science; Wittgenstein, on the other hand, tolerated no critical examination by others, once the insight had been gained by an act of inspiration. I sometimes had the impression that the deliberately rational and unemotional attitude of the scientist and likewise any ideas which had the flavour of "enlighten-ment" were repugnant to Wittgenstein . . . Once when Wittgenstein talked about religion, the contrast between his and Schlick's position became strikingly apparent. Both agreed of course in their view that the doctrines of religion in their various forms had no theoretical content. But Wittgenstein rejected Schlick's view that religion belonged to the childhood phase of humanity and would slowly disappear in the course of cultural development. When Schlick, on another occasion, made a critical remark about a metaphysical statement by a classical philos-opher (I think it was Schopenhauer), Wittgenstein surprisingly turned against Schlick and defended the philosopher and his work . . . Earlier, when we were reading Wittgenstein's book in the Circle, I had erroneously believed that his attitude toward metaphysics was similar to ours. I had not paid sufficient attention to the statements in his book about the mystical, because his feelings and thoughts in this area were too divergent from mine. Only personal contact with him helped me to see more clearly his attitude at this point.'[21]

We should not, in this respect or others, allow ourselves to slip into the common mistake of thinking as if the members of the Vienna Circle all held the same views. On most issues they constituted a spec-trum of opinion which ranged from the more traditional to the more radical, and there was perpetual controversy among them. The closest of them in spirit to Wittgenstein were Waismann and Schlick. But the really hard-nosed positivists such as Carnap and Neurath were so intellectually uncongenial to him that after a time he refused to engage in further discussion with them. These were the people who were most insistent of all that there was nothing 'behind' the world as representation — a position dramatized by Neurath in his slogan 'everything is surface' — and this seems in Wittgenstein's view to have rendered them incapable of understanding his philo-sophical aims and utterances. Unfortunately, by historical accident, the person who introduced logical positivism into the English-speaking world, A. J. Ayer, did so in its most simple-minded and uncritical form, with the result that ever since the 1930s a 'tough' and impoverished image of the attitudes represented by the Vienna Circle has been current on both sides of the Atlantic. More to the point of our present concerns, the most uncomprehending of the

---

[21] *The Philosophy of Rudolf Carnap*, ed. Paul Schilpp, pp. 26–7.

available views of the *Tractatus* was the one the Anglo-Saxon countries imported and spread.

I would like to conclude this account of the prolonged, and in many quarters continuing, failure to appreciate the extent and nature of Schopenhauer's influence on Wittgenstein by giving additional body to two elements in the explanation that have been touched on in passing. The first is Wittgenstein's failure to explain himself, the second the ignorance of Schopenhauer's work prevailing among the philosophers who were interested in Wittgenstein. With regard to the first, Wittgenstein almost never gave sources, and throughout his life he went out of his way to draw attention to his lack of acquaintance with other peoples' work. There must, I think, have been an element of vanity in this, but I do not think it was vanity of a superficial kind. The depth to which Wittgenstein penetrated the thought of others is abnormally impressive: what he absorbed from them was re-thought to the very bottom, so that it became his own possession and part of his living tissue; and I believe that for this reason he genuinely believed that to attribute to others what was thus authentically his own could serve only to mislead. He used to say[22] that if a man had been physically nourished on bacon and potatoes we should all see the folly of trying to identify which bits of his person derived from bacon and which bits from potato, and yet we make exactly that mistake with regard to whatever intellectual nourishment he may have metabolized into himself.

The concealments which in practice resulted from Wittgenstein's hostility to any consideration of intellectual antecedents were further and strongly reinforced by an almost uniquely cryptic style of prose composition. In each of these two respects, it must be said, Wittgenstein stood at the very opposite end of the spectrum from his chief mentor. Schopenhauer strove all his life to express himself with the minimum ambiguity and the maximum clarity. He despised oracular utterance, which he regarded as an infallible indication of inauthenticity; and even though for most of his life oracular contemporaries of his were fêted while he was ignored, he remained unshakeably committed to an all-revealing lucidity of expression. Furthermore, he always went out of his way to draw his readers' attention to his own forerunners: his most characteristic way of opening a discussion of any important subject is to trace the development of its treatment by his predecessors in the history of thought, with ample quotation and full attribution. This approach never becomes pedantic or pedestrian, nor do the generous helpings of other peoples' ideas to which he treats us diminish our appreciation of his own, or lessen our sense of the distinctiveness of

---

[22] I owe this illuminating piece of information to Professor Anscombe.

his philosophical personality. On the contrary, he combines this approach with a personal vision every bit as deep as Wittgenstein's, and incomparably more self-disclosing.

To Wittgenstein's characteristics in this regard must be added certain enigmatic and hermetic attributes not only in his writing but in his personality. He was a proud, fastidious loner, passionately committed to the pursuit of understanding but comparatively little concerned to communicate it beyond the circle of people he knew. He seems almost to have taken it for granted that outside the boundaries of that circle he would be misunderstood. Nevertheless, when all these things have been said, there is something odd about his refusal — whether it was vain, or esoteric, or lofty, or despairing, or indifferent, or whatever its cause may have been — to at least *try* to correct so widespread and persistent a misunderstanding of his work. As Janik and Toulmin put it: 'The question remains: Why, in the face of all of this misrepresentation, did Wittgenstein himself remain silent? To explain this reaction fully might well require an exercise in psychobiography that would involve laying bare the whole development of his personality. Such an interpretation would suit the existentialist attitudes of the author of the *Tractatus*, who could no more have explained his book to anyone else than the author of *Either/Or* could have written a scholarly commentary on his own work . . .'.[23] I suspect that part of the answer may lie in Carnap's observation that Wittgenstein seemed to regard his most important insights as inhabiting a level deeper than any to which rational and scientific modes of enquiry, such as his colleagues were committed to, could penetrate, and he could find no way of establishing them other than by bald assertion to sympathetically minded people. The very first words of the *Tractatus* are: 'Perhaps this book will be understood only by someone who has himself already had the thoughts that are expressed in it — or at least similar thoughts.' Certainly Wittgenstein did not suppose that the most important of his thoughts could be established by argument: rather, he regarded them as nearer to the sort of perceptions that furnish the premisses of arguments (see pp. 38–40). I have a strong suspicion, too, that both in Anglo-Saxon philosophical circles and in Viennese positivist circles he may have found that whenever he said anything incorporating any of the assumptions of transcendental idealism he was misunderstood almost automatically, and by people who were impervious to any suggestion that they were misunderstanding, and still more to any suggestion that they might try to understand. And after all, it is almost impossible to say anything about the noumenal — indeed, that was the young Wittgenstein's main point.

[23] Allan Janik and Stephen Toulmin: *Wittgenstein's Vienna*, p. 201.

In these circumstances it is not surprising that for a long time professional philosophers failed almost universally to perceive Schopenhauer's influence on Wittgenstein — given not only that he gave little indication of its existence, and none of its extent, but also that scarcely any of them had read Schopenhauer and virtually none were inclined to take him seriously. The first of the historically important misunderstanders, as has been said, was Bertrand Russell, and it is obvious from the chapter on Schopenhauer in Russell's *History of Western Philosophy*, published twenty-four years later, that he had not read *The World as Will and Representation*. (In view of this, I suppose he must have accepted on trust from Wittgenstein the judgement that there was 'a certain shallowness' in Schopenhauer's philosophy, without appreciating that what Wittgenstein meant by it was what has just been indicated on p. 298.) Carnap's testimony has already been quoted. A book still regarded by many professional philosophers as providing the most comprehensive discussion of the *Tractatus* — Max Black's *A Companion to Wittgenstein's Tractatus*, published in 1964 — betrays a near-total unfamiliarity with Schopenhauer's work and a near-complete obliviousness of its importance for an understanding of Wittgenstein. The former defect is piquantly revealed by the fact that Black ascribes the derivation of the metaphor about the eye's not appearing in its own field of vision to, of all people, Stendhal, giving no reference for it to Schopenhauer. Yet Schopenhauer used it in three different places in his writings; and — unlike Stendhal — did so to make exactly the same philosophical point with it as Wittgenstein; and his use of it was published three-quarters of a century before Stendhal's. (Similarly, Black gives Mauthner and Sextus Empiricus as Wittgenstein's forerunners in the use of the metaphor of the ladder, without mention of Schopenhauer, who was almost certainly Mauthner's own source for it.) The latter defect is betrayed by Black on the very first page of his book and in his very first reference to Schopenhauer: 'Parts of [the *Tractatus*] date back to 1913 and some of the concluding remarks on ethics and the will may have been composed still earlier, when Wittgenstein admired Schopenhauer.' As we have seen, the implications of this remark had been demolished three years before Black published it — by the publication, in 1961, of Wittgenstein's *Notebooks 1914–1916*. But these are small points. Both of the defects of Black's approach which they illustrate consist more massively and all-pervadingly in the *absence* from his book of any serious discussion of Schopenhauer's influence on Wittgenstein. There are no more than half a dozen references in passing.

It is this — of its nature unquotable — absence of discussion where discussion is called for, a persistent failure to point to Schopenhauerian

connections and allusions when what is being said can be understood
only with reference to them, that betrays ignorance of Schopenhauer on
the part of most commentators on Wittgenstein. A common indicator
of such ignorance is the attribution to Kant of something which Wittgenstein took directly from Schopenhauer, and perhaps reproduced in
much the same words.

Discussion of Wittgenstein without large-scale reference to
Schopenhauer is bound to be inadequate but may still be valid within
its limitations. What is not permissible is discussion of Schopenhauer's
influence on Wittgenstein without familiarity with Schopenhauer.
Several writers are guilty in this respect. One of the best-known discussions of Schopenhauer's influence on Wittgenstein to have appeared in
recent years is contained in P. M. S. Hacker's book *Insight and Illusion*,
published in 1972. In it we find Mr Hacker asserting (pp. 67–8): 'My
awareness of my will constitutes, according to Schopenhauer, an
awareness of noumenal reality, the underlying thing-in-itself.' This is,
of course, false. On p. 75 Mr Hacker tells us: 'Schopenhauer associated the philosophic and artistic spirit with self-consciousness.' This is
the diametrical opposite of the truth: Schopenhauer associated these
things with 'a complete forgetting of our own person and of its relations
and connexions . . . the ability to leave entirely out of sight our own
interest, our willing and our aims, and consequently to discard entirely
our own personality for a time.'[24] And so Mr Hacker's discussion goes
on. He exhibits a rare and welcome realization that Wittgenstein was a
transcendental idealist of some kind,[25] but shows himself unfamiliar
with even the most central doctrines of transcendental idealism: for
instance, after referring to Wittgenstein's view that certain things lie
'outside space and time', he can write: 'These are mysterious claims,
and are usually dismissed as poetic licence or mystical metaphor.'[26]
Furthermore, Mr Hacker's non-acquaintance with transcendental
idealism leads him to confuse it systematically with solipsism, and this
in turn leads him to suppose both that Schopenhauer was a sort of
solipsist and that the theme of solipsism is of central significance in the
early philosophy of Wittgenstein. Schopenhauer in fact dismissed solipsism out of hand (see p. 122), and the subject is touched on only
rarely, and briefly at that, in the early philosophy of Wittgenstein. Mr

[24] *The World as Will and Representation*, i. 185–6.
[25] On p. 83 of his book he refers to 'the implicit transcendentalism' of the *Tractatus*.
A footnote on p. 76 ends with the sentence: 'The views already examined on death,
the significance of life and the solution of its riddle; as well as the conception of the
aesthetic or mystical vision, commit Wittgenstein to some form of the doctrine of the
ideality of time.'
[26] P. M. S. Hacker: *Insight and Illusion*, p. 72.

Hacker's ignorance in all these respects goes hand in hand with a complacent dismissal-in-advance of what he is ignorant of. The following paragraph, given here complete, beggars any comment of mine. 'Wittgenstein's remarks about death are now recognizably derived from Schopenhauer. Most important of all is the fact that little sense can be made of his thinking these thoughts without presuming that he saw some deep truth in the Schopenhauerian metaphysical vision and the transcendental ideality of time. Nothing thus far said, however, suggests that it is possible to make sense of *what* he thought. This should not be surprising.'[27]

It should not be necessary at this stage to digress into the philosophical substance of these muddles and misrepresentations. However, so much has been written about Wittgenstein's alleged solipsism that it is worth pointing out that what he has to say on that topic carries a comparatively straightforward significance to a reader familiar with Schopenhauer. For he points out that in each of the noumenal and phenomenal realms taken separately there is a sense in which the world and the individual are at one with each other — and therefore a sense in which what the solipsist asserts might, *in a manner of speaking*, be said to be true. In the noumenal realm all is undifferentiable, and therefore at one with my noumenal self, as my noumenal self must be at one with it. ('There really is only one world soul, which I for preference call *my* soul, and as which alone I conceive what I call the souls of others. [This] remark gives the key for deciding the way in which solipsism is a truth.' *Notebooks 1914–1916*, p. 49.) On the other hand, with regard to the world as representation, the very separation of subject and object, and their correlativity, means that any or all of empirical reality can exist only for a perceiving subject, yet that the perceiving subject is not *in* the empirical world. ('Here it can be seen that solipsism, when its implications are followed out strictly, coincides with pure realism. The self of solipsism shrinks to a point without extension, and there remains the reality co-ordinated with it.' *Tractatus Logico-Philosophicus*, 5. 64.) Both of these doctrines of Schopenhauer's, which Wittgenstein merely reasserts, have been referred to in the main text of the present volume. And just as it was made clear there that Schopenhauer was not a solipsist of any kind whatsoever, so it needs to be understood here that 'Wittgenstein has never held to solipsism, either in the *Tractatus* or at any other time.'[28]

One of the most important respects in which Schopenhauer anticipated Wittgenstein was in what Patrick Gardiner has called 'the philo-

[27] P. M. S. Hacker: *Insight and Illusion*, p. 73.
[28] R. Rhees in *Mind*, 56 (1947), 388.

sophical challenge to the entire Cartesian approach — exemplified by
the later writings of Wittgenstein and by the work of Gilbert Ryle — in
the present century.'[29] In Schopenhauer's case this had nothing to do
with the dethronement of epistemology referred to on p. 298: it consisted chiefly in his rejection of the mind–body dualism which Descartes had succeeded in establishing as one of the classical doctrines of
Western philosophy. Wittgenstein did indeed follow Schopenhauer in
this; but the philosopher — much influenced by Wittgenstein — who
became most famous on this score was Gilbert Ryle for his book *The
Concept of Mind*, published in 1949. Because this is so, I hope it will not
appear out of place if I conclude this Appendix with a paragraph on the
question of Schopenhauer's influence, or lack of it, on Ryle — with
respect to doctrines which, after all, Ryle shared with Wittgenstein,
and in the formulation of which he had acknowledgedly been influenced by Wittgenstein.

   In the main text of this book I have shown how the doctrine for which
Ryle is best known was expounded at some length by Schopenhauer
(see pp. 124–125), as was also Ryle's well-known doctrine of the systematic elusiveness of 'I' (see p. 127). I will not repeat those demonstrations. The question is, did Ryle get these doctrines from
Schopenhauer? I once asked him if he realized that he had been
unequivocally anticipated in them by Schopenhauer, and he replied
that he did, but that he had learned of the fact only when Patrick
Gardiner pointed it out to him after *The Concept of Mind* was published. I
then asked him if he had read Schopenhauer's work, and he replied that
he had, during his student years, but that he remembered scarcely
anything of it and did not believe he had been influenced by it. Now this
presents a problem. I have no doubt that Ryle was speaking the truth
— I do not think I have ever known a man whose word I would more
confidently trust. On the other hand he did once say to me that the
frame of mind in which he had written *The Concept of Mind* seemed to
him, looking back on it, a strange one, and not at all normal to him.
Even as he said it there was a note of surprise at himself in his voice. It
suggested to me that a good deal of the book derived from sources and
drives in his mind and personality which were normally unconscious to
him. (For the matter of that, I believe this to be so with most creative
work, especially if it has the animal vitality and drive that Ryle's had.)
If this is so, it may be that Ryle got his central doctrines from
Schopenhauer after all. Given that he was a person of outstanding
philosophical ability, is it really likely that he would have read — at the
most formative stage in his intellectual development, when he was, as

[29] Patrick Gardiner: *Schopenhauer*, p. 169.

he described himself later, 'philosophically eager' — a philosopher of genius uniquely akin to him in doctrines for which he himself was subsequently to become famous without these doctrines leaving any traces in his mind at all, not even subliminally? It seems to me implausible.

Appendix 4

A Note on Schopenhauer and Buddhism

There is nothing controversial in saying that of the major figures in Western philosophy Schopenhauer is the one who has most in common with Eastern thought. Less adequately pondered is the fact that much of what it is that the two have in common was taken by Schopenhauer from Kant. To suppose that Schopenhauer's philosophy was formed to any decisive degree under the influence of Eastern thought is not only a mistake, but misses the crucial point that in Kant and Schopenhauer the mainstream of Western philosophy threw up conclusions about the nature of reality which are strikingly similar to some of those propounded by the more mystically oriented religions or philosophies of the East, yet arrived at by an entirely different path. It would be an error, though one characteristic of Western intellectual provincialism, to suppose that the Oriental doctrines in question were not supported by rational argument: in the case of Buddhist philosophy, in particular, they conspicuously are. But the Kantian–Schopenhauerian conclusions were reached by processes internal to a tradition of thought which is fundamentally rooted in the development of mathematical physics, and this is something with which Buddhist philosophy has been little concerned until the present century. Incidentally, both the Kantian–Schopenhauerian philosophy and the more sophisticated of the mysticisms of the East have received, and continue to receive, extensive corroboration from the revolutionary developments of the twentieth century in the natural sciences. (There is a growing literature on this in the case of Eastern mysticism — a good introduction is *The Tao of Physics* by Fritjof Capra, which also contains a useful bibliography.)

The Eastern religion most congruent with contemporary science is Buddhism. This fact is relevant, albeit indirectly, to the subject of the present appendix, for there are a set of interesting three-way comparisons to be made between Schopenhauer's philosophy, Buddhism and the science of the twentieth century. I do not wish to pursue the parallels between the latter two, but it is worth citing a quotation which indicates their main character. 'One of the main attractions of Buddhism is the modernity of its ideas about events and causality: for in reducing the visible world to a vast interconnected swarm of events it echoes the findings of modern science. An event is where a certain characteristic manifests itself at a particular point in space and time. Its coming into being is due to a set of conditions, themselves similar events. In Hua-yen's extension of this picture each event is a result of the total conditions of the universe and likewise is itself part of the conditions which brought about the state of the total universe. Because each event is empty of "own essence" in the sense that its nature arises from the conditions which bring it into being, every event is, considered in itself, empty. Moreover the Mahayana metaphysics echoes the kind of view of reality which we find in science in that we transcend, in the latter, common sense and common perception. The theoretical constructs of science are very far removed from what we perceive with our sensory apparatus. The latter simplifies the world, and presents it to consciousness in a way which suggests substantiality, relative permanence, large-scale qualities such as broad patches of colour and so on. But actually behind the ways in which the mind sifts and translates the messages coming into the conscious organism are a vast swarm of small-scale events and processes. Buddhist atomism is more advanced, from a modern point of view, than Hindu atomism, where atoms are everlasting, tiny building blocks of the universe. There is no need for the hypothesis of lasting atoms: better to see the world as a vast set of short processes, the one giving rise to the next according to a complex pattern. Perhaps too we may say that modern science has acquired a sense of philosophical idealism, in that discovery is the result of an interplay between the scientist and the natural world in which constructs, theories, revolutionary new conceptualizations play a vital part. It is folly to think of theories simply standing in one–one relationship to a reality out there. The correspondence theory of truth, which implies this kind of mirroring by language of what it is it describes, is naïve. So it is not possible really to say how things and events are in themselves. Rather it is possible to say that certain theories in a general way give a kind of purchase both in understanding and in practical manipulation on the facets of the world which they are "about". There is a beginning and a schematic account of this relationship between things in themselves and our thought in Kant: though it would be much better to think of "processes in themselves". Given this modification there is a strong affinity between Kant and the Buddhist semi-idealist metaphysics of the Great Vehicle. In brief, there is a congruence between this metaphysics and the situation in which modern knowledge about the world finds itself. This undoubtedly is one of the latter-day attractions of Buddhism. It seems not to have those clashes between the spiritual and the scientific which have seemed to plague Western faith.'[1]

What I wish now to extend are the similarities, touched on in this quotation, between Buddhism and the Kantian–Schopenhauerian philosophy. Common to Schopenhauer on the one hand and Buddhism on the other is the notion that the world of experience is something in the construction of which the observer is actively involved; that it is of its nature permanently shifting and, this being so, evanescent and insubstantial, a world of appearances only; and that as such it screens us off from ultimate reality, which somehow lies 'behind' it, or perhaps one should say 'within' it, and is timeless and changeless. The fact that the world of our experience is a variegated world of disparate objects and events misleads us as to the character of ultimate reality, which is not differentiated but is the same in and through everything. Contrary to appearances, everything is, in its inner nature, one. There are no concepts or categories in terms of which this undifferentiated inner reality of everything can be described, so it cannot be an object of discursive knowledge, and cannot be talked about. But prolonged reflection may enable us to free ourselves from the illusion that the world of experience is the world of permanent reality, and in that sense philosophy may be an indispensable vehicle of insight. However, achievement of this insight is an unavoidably lengthy and difficult task, and any direct apprehension or even mere glimpse of reality that may be achieved is bound to be ineffable. It would be further agreed that the fact that all living things are, in their inner nature, one is the explanation of compassion and the foundation of morality: in hurting any living thing I am damaging my own permanent being; thus wrongdoing is its own punishment. It would be agreed too that happiness is not to be found in attachment to the things of this world but, on the contrary, in detachment from them, which means the overcoming of desire and the will — thus asceticism is held in high esteem.

These constitute a great many fundamental ideas for two bodies of doctrine arrived at independently of each other to have in common. But the similarities go further. The following quotations are taken from the article on 'Buddhism' in *Macmillan's Encyclopaedia of Philosophy*, and at no time did the writer of it have Schopenhauer in mind, yet almost every one of his formulations could be taken as applying, *mutatis mutandis*, to Schopenhauer's work. 'The doctrine of *dharma* (in Pāli, *dhamma*) taught by the Buddha was summed up in the Four Noble Truths. They affirm that (1) life is permeated by suffering or dissatisfaction (*dukkha*);

---

[1] Ninian Smart: *Beyond Ideology: Religion and the Future of Western Civilization* (Gifford Lectures, 1979–1980), pp. 169–70.

(2) the origin of suffering lies in craving or grasping (*tạnhā*); (3) the cessation of suffering is possible, through the cessation of craving; and (4) the way to the latter is the Noble Eightfold Path (*ariya aṭṭhangilea magga*) . . . This attainment of peace and insight is called *nirvāṇa* (in Pāli, *nibbāna*) and implies that the saint (*arhat*) will upon death be no more reborn . . . Individuals are described by the Buddha as having three characteristics — suffering (*dukkha*); *anattā*, or absence of an eternal self; and *anicca* or impermanence. The no-self doctrine (*anattā*) implies both that living beings have no eternal souls and that there is no cosmic Self. The Buddha, indeed, did not believe in a Creator and seems to have found the existence of evil and suffering to be an unsuperable obstacle to such a belief. Also, he deemed questions as to the finitude of the cosmos in space and time, and certain other cosmological and metaphysical questions, as "undetermined" — intrinsically unanswerable . . . Metaphysically, there was during this period (second century B.C. – third century A.D.) a development of absolutistic and idealistic views. These are represented by the Mādhyamika and Yogācāra schools of philosophy respectively. According to the Mādhyamika, all views about ultimate reality involve contradictions, and the only thing that can be said is that reality is void (*śūnya*). This indescribable Absolute that, as it were, underlies empirical phenomena (which are thus also essentially void) is conceived, in effect, as a shadowy substance and is identified with nirvana . . . ultimate reality can be conceived as the inner essence of the observable world. The Yogācāra school is an extension and transformation of these ideas, holding that phenomena are the product of the mind. Thus, the existence of matter is denied and things are analysed as complexes of perception . . . the external world is independently unreal.'[2]

There are yet other doctrines in common between Buddhism and Schopenhauer — for instance the doctrine that reality has a fundamentally moral significance, and the doctrine that some sort of *karma* is at work in the fate of each individual. And quite apart from specific doctrines, there is something in common to the mental climate of the two philosophies, for instance their pessimism. Perhaps the school of thought within Buddhism which is closest to Schopenhauer is Vijñāna-vāda — which used to be translated as 'consciousness only' but now, interestingly enough, is more accurately translated as 'representation only'. Vijñānavāda teaches that every phenomenon has to be both presented to and grasped by a percipient, with the result that all empirical perception and knowledge takes a dual *grasper-graspable* form;

---

[2] To discussion with the author of this article, Ninian Smart, I am indebted for much else in this appendix.

but that independent reality, as it is in itself, cannot possibly have this structure, so that there must be something radically, categorially different between reality and our knowledge of it, the latter being inherently subject-dependent. It also teaches that there is what it calls a 'store-representation' (*ālayavijñāna*), a kind of Unconscious which gives rise to perceptions, the suggestion being, exactly as in Schopenhauer, that there is a sense in which the subjects of perception choose to come into being out of an undifferentiated *x* which also produces the objects of perception. It teaches that, by meditation, one might be able to reach a non-dualistic apprehension of ultimate reality, but that if so it will be incommunicable. On this last point compare Schopenhauer: 'If, however, it should be absolutely insisted on that somehow a positive knowledge is to be acquired of what philosophy can express only negatively as denial of the will, nothing would be left but to refer to that state which is experienced by all who have attained to complete denial of the will, and which is denoted by the names ecstasy, rapture, illumination, union with God, and so on. But such a state cannot really be called knowledge, since it no longer has the form of subject and object; moreover, it is accessible only to one's own experience that cannot be further communicated.'[3]

It would take a Buddhist scholar, which I am not, to pursue these and other similarities in detail. However, it is perhaps these very big, broad comparisons which I have drawn that are the most revealing and interesting ones. I have concentrated on Buddhism among religions because it yields the most and the closest comparisons of any of them with Schopenhauer's philosophy, and was recognized by Schopenhauer as doing so; but he pointed out parallels with Hinduism also, and with Christianity. He sometimes even has ambivalences in common with a religion — for instance Hindu scholars are divided as to whether *māyā* is or is not illusion, and Schopenhauer is similarly divided. Although in no sense whatsoever a religious believer, indeed a declared atheist, he had the profoundest respect for Hinduism, Buddhism and Christianity, while on the other hand he despised Judaism and Islam. He thought that Christianity, rightly understood, was much closer to Buddhism than is generally realized. He regarded the history of the Church, and indeed of Christendom, with a good deal of contempt, but this was because the teachings of the founder to whom lip service was paid had been so monstrously perverted or disregarded.

[3] *The World as Will and Representation*, i. 410. Compare also: 'The solution of the problem of life is seen in the vanishing of the problem. (Is not this the reason why those who have found after a long period of doubt that the sense of life became clear to them have then been unable to say what constituted that sense?)' Wittgenstein: *Tractatus Logico-Philosophicus*, 6. 521.

When one confronted his teachings themselves one discovered marvellously insightful doctrines of love and self-abnegation, asceticism and
suffering, and an insistence throughout on authentic values.
Schopenhauer regarded Jesus the man as being almost a sort of natural
Buddhist, and believed that he must have been under influences from
further East: 'Whatever anyone may say, Christianity has Indian blood
in its veins.'[4] It had brought to Europe some of the profoundest of the
insights which had spread out from India centuries before, through
Hinduism and Buddhism. 'Through Christianity Europe acquired a
tendency which had hitherto been foreign to her, by virtue of a knowledge of the fundamental truth that life cannot be an end in itself, but
that the true purpose of our existence lies beyond it . . . Christianity
preached not merely justice but loving kindness, sympathy, compassion, benevolence, forgiveness, love of one's enemy, patience, humility,
renunciation, faith, and hope. In fact it went further; it taught that the
world is evil and that we need salvation. Accordingly, it preached a
contempt for the world, self-denial, chastity, giving up of one's own
will, that is, turning away from life and its delusive pleasures. Indeed, it
taught one to recognize the sanctifying force of suffering; an instrument
of torture is the symbol of Christianity. I am quite ready to admit that
this serious and only correct view of life was spread in other forms all
over Asia thousands of years earlier, just as it is even now, independently of Christianity; but for humanity in Europe it was a new and
great revelation.'[5]

[4] *On the Fourfold Root of the Principle of Sufficient Reason*, p. 187.
[5] *Parerga and Paralipomena*, ii. 347 and 348.

Appendix 5

Schopenhauer's Addendum on Homosexuality

Chapter 44 of volume II of *The World as Will and Representation* is called 'The Metaphysics of Sexual Love'. For the third edition of the book, published in 1859, when Schopenhauer was seventy-one, he tacked on to it an addendum which he called simply 'Appendix to the Preceding Chapter', and which is about male homosexuality — a subject to which there had been only the most glancing reference in the second edition, and none at all in the first. The sudden appearance of this appendix is surprising in more ways than one. First, no other such self-contained addition was made on any other subject in either volume of the work. Second, in it the author discusses coolly, and attempts to understand and explain, a phenomenon which in his day was felt to be shocking in the extreme, and was either not mentioned at all or was discussed with much show of horror and moral outrage. It was a topic, moreover, which no other philosopher had dealt with since the Greeks, and which readers would not expect to be discussed in a philosophical work. Schopenhauer succeeds ingeniously enough in offering an explanation of homosexuality which fits into the general framework of his theoretical system. But reading between the lines I get an irresistible impression that the subject is brought in because of personal experiences which fell to him comparatively late in life, and which took him by surprise.

His explanation of homosexuality is as follows. We know, he says, that only parents who are physically mature and yet not too old produce strong, healthy children. Parents who are either too young or too old produce children who are 'weak, dull, sickly, wretched, and short-lived'. However, since Nature never proceeds by sudden jumps, sexual appetites do not conveniently switch on and switch off at the appropriate ages: on the contrary, the desire for sexual activity grows from puberty, which after all occurs in childhood, and in most cases wanes only late in middle age, if then. So Nature has to find some way of seeing to it that in the adolescent and the elderly the sexual impulse is directed away from the procreation of children. This she does by the introduction of homosexual inclinations at these two stages of life. Thus what appears at first sight to be an unnatural, indeed perverted impulse, and an obviously unproductive one, is planted in us by Nature herself for the benefit of the species. This fact — that homosexual inclinations are natural and not unnatural — explains why homosexual activity goes on in all communities at all times, regardless of whether it is viewed with horror or even punishable by death. In many cultures, to be sure, it is tolerantly accepted, and presumably in those cultures individuals who feel homosexual inclinations would have no reason to suppress them. 'In Europe, on the other hand, it is opposed by such powerful motives of religion, morality, law, and honour, that almost everyone shrinks at the mere thought of it, and we may assume accordingly that out of some three hundred who feel the tendency, hardly more than one will be so feeble and crazy as to give way to it.'[1] In our own culture, therefore, literally hundreds of times more people feel a homosexual temptation than show any outward indication of doing so: indeed, 'only a thoroughly depraved nature will succumb to it'.

With exceptions whose context usually makes them obviously so it can, I think, be taken that if an individual puts forward a serious general statement about human beings or human behaviour as such, he accepts it as applying to himself, since if it did not he would know it to be false, or at least he would know that (and also something about how) it needed to be qualified. What Schopenhauer's treatment of homosexuality suggests to me is that he himself had felt homosexual inclinations not only in adolescence but also in late middle age or old age. We know that as a young man he had an overmastering sexual drive; so much so that, like Sophocles, he felt himself to be like a slave in thrall to 'a mad and savage master'. It would be entirely unremarkable for such a person to have passed through a homosexually oriented phase in adolescence: in fact most of us do so as a normal stage of our development. However, it also looks as if such impulses stirred in him again in later life, and furthermore that he was horrified by them and did not give way to them, but was moved by the experience to think about homosexuality afresh; and this led him to see it in a new light, not as a crazy perversion which only a monster could practise but as a natural impulse which anyone, even an Arthur Schopenhauer, could feel a temptation to indulge. If one reads his treatment of the subject with close attention the following personal history suggests itself.

'At about the age stated by Aristotle' (p. 564) as being that at which men should stop having children, that is to say the age of fifty-four (p. 563), Schopenhauer became aware in himself of homosexual feelings towards young men. These feelings grew as the years went by (p. 564), and the process was accompanied by a diminution of sexual interest in women, towards whom he developed an 'aversion' which became in the

---

[1] *The World as Will and Representation*, ii. 564–5.

324 *Schopenhauer's Addendum on Homosexuality*

end 'loathing and disgust' (p. 565). During this period he was, 'unfortunately' (p. 565), importuned by young homosexuals in Frankfurt. It
is unclear whether or not this was by way of prostitution, but
Schopenhauer does mention that the soliciting of 'elderly gentlemen'
by 'young pederasts' in 'not uncommon in large cities' (p. 565), and
this suggests male prostitution of a character which is commonplace
enough in our own day. Though tempted, he resisted the temptation,
and never committed a homosexual act. (I think this is both the
confession and the claim implied by the epigraph to the whole appendix, an exchange from Sophocles' *Oedipus Rex* which reads: ' "Do you
make bold so shamelessly to utter such a word, and think to escape
punishment?" "I have escaped, for truth bears me witness." ') However, he had been singed by the experience, and emerged from it
shaken. He had always regarded sodomy as 'a monstrosity' to which
only the most utterly depraved natures could descend, but now he
found himself re-examining the question in the light of personal experience. The result was a sort of Gestalt shift in his perceptions. He saw
what, in a sense, had always been staring him in the face, namely that
homosexual interest and activity are omnipresent. 'Considered in itself,
pederasty appears to be a monstrosity, not merely contrary to nature,
but in the highest degree repulsive and abominable; it seems an act to
which only a thoroughly perverse, distorted and degenerate nature
could at any time descend, and which would be repeated in quite
isolated cases at most. But if we turn to experience, we find the
opposite; we see this vice fully in vogue and frequently practised at all
times and in all countries of the world, in spite of its detestable nature'
(p. 561). In demonstrating this as far as ancient Greece and Rome are
concerned 'there is no need of proofs for well-informed readers; they
can recall them by the hundred, for with the ancients everything is full
of it. But even among less cultivated peoples, particularly the Gauls,
the vice was very much in vogue. If we turn to Asia, we see all the
countries of that continent permeated with the vice from the earliest
times down to the present day, and likewise with no special attempt to
conceal it; Hindus and Chinese, no less than the peoples of Islam,
whose poets also we find much more concerned with love of boys than
with love of women' etc., etc. (p. 561) . . . 'Thus the universal nature
and persistent ineradicability of the thing show that it arises in some
way from human nature itself' (p. 562) . . . 'That something so thoroughly contrary to nature, indeed going against nature in a matter of
the greatest importance and concern for her, should arise from nature
herself is such an unheard-of paradox, that its explanation confronts us
as a difficult problem' (p. 562). And so he goes on to offer his solution,
which I outlined earlier.

Not only does Schopenhauer's appendix on homosexuality indicate on internal evidence a personal history of the kind I have just conjectured, but such an interpretation would also fit the chronology of his writings in general: the absence of any discussion of homosexuality in the first edition of *The World as Will and Representation*; the insertion of a reference to it in the second edition, which came out when he was fifty-six; the famous onslaught on women in *Parerga and Paralipomena* which appeared when he was sixty-three; and then finally the explicit confrontation of the subject at the age of seventy-one. He knew that to write with such directness on this shocking subject might do him harm, but was undeterred — he ended the appendix with the words: 'Finally, by expounding these paradoxical ideas I wanted to grant to the professors of philosophy a small favour, for they are very disconcerted by the ever-increasing publicization of my philosophy, which they so carefully concealed. I have done so by giving them the opportunity of slandering me by saying that I defend and commend pederasty.' But the most impressive aspect of it all was that characteristic in Schopenhauer which most influenced Nietzsche, who tried consciously to copy it, namely his utterly fearless honesty not only with society but with himself — his ability not just to speak out the unmentionable but to confront, within himself, the unthinkable.

Appendix 6

Schopenhauer and Wagner

One thing that can probably be said of Richard Wagner (1813–1883) is that he was the only composer of the very front rank who was in any significant sense an intellectual. He had a lively interest in ideas not only to do with music and theatre but across a wide range of subject-matter which included literature, philosophy, politics and history. Nor was he only a consumer in these fields: he poured out books, pamphlets, articles, short stories, poems and other published communications of every kind — the standard edition of his collected writings, which does not include his letters, extends to sixteen volumes. Most important of all, this interest in ideas had a shaping influence on both the form and the content of his greatest works of art. Of course, those works can be, and mostly are, loved by people with little or no knowledge of the ideas that helped to nourish them: but such knowledge enriches our understanding of them none the less.

The special significance of Schopenhauer for Wagner lies in the fact that when Wagner first read *The World as Will and Representation* — towards the end of 1854, at the age of forty-one — he was composing operatic masterpieces in a form which he had elaborated intellectually to a highly sophisticated degree; that Schopenhauer's ideas were incompatible with his approach; that he came under their influence nevertheless; and that his development as a creative artist, and therefore all his subsequent work, was changed as a consequence.

Wagner's first three operas imitated in turn all three of the established operatic forms of his day. The first, *Die Feen* (*The Fairies*, 1834), was in the style of German romantic opera as represented by Weber and Marschner; the second, *Das Liebesverbot* (*The Ban on Love*, 1836), was in the Italian style of Bellini; and the third, *Rienzi*, 1840, imitated Parisian grand opera in the manner of Meyerbeer, Auber and Halévy. (Hans von Bülow once tartly described *Rienzi* as 'Meyerbeer's best opera'.) Having thus boxed the compass, and needing now to decide in which direction to steer, Wagner paused and evaluated his models. He came to the conclusion that, as they existed in his day, French and Italian opera constituted degenerate forms: they were hangovers from a past, not harbingers of a future. So he turned his back on them and, returning to the Weber–Marschner model with which he had begun, devoted himself to developing the possibilities of German romantic opera. Subsequently he excluded his three earliest operas from the established canon of his works: none of them, for instance, has ever been performed at Bayreuth.

The Wagner canon begins with his fourth opera, *The Flying Dutchman*, 1841. This and his next two works, *Tannhäuser*, 1845, and *Lohengrin*, 1848, would be widely agreed, I think, to be the finest German romantic operas ever written — certainly they remain to this day the best-known and loved, and the most often performed. But in them Wagner exhausted the possibilities of the form, or so he felt: after *Lohengrin* it seemed to him that in this direction there was nowhere left to go.

So again he paused and took stock. This time he composed nothing at all for nearly six years, during which he devoted himself to a complete revaluation of the possibilities of opera as such. This led him to the creation of a form of his own which he described and defended in a series of books and articles which have remained the most famous of his critical writings. The chief of these are *The Work of Art of the Future*, 1849, *Opera and Drama*, 1850–1851, and *A Message to My Friends*, 1851. After finishing these he plunged into the creation of his gigantic *Ring* cycle, which was to embody the revolutionary theory of opera which they contained. The exposition of that theory to which I devoted the first chapter of my book *Aspects of Wagner* has been widely quoted, and I feel I would be better advised to select a quotation from it myself than to try here to re-express the same things differently and perhaps less well. There is also the advantage that I wrote it, just as Wagner formulated his theory, before encountering Schopenhauer.

The highest point ever reached in human creative achievement was Greek tragedy. This is for five main reasons, which should be considered together. First, it represented a successful combination of the arts — poetry, drama, costumes, mime, instrumental music, dance, song — and as such had greater scope and expressive powers than any of the arts alone. Second, it took its subject matter from myth, which illuminates human experience to the depths, and in universal terms. 'The unique thing about myth is that it is true for all time; and its content, no matter how terse or compact, is inexhaustible for every age.' Third, both the content and the occasion of performance had religious significance. Fourth, it was a religion of 'the purely human', a celebration of life — as in the marvellous chorus in the *Antigone* of Sophocles which begins

> *Numberless are the world's wonders, but none*
> *More wonderful than man . . .*

Fifth, the entire community took part.

This art-form was ideal because it was all-embracing: its expressive means embraced all the arts, its subject matter embraced all human experience, and its audience embraced the whole population. It was the summation of living.

But with the passage of time it disintegrated. The arts all went their separate ways and developed alone — instrumental music without words, poetry without music, drama without either, and so on. In any case its available content dissolved when Greek humanism was superseded by Christianity, a religion which divided man against himself, teaching him to look on his body with shame, his emotions with suspicion, sensuality with fear, sexual love with feelings of guilt. This life, it taught, was a burden, this world a vale of tears, our endurance of which would be rewarded at death, which was the gateway to eternal bliss. In effect this religion was, as it was bound to be, anti-art. The alienation of man from his own nature, especially his emotional nature; the all-pervading hypocrisy to which this gave rise throughout the Christian era; the devaluation of life and the world and hence, inevitably, their wonderful-ness; the conception of man as being not a god but a worm, and a guilty one at that; all this is profoundly at odds with the very nature and existence of art. Such a religion, based as it is on the celebration of death and on hostility to the emotions, repudiates both the creative impulse and its subject matter. Art is the celebration of life, and the exploration of life in all its aspects. If life is unimportant — merely a diminutive prelude to the real Life which is to begin with death — then art can be only of negligible importance too.

The descent from the Greek achievement had reached rock bottom by the nineteenth century. Theatrical performance had degenerated from being a religious occasion in which the entire community took part to being entertain-ment for tired business men and their wives. It was frivolous, often to the point of contentlessness, and such values as it embodied were those of the Christian-bourgeois society around it. The most frivolous, vulgar, socially exclusive and contentless of all theatrical forms was opera. Its conventions were grotesque, its plots ridiculous, its libretti fatuous. Yet none of this was thought to matter, neither by its audiences nor its creators, for these things were there only to provide a framework for stage spectacle, catchy tunes and vocal display by star singers. Even so opera was potentially the greatest of the arts, for it alone in the modern world could combine all the others, as Greek tragedy had done. What was needed, therefore, was a revolution in opera that would turn it into the comprehensive art-form it was capable of becoming, in which all the resources of drama, poetry, instrumental music, song, acting, gesture, costumes and scenery would once more combine in the theatrical presentation of myth to an audience of all the people. The subject matter of such works, though purely human, would be the deepest things of life. Far from being mere entertain-ment, therefore, they would be almost religious enactments.

This, in a nutshell, was the Wagnerian programme. It was not just based on the slogan '*Back to Greek tragedy!*', for it looked forward to a new and better way of doing what the Greeks had done — better, because it would draw on resources which the Greeks had not had. Shakespeare, 'a genius the like of which was never heard of', had developed poetic drama beyond anything the Greeks could have conceived. Beethoven had developed the expressive powers of music beyond the limits of speech altogether, even the speech of a Shakespeare. The artist of the future (no marks for guessing who) would combine the achievements of Shakespeare and Beethoven in a single art form, something which, on the analogy of poetic drama, might be called music drama.

How would music drama differ from existing opera and existing drama? Traditional drama depicts, for the most part, what goes on outside people, specifically what goes on *between* them. Its stuff is personal relationships. As for what goes on inside them, almost its only concern here is with their motives. Dramatic development is a chain of cause and effect, one motivated action bringing about or conflicting with another, the whole adding up to a self-contained interlocking system that constitutes the plot. This requires that the forces which act on the characters be convincingly shown, and this in turn requires that they be placed in their social and political context, and their interaction with it articulated. The more motive is explored and displayed, the more 'political' the play has to be — the plays of Shakespeare conjure up whole courts and governments and armies, ruling classes, city states, feuding families and the rest, with a vividness which would be unbelievable had he not done it, and always in terms of warmly alive individuals.

Music drama would be the opposite of this in almost every respect. It would be about the insides of the characters. It would be concerned with their emotions, not their motives. It would explore and articulate the ultimate reality of experience, what goes on in the heart and the soul. This had been made possible by Beethoven, who had developed in music the power to express inner reality in all its fullness, unfettered by the limitations of language with its dependence on the use of specific concepts and its permeation by the laws of logic. In this kind of drama the externals of plot and social relationships would be reduced to a minimum. Its chief requirement was for situations which remained unchanged long enough for the characters' full inner experience of them, and response to them, to be expressed. Myth was ideal for this, because it dealt in archetypal situations and because its universal validity, regardless of time and place, meant that the dramatist could almost dispense with a social and political context and present, as it were 'pure', the inner drama.

Music drama would also be the reverse of traditional opera, for in traditional opera the drama was merely a framework on which to hang the music — drama was the means, music the end — whereas the object of music drama was the presentation of archetypal situations *as experienced by the participants*, and to this dramatic end music was a means, albeit a uniquely expressive one.[1]

The term Wagner used for his projected all-embracing work of art was *Gesamtkunstwerk*. Within it, none of the arts was to be subordinate to any other; each was to speak out in all its fullness, supported and amplified by the others; and thus what would be expressed at any given moment about any situation or emotion would be the totality of what

[1] Bryan Magee: *Aspects of Wagner*, pp. 12–18.

330 Schopenhauer and Wagner

all the arts could express. So this art form would make possible the very maximum of artistic expression *as such*. But the way the arts were synthesized would have to be just right to achieve that purpose. They must not be too loosely related to each other, but nor must they get in each others' way. In particular, there must be no question of making the poetic text or the development of the drama subordinate to the music, as in conventional opera. Some of Wagner's most detailed and technical discussions are about these problems of synthesis: how to set words to music so that both carry equal weight, how to relate modulations of key to changes of verbal meaning or shifts in the dramatic situation, what sort of verse forms are best suited to music drama, the comparative merits of rhyme and alliteration, how to integrate the rhythms of music and the rhythms of speech, how to match music to gesture, how to get the orchestra in a music drama to perform the same function as the chorus in a Greek drama by endowing orchestral motives with a reference to specific elements in the stage action; and so on.

At the time when Wagner was pouring out these theories he was living in Switzerland as a political exile. This was because of his active role in the Dresden uprising of 1849. His closest associates among the insurgents, such as August Röckel and the anarchist Bakunin, had been arrested and put in prison, where they remained for several years, and it is certain that Wagner had escaped a similar fate only by fleeing his native land. At this period of his life his revolutionary theories about art were bound up in his mind with revolutionary political and social theories. He believed that the decadence of opera and the theatre were part and parcel of the decadence of society generally, and that so long as social conditions remained unchanged it would be impossible for him or anyone else to achieve the artistic reforms he was aiming at. (This view too, characteristically, was put forward in an article, *Art and Revolution*, 1849.) Wagner was not greatly interested in politics for its own sake — it was more a matter of politics for art's sake — but he did believe that improvements in the most important matters in life could be, and were going to be, brought about by political activity.

While, and immediately after, publishing these ideas Wagner also wrote the libretti for the four operas that constitute the *Ring* cycle: *Rhinegold, The Valkyrie, Siegfried* and *Götterdämmerung*.[2] There is probably

---

[2] I refer to Wagner's operas by the names most commonly given to them by English opera-goers, in spite of the fact that this results in such inconsistencies as referring to *Götterdämmerung* in German and *The Valkyrie* in English (instead of *Die Walküre*). For some reason *Die Feen, Das Liebesverbot* and *Götterdämmerung* are usually referred to by their German titles whereas *The Flying Dutchman, The Valkyrie* and *The Mastersingers* are more often referred to in English. Furthermore, the abbreviations *The Ring, The*

no more capacious work of art in existence. It can almost be said without facetiousness to be about everything. It begins with the emergence of Nature out of nothingness and ends with the destruction of the world. In between, various races of beings — gods, dwarfs, giants, humans and animals — interact with each other and with Nature in the multifarious ways of love, parenthood, play, work, assertions of dominance and independence, the creation of families, dynasties, societies, races; mutual succour and support, betrayal, mortal strife, conquest, failure, success. The interweaving plots and sub-plots articulate such counterpointed meanings as only myth can express. At one level the whole thing is a gigantic metaphor for developments and conflicts within the individual in his uniquely possessed world, the world between the emergence of his conscious self and its destruction. On this level of interpretation — a level on which Wagner shows himself a psychologist of the most penetrating and subtle genius — the main theme is the centrality of love, and the irreconcilability of inner harmony with domination over others. Alongside this, and interrelated with it at every point, there is a continuous level of moral significance: *The Ring* explores the irreconcilable conflict between the morality of the heart and social morality, and shows how those who live in accordance with the former are punished and destroyed by the guardians of the latter — who nevertheless themselves atrophy because of their denial of the former within themselves. Alongside this, and interpenetrating it, is a social and political level of import which traces successive attempts to preserve or destroy a corrupt world order presided over by degenerate gods. The harbinger of the new order is Siegfried (traditionally said to be modelled in part on Bakunin) but he perishes even before the gods, whose physical downfall is brought about by the conflagration of his funeral pyre. I need not go into the details of an involved plot; suffice it to say that *The Ring* can be interpreted all the way through on the level of individual psychology, on the level of a conflict between moral systems, and on a level of social and political ideas. I single these out, however, only because they are the most important for purposes of our present discussion. There are other levels too. To quote the best of its English translators, '*The Ring* is on the first level a rousing and splendid old tale of gods and dwarfs and men, of giants and dragons, loves and hates, murder, magic, and mysteries, unfolded amid vast and picturesque scenery. Beyond that it is about (among other things) man's conquest of the natural world for his own uses (the first action recorded is Wotan's tearing a branch from the World Ashtree); about man's

Mastersingers and *Tristan* are commoner than the full titles *The Nibelung's Ring, The Mastersingers of Nuremberg* and *Tristan and Isolde*.

dominion over men (well-intentioned oligarchy and capitalist tyranny are both condemned); and about man's understanding of himself (the forces influencing his action, at the start located in gods, are finally discovered to lie within himself). By intention, Wagner patterned his drama on Attic tragedy but chose as his symbolic matter the ancestral myths of the North. To mankind's collective unconsciousness he gave form . . .'.[3] All these meanings, and others besides, are genuinely there in the work, and so different interpretations, far from cancelling each other out, are necessary, and supplement each other.

The first music that Wagner composed after formulating his new theory of opera was that of *Rhinegold*, which he completed in May 1854. Thus *Rhinegold* bears the same relation to his subsequent operas as *Die Feen* does to *The Flying Dutchman, Tannhäuser* and *Lohengrin*: that is to say, it is his first attempt at something which was new to him, and in the doing of which lay the learning: so in the context of his work as a whole it appears as a fledgeling essay in a form whose full possibilities he was to realize only subsequently. *Rhinegold* thus has the odd character of being an apprentice work in the middle of Wagner's output — almost literally in the middle too, for there were six operas before it and six after. It fits the new theory as well as a living work of art can be expected to fit a theory. As has been said, the ultimate model is Greek tragedy, and the subject-matter is derived from myth — not from the German myths, a false assumption from which much anti-Wagner prejudice has proceeded, but mostly from the Scandinavian myths, freely altered and added to by Wagner himself. The verse is written in accordance with his detailed theories concerning line-length, compression, alliteration, and so on. And in keeping with other of his theories there are no arias, duets or other set numbers, and no concerted singing — no two characters ever talk at once — and no verbal repetition. The drama proceeds naturalistically, serviced by words and music integrated in an unprecedented manner — not 'melodically' but 'dramatically expressively', as one might say. The fit between theory and work is, even so, not perfect altogether. In some respects Wagner leant over so far backwards to avoid the shortcomings of conventional opera that he fell down in the opposite direction. For instance, for most (though by no means all) of the work everything that goes to make up the melodic line in the voice parts — not only the rise and fall of pitch but the apportionment of stress, the phrasing, changes of rhythm, and so on — is dictated by the words and their dramatic significance. This subordinates musical to other considerations. It heightens the intensity of the verbal and dramatic expression to an impressive degree, but without

[3] From Andrew Porter's Introduction to his translation of *The Ring*, p. xviii.

the vocal line itself acquiring much independent value — that is to say, without its becoming very interesting in itself *as music*. There are long stretches of dramatically effective singing in *Rhinegold* which not even the most fanatical Wagnerian is ever likely to find himself singing in his bath. And this is not what the theory ideally calls for. It asks that each of the constituent arts — and therefore the melody, like the words — should be interesting and significant in itself, as well as making a contribution to the comprehensive work as a whole. This was achieved by Wagner in his subsequent operas — in which, however, there are still occasionally, if rarely, patches of *Rhinegold*-like uninterestingness in the vocal line considered solely as music.

The other important respect in which Wagner's practice in *Rhinegold* departs from his theories of that time is in his use of the orchestra. In theory, the orchestra should withdraw into the background when the characters on stage are expressing themselves through words with poetic intensity: at these times it should not distract attention from the words but should play a subdued, supportive role. By contrast, when the requirements of the drama call on the characters to talk in ways which are less poetic, more in the vein of everyday life — for purposes of exposition, perhaps, or explanation — then, to prevent too steep a drop in the artistic temperature, the orchestra should move into the fore-ground, heightening the emotional level and at the same time relating current stage action to past and future by using motives in ways that insinuate reminiscence or foreboding. The motives themselves, it must be remembered, are seen as highly malleable material. They are not expected simply to recur in unchanging form, unless this is itself to make a point. They are to be subject to symphonic development — to metamorphoses of melodic shape, harmonization, orchestration, tempo, rhythm, and so on — with always a dramatically expressive purpose. This use of motives by the orchestra is to be made possible by the fact that their first appearance in the work is associated in each case with specific words sung to it, or with a specific character, or aspect of a situation, which will then automatically be recalled to the listener's mind by any subsequent uses of the motive. All this, as I say, is according to the theory. But in practice Wagner's orchestra had already acquired a life of its own. What it actually does in *Rhinegold* and thereafter is in some ways the opposite of the theory: some of the most eloquent orchestral outpourings flow through scenes in which the verbal utterances of the characters are at their most poetically and dramatically intense; and when the text subsides to a functional level the orchestra is often pared down to the level of a functional accom-paniment. Furthermore, even in *Rhinegold*, a good many of the musical motives make their first appearance in the orchestra, not in any of the vocal lines, and therefore not sung to words — and also not in any particularly obvious association with a character, or with one identifiable aspect of a situation. In consequence their associations, whatever these may be, are not verbally fixable. This is illustrated by the fact that different published commentaries on *The Ring*, of which there are many, allot different and incompatible labels to some of the motives. Wagner, it should be said, was opposed to this verbal labelling of motives altogether. He did not coin, nor did he use, the term *Leitmotiv*. He knew that what he was doing was more subtle — musically, dramatically, psychologically — than words could imply.

Having finished *Rhinegold* he moved on to compose the music for *The Valkyrie*. After the non-human world of *Rhinegold*, a world of gods, immortality and magic power, we begin *The Valkyrie* in an everyday world of vulnerable and mortal human beings. One of the salient points which Wagner had been concerned to make in *Rhinegold* had been made by omission: he had presented us there with a loveless order of things held together by power, cunning and self-interest but no ties of affection. Act I of *The Valkyrie*, in immediate contrast, is the love story of Siegmund and Sieglinde from their first meeting to their first love-making — or perhaps I should say from their first meeting *in adult life*, for they are twin brother and sister who have been separated and lost to each other in early childhood, though this truth does not dawn on them until they have been swept irrevocably into each other's arms by sexual passion. There is something deeply marvellous about this Act. It is no surprise to me that it is the only act in the whole of Wagner which has a sustained life of its own as a musical item in the programmes of symphony concerts, or that it has been recorded by itself so frequently. Here, for the first time in his work, Wagner hit the gusher to the unconscious, and out poured a flow of molten material from the innermost core of the world of human feeling, from that buried, remote and dangerous interior to which he was to retain access ever after. The fact that this is its first free emergence gives its expression an unsulliedness, a cleanness and freshness of emotional atmosphere, that was never to recur. The most forbidden emotions are spoken out in all their uninhibited fullness without the least trace of awareness of any counter-pressure or strain. By comparison *Tristan*, though greater in its way, has something of the hot-house about it, something steamy, which is wholly absent from Act I of *The Valkyrie*. What is astonishing is that this unconstrained emotionalism is contained in a form that fits a pre-existing theory, and this time more or less to perfection. For while the various components of the work, especially the music, unfold with seeming freedom, at the same time the synthesis of universal psychological significance with specific dramatic action, and of word-by-word and line-by-line poetic text with note-by-note and bar-by-bar music, is seamless. The words and the music are so integrated that they sound as if they had been conceived simultaneously, and they also fit character and dramatic action at every point in the subtlest and most finely nuanced ways. The vocal line, never the orchestra, is the natural focus of attention whenever anyone is singing; yet when the characters fall silent the orchestra moves into the foreground and speaks to us of the inwardness of their situation with an eloquence that no music surpasses. The vocal lines too, like the orchestral commentary, are hauntingly beautiful even if taken only by themselves, simply as music, without any of the other elements — as thousands of non-German-speaking music lovers have experienced in the concert hall. Compared to this, the musical fabric of *Rhinegold* is as prose to poetry — distinguished prose, no doubt, but not incandescent, not lit up from inside as this is.

Wagner composed the music to Act I of *The Valkyrie* between 28 June and 1 September 1854, to Act II between 4 September and 18 November, and to Act III between 20 November and 27 December. When I say 'composed' I should perhaps explain that Wagner, like most composers of large-scale orchestral music during the last 150 years, was accustomed to work in at least two stages — first a preliminary draft, then the fully realized orchestral score — and my dates refer to the preliminary draft. (This, for him, was the real composing; he once said: 'The moment of joy is when the nebulous idea transmitted to my pencil suddenly stands before me, clear and plain. Orchestration, by comparison, is already a public process.') It was while thus composing the music to Acts II and III of *The Valkyrie* that he read *The World as Will and Representation* for the first time.

It will be remembered that Schopenhauer's fame had begun in 1853, in England, and spread from there to Germany. Before long the growing band of early enthusiasts included some of Wagner's fellow German exiles in Switzerland. The one who happened to introduce him to Schopenhauer was the poet Herwegh. It was the most important intellectual event in Wagner's life. The doyen of Wagner scholars, Ernest Newman, has written in his classic four-volume biography that Schopenhauer's intellectual impact on Wagner 'was the most powerful thing of the kind that his mind had ever known or was ever afterwards to know'.[4] Thomas Mann has written: 'His acquaintance with the philosophy of Arthur Schopenhauer was the great event in Wagner's life. No earlier intellectual contact, such as that with Feuerbach, approaches it in personal and historical significance. It meant to him the deepest

---

[4] Ernest Newman: *The Life of Richard Wagner*, ii. 431.

consolation, the highest self-confirmation; it meant release of mind and spirit, it was utterly and entirely the right thing. There is no doubt that it freed his music from bondage and gave it courage to be itself.'[5] In much more recent times we find one biographer describing Schopenhauer as 'the greatest single influence in Wagner's creative life',[6] and another referring to 'the most profound intellectual experience of Wagner's whole life — his encounter with the philosophy of Schopenhauer'.[7] Some such sentence occurs in a great many books about Wagner, and almost unavoidably so. He had been influenced by philosophers before, especially by Feuerbach, to whom he had dedicated *The Work of Art of the Future*, and some of whose notions of godhead are enshrined in the text of *The Ring*. But Schopenhauer penetrated to Wagner's core in a way that was unique; and both Wagner's outlook and his work were never the same again.

Wagner wrote subsequently in his autobiography that 'for years Schopenhauer's book was never completely out of my mind, and by the following summer I had studied it from cover to cover four times. It had a radical influence on my whole life.'[8] He continued to re-read it for the rest of his days, and new bouts of re-reading seemed to occur at, among other times, his own creative periods. For instance, later in his autobiography he tells how, in 1857, 'working on the orchestration of the first act of *Siegfried*, I plunged anew into the philosophy of Schopenhauer' (*My Life*, p. 659). In Venice in November 1858, when his work on the second act of *Tristan* was disrupted by illness, 'I once more took up, by way of a restorative, as I had often done before, a volume of Schopenhauer, with whom I became on intimate terms, and I experienced a sensation of relief when I found that I was now able to explain the tormenting gaps in his system by the aids which he himself provided' (*My Life*, p. 699). Nearly twelve years after that, in a letter dated 16 July 1870, we find his second wife Cosima informing Nietzsche that Wagner was composing *Götterdämmerung* in the mornings and reading Schopenhauer in the evenings.

The index to Cosima's published diaries, which give a day-by-day account of her husband's doings and sayings for the last fourteen years of his life, contains over 200 references under 'Schopenhauer' — for, as she says in one of them (25 January 1870): 'Time and again R. harks

---

[5] Thomas Mann in his essay 'Sufferings and Greatness of Richard Wagner', reprinted in *Essays of Three Decades* (p. 330).

[6] John Chancellor: *Wagner*, p. 132.

[7] Ronald Taylor: *Richard Wagner: his Life, Art and Thought*, p. 111.

[8] This translation is Ronald Taylor's, from p. 124 of his *Richard Wagner: his Life, Art and Thought*. The corresponding passage in the standard English translation of *My Life* will be found on p. 616 of that volume.

back to the greatness of Schopenhauer.' Many of these references are simply to phrases like 'in the evening Schopenhauer'[9] or 'In the evening we read Schopenhauer'.[10] So much an integral part of their lives was the reading of Schopenhauer that one begins to feel that at some periods it was almost more noteworthy when they did not read Schopenhauer. (Cosima does indeed note one such occasion: on 12 December 1874 she writes: 'In the evening no Kant–Schopenhauer.') Not surpisingly in these circumstances, Wagner even dreamt about Schopenhauer. One such dream seems to me to articulate in a symbolic way what he felt in his inmost self about the relationship between the two of them. On 4 February 1883, less than ten days before his death, Cosima wrote in her diary: 'R. tells me the nice dream he had: he was with Schopenhauer, who was extraordinarily cheerful and friendly (and completely white, causing R. to ask himself, "Who would ever think that this is the great philosopher?"). Then R. drew Sch.'s attention to a flock of nightingales, but Sch. had already noticed them.'

It is clear, I think, that Wagner deferred to Schopenhauer, regarding him at least as his equal if not as his superior. I do not believe the same can be said of anyone else whose adult life overlapped with his, and probably not of anyone else at all. In one sense he regarded himself and Schopenhauer as complementary. He noted in his diary on 8 December 1858 that he was contemplating a 'correction of certain of [Schopenhauer's] imperfections . . . The subject becomes more interesting to me daily, because it is a question here of conclusions which I am the only person able to draw, because there never has been a man who was poet and musician at the same time as I am, and to whom therefore insights into inner processes are possible such as are not to be expected from anyone else.' In the last decade of his life he came to think of 'Schopenhauerian philosophy and *Parsifal* as the crowning achievement!'[11] Yet although he had these unique attitudes towards Schopenhauer, and the two men had a number of acquaintances in common, they never met, nor was there ever any serious attempt on Wagner's side to arrange a meeting. In the first heady weeks of discovery, at Christmas 1854, he sent the philosopher a published copy of his *Ring* libretto inscribed 'With reverence and gratitude', but he felt too diffident to enclose a letter. He received no acknowledgement. In 1860 he stayed for a time in Frankfurt, where Schopenhauer was, of course, living (Schopenhauer was then seventy-two, Wagner forty-seven) but although he ostensibly toyed with the idea of calling on the philosopher he never did it. The prospect made him feel inadequate:

[9] e.g. 30 November 1871, 1 December 1871 and 6 December 1871.
[10] e.g. 5 March 1872.
[11] *Cosima Wagner's Diaries*, i. 851.

he felt he would have nothing to say. Schopenhauer, on his side, gave very little thought to Wagner: he regarded him as having a genuine but minor poetic gift, though having seen both *The Flying Dutchman* and *Tannhäuser* he rated him of little account as a composer. Wagner was bruised by Schopenhauer's disregard, and felt something of the resentment of a rejected lover for the rest of his life, though it never mitigated his adulation. Eighteen years after Schopenhauer's death he remarked to Cosima: 'It does not say much for Schopenhauer that he did not pay more attention to my *Ring des Nibelungen*. I know no other work in which the breaking of a will (and what a will, which delighted in the creation of a world!) is shown as being accomplished through the individual strength of a proud nature *without the intervention of a higher grace*, as it is in Wotan . . . I am convinced Sch. would have been annoyed that I discovered this before I knew about his philosophy — I, a political refugee, the indefensibility of whose theories had been proved by his disciple Kossak on the basis of his philosophy, since my music is supposed to have no melody. But it was not very nice. It's the way Goethe treated Kleist, whom he should have acclaimed . . .'.[12]

When Wagner began to study Schopenhauer, and indeed for a long time after, he had difficulty in grasping the doctrines of the transcendental ideality of space and time. But the epistemology was what was of least interest to him, except that he enthusiastically went along with Schopenhauer's contention that intuitive apprehension yields a knowledge more significant than sensory experience, and sensory experience a knowledge more significant than any purely conceptual processes can do. What he gulped down, and metabolized into his own tissue, were the ontology, the ethics and the aesthetics — the distinction between the noumenal and the phenomenal, and such notions as the independent nothingness of the phenomenal world, the inevitability within it of frustration, suffering and death, the ultimate reality of the metaphysical will, the noumenal identity of everything, the tragedy of individuation and the desire to return to an all-embracing oneness, death as our redemption from the nullity of the phenomenal world, and therefore a denial of the will to live as the supreme achievement of individual consciousness; compassion as the basis of all morality, the noumenal significance — above all other things in our life in this phenomenal world — of the arts and of sex, and the unique status among the arts of music as the direct expression of the metaphysical will. Along with all this went explicit rejection of belief in God, hostility to historical Christianity, scepticism about science, contempt for the neo-Kantian philosophers, and some special views about the nature of genius (not to

[12] *Cosima Wagner's Diaries*, ii. 52.

mention a voracious sense of being one). In the course of time Wagner followed out all Schopenhauer's chief recommendations with regard to reading — he studied Kant and Plato and Buddhism, bought the Oupnekhat, read the approved poets and novelists. For the rest of his life after 1854 he was given — not always, of course, and not even usually, but often — to proffering Schopenhauer's views as his own, both in speech and in writing, without bothering to credit them to their originator. Not that there was ever any attempt to conceal his debt: on the contrary, he talked about Schopenhauer to almost everybody he knew or met, and quite a number of jokes were made by his friends, sometimes complaints indeed, about this endless going-on about Schopenhauer.

Looked at the other way round, Wagner was no mean proselytizer. He made all his friends read Schopenhauer and then insisted on discussing him with them; he sent copies of Schopenhauer's books to his correspondents; he wrote at great length about him in his letters, and quoted him in his published writings. As one of his biographers has written, Wagner 'after the middle of the fifties was probably [Schopenhauer's] most fervent disciple in Germany'.[13] So the debt was by no means all in one direction. Ernest Newman has pointed out that 'Schopenhauer never realized how much of the vogue that was now [1854 and after] beginning for him he owed to Wagner. The old man, whom years of misunderstanding, neglect and disappointment had made excessively self-centred, did not even know that it was Wagner (not Sulzer, with whom the official correspondence was carried on) who was responsible for a movement which, however, came to nothing, to found a chair of Schopenhauerian philosophy at the Zürich University.'[14] Wagner, for his part, never lost a sense of being a committed public advocate for Schopenhauer. Twenty years later, by which time one might have thought that Schopenhauer was satisfactorily famous, Cosima wrote in her diary (13 November 1874): 'R. is always roused to indignation by new evidence of how little known Schopenhauer is.' And Wagner's wondering sense of his own indebtedness never weakened either. 'How can I thank him enough?'[15] remained a positively active feeling in him for the rest of his life.

As in the case of Schopenhauer's influence on Nietzsche, his influence on Wagner consisted before all else in a process of liberation: he helped Wagner, perhaps even enabled him, to become himself. This was Wagner's own estimate. In a letter written to Mathilde Wesendonk in 1860, before Schopenhauer's death later that year, he said:

[13] Sir W. H. Hadow: *Richard Wagner*, p. 114 n.
[14] Ernest Newman: *The Life of Richard Wagner*, ii. 432.
[15] *Cosima Wagner's Diaries*, i. 618.

'How beautiful it is that the old man knows nothing at all of what he is to me, *or of what I am to myself through him!*' (my italics). As Wagner now began to see it, his early self had developed an ever-widening schism between the conscious and the unconscious sides of his personality. At the conscious level he had evolved a sophisticated assortment of culturally-derived views (stemming ultimately from ancient Greece) about the all-importance of this life, of man and of Nature, as if the phenomenal world were all that existed. He had believed that morality, values and art all had social foundations, and he had been an unthinking meliorist, assuming both that society and art could be made better by political activity and that the individual could achieve personal fulfilment and happiness by his own striving. But deep down in the recesses of his unconscious he had not really subscribed to any of this. And his works of art, sprung as they were from the intuitive and unconscious levels of his personality, reflected what he really believed and not what he believed he believed. In a way, he had become increasingly puzzled by his own work. Then at last, in Schopenhauer, he found the unconsciously held convictions and intuitions of his buried self raised to the level of consciousness and articulated verbally in the form of a systematic philosophy. This moved him to the roots of his being, and caused him to embrace consciously the view of reality to which his unconscious had been subscribing. And by putting his conscious self fully in touch with his unconscious self for the first time it rendered him whole. It also greatly enhanced that intellectual awareness of the workings of his creative self which never ceases to astonish, and which perhaps makes him unique among the supremely great creative artists. He may even have had a subliminal apprehension of his need for this before it happened: already in *Opera and Drama* he had stated that one characteristic of the more developed human being of the future would be his consciousness of the unconscious (*'Bewusstsein des Unbewussten'*).

Of his many attempts to explain all this to his friends there is one which is so remarkable for its insight that it is worth quoting at length. The friend was the unfortunate Röckel — still, and for a long time yet to come, in prison for his part alongside Wagner in the Dresden uprising of 1849. Wagner wrote to him, in a letter dated 23 August 1856:

How can an artist expect that what he has felt intuitively should be perfectly realized by others, seeing that he himself feels in the presence of his work, if it is true Art, that he is confronted by a riddle about which he too might have illusions, just as another might? Now, would you suppose it possible for an artist to be helped to a clear understanding of his own work by an intelligence other than his own? As to this, I am in a position to speak, as on this very point I have had the strangest experiences. Seldom has there taken place in the soul of one and the same man so profound a division and estrangement between the intuitive or impulsive part of his nature and his consciously or reasonably formed ideas. For I must confess to having arrived at a clear understanding of my own works of Art through the help of another, who has provided me with the reasoned conceptions corresponding to my intuitive principles.

The period during which I have worked in obedience to my intuitions dates from 'The Flying Dutchman'. 'Tannhäuser' and 'Lohengrin' followed, and if there is any expression of an underlying poetic motive in these works it is to be sought in the sublime tragedy of renunciation, the negation of the will, which here appears as necessary and inevitable, and alone capable of working redemption. It was this deep underlying idea that gave to my poetry and my music that peculiar consecration, without which they would not have had that power to move profoundly which they have. Now, the strange thing is that in all my intellectual ideas on life, and in all the conceptions at which I had arrived in the course of my struggles to understand the world with my conscious reason, I was working in direct opposition to the intuitive ideas expressed in these works. While as an artist I *felt*, and with such convincing certainty that all my creations took their colour from my feelings, as a philosopher I sought to discover a totally opposed interpretation of the world; and this interpretation once discovered, I obstinately held to it, though to my own surprise I found that it had invariably to go to the wall when confronted by my spontaneous and purely objective artistic intuitions. I made my most remarkable discovery in this respect with my Nibelung drama. It had taken form at a time when, with my ideas, I had built up an optimistic world, on Hellenic principles; believing that in order to realize such a world it was only necessary for men to wish it. I ingeniously set aside the problem why they did not wish it. I remember that it was with this definite creative purpose that I conceived the personality of Siegfried, with the intention of representing an existence free from pain. But I meant in the presentment of the whole Nibelung myth to express my meaning even more clearly, by showing how from the first wrong-doing a whole world of evil arose, and consequently fell to pieces in order to teach us the lesson that we must recognise evil and tear it up by the roots, and raise in its stead a righteous world. I was scarcely aware that in the working out, nay, in the first elaboration of my scheme, I was being unconsciously guided by a wholly different, infinitely more profound intuition, and that instead of conceiving a phase in the development of the world I had grasped the very essence and meaning of the world itself, in all its possible phases, and had realized its nothingness; the consequence of which was, that as I was true to my living intuitions and not to my abstract ideas in my completed work, something quite different saw the light from what I had originally intended. But I remember that once, towards the end, I decided to bring out my original purpose, cost what it might, namely, in Brünnhilde's final somewhat artificially coloured invocation to those around her, in which, having pointed out the evils of possession, she declares that in love alone is blessedness to be found, without (unfortunately) making quite clear what the nature of that Love is, which in the development of the myth we find playing the part of destructive genius.

To this extent was I led astray in this one passage by the interposition of my intellectual intention. Strangely enough, I was always in despair over this said passage, and it required the complete subversion of my intellectual conceptions, brought about by Schopenhauer, to discover to me the reason of my dissatisfaction, and to supply me with the only adequate key-stone to my poem in keeping with the whole idea of the drama, which consists in a simple and sincere recognition of the true relations of things, and complete abstinence from the attempt to preach any particular doctrine.

My reason for imparting to you this mental process, which cannot be considered devoid of interest, is to make my own position clear to you. Once this problem of the difference between intellectual conceptions (*Begriff*) and intuitions (*Anschauung*) had been solved for me by Schopenhauer's profound and inspired penetration, I ceased to think of it as a mere abstract idea, for I realised it as a truth, which was borne in on me with such convincing force that, having fully recognized its nature, I was satisfied to accept it for myself, without committing myself to the presumptuous mistake of attempting to force it on others by means of dialectic. I am profoundly conscious myself that I should never have been convinced by such means unless my own deepest intuitions had been satisfied; and therefore I see that if the truth of which I have spoken is to be brought home to any one, he must have felt it intuitively before he can grasp it intellectually.[16]

It should be said in qualification of Wagner's self-analysis that even at the level of his conscious thoughts he had been a Schopenhauerian in many, if uncoordinated, ways before reading Schopenhauer. At the age of only twenty-one he had written, in an article published in Schumann's *Neue Zeitschrift für Musik*: 'The essence of dramatic art does not consist in the specific subject or point of view, but in this: that the inner kernel of all human life and action, the Idea, be brought to show.'[17] On pp. 186–7 I showed by juxtaposed quotations how astonishingly close he was to Schopenhauer in the view he took of what one might call the metaphysics of orchestral music. One could give a great many other such examples. At the age of twenty-seven Wagner had written: 'What music expresses is eternal, infinite and ideal. It speaks not of the passion, love and longing of this or that individual in this or that situation, but of passion, love and longing in themselves.'[18] Set this alongside: 'Music does not express this or that particular and definite pleasure, this or that affliction, pain, sorrow, horror, gaiety, merriment, or peace of mind, but joy, pain, sorrow, horror, gaiety, merriment, peace of mind *themselves*.'[19] Such parallels had already occurred over

[16] *Richard Wagner's Letters to August Roeckel*, translated by Eleanor C. Sellar, pp. 146–53.
[17] W. Ashton Ellis: *Richard Wagner's Prose Works*, volume 8, p. 65.
[18] Richard Wagner: 'A Happy Evening', to be found in *Wagner writes from Paris . . .* (ed. Robert Jacobs and Geoffry Skelton), p. 187.
[19] *The World as Will and Representation*, i. 261.

and over again, often with insights of great depth. On some points Wagner had gone beyond Schopenhauer. A couple of pages back I quoted him on the supreme importance of raising the contents of the unconscious to consciousness: it has been claimed for him that he may have been the first individual in the history of European culture to express that thought.[20] In the same chapter of *Opera and Drama* as that in which he makes this observation he writes approvingly of Antigone that 'out of compassion she had to obey this unconscious compelling necessity for self-annihilation (*Selbstvernichtung aus Sympathie*)'. Any attempt at a full list of Schopenhauerian observations by Wagner before he read Schopenhauer would be long, highly varied in subject-matter, and somewhat tedious to compile and read, but it would demonstrate a deep-lying affinity between the two men in their intuitive perceptions with regard to most subjects.

Obviously, then, with Wagner, as with others we have considered who were also influenced by Schopenhauer, there was a predisposition to such influence in the form of already deep-lying affinities. And by no means all of these affinities were intellectual. Writing to Wagner on 16 January 1862, Mathilde Wesendonk said to him: 'I have been reading Schopenhauer's biography, and felt myself indescribably attracted by his personality, which has so much in common with yours.' Both men were hugely life-enhancing to those who were not repelled by the force of their personalities. Both were psychologists of the profoundest genius, with a passion also for ideas, a quasi-religious attitude towards art, and a special insight into the nature of music. Both, as Nietzsche was to find, were phenomenally effective liberators, confronting whatever had to be confronted, and thus helping others to confront what hitherto they had evaded. As the older Wagner was to put it, 'everything depends on facing the truth, even if it is unpleasant. What about myself in relation to Schopenhauer's philosophy — when I was completely Greek, an optimist? But I made the difficult admission, and from this act of resignation emerged ten times stronger.'[21] Paradoxically, though, both of these supreme liberators were also dominators, men of ferocious and tireless will; both were polymaths, with a need to know everything and be right about everything; both were erotic to an

[20] See L. J. Rather: *The Dream of Self-Destruction: Wagner's Ring and the Modern World*, p. 110: 'Wagner may have been the first to formulate the task confronting European humanity of the present age as *the making conscious of the unconscious*. In so doing he anticipated Eduard von Hartmann's use of the same words in 1868 (with reference to a philosophical and social task) and Freud's use of them in 1896 (with reference to a psychological task). Wagner's use of the Oedipus myth to point up a present political necessity may also be without precedent.'
[21] *Cosima Wagner's Diaries*, i. 291.

uncommon degree, and yet each was his own man who, with respect to his creative work, never made a significant compromise once he had found his feet; each was the centre of his world, yet had a deep-rooted feeling of isolation; and although each had that engulfing zest which others found so exciting, each was deeply pessimistic in his view of ultimate reality; and in spite of that, each was unshakeably convinced of his own unique greatness in his chosen field. Both were vibrantly neurotic personalities with a lifelong tendency to psychosomatic disorders. Taken all in all, perhaps it is not surprising that there were already fundamental similarities in the way they viewed the world.

The similarities extended even to personal appearance. When Cosima Wagner took delivery of the portrait of Schopenhauer which she had commissioned from Lenbach as a present for her husband, her immediate reaction was 'Resemblance to R.: chin, the relationship of the head to the face, one eye half closed, the other wide open, the sorrowful acute gaze which is peculiar to all geniuses.'[22]

But for us the most significant of all the already-existing affinities are those that were present in Wagner's creative work. The supreme one of these is not amenable to discussion in words: I profoundly agree with Curt von Westernhagen when he writes: 'More than the thoughts expressed, Schopenhauer's metaphysics and Wagner's music share something that is outside the province of reason.'[23] Nevertheless many of the other affinities can be discussed. Let us consider, for instance, the main characters in the operas Wagner had written already when he came to Schopenhauer. As one of his innumerable biographers has put it, 'Many of Wagner's characters were disciples of Schopenhauer before their creator grasped the doctrine guiding their steps.'[24] What the flying Dutchman was seeking was an end to the perpetual striving of unnumbered lifetimes, release from the necessity to renew life on any terms: what he specifically longed for was a state of timeless negation of all being, as against the traditional conception of death as a transmutation to a different order of being. 'When all the dead arise, then shall I dissolve into nothing. Worlds, end your course! Eternal nothingness, absorb me!'[25] Tannhäuser, having been torn between the equally compulsive demands of art and sexual love, is overwhelmed by a sense of the nullity of the world, and wishes to renounce it. Like the Dutchman,

[22] *Cosima Wagner's Diaries*, i. 818.
[23] Curt von Westernhagen: *Wagner*, p. 197.
[24] Robert W. Gutman: *Richard Wagner: The Man, his Mind, and his Music*, p. 117.
[25] 'Wann alle Toten aufersteh'n,
  dann werde ich in Nichts vergeh'n.
  Ihr Welten, endet euren Lauf!
  Ew'ge Vernichtung, nimm mich auf!'

he is finally enabled to do this by the compassionate, self-sacrificing love of a woman. Lohengrin's true home is in some noumenal other-where, from which he mysteriously arrives at the beginning of his opera into the ordinary human world. He comes prepared, out of compassionate concern for another individual, to take on this world's burdens and involvements — and hopefully too its pleasures, especially those of sexual love — but the world is unequal to his demands on it. This time the woman in the case fails to keep her promise of self-sacrifice, with the result that her own happiness is destroyed, while Lohengrin has to renounce the world and return to the noumenal realm from which he came.

The subject of 'redemption through love', as it is usually labelled, runs through the whole of Wagner's output, from his very first opera to his very last. Although the love is usually between the sexes it is also compassionate and self-sacrificial, and in most cases does not demand sexual fulfilment as a condition of the sacrifice. The Oedipal implications of this are obvious, and indeed Wagner wrote most penetratingly about the Oedipus myth in *Opera and Drama*, and consciously derived from it some of the most significant elements in *The Ring*. As for his notion of redemption, he never spelled out what he meant by it, but it obviously is, or at least involves, liberation and release from this phenomenal world, and is seen as being the supremely desirable good, and is to be achieved by a combination of compassionate concern for others with a denial of one's own will to live. All these things are, if anything, more clearly articulated in the operas Wagner composed before he read Schopenhauer than in those he wrote after.

In this context is must be remembered that although he composed most of the music of *The Ring* after reading Schopenhauer, the text had been written before. And it contains passages like Wotan's great monologue in Act II of *The Valkyrie*, which lies at the heart of the cycle and in which occur such lines as

> I am sick of finding
> eternally only myself
> in everything I achieve

and

> Farewell, then
> glory and pomp
> and boastful shame
> of godlike splendour.
> Let what I have built
> fall apart.

> I renounce my work.
> There is one thing only I still want:
> the end —
> the end!

In a letter to Röckel written on 25 January 1854, some nine months before he started to read Schopenhauer, Wagner says of Wotan that he 'rises to the tragic height of *willing* his own destruction'. And in the same letter he says of us all: 'We must learn *to die*, and to die in the fullest sense of the word', by which is is clear in context that he means that we have to embrace non-being as *the negation of being as such*, without supposing death to be a change to a different mode of existence.

In Wagner's first draft for the text of *The Ring* he gave it, incredibly, what might be described as a happy ending, with Siegfried carried off in triumph to a Valhalla in which Wotan and all the gods are restored to their former power, presumably to rule with greater insight as a result of their chastening experiences. But Wagner knew that this was not right, and he dropped it long before reading Schopenhauer. The ending of *The Ring* gave him trouble over a number of years, because he had no confident intuition as to what ending was 'right'. The last of several false attempts, made after he had read *The World as Will and Representation*, was to tack on to Brünnhilde's closing monologue a passage of pure Schopenhauer which still appears in many printed editions of the text, but which he never set to music.[26]

> From the realm of desire I depart,
> the realm of illusion I abjure for ever;
> I close behind me
> the open gates
> of endless becoming:
> to the free-from-desire, free-from-illusion,

[26] The chief reason, I fear, why Wagner found it so difficult to hit on the right ending for *The Ring* is that the work itself is incoherent. When he began the text it was consciously intended by him to articulate the world-view of the revolutionary meliorist which he then thought of himself as being, yet for reasons given in the letter to Röckel quoted on pages 340–2 it turned into a tragedy under his pen, guided as this was by his unconscious intuitions. As Deryck Cooke has rightly said: 'In fact, the tetralogy cannot be consistently interpreted on a single level . . . *The Rhinegold*—whatever happens later — begins the tetralogy unmistakably in the world of social and political actuality: Wagner's first conception of *The Rhinegold* — as "showing the original injustice from which a whole world of injustice arose" — remains embedded in that work, and is its manifest overt meaning. Although he eventually came to change his ideas about the nature of the *sovereign remedy* for the world's ills, and represented it in *The Twilight of the Gods* as a metaphysical, not a political one, he nevertheless felt no need to go back and alter the basic content of *The Rhinegold*.' (Deryck Cooke: *I Saw the World End*, p. 247.)

holiest, chosen land —
the goal of worldwide wandering —
she who has achieved wisdom now goes.
Do you know how I reached
this blessed end
of all that is endless?
My eyes were opened
by the profoundest suffering
of grieving love.
I saw the world end.[27]

So in the final outcome Wagner's reading of Schopenhauer did not result in any textual alterations in *The Ring*. Yet it transformed his view of what the text meant, and thus his attitude to the work as a whole: after 1854 he saw its conceptual significance very largely in Schopenhauerian terms. For instance, having come to accept Schopenhauer's doctrine of the nothingness of the phenomenal world, he came to see the closing scene of *Götterdämmerung* as articulating this. And having come to accept Schopenhauer's doctrine of the self or ego as the bearer of the world, he came to see the fact that the *Ring* begins and ends with the beginning and end of the world as being equivalent to its beginning and ending with the emergence and destruction of the self. On matters of character-interpretation, a typical observation is that Wotan 'recognizes the guilt of existence and is atoning for the error of creation'.[28] Twenty years after his discovery of Schopenhauer he remarked to his wife how extraordinary it was that he had fashioned the text of *The Ring* in the way he had without knowing Schopenhauer's philosophy — but he at once went on to say that his ignorance had been a blessing, since 'if I had known it, I should have been less uninhibited in my choice of expressive means'.[29]

However, the text is not the whole work. When Wagner discovered *The World as Will and Representation* he had still to compose more than half the music of *The Ring*. And although his reading of Schopenhauer may not have brought about any changes in the text, its influence on the music, and on the synthesis of the music with the drama, was prodigious. It is here at last that we come to Schopenhauer's positive influence on Wagner's work.

The theory of opera which Wagner had already worked out for

[27] This passage may also remind us that when in 1873 a house was built for Wagner to end his days in he called it *Wahnfried*, which means 'Peace from Illusion', a name that has caused much puzzlement but can be understood clearly in a context of Schopenhauerian-cum-Buddhist ideas.

[28] *Cosima Wagner's Diaries*, i. 506–7.

[29] Ibid. i. 812.

himself before reading Schopenhauer was in contradiction with Schopenhauer's aesthetics on point after point. Wagner saw art as a celebration of the purely human, of this life of ours in the world of experience, whereas Schopenhauer saw this life as a burden and this world as a vale of tears, and regarded art as concerned with Platonic Ideas and the noumenal; Wagner's theories were historicist, which Schopenhauer would have despised; Wagner believed that the creative artist should address himself to 'the people', whereas Schopenhauer considered only a minority capable of being interested in great art; Wagner considered the main function of art as expressive, whereas Schopenhauer saw it as cognitive. But the most important difference of all, in its practical consequences, was the difference between their two views of the nature of music and its relation to the other arts. Wagner's notion of the *Gesamtkunstwerk* implied some sort of family relationship among all the arts, one might say a more or less equal relationship, and his detailed theories about synthesis naturally rested on the premiss that synthesis was possible. Schopenhauer saw the arts as constituting an exceedingly unequal hierarchy, and music as standing outside the hierarchy altogether as an art of a different order from the rest, incapable of synthesis with the others. 'The music of an opera, as presented in the score, has a wholly independent, separate, and as it were abstract existence by itself, to which the incidents and characters of the piece are foreign, and which follows its own unchangeable rules; it can therefore be completely effective even without the text . . . It never assimilates the material, and therefore, when it accompanies even the most ludicrous and extravagant farces of comic opera, it still preserves its essential beauty, purity and sublimity.'[30]

The long and short of the matter is that when Wagner encountered Schopenhauer's aesthetics he was, after a brief initial resistance, won over by them in preference to his own. But, as with the other cases of influence which we have discussed, it was not a bolt-from-the-blue conversion so much as a case of Wagner discovering intuitions which were already his in the hidden-from-himself depths of his creative personality, now openly and boldly expressed for the first time. In aesthetics, as in other matters, Schopenhauer put Wagner in touch with his own unconscious. (As this is the key to what Wagner himself does for those who are susceptible to his art, it explains why his attitude towards Schopenhauer is similar to their attitude towards him.) What Wagner had always felt about music in his heart of hearts, as against what he said about it in his verbal theorizing, was raised to the surface of his conscious mind. In particular the 'glorification of music as a

[30] *The World as Will and Representation*, ii. 449.

super-art Wagner found irresistibly fascinating. He not only accepted it fully, but it so affected his views on art and his creative faculties that one can say he was never again the same as an artist after having read it. I do not believe it is overstating the case to say that Wagner's creative work from this time on takes a new direction and that everything subsequently produced would have had a very different form if Schopenhauer's influence had been absent.'[31] The first person to perceive and state this clearly was, not surprisingly, Nietzsche, who in 1887 wrote in *The Genealogy of Morals* (third essay, section v): 'Consider Schopenhauer's curious, and to some of us most fascinating, attitude to art. It was doubtless that which first converted Wagner to Schopenhauer (at the instance, as everyone knows, of the poet Herwegh) to such a degree that his later aesthetic views completely contradict his earlier ones. As an example of the earlier views, we may take the treatise *Opera and Drama*, of the latter, his articles from 1870 onwards. What most impresses one is the radical change in his notion of the position of music itself . . . music seen as apart from all the other arts, the triumphant culmination of all art, not concerned like the others with images of the phenomenal world but, rather, speaking the language of the will directly from the deep source of Being, its most quintessential manifestation.'

Since, as Nietzsche points out, this change occurs not only in Wagner's creative works but also in his theorizing about art, the best way for us to proceed towards a clear view of it in his operas is first to consider the changes in his verbal formulations of what it was he was doing. These begin to appear much earlier than Nietzsche suggests. Already at the beginning of 1857, in his essay *On Franz Liszt's Symphonic Poems*, we find Wagner writing: 'Hear my creed: music can never, regardless of what it is combined with, cease being the highest, the redemptive art. Its nature is such that what all the other arts only hint at becomes in it the most indubitable of certainties, the most direct and definite of truths.' And whereas in 1849, in *The Work of Art of the Future*, he had dismissed that uniquely musical phenomenon counterpoint as 'artificial art . . . the mathematics of feeling', by 1861, in '*Music of the Future*',[32] he was describing it as 'an absolutely unique effect of the most irresistible power'. Most important of all, in the same essay he for the first time puts forward the view that the nub of the relationship of the music to the rest of an opera consists not in an integration but in a parallelism: the music is, as it were, a running commentary on the

---

[31] Jack Stein: *Richard Wagner and the Synthesis of the Arts*, p. 114.

[32] The title is ironic, as the quotation marks round it were intended to make clear, but this fact has been lost on all those who, contemporaneously and since, have turned the phrase derisively against Wagner himself.

inwardness of the drama, not only when no one is singing but all the time. Technically this is a looser relationship altogether than the one envisaged in *Opera and Drama*, and one which allows the music greater independence of development and expression. The most revealing quotation from Schopenhauer in this regard is: 'This close relation that music has to the true nature of all things can also explain the fact that, when music suitable to any scene, action, event, or set of surroundings is played, it seems to disclose to us its most secret meaning, and appears to be the most accurate and distinct commentary on it.'[33] In terms of Schopenhauer's philosophy this parallelism between music and stage drama is of a fundamentally metaphysical character. The stage action simulates the world of experience, which is the manifestation in terms of phenomena of the metaphysical will, while music is the direct, unmediated articulation of that will; so music is the interior of that of which the stage action represents the exterior. Taken together they bring us as near as it is possible for us to come to an apprehension of the ultimate significance of life — which is something inexpressible in concepts, and therefore inexpressible in words. By this route Wagner came to regard himself as doing *in concreto* what Schopenhauer as a philosopher was doing *in abstractio* — which is precisely what Schopenhauer's own view had been of the relationship between himself and a great composer (see p. 183).

In 1870, in his essay *Beethoven*, Wagner for the first time explicitly repudiated his earlier notions of synthesis. 'The relation of music to poetry is a sheer illusion: for it can be confirmed that when words are sung to music, it is not the poetic thought which is comprehended . . . but at most the mood it engendered in the musician as music and to music.' In the same essay he goes beyond Schopenhauer to the assertion that, because both the stage action and the music are articulations of the metaphysical will, the underlying principles of their inner organization must be the same. He refers to the drama as 'a visible image of the music'. The following year, in *The Destiny of Opera*, he writes: 'I would almost like to call my dramas deeds of music become visible.' A year later, in an essay *On the Term 'Music-Drama'*, he writes: 'The music sounds, and what it sounds you may see on the stage before you.'[34] By

---

[33] *The World as Will and Representation*, i. 262

[34] The reader may be reminded by these quotations of the central thesis of Nietzsche's first book, summed up in its full title *The Birth of Tragedy From the Spirit of Music*. One of Wagner's biographers, Curt von Westernhagen, is of the opinion that it was from Wagner that Nietzsche got the idea that drama derives from music, and I find his conjecture persuasive. We have seen the process by which Wagner arrived at the view: he clearly did not get it from Nietzsche. On the other hand, Nietzsche was writing *The Birth of Tragedy* during the two years 1870–71, the former being the year in which Wagner published *Beethoven* and the latter the year in which he published *The Destiny of*

now music is seen as the overwhelming predominantly, all-creative element. The earlier conception, which the younger Wagner had spent years working out, of an equal synthesis of word-by-word poetic text and note-by-note vocal line and gesture-by-gesture stage action has given place to something quite different, to a primarily musical conception of a stage drama whose inner and most vital significance is articulated by a flow of symphonically constructed music, developed according to musico-dramatic principles which treat music not only as the primary medium of expression but as the main depository of what it is that is being expressed.

Having thus followed out the changes which Wagner's theories went through under Schopenhauer's influence we are now prepared to trace the course of the corresponding reality in his creative works. In doing so we should keep certain warnings and qualifications before our minds. The most important of these is that at no time after his first three operas did Wagner take any theory or aim which was expressible in concepts as the starting-point from which to begin the creation of a work of art. It was clear to him, as it was to Schopenhauer, that this could result only in dead art. The primary source of his work lay always in creative intuitions which were rooted in his subconscious, and which he followed even when he did not understand them, so that the chief value to him of any form of theoretical understanding was that it made a rationale of the workings of his creative self available to his conscious mind. This meant that his theories could change only after his artistic apprehensions had changed. Even if these apprehensions then found public expression as theories before being incorporated in works of art, it was the theoretician who followed the artist, not the artist the theoretician. The chief reason why he embraced Schopenhauer's philosophy was that it boldly articulated what in the depths of his intuition he already believed, and was already inclined to pursue. He remarked to Cosima in 1872 that at the time when he had written *Opera and Drama* 'I didn't dare to say that it was music which produced drama, although inside myself I knew it.'[35] He was perpetually acquiring retrospective

---

Opera. Most important of all, this was the high tide of the personal friendship between the two men — which was an exceedingly unequal relationship between idol and idolator, Wagner being 57 and world famous, with all his works up to *Tristan* and *The Mastersingers* behind him, while the young visitor and house-guest Nietzsche was 26 and writing his first book. All the evidence known to me suggests that the influence between these two was largely one way, and this seems to be borne out by Nietzsche's subsequent dithyrambic accounts of the influence on him of his conversations with Wagner at that stage in his life. I suspect that this debt to Wagner over *The Birth of Tragedy* is acknowledged in the fact that the book is dedicated to Wagner.

[35] *Cosima Wagner's Diaries*, i. 457.

understanding of what, as a creative artist, he had already accomplished, or at least had already perceived the possibility of. We saw earlier how from the beginning he reinterpreted his existing work in the light of his first encounter with Schopenhauer. His theories thereafter continued to illuminate not so much what he was currently doing, or was about to do, as what he had just done. It is true that the increased self-awareness he was thus perpetually acquiring had a creative usefulness, but this consisted not in providing him with material but in enriching the technical means available to him as a craftsman for the working-out and integration of the material that flowed to him from his subconscious.

This leads us to another important caveat. The amount of his earlier theory which continues to apply to his later practice is much greater than one might suppose in the light of the overt theoretical change. This is partly because, as I have said already, he never did work out a coherent theory and *then* apply it: his actual practice was always governed by instinct, and was always therefore eclectic and inconsistent. In any case, even if, *per impossibile* as a great artist, he had taken his starting-point from theory, a creative genius entering middle-life but having only just reached the height of his powers could scarcely be expected to throw overboard in a single moment the hard-won practices of half a lifetime, to embrace on the instant a wholly new set of creative procedures. Any such change, inevitably, would be bound to take time, during which elements of a new approach might increasingly intermingle with continuations of the old. Finally, there is the purely practical consideration that for Wagner, working as he was in the most complicated of all art-forms, it remained the case that even after he had gone through the important change of approach I have described, most of the same subsidiary tasks as before had still to be done: libretti had still to be written, preferably in verse form, and words matched to music, and melodic phrases harmonized, and voices integrated with the orchestra, and orchestral themes developed, and keys related, and modulations effected — and in these and other such detailed respects he continued with his earlier practices, while of course developing and extending them. It would seem from his writings that what he regarded himself as doing was not so much rejecting one overall theory of opera and replacing it with another as accepting a radical shift of emphasis within his earlier theories, preserving the same constituent elements as before but giving them a new order of priority which placed music at the head. Certainly it is possible, and generations of analysts have done it, to interpret the later works in the light of the earlier theories. But I think Jack Stein has the balance about right when he says, with reference to *Tristan*: 'Although the principles of synthesis from *Opera and*

Drama are the basis for the work, and certain portions of the drama (particularly Isolde's narrative, the drinking of the love potion, and the great speech of King Marke) are as magnificent examples of the *Opera and Drama* synthesis as are to be found anywhere, it can be shown that in most of the work (from the drinking of the potion to the end), the music is so overwhelmingly dominant that what seems to be a synthesis on the basis of a three-fold relationship of words, music, and action is closer to a glorification of music as a virtually independent super-art.'[36] In other words, the later theoretical approach subsumes most of the earlier, rather than replaces it.

Wagner, it will be remembered, first read *The World as Will and Representation* while he was composing Acts II and III of *The Valkyrie*. There is no knowing how soon the liberation it initiated began to work its way through to his compositional practices, and it may well not have affected *The Valkyrie* at all, though Act III of that work does end with a scene (standardly referred to as *Wotan's Farewell*) which is regarded by many Wagnerians as surpassing anything Wagner had achieved before in its combination of lyrical and orchestral magnificence. The score has the same dramatic relevance yet musical freedom as in Act I, and if anything an even greater emotional depth, yet somehow the orchestral fabric seems to be woven with a combination of mastery and adventurousness that is new, as if the whole world is now effortlessly within its compass. Be that as it may, when we come to the next work Wagner composed, *Siegfried* — the music for which was begun in the summer of 1856 — there is no doubt that the relationship between music and word has changed.

A moment ago I remarked that in *Rhinegold* Wagner used the orchestra with a degree of freedom which was at odds with the theory he was supposed to be exemplifying. Nevertheless in both *Rhinegold* and *The Valkyrie* all the various expressive media, including the orchestra, are devoted to the same end, that of bringing out the full significance of the dramatic text. For most of the time, at least, the words are the point of common focus. But suddenly, in *Siegfried*, it becomes difficult at times to hear words at all. This is because an urge towards freeing the orchestra, allowing it to become an independent means of expression within the total work — an urge which had always been there with Wagner, but which had been reined in hitherto — now starts to get its head. The sheer weight of orchestral sound is unprecedented. This cannot be because it is called for by the subject-matter of the drama because, on the contrary, the story of young Siegfried in the springtime of the world would of itself require a lighter touch than the earlier

[36] Jack Stein: *Richard Wagner and the Synthesis of the Arts*, p. 132.

dramas — the four operas of *The Ring* have frequently been likened to
the four movements of a symphony with *Siegfried* as its scherzo. The
new approach, then, is not specific to the work but marks a change
which continues to develop throughout the rest of Wagner's output.
The orchestra is ceasing to be 'accompaniment' or 'support'; it is no
longer subordinate to the voices, but is entering into partnership with
the totality of what is happening on the stage — with the result that it
always claims the direct attention of the spectator no matter what else
is going on. In *Siegfried* a character has only to mention the fluttering of
a wing or the movement of a fish for the orchestra to evoke it more
vividly than words, thus perpetually drawing attention away from the
words, and away from the stage itself, to the orchestra. However, the
most important thing of all is that we now begin to get, for the first time,
the creation of a sustainedly massive and complex orchestral sound out
of the ceaseless interweaving of already-existing motives, often two and
sometimes three of them to a bar. At such a rate of density it is difficult
to believe that Wagner expected us, in practice, to 'decode' them all
into their specific dramatic reminiscences and forebodings. They now
have a musical life of their own, in addition to whatever may be their
dramatic and psychological evocations. And this symphonic orchestral
organism is evolving side by side with the stage drama, the two of them
being laced together at the most fundamental level by emotional signi-
ficances which are multiple but which relate to the non-visible, and are
no longer connected at each point by specific matchings of individual
notes with individual words and individual gestures, of which there are
nevertheless many.

Siegfried is a transitional work as regards Schopenhauer's influence
on Wagner. Its text, which was the first of the *Ring* opera libretti to be
completed, had been written long before Wagner read Schopenhauer.
In the scores of *Rhinegold* and *The Valkyrie* there was already a treasure
house of musical material ready and waiting for use in *Siegfried*. So the
pre-Schopenhauerian legacy is large. The first wholly new project
which Wagner conceived after encountering Schopenhauer was *Tristan
and Isolde*. This was unique among his mature works in that it was
produced under pressure from a single intense and sustained impulse
— the period from its conception to its completion was less than five
years, and he broke off work on *The Ring* to compose it, whereas all the
other works of his maturity were literally decades in the making, being
based on ideas which marinated in his mind while he did other things.

The whole project of *Tristan and Isolde*, including its very first conception, was bound up in a deep-lying way with *The World as Will and
Representation*. In his autobiography Wagner refers at one point to 'the
serious mood created by Schopenhauer, which was trying to find

ecstatic expression. It was some such mood that inspired the conception of *Tristan and Isolde*' (*My Life*, p. 617). His first reference to *Tristan* occurs in the same comparatively short letter as his first extended reference to Schopenhauer. It was a letter to Liszt written in December 1854, and in it Wagner says: 'Apart from slowly progressing with my music [the composition of Act III of *The Valkyrie*] I have of late occupied myself exclusively with a man who has come like a gift from heaven, although only a literary one, into my solitude. This is Arthur Schopenhauer, the greatest philosopher since Kant, whose thoughts, as he himself expresses it, he has thought out to the end. The German professors ignored him very prudently for forty years; but recently, to the disgrace of Germany, he has been discovered by an English critic. All the Hegels, etc., are charlatans by the side of him. His chief idea, the final negation of the desire of life, is terribly serious, but it shows the only salvation possible. To me of course that thought was not new, and it can indeed be conceived by no one in whom it did not pre-exist, but this philosopher was the first to place it clearly before me. If I think of the storm of my heart, the terrible tenacity with which, against my desire, it used to cling to the hope of life, and if even now I feel this hurricane within me, I have at least found a quietus which in wakeful nights helps me to sleep. This is the genuine, ardent longing for death, for absolute unconsciousness, total non-existence. Freedom from all dreams is our only final salvation.' Then, in the next paragraph but one, he writes: 'As I have never in life felt the real bliss of love, I must erect a monument to the most beautiful of all my dreams, in which, from beginning to end, that love shall be thoroughly satiated. I have in my head *Tristan and Isolde*, the simplest but most full blooded musical conception. With the black flag that floats at the end of it I shall cover myself to die.'

Satiation with love followed by a desire for death is, of course, central to what the stage action of *Tristan and Isolde* is about. But it will have struck the reader that in his letter Wagner referred to *Tristan* as a 'musical' conception, and furthermore as a 'simple' one. Long before he wrote any of the words for *Tristan* the music for it started to interfere with his work on *Siegfried*, 'in the shape of a melodic thread which . . . kept on spinning itself, so that I could have spent the whole day developing it'.[37] Three days after writing these words he complained that he was unable to get into the mood for composing *Siegfried* at all.[38] He broke off work on it at the end of Act II in order to devote himself to *Tristan*. But some months later he still referred to *Tristan* as '*only music* as

[37] Letter to Marie Wittgenstein, 19 December 1856.
[38] Letter to Otto Wesendonk, 22 December 1856.

yet'.[39] The finished work is, as Ernest Newman puts it, '*musical* from centre to periphery — so much so that the bulk of the opera would make an organic musical whole if played through by the orchestra without the voices. . . . The musical texture of *Tristan* is different from that of any other of Wagner's works in that it is almost purely "symphonic"; often he abandons himself to the sheer intoxication of "developing" the mood symbolized by a particular motive for pages at a time, the stage situation meanwhile remaining stabilized . . . The real drama, as has been already pointed out, is not external but internal, a state of affairs made possible to the musical dramatist only in virtue of the vast superiority of music to speech and to the pictorial arts in range and subtlety and intensity of emotional expression.'[40] Wagner himself wrote: 'This work is more thoroughly musical than anything I have done up to now.' The third act in particular, he said, had received 'a most independent orchestral treatment'.

The very first chord of *Tristan*, perhaps the most famous in the history of music, contains two dissonances, one of which is then re-solved but the other not; the same is true of the second chord, and the third and the fourth; and throughout the work the perpetual longing of the ear for the resolution of discord is at every moment partially satisfied and partially not. This goes on for more than four hours of music, until finally, on the very last chord — when Isolde joins Tristan in death — resolution is at long last achieved, and a full close reached: the striving, indeed everything, stops. The entire work is a sort of musical equivalent of Schopenhauer's doctrine that existence is an inherently unsatisfiable web of longings, willings and strivings from which the only permanent liberation is the cessation of being. The chief musical device by which this equivalence is achieved is known as 'suspension', the holding-over of a note from one chord to the next in such a way as to make the second chord dissonant and thus to delay an expected resolution; it is one of the standard procedures of harmony, often used at the end of a work to produce a feeling first of surprise and then of heightened satisfaction; but what Wagner has done, incredibly, is to extend it over an entire work, indeed an entire evening. In *The World as Will and Representation* — which by the time he composed *Tristan* Wagner had re-read several times — Schopenhauer writes about the connection between this harmonic device and the satisfaction of the will. 'Now the constant *discord and reconciliation* of its two elements which occurs here [in melody] is, metaphysically considered, the copy of the origination of new desires, and then of their satisfaction. . . . The effect

[39] Letter to Marie Wittgenstein, 4 March 1857.
[40] Ernest Newman: *Wagner Nights*, pp. 215–16.

of the *suspension* also deserves to be considered here. It is a dissonance delaying the final consonance that is with certainty awaited; in this way the longing for it is strengthened, and its appearance affords the greater satisfaction. This is clearly an analogue of the satisfaction of the will which is enhanced through delay . . . Music consists generally in a constant succession of chords more or less disquieting, i.e., of chords exciting desire, with chords more or less quieting and satisfying; just as the life of the heart (the will) is a constant succession of greater or less disquietude, through desire or fear, with composure in degrees just as varied.'[41]

This makes it clear what Wagner had in mind when he described *Tristan* as a simple musical conception, and as giving ecstatic expression to a mood induced by the reading of Schopenhauer. The stage action with which he makes this musical conception visible concerns a man and a woman who at first love each other with a passionate but undeclared love which they both assume impossible to satisfy in this world. They seek escape from their intolerable longing in a suicide pact which is itself undeclared; but the devoted and horrified attendant who is ordered to bring poison from a chest of magic liquids deliberately brings the wrong phial. It is a love potion. After drinking it the pair are astounded to find themselves not dying but swept away by the love they had repressed. They slake their longings to the utmost limits of possibility: but their desire for unity is impossible of fulfilment in this world of differentiated phenomena; it is possible only in the noumenal realm, a world which is not this, the world of before birth and after death, outside space and time. So they find themselves longing for that as the only mode of being in which their love can achieve its end. Each finally embraces death not only as the cessation of an otherwise unfulfillable longing but also as the loss of self-identity in an ultimate merging with the other.

The basic notions here are all Schopenhauerian — not only the unsatisfiability of the will in the phenomenal world but the inescapable tragedy of differentiation in it, the profound metaphysical significance of sexual love, the distinction between the phenomenal and the noumenal, and the undifferentiated oneness of the noumenal. Much of this finds direct and literal expression in the text — for instance in Act III, Tristan, after being cheated of death for the third time, cries

> Longing, longing
> even in death still longing
> not to die of longing.
> That which never dies,

---

[41] *The World as Will and Representation*, ii. 455–6.

> longing, now calls out
> for the peace of death . . .

and

> No cure now,
> not even sweet death,
> can ever free me
> from this agony of longing.
> Never, no never
> shall I find rest.

However, as in Tristan's next four lines —

> Night has flung me
> to day
> so that the eye of the sun can eternally
> gloat over my sufferings[42]

— most of the text is permeated with imagery; and, as in this instance, Wagner uses 'day' and 'night' as his key symbols for the phenomenal and the noumenal. If one traces this imagery to its source in Schopenhauerian philosophy one is reminded that the fundamental constituent of day is light, that light can exist only in a space, and that space is a category of outer experience alone. 'Day' then, represents the world of outer sense, the world with which our consciousness and our senses are equipped to deal — the phenomenal world and everything associated with it. It is a world of appearances only, of ephemera and illusions, both material and social. Attachment to it is of the essence of false values. 'Night', by contrast, is the noumenal, the realm of permanent reality, the only something that timelessly and undifferentiatedly is, the aboriginal spaceless — and therefore lightless — oneness of

[42] There seems to be an echo here of the following passage in Schopenhauer: 'The form of the present is essential to the objectification of the will. As an extensionless point, it cuts time which extends infinitely in both directions, and stands firm and immovable, like an everlasting midday without a cool evening, just as the actual sun burns without intermission, while only apparently does it sink into the bosom of the night. If, therefore, a person fears death as his annihilation, it is just as if he were to think that the sun can lament in the evening and say: "Woe is me! I am going down into eternal night." Conversely, whoever is oppressed by the burdens of life, whoever loves life and affirms it, but abhors its torments, and in particular can no longer endure the hard lot that has fallen to just him, cannot hope for deliverance from death, and cannot save himself through suicide. Only by a false illusion does the cool shade of Orcus allure him as a haven of rest. The earth rolls on from day into night; the individual dies; but the sun itself burns without intermission, an eternal noon.' (*The World as Will and Representation*, i. 280–1.) In a footnote to this passage Schopenhauer points out that Goethe also appropriated its central metaphor from him.

being from which we were expelled at birth and to which we long to
return, reverberations from which echo within us in our (again) spaceless, lightless inner world, strongest of all in the hidden-from-ourselves
depths of our unconscious selves. Thus we get episodes like that in
which the lovers recall Tristan's arrival in Ireland to woo for his king
the princess whom, unacknowledged by himself, he himself loved.

ISOLDE: Was it not the day
that lied from within you
when you came to Ireland
as a suitor
to court me for Marke
and destine her who loved you to death?

TRISTAN: The day! The day
that shone around you,
there where you
matched the sun
in loftiest honour's
brightness and radiance,
removed you, Isolde, from me . . .

ISOLDE: What lies did evil
day tell you,
that the woman destined for you
as your lover should be thus betrayed by you?

TRISTAN: You were haloed
in sublimest splendour,
the radiance of nobility,
the authority of fame.
Illusion ensnared me
To set my heart on them . . .

ISOLDE: From the light of day
I wanted to flee
and draw you with me
into the night,
Illusions would end there . . .

TRISTAN: Now we have become
night's devotees.
Spiteful day
armed with envy
could still delusively keep us separate
but never again deceive us with its illusions.
Its idle pomp,
its boastful seeming

> are derisory to those whose vision
> has been consecrated by night.
> The transient flashes
> of its flickering light
> hoodwink us no more.
> To us who have looked lovingly
> on the night of death
> and been entrusted
> with its deep secret
> the day's illusions —
> fame and honour
> power and profit —
> have the glitter of mere
> dust in the sunlight
> into which it disperses . . .

And so on and so forth. This imagery of day and night dominates much of the text, especially in Act II. In the final episode Tristan turns to Isolde and says:

> Where Tristan is going now
> Will you, Isolde, follow him?
> The light of the sun does not illumine
> the land that Tristan means:
> It is the dark
> land of night
> out of which
> my mother sent me . . .

In Act III, when Tristan returns to consciousness after an oblivion so deep as to be an intimation of death, he says to Kurwenal:

> Where I awoke —
> I did not stay:
> But where I stayed
> I cannot explain to you.
> I did not see the sun,
> did not see land and people:
> yet what I saw
> I cannot explain to you.
> I was
> where I have always been,
> where I am going for always:
> the broad realm
> of the night of the world.

Only one kind of knowledge
belongs to us there:
godlike, eternal
pristine oblivion!

Passage after passage in the text is thus poeticized Schopenhauer, and
for anyone familiar with Schopenhauer the verbal imagery is unproble-
matic throughout the work — but alas, only for someone familiar with
Schopenhauer. In consequence, most spectators and commentators
have found it obscure. The assertion has quite often been made that the
words cannot have been intended to mean anything much at all, and
are there chiefly as carriers for the music. The textual passages which
have been found least informative are the long disquisitions on day and
night (only brief extracts from which have been quoted here). It is
obvious to any spectator that day, in a literal sense, keeps the lovers
apart, whereas night unites them, but beyond that what makes Wagner's imagery so impenetrable to someone without prior knowledge is
that its meanings are directly at variance with those which are customarily accorded in our culture to these images. The association of
'truth' with 'light' pervades not only our poetry and our imaginative
literature but our everyday speech, in such terms as 'enlighten', 'in the
light of', 'cast light on', 'bring to light', 'as clear as daylight', and so on.
Conversely, we speak of things being 'shrouded in darkness' or of
'keeping someone in the dark', and so on. These associations seem to
occur in all European languages, and in the oldest literature with which
we are familiar, such as the Old Testament. Yet *Tristan* stands them on
their heads. Here, day and the world of daylight are not the realm of
truth, of reality, of things as they actually are, perceived clearly and
without illusion, but, on the contrary, they *are* the realm of illusion, of
lies, mere appearance, unreality — of 'dreams', paradoxically. And
night is not the realm of ignorance, of delusive appearances, of dreams
and unfulfillable longings, but of ultimate truth, the one and only
timeless reality, and of the only true knowledge of this reality, and thus
escape from unsatisfiable longing.

Ever since its appearance, *Tristan* has been regarded by many people
as a work of unsurpassed greatness. It is also something else which is
unique, and which might never have existed at all: both as a totality
and in its details, and both in its music and in its verbal text, it is a
fusion, effected at white heat, of insights from a great philosopher with
the art of a consummate musical dramatist. This not only makes it *sui
generis* as a work of art but gives it a *kind* of significance which would be
uncapturable in any other form. Some commentators, apprehending
that the work is pervaded with metaphysical significance, have denied

that it is, understood seriously, erotic; but this can be done only in ignorance of Schopenhauer's doctrine of the metaphysical implications of sexual love, a doctrine of whose essential kernel of truth Wagner was consciously persuaded before he read Schopenhauer. According to Schopenhauer's philosophy the two specific involvements of ordinary life which bring us closest to a direct contact with the noumenal are sexual love and music. *Tristan and Isolde* — the very work itself, merely by existing — is a celebration of this affinity. Its content includes an ecstatic (Wagner's word) celebration of sexual love. Significantly, his next opera, *The Mastersingers*, was to be a celebration of music. When we consider the content of *Tristan*, almost everything in the work itself refutes the notion that it is not erotic. The music is some of the most erotic ever composed — especially in the second act, rising to an orgastic climax with the words, on which the two voices come together:

> then I myself
> am the world:
> woven of sublime bliss,
> life of holiest love,
> the marvellously aware
> undeluded wish
> never to waken again.[43]

These words are followed by an episode saturated with the mutual tenderness that follows lovemaking. Then the pair's passions stir again, until they are once more heatedly aroused, and they are in the throes of combined orgasm for a second time when the phenomenal world bursts in on them in the differentiated shapes of King Marke and the returned hunting party, ghosts from the world of day, catching them 'openly in the act (*in offner Tat*)' as Melot says. Apart from the clear evidence of the music and the words, there is the fact that the love potion which the two have drunk had been intended by Isolde's mother for King Marke in order to keep him faithful to Isolde in marriage, and thus to ensure the permanence of their union. And as I have said, there was in Wagner already, before he read Schopenhauer, an unqualified acceptance of the fundamentality of sex to love. In a letter which he wrote to Röckel on 25 January 1854 there occurs the following passage:

[43] *selbst dann*
  bin ich die Welt:
  Wonne-hehrstes Weben
  Liebe-heiligstes Leben
  Nie-wieder-Erwachens
  wahnlos
  hold bewusster Wunsch.

'Love in its most perfect reality is possible only between the sexes; it is only as man and woman that human beings can truly love. Every other manifestation of love can be traced back to that one absorbing real feeling, of which all other affections are an emanation, a connection, or an imitation. It is an error to look upon this as only one of the forms in which love is revealed, as if there were other forms co-equal with it, or even superior to it. He who after the manner of metaphysicians prefers *unreality* to *reality*, and derives the concrete from the abstract — and, in short, puts the word before the fact — he may be right in esteeming the idea of love as higher than the expression of love, and may affirm that actual love made manifest in feeling is nothing but the outward and visible sign of a pre-existent, non-sensuous, abstract love; and he will do well to despise that love and sensuous function in general. In any case it would be safe to bet that such a man had never loved or been loved as human beings can love, or he would have understood that in despising this feeling, what he condemned was its sensual expression, the outcome of man's animal nature, and not true human love. The highest satisfaction and expression of the individual is to be found only in his complete absorption, and that is only possible through love. Now a human being is both *man* and *woman*, and it is only when these two are united that the real human being exists, and thus it is only by love that man and woman attain to the full measure of humanity. But when nowadays we talk of a human being, such heartless blockheads are we that quite involuntarily we think only of man. It is only in the union of man and woman, by love (sensuous and super-sensuous) that the human being exists; and as the human being cannot rise to the conception of anything higher than his own existence — his own being — so the transcendent act of his life is this consummation of his humanity through love.'

Tristan really is, then, as it so obviously appears to be, all-engulfingly erotic. However, on the basis of Schopenhauer's philosophy there is an unsolved problem posed by the work, and it is this: the lovers speak endlessly of unity with each other in death, but they will be united in death only in the sense that they will also be united with everything and everybody else, including all the other characters in the opera. There cannot be a more specific sense in which they will be united *with each other* in death because the terms 'each other' derive their significance from the fact of differentiation, and could have neither sense nor reference in an undifferentiated noumenal realm. Only in the phenomenal world would oneness with each other as individuals be possible, and that would be on the basis of compassionate, not sexual, love,

a love in which the will was denied. Wagner was aware of this inconsistency with Schopenhauer's teaching, and he considered that it was a
point on which Schopenhauer was wrong. Characteristically, while
working on *Tristan*, he sat down and started writing a letter to the
philosopher to put him straight; but the letter was never finished.
However, the fragment he completed has been included in his collected
published works, and it makes the crucial point that sexual love is also a
way in which the will can be led to self-awareness and self-denial — and
Wagner specifically says that he is talking here not only about the wills
of individuals. This explains, he says, something which Schopenhauer
admits he finds inexplicable. Wagner begins the letter with the following quotation from *The World as Will and Representation*: 'Every year
provides us with one or two cases of the common suicide of two lovers
thwarted by external circumstances. But it is inexplicable to me why
those who are certain of mutual love do not withdraw from every
connexion by the most extreme steps, and endure every discomfort,
rather than give up with their lives a happiness that for them is greater
than any other they can conceive.'[44] Such a suicide pact is, of course,
precisely what is made by Tristan and Isolde, and Wagner thinks he
understands it. However, even if he is right, his view still does not give
us any grounds for regarding such a pair of lovers as united in any
specific way *with each other* after death. The problem of noumenal
oneness between individuals was to be resolved only in a separate work,
Parsifal, and then it was resolved in an orthodox Schopenhauerian
way.

The year in which Wagner conceived *Tristan*, 1854, was something of
an *annus mirabilis* for him, for in it he also drafted all the music for both
Rhinegold and *The Valkyrie* — after having composed nothing for almost
six years — and read *The World as Will and Representation* for the first
time. A year or two later, in response to his reading of Schopenhauer
and his consequent studies in Buddhism, he formed the project of
writing a 'Buddhist' opera to be called *The Conquerors* (*Die Sieger*). This
work, as Ernest Newman tells us, 'haunted his imagination for another
twenty years or so, but never came to fruition, partly because much of
the emotional and metaphysical impulse that would have gone to the
making of it had been expended on *Tristan*, partly because, in the late
1870s, he found that a good deal of what he would have to say in
connection with it was finding its natural expression in *Parsifal*.'[45] This
means that by the end of 1854 all the operas that he was actually to
compose during the remaining three decades, almost, of his life, includ-

[44] *The World as Will and Representation*, ii. 532.
[45] Ernest Newman: *Wagner Nights*, pp. 204–5.

ing his four last and greatest works — *Tristan, The Mastersingers, Götter-dämmerung* and *Parsifal* — were specifically formed projects in his mind. Since this was his forty-second year one is disconcertingly reminded of Schopenhauer's dictum that at the most fundamental level the sum of what we are does not increase after the age of forty-two though the sum of what we are able to make of what we are may go on growing. Up to forty-two, he says, our life is like the text of a book of which the remainder is commentary: the commentary may be as wise, as penetrating, as illuminating as one likes, but it does not add to the store of original material.

The next opera Wagner wrote after *Tristan, The Mastersingers*, had been conceived by him as far back as 1845, within a few weeks of his first thoughts also of *Parsifal*. He had actually written a twelve-page scenario for *The Mastersingers*, to which he appended the date 16 July 1845, but he then put it to one side to ferment. He knew he was not yet ready to compose it. It was finally created over the period of nearly six years between January 1862 and October 1867. All the summers of those intervening twenty years seem to have contributed to the process of its maturation: what began as a skit became a massive hymn to the supreme position in social life of art, and above all of music. This is, of course a thoroughly Schopenhauerian theme. It is also something which it could not possibly have been had it been written earlier: it is the paradigm work in the form subsequently adumbrated by Wagner in *Beethoven* and *The Destiny of Opera*. As such it breaks most of the chief rules and proposals of his earlier theoretical writings — one of the most interesting things that is worked out in the opera, symbolically, is a confrontation between Wagner's older and younger selves. The setting is not mythical but an actual place and time — Nuremberg in 1560 — and the central character, the cobbler and poet Hans Sachs, is someone who had actually lived there and then. The text and the stage action are cast in the conventional operatic forms outlawed or scorned by the younger Wagner: stanzaic songs with conventional rhyme schemes abound, in which different words are sung to the same music in successive verses; and there are chorales and choruses, duets, a quintet, even a brief ballet of sorts. It is as if the mature Wagner is saying — as his *alter ego* in the opera does say to the headstrong young natural genius, Walther — that however it may look to the brilliant young, tradition is not an incubus, not a concatenation of dead or empty forms to be swept aside by the spontaneously creative, but a rich support-system of wisdom and experience which, rightly used, nourishes a genius on his journey into the unknown. This attitude to the cultural legacy of the past exactly corresponds to Schopenhauer's, and is the opposite of what Wagner's had been before he read Schopenhauer. The place of words in this opera has fallen back to a position from which Wagner had once sought to rescue it. Lines of text are repeated for purely musical reasons. Different characters talk at once. At the climax of Act I, sixteen different vocal lines are going at the same time, so there can be very little question of many of the words being heard at all in such circumstances. Altogether, words in this work are relegated to an unmistakably subsidiary role — which, though at first this may seem paradoxical, is why it can be so effective in a good translation: so little is lost. Never is there any attempt to conjure the musical line out of the poetic text in the manner of Act I of *The Valkyrie*. The synthesis is not of words and music but of stage action and orchestra, and the orchestral tapestry is woven with scant regard for individual words. One of Wagner's standard procedures is to introduce a musical motive at the beginning of an episode and then develop it orchestrally in a rich polyphonic style that goes weaving on alongside the stage action for the rest of that episode — the contrapuntal lyricism of these inner parts is one of the marvels of all music — with the result that each episode has its own characteristic music in the form of a symphonically developed commentary on what can be called the internality of the scene. This orchestral presence is so massive that it at least equals the stage drama in the extent to which it impinges on the spectator. The sheer bulk of it can be illustrated by the fact that when the score was published it was the largest in the history of music up to that time.

As in the case of *Tristan*, the unifying, overall form of the work is musically derived. The relationship of the three acts to each other corresponds to that, much discussed within the opera itself, of the verses of a Master-song. And the primacy of music which this work exemplifies shows also in the history of its composition: Wagner wrote the music for the most important of its many set pieces, the Prize Song, a long time before he wrote any of the words; and the overture, which contains all the most important themes in the opera, was composed, indeed publicly performed, before any of the text had been set to music. As one of the more astute commentators on Wagner's operas has written: 'The "thematic image" of the whole work — Senta's ballad in *Der fliegende Holländer* — is in *Die Meistersinger* the overture, a piece of instrumental music. (The form is that of a symphonic poem after the Lisztian pattern. The four movements of classical symphonic form are compressed into a single movement, to whose four parts — first subject, second subject, development and reprise — Wagner gives the character of the various movements of the conventional symphony: Allegro, Andante, Scherzo and Finale.)'[46]

---

[46] Carl Dahlhaus: *Richard Wagner's Music Dramas*, p. 71.

Since our aim here is not to launch into a discussion of *The Master-singers* for its own sake, but merely to draw attention to those aspects of it over which the shadow of Schopenhauer's influence has fallen, I confine my remaining remarks to the most important of the Schopenhauerian references in its text. Schopenhauer believed that our unconscious really is unconscious, and that we have no direct access to it at all. The dreams that we dream in the depths of sleep are unrememberable to our waking selves. However, the dreams that we dream while we are drifting to the surface — what are often called 'morning dreams' — face both ways, as it were: they are largely shaped by the unconscious mental activities which have immediately preceded them, but they are still in our minds when we wake. Thus the dreams that we can remember constitute something intermediate through which we can gain knowledge of unconscious processes to which we have no direct access. All this is marvellously previsionary of Freud; but Schopenhauer stresses the additional point that it means that remembered dreams have something fundamentally in common with art. Both are inwardly created worlds which are symbolically representative of a noumenal reality to which we do not have direct access; and the creation of neither can be willed. Not only do they speak of the same things, they spring from the same subconscious, as distinct from unconscious, level of the personality. In short, dreams and art are of the same stuff: one is merely a transmutation of the other. All this comes into *The Mastersingers*. The Prize Song is an account of a morning dream, and when its melody has to be given an elaborate name, in the manner of the time, Hans Sachs christens it 'The blissful Morning-Dream-Interpretation melody' (*Die selige Morgentraum-Deutweise*). The famous quintet is the baptismal scene, the bestowing of this name. And it should be noted that the name includes the term 'interpretation' — we are specifically concerned here with *the interpretation of dreams*. When Sachs first persuades Walther to put the dream on paper, in the form of a song, he delivers him a Schopenhauerian lecture on the connection between art and dreams, telling him that it is dreams that disclose to us the truest depths of our inner world, and therefore that all creativity and poetizing are nothing but the elucidation of significant dreaming.[47]

As in *Tristan*, it is some of the elements which are derived most directly from Schopenhauer that audiences and commentators — most

[47] *Mein Freund, das grad' ist Dichters Werk*
dass er sein Träumen deut' und merk'.
Glaubt mir, des Menschen wahrster Wahn
wird ihm im Traume aufgetan:
all' Dichtkunst und Poeterei
ist nichts als Wahrtraum–Deuterei.

of whom, reasonably enough, have no particular knowledge of the philosopher — have found the most puzzling. A Schopenhauerian term of which Sachs makes repeated use is *Wahn*, meaning sometimes the follies of mankind, sometimes madness, sometimes illusion; and sometimes the self-created significance, albeit illusory, that makes art possible and life meaningful. The great *Wahn monologue* starts with the first of these meanings and transubstantiates it via the remainder into the last. In the process Sachs refers to Schopenhauer's doctrine that 'the difference between the inflicter of suffering and he who must endure it is only phenomenon, and does not concern the thing-in-itself which is the will that lives in both. Deceived by the knowledge bound to its service, the will here fails to recognize itself; seeking enhanced well-being in *one* of its phenomena, it produces great suffering in *another*. Thus in the fierceness and intensity of its desire it buries its teeth in its own flesh, not knowing that it always injures only itself, revealing in this form through the medium of individuation the conflict with itself which it bears in its inner nature. Tormenter and tormented are one.'[48] Sachs repeats one of Schopenhauer's images here:

> driven into flight
> he is under the illusion he is hunting
> and does not hear his own
> cry of pain;
> when he tears into his own flesh
> he imagines he is giving himself pleasure![49]

About Sachs altogether there is an unmistakably Schopenhauerian air of resignation. In a letter to King Ludwig II written in 1869 Wagner described him as a 'resigned man who shows the world a cheerful, energetic countenance'. The chief of the things he is renouncing is the demand of the will in its most life-warming form, sexual love, and one of the greatnesses of the opera lies in the way this inner resignation, concealed beneath an apparent affirmation of life, is somehow given expression *within* the life assertion that characterizes the whole work. Such simultaneous expression of conflicting emotions, to the degree of complexity exhibited in this opera, is something which only music and

---

[48] *The World as Will and Representation*, i. 354.
[49] *in Flucht geschlagen*
   wähnt er zu jagen.
   Hört nicht sein eigen
   Schmerz-Gekreisch,
   wenn er sich wühlt ins eig'ne Fleisch
   wähnt sich Lust zu erzeigen!

drama together can accomplish. I would not say that Wagner's achievement in this respect is unique: similar claims might be made for Mozart, though I think only for Mozart.

After *The Mastersingers*, Wagner turned back to *The Ring*. He had been away from it for twelve years, during which time he had created not only *The Mastersingers* but also *Tristan*, one of the most original, revolutionary and influential works of art in the history of European culture. The surprising thing therefore is not that the music of Act III of *Siegfried* and the whole of *Götterdämmerung* is in a more evolved style than that of the earlier parts of the cycle — something of the sort must have been inevitable — but that the artistic unity of the cycle is nevertheless maintained. Given that Wagner was returning to a libretto which had been written so many years before, in the first flush of his *Opera and Drama* approach, and was taking up again hundreds of pages of completed musical score which were overflowing with dozens or even hundreds of musical motives and themes of already established significance in the drama, there was only one respect in which his changed approach could even possibly have revealed itself without turning the work as a whole into a hybrid, and that was in the orchestral treatment and its relation to the stage action — and this precisely is what occurred. 'A difference is at once noticeable in the prelude to Act III of *Siegfried*. Here only the old *Ring* motives are used, but their combination and musical treatment are bolder, freer and more lavish than in any of the preludes to the previous acts of the *Ring* dramas. No less than nine familiar motives are brought into this short introduction, a considerably higher concentration than in any of the others, and they are combined with an improvisational freedom that reminds one of *The Mastersingers* orchestra far more than the earlier *Ring*. This heralds a noticeable difference in the use of leitmotifs throughout; they are used in a profusion which is not in evidence even in the first two acts of *Siegfried*, where we already noted a deviation from the strict use that characterized *The Rhinegold* and *The Valkyrie*. The motives come at one in such swift succession, often combined, that it is impossible to associate them, as they were originally intended, with reminiscences of previous scenes. In Act III of *Siegfried*, for instance, as the hero is ascending the mountain to Brünnhilde's rock, the Slumber motive from *The Valkyrie*, Siegfried's Horn Call from *Siegfried*, the Bird Call from *Siegfried*, and the Bondage motive from *The Rhinegold* are contrapuntally interwoven into a single [bar]. Three-fold and four-fold combinations of this kind are numerous. Because of this more lavish use of leitmotif, the total number of separate occurrences is much higher than in the earlier *Ring* dramas. The number in *Twilight of the Gods* (1003) is more than double the number in *The Valkyrie* (405). (Immediate repetitions in the same scene or portion of a scene are not included in these figures.)'[50]

As another commentator has put it, 'there is hardly a bar in *Götter-dämmerung* that does not refer forward or back or sideways or all three, as well as to the situation in hand.'[51] Herein lies the secret of this work's miraculous texture. A polyphonic orchestral technique which had been raised to perfection only with the composition of *The Mastersingers* is brought to bear on the already existing and incredibly rich motivic material of *The Ring*. That masterful interweaving of the inner orchestral parts now inherits an inexhaustible supply of highly distinctive symphonic-dramatic themes to work with, themes which are not only unforgettable in themselves but are also imbued with a complex dramatic and psychological significance which has accrued to them over no less than three whole evenings. The metamorphoses to which they are subjected are of the utmost subtlety and elusiveness in themselves, and at the same time intertwine contrapuntally with each other, and grow seamlessly into and out of each other, in a texture which is unique — but which also has this in common with the orchestra of *The Mastersingers*, that it relates to the total dramatic situation rather than to the individual words being sung. Wagner also carried over from *The Mastersingers* the habit of introducing a dominant musical theme at the beginning of an episode and then subjecting it to an extended symphonic development which goes on alongside the stage action. The resulting complexities are inexhaustibly beautiful simply as music, and have at the same time a many-tongued dramatic and psychological eloquence; indeed, Wagner's psychological insight is here at its very deepest. For what is happening is the recollection, from a state of achieved resignation, of previous experience, its absorption and digestion at the profoundest level, and its transubstantiation into emotional understanding, which is to say into insight and wisdom. And this metabolism of feeling is at one with the orchestral texture: the most profound and significant process of human life has at last found its objective correlative in art. Only towards the end of a total work of a very much greater length could any such process be possible. Only a symphony orchestra — and indeed, only a symphony orchestra used in this way — could articulate it. And only because Wagner had broken off his labours on *The Ring* in order to compose *Tristan* and *The Mastersingers* had he acquired the ability to do it. We have seen how, in this whole process of development, the influence of Schopenhauer was vital, and was regarded by Wagner himself as being so.

[50] Jack Stein: *Richard Wagner and the Synthesis of the Arts*, p. 190.
[51] Richard David: 'Wagner the Dramatist' in *The Wagner Companion*, ed. Peter Burbridge and Richard Sutton, p. 119.

To achieve the same thing again Wagner would have had to write another work of comparable dimensions to *The Ring*, and that can scarcely be regarded as feasible. So the scaling of the combined musical, dramatic and psychological heights attained in *Götterdämmerung* was an unrepeatable achievement. For technical reasons, I doubt in any case whether it would have been likely to be surpassed: we have now arrived at an orchestral texture whose density is just about the maximum compatible with clear intelligibility, and any attempt to make an orchestra articulate yet more would be almost bound to result in an over-dense sound which, because of its greater homogeneity, would in practice communicate less. Even if this were not so, any further enlarging of the orchestral contribution would unbalance the whole in the direction of becoming an orchestral work with stage accompaniment, thereby ceasing to be essentially dramatic. As it is, *Götterdämmerung*, unlike any of the previous *Ring* dramas, contains not just one but several colossal outpourings for orchestra alone which have become famous in their own right, such as Siegfried's Journey to the Rhine, Hagen's Watch, Siegfried's Funeral March, and the closing scene of the work. The role of music has now grown about as big as it can be and still remain contained within, and make a contribution to, a larger dramatic whole.

Each one of Wagner's operas has its own characteristic sound: there is an utterly distinctive *Tristan* sound, *Mastersingers* sound, and so on; and within the *Ring*, for reasons I have gone into, each of the four operas has its own sound too, that of *Götterdämmerung* being far and away the most subtle and sophisticated. In *Parsifal*, the only opera Wagner was to write after *Götterdämmerung*, this aural image is the most markedly individual of all — and it is a purely orchestral sound. In fact it is the first appearance in music of the sound-world from which were to emerge the great adagios of the late Bruckner symphonies and the symphonies of Mahler. In this context it is illuminating to recall that Wagner intended *Parsifal* to be the last of his operas, after which he was going to devote himself to the writing of symphonies. But, tragically, he died too soon, a loss to music comparable only to the premature death of Schubert. What those symphonies would have been must remain forever a matter of speculation. *Parsifal* was his last work. In it, all the thematic motives except for one originate in the orchestra, which develops them symphonically as an equal counterpart to the stage action in virtual independence of the words. For long stretches of the opera there is no dialogue between the characters at all, in consequence of which there is more music to less text than there is even in *Tristan*; in fact, although in performance *Parsifal* is one of the longest of Wagner's operas, its text is the shortest. Harmony is developed with a daring that

carries it to the outermost limits of tonality and lights the path towards
the post-tonal world of twentieth-century music. To quote Ernest
Newman: 'The third act opens with a grave orchestral prelude the
subtle chromaticisms of which are a foretaste of a harmony, throughout
the act, the like of which had not been known in music until then, even
in the work of such a master of chromatic nuance as Wagner: in some
places it marks an advance upon *Tristan* in this field as great as that of
Tristan — which is the great dividing line between the older harmony
and the new — had been upon the *Rhinegold* and the *Valkyrie*.'[52] The
score of *Parsifal*, like that of *Tristan*, has proved to be one of the most
influential in the history of music.

   With *Parsifal*, unlike *Götterdämmerung*, Wagner was free to create an
entire work in accordance with his current conceptions. The result was
an opera which, in its different way, was as Schopenhauerian as *Tristan*.
It will be remembered that Schopenhauer had regarded the whole of
morality as being based on compassion, and taught that this functioned
independently of the intellect, consisting for each of us in an intuitive
understanding that what is essential to our own nature, our noumenal
self, is at one with the inner nature of everything and everybody else.
All value and all significance lie in the noumenal, outside the world of
phenomena. He regarded the great religions — by which he meant
Hinduism, Buddhism and Christianity — as embodying the most
fundamental truths of all, namely that this world is ephemeral and
paltry, that we do not belong to it, and that nothing in it is to be
regarded as an end in itself; that we should therefore try to detach our
desires and our wills from it; that — next to the will-to-live itself — the
chief focus of the will, and therefore the most difficult of its demands to
deny, is the sex drive, which in most of us overcomes our better selves;
that altogether our life in this world is an interim condition of suffering,
guilt, trial, struggle, and perhaps purification, through which it may be
possible for us to lift ourselves to a better existence — not by any
amount of intellectual activity but by renunciation and the denial of
our self-will. He also believed that such truths stated generally in this
way do not make much impression on mankind at large, and that for
this reason the great religions present them in more interesting forms,
more concretely and specifically, in the shape of history, myth, legend,
fable, parable, prophecy, song, commandment, ritual, social institutions, architecture, art, and so on. To the simple-minded all these
metaphorical constructs are presented as literal truths, and are
believed in by them as literal truths; but literally they are not true: it is
their symbolic content that is true. Thus, for instance, Schopenhauer

[52] Ernest Newman: *Wagner Nights*, p. 745.

positively disbelieved in the existence of a personal god, and *a fortiori* did not believe in the divinity of Jesus, and therefore cannot in any serious sense whatever be said to have been a Christian — and yet he believed that 'that great fundamental truth contained in Christianity as well as in Brahmanism and Buddhism, the need for salvation from an existence given up to suffering and death, and its attainability through the denial of the will, hence by a decided opposition to nature, is beyond all comparison the most important truth there can be.'[53]

All this is absorbed into *Parsifal*. The familiar diatribes against Wagner either for having 'succumbed' to Christianity in this work or else for having 'pretended' to believe in it when really he did not are point-missing. Wagner was never a Christian, and never believed in God. 'Wagner's faith was philosophical, not religious, a metaphysics of compassion and renunciation, deriving its essential elements from Schopenhauer's *World as Will and Representation* and — via Schopenhauer — from Buddhism.'[54] In the last of his theoretical writings, *Religion and Art* — written in 1880, while he was working on *Parsifal* — he made his Schopenhauerian position plain on the specific point of the use of religion in art. 'One could say that when religion becomes artificial it is for art to salvage the essence of religion by construing the mythical symbols which religion wants us to believe to be literal truth in terms of their figurative value, so as to let us see their profound hidden truth through idealised representation. Whereas the priest is concerned only that the religious allegories should be regarded as factual truths, this is of no concern to the artist, since he presents his work frankly and openly as his invention.'

The story told by Wagner in *Parsifal* is as follows. The human beings who are the guardians of the things of greatest value on this earth (having come to them from outside the world, as the gift of angels) are the knights of the grail, keepers of both the cup from which Christ drank at the Last Supper and the spear that pierced his side on the cross. But individual members of this knighthood are perpetually being lured from their calling by seductive women who are working in the service of Klingsor, an evil magician. Klingsor had once been a knight who himself wished to join the order, but he had been unable to rid himself of lustful desires, whereas only the pure could serve. He had sought to extirpate the lust that excluded him by castrating himself — but far from giving him entrance to the order this made him an object of horrified revulsion, an eternal outcast. Now, being forever unable to reach the grail and the spear through membership of the order, he is

[53] *The World as Will and Representation*, ii. 628.
[54] Carl Dahlhaus: *Richard Wagner's Music Dramas*, p. 143.

determined to get possession of them by destroying the order. That same self-mutilation which shuts him out from it also makes him immune to the temptations which destroy its members, enabling him to be lord and master of the temptresses whom he can thus use for his purpose. The chief of these is Kundry, who had once displayed the ultimate in lack of compassion by laughing at the dying Christ as he hung on the cross. She has ever since been pursuing atonement through existence after existence — in fact through a dual existence as the two aspects of archetypal Woman: alternately she is the caring, self-sacrificing, dowdy minister to the needs of others and the delectable seductress; and in each of these roles she has no awareness of her existence in the other. At Klingsor's bidding she seduces no less a person than the King of the knightly order, Amfortas. When Amfortas lays aside his spear — the holy spear — to make love to her, the watching Klingsor rushes in on the scene and seizes it, plunges it into Amfortas, and makes off with it. Amfortas, direly wounded, manages to get back to Monsalvat, the home of his order. But thereafter he has a terrible wound of which he does not die, yet which never heals, with the result that he lives suspended in a permanent state of mortal agony. Despite this, as King of the order he is still required to carry out the religious ritual — the continued use of the grail to celebrate the Holy Feast — which is the order's *raison d'être*. This duty pushes him each time to the limits of humiliation, mortification and suffering. Over the years, knight after knight seeks to retrieve the situation by venturing forth to recover the spear, and with it Amfortas's release and the order's honour, but without exception they succumb to Klingsor's temptresses and never return. A prophecy emanating from the grail tells Amfortas that redemption will come only at the hands of an innocent whom compassion, not pre-existing knowledge (still less cleverness), has rendered understanding. This is Parsifal. When he comes on the scene he is as ignorant and as lacking in compassion as a human being can well be: he has no idea who he is or where he comes from; he has allowed his mother to die by his sheer disregard of her loving concern for him; and he kills merely for something to do. Religious enactments have no meaning for him. When faced with the torture of Amfortas this does stir something in him, but he has no idea what it is. Then Kundry attempts to seduce him. Her subtle arousal of his sexual awareness by associating herself with his mother brings home to him for the first time his responsibility for his mother's death.[55] Then he experiences the full

---

[55] 'It is not inconceivable . . . that the second act of *Parsifal* and the third act of *Siegfried* exercised an unacknowledged influence on the development of psycho-analytical theory.' (Carl Dahlhaus: *Richard Wagner's Music Dramas*, pp. 147–8.) When Siegfried encounters the first woman he has ever seen, Brünnhilde, he simultaneously

onslaught of sexual desire — and it is this, the rack of passion, that makes him realize what it is that has happened to Amfortas, and thus the nature of the wound. Further, it leads him to apprehend for the first time the condition of the whole of suffering mankind, the rack of unsatisfiable willing on which it is endlessly stretched out — and hence to understand the compassion of a Christ for humanity at large — and hence to understand the significance of the religious ceremony he has witnessed. Armed with these insights, he is enabled to withstand Kundry's temptations, and thus to regain the spear from Klingsor. With this he returns to Monsalvat and touches the wound of Amfortas — which at once heals, thereby releasing Amfortas from any further compulsion to live with his disgrace. The return of the spear to Monsalvat opens up a new era for the depleted, dishonoured and decaying order. Parsifal, succeeding Amfortas as its king, takes up with full consciousness the task of restoring it, and leading the religious ceremonies that express the purpose of its being.

In the medieval poem by Wolfram von Eschenbach from which Wagner got the original story the sexual nature of Amfortas's wound is made brutally explicit: he is 'pierced through the testicles'. But in a nineteenth-century European stage work it was not possible to say this, still less to represent it in any way, so Wagner relocated the wound in Amfortas's side. But its symbolic significance remains the same. It is the rack of willing in its most extreme form. Such a devastating wound — which refuses to kill yet also refuses to heal, so that its victim longs for death but can neither die nor live — had also been suffered by Tristan in Act III of *Tristan and Isolde*. There this unassuageable willing that constitutes human life, and is at its most imperious in the sex demand, took the form of an overmastering need for Isolde which kept Tristan in this world, yet was inherently unsatisfiable. Wagner was clear about the identity of the two cases. In a letter to Mathilde Wesendonk dated 30 May 1859 he wrote: 'It has suddenly become terribly clear to me: [Amfortas] is my Tristan of the third act, but inconceivably intensified.' This was twenty years before *Parsifal* was composed!

For reasons which must by now be self-evident to the reader, *Parsifal* and *Tristan* were intimately bound up with one another in Wagner's mind. At one point when he had been working on *Tristan* he had toyed with the idea of having the wandering Parsifal appear on the stage in Act III. 'Parzival, questing for the Grail, was to come in the course of

experiences hitherto unknown sexual feelings and thinks of his mother — in fact he wonders whether perhaps this *is* his mother. All attempts up to now to teach him the meaning of fear have failed, but his very first sexual emotions are accompanied by anxiety — and suddenly he knows what fear is.

his pilgrimage to Kareol, and there find Tristan lying on his death-bed, love-racked and despairing. Thus the longing one was brought face to face with the renouncing one, the self-curser with the man atoning for his own guilt, the one suffering unto death from love with the one bringing redemption through pity. Here death, there new life.'[56] This seems to imply that Wagner did after all see *Parsifal* as providing the solution to a problem insoluble in *Tristan*: both redemption from un- assuageable longing and a full and true union with another human being are available *in this life*, but the path to them lies through renunciation of the will, and therefore involves the repudiation of sexual desires — which was out of the question for Tristan. In *Parsifal*, all the characters except Parsifal himself are looking for redemption in the wrong place. The dishonoured knights are desperately hoping for it from an endless repetition of religious ceremonial whose significance is draining away over time. Amfortas, like Tristan, seeks it in death. Klingsor's attempt to deny the will in himself by doing violence on himself is wilful self-assertion of the most horrific kind, reminding one of Schopenhauer's condemnation of suicide. Kundry is in search of salvation through sexual fulfilment, though in fact she can reach it only by transcending her sexuality altogether. It is Parsifal alone who experiences the demands of the will in all their unmitigated fullness, and lives them through, but in doing so masters them and puts them behind him. And this alone, we are being told, is the path to salvation.

The spear in *Parsifal*, as in *The Ring*, is a symbol of power, but whereas in *The Ring* it was a symbol of power over others in *Parsifal* it is a symbol of power over oneself — the sort of morally desirable auton- omy which is rooted in the authenticity and integrity of the personality. The generality of people are unable to attain it. Amfortas loses it because of his inability to resist the will's demands. Klingsor achieves self-sufficiency, but of the wrong kind, and at a price he would have done better not to pay: all he gains is the forever diminished autonomy of compassionless self-isolation. (Like Alberich in *The Ring*, he trades away the possibility of love in return for the exercise of power over others.) It is only Parsifal who comes into full and permanent posses- sion (i.e. full and permanent self-possession) by being open to the demands of experience and yet not losing his integrity in them, but achieving *through* them a compassionate self-indentification with others and a sense of oneness with the inner identity of others.

'Compassion' (*Mitleid*) is the key word in *Parsifal* — as it is, and because it is, in Schopenhauer's ethics. The sole musical motive in the opera that does not originate in the orchestra comes on the words

---

[56] Hans von Wolzogen, quoted by Ernest Newman in *Wagner Nights*, p. 698.

'Given knowledge by compassion, the stupid innocent . . .'.[57] Although the opera was composed during the period 1877–82, the centrality of compassion to Wagner's conception of it stretches back over two decades to his first reading of Schopenhauer. 'In the late 1850s Wagner's whole thinking about life and the cosmos took a mystical–metaphysical turn, the result partly of his study of Schopenhauer, partly of his contact with Buddhist literature, partly of his own tortured broodings upon the nature of the world and the destiny of man and beast, partly of the flood of new emotion set coursing in him by the sorrowful Tristan subject. The centre of his ethic now was pity for everything doomed to carry the burden of existence; and it was from this centre outwards that he had already come to survey the Parzival subject afresh.

'The biographical record now shifts to the autumn of 1858, when Wagner began for Frau Wesendonk's benefit that "Venice Diary" that is of the first importance for our understanding of him at that time. "Nothing touches me seriously", he wrote, "save in so far as it awakes in me fellow-feeling, that is, fellow-suffering. This compassion I recognize as the strongest feature of my moral being, and presumably it is also the fountain-head of my art." Even more with animals than with man, he says, does he feel kinship through suffering, for man by his philosophy can raise himself to a resignation that transcends his pain, whereas the mute unreasoning animal can only suffer without comprehending why. "And so if there is any purpose in all this suffering it can only be the awakening of pity in man, who thus takes up the animal's failed existence into himself, and, by perceiving the error of all existence, becomes the redeemer of the world. This interpretation will become clearer to you some day from the third act of *Parzival*, which takes place on Good Friday morning." Manifestly, then, the Parzival drama had already defined itself within him as the drama of compassion.'[58]

If 'compassion' is the key word in the *Parsifal* text, any attempt to describe the music should make special use of the word 'resignation'. This music has an extraordinary sound, perhaps best characterized by

---

[57] *Durch Mitleid wissend,*
der reine Tor . . .

Cf. Schopenhauer's: 'Genuine goodness of disposition, disinterested virtue and pure nobleness of mind do not come from abstract knowledge; yet they do come from knowledge. But it is a direct and intuitive knowledge that cannot be reasoned away or arrived at by reasoning; a knowledge that, just because it is not abstract, cannot be communicated, but must dawn on each of us.' (*The World as Will and Representation*, i. 370.) He goes on, on the same page, to say that what brings us to such knowledge is compassion.
[58] Ernest Newman: *Wagner Nights*, pp. 701–2.

contrast with Wagner's other mature works. In them there is an overmastering insistence, a lust to assert which comes close to attempting the subjugation of the listener. In short, there is an assertion of will, which is widely felt to be unique in music, and perhaps unique in art. Very many people have found it alienating, even repellent, and on the whole it is the characteristic of Wagner's work which those who dislike it dislike in it most. This unremitting vehemence is absent from *Parsifal*. The motor that powers those other works is not present at all in this one, which seems to unfold in a relaxed, inevitable way, without impetus, as if altogether un-driven from inside. It is a music that radiates acceptance. It is resignation in orchestral sound. With this opera, which Wagner knew was to be his last, the crucial point is not that he advocates renunciation of the will but that he achieves it.

Appendix 7

Schopenhauer's Influence on Creative Writers

I have dealt with Schopenhauer's influence on Wagner at such length
because it is probably the outstanding instance in our culture of a great
artist's work being importantly influenced by a great philosopher's —
or, as Thomas Mann has put it in his somewhat more lurid idiom:
'Never probably in the history of the mind has there been so wonderful
an example of the artist, the dark and driven human being, finding
spiritual support, self-justification, and enlightenment in another's
thought, as in this case of Wagner and Schopenhauer.'[1] There is not
space, however, to give proportionate treatment to every other artist
influenced by Schopenhauer. So I shall offer no more in this appendix
than the roughest of sketch-maps to indicate where most of the treasure
trove lies.

Tolstoy (1828–1910) worked on *War and Peace* from 1863 to 1869, and
on *Anna Karenina* from 1873 to 1877. As soon as he had finished *War and
Peace* he plunged into the study of Schopenhauer, and at once became
intoxicated. In a letter written on 30 August 1869 to his closest friend,
A. A. Fet, he wrote:

'Do you know what this summer has meant for me? Constant rap-
tures over Schopenhauer and a whole series of spiritual delights which
I've never experienced before. I've sent for all his works and I'm
reading them (I've also read Kant), and probably no student has ever
studied so much on his course, and learned so much, as I have this
summer.

'I don't know if I'll ever change my opinion, but at present I'm
certain that Schopenhauer is the most brilliant of men.

'You said that he wrote something or other on philosophical subjects, not too badly. What do you mean, something or other? It's the
whole world in an incredibly clear and beautiful reflection.

'I've begun to translate him. Won't you also take it on? We could
publish it jointly. As I read him, it's inconceivable to me how his name
can remain unknown.'

Fet did indeed take on the translation of Schopenhauer, and carried the

[1] Thomas Mann: *Essays of Three Decades*, p. 331.

project through single-handed, his translation of *The World as Will and Representation* being published in 1881. Tolstoy dropped out almost at once: while Fet was working on Schopenhauer he wrote *Anna Karenina*. But he continued for years to be interested in Schopenhauerian problems. On 30 November 1875, while in the very middle of *Anna Karenina*, he referred in a letter to N. N. Strakhov to 'genuine philosophy, whose task is to answer Kant's questions'. And his Schopenhauerian concerns were being quietly woven into his second great novel as one of the unobtrusive strands in the texture. As his biographer Henri Troyat puts it: 'In the world of Levin and Anna, as in Tolstoy's own world, conversation centers on Gustav Doré's illustrations of the Bible, the novels of Daudet and Zola, the physicist Tyndall's theories on radiant heat, the teachings of Spencer and Schopenhauer, Lassalle's scheme for workers' unions . . .'.[2]

Tolstoy bought a portrait of Schopenhauer and (like Wagner at the same time) hung it on the wall of his study. He had come to the conclusion that Schopenhauer takes us as far as philosophy can. He never altered that judgement, and Schopenhauer remained for him an important point of reference, but its significance for him went through a revolution of 180 degrees: for, having started out by thinking philosophy all-important, he ended by considering it dispensable. In his *Confession* of 1884 he tells us that it was the inability of even the greatest of philosophers to answer the only question that really matters in the end, namely, what is the point of living, that impelled him into religion. Incidentally, those later writings of his that wrestle with the problem of whether life has a meaning, and if so how we can find out what it is, were to have a profound influence on Wittgenstein.

A great Russian novelist in whose books the influence of Schopenhauer was much more to the fore, and more lasting, was Turgenev (1818–1883). 'Arthur Schopenhauer was Turgenev's favourite philosopher from the early sixties until the end of his life . . . Schopenhauer's philosophy became for Turgenev an inestimably valuable framework for the integration of his views . . . his "Schopenhauerism" was much more genuine than the "Schopenhauerism" of Lev Tolstoy.'[3] In Leonard Schapiro's biography of Turgenev there is a passage which begins by considering one

[2] Henri Troyat: *Tolstoy*, p. 365. Troyat translates the opening of Tolstoy's letter to Fet of 30 August 1869 much more full-bloodedly than the standard translation drawn on above. 'Do you know what my summer has been? One continuous roar of approval of Schopenhauer . . .'. (Ibid., p. 316.)

[3] A. Walicki: 'Turgenev and Schopenhauer', *Oxford Slavonic Papers*, X (1962), 1, 17 and 15.

example of Schopenhauer's influence and then broadens out to consider that influence in general.

'Ghosts' is a work of profound pessimism and of lack of faith in or hope for the future of mankind. Turgenev was much depressed at the time of writing the work by the rejection of *Fathers and Children* by the younger generation, which he had not expected. He was probably also much influenced by Schopenhauer, whose *World as Will and Idea* he was reading around this time. There is indeed a direct reminiscence of Schopenhauer in the description which he gave in 'Ghosts' of the earth as seen from above, when the humans look small and unimportant and are locked in eternal struggle with blind forces which they cannot control — creatures who have emerged from the slime that covers the earth's surface. This recalls the first paragraph of the second volume of *The World as Will and Idea*, and in the draft of the story there appears an entry 'View of the earth (Schopenhauer)' which shows that the borrowing was conscious.

Statements are sometimes made that Schopenhauer is repeatedly mentioned in Turgenev's letters. But there are only two references, one in 1862, and a second, much later, which is merely an enquiry of Fet about how he is getting on with his translation of Schopenhauer. Nevertheless, it is clear from a number of his works that Turgenev was much influenced by this philosopher's sombre pessimism. The most striking influence of Schopenhauer's view of the nature of sexual passion occurs in two later works, *Spring Torrents* and *Song of Triumphant Love* (see chapters 14 and 16). But Schopenhauer's themes abound in Turgenev's writings. For example, the illusion that man can attain happiness, which is in essence nothing but deliverance from pain; this deliverance once achieved, boredom sets in, and the striving after satisfaction reasserts itself. Or again, that temporary escape from the driving of the cosmic will is to be found in aesthetic contemplation; or that in the hierarchy of art the pride of place belongs to music, which exhibits no ideas, only the will itself, so that in listening to it one obtains a direct revelation (in non-conceptual form) of the reality, the will which underlies all phenomena. Above all, the insignificance of man in the scheme of nature which pursues its own course, its will, with total disregard for his existence.[4]

In France it was a little later before writers of the front rank began to fall under Schopenhauer's spell. But in the early 1880s Zola (1840–1902) wrote a whole Schopenhauerian novel, over which he laboured with unusual deliberation, and called it ironically *The Joy of Living*. His biographer says particularly of this book that it 'encompasses his obsessions and his metaphysical sorrows'.[5] In it Zola tells us of his young hero that, through pondering on 'the ruses of the Will which directs the world, the blind stupidity of the will-to-live, all life seen as pain, he arrived at the morality of the Indian fakirs, at deliverance

[4] Leonard Schapiro: *Turgenev: His Life and Times*, pp. 207–8.
[5] Matthew Josephson: *Zola and his Time*, p. 290.

through Nirvana'.[6] As for Zola's admirer Maupassant (1850–1893), one of his biographers tells us that Schopenhauer 'was one of the few authors whom Maupassant had read'.[7] And another says he 'professed to be Schopenhauer's admirer', speaks of 'his Schopenhauer', and attributes to him 'a metaphysical curiosity, probably enhanced by his reading of Schopenhauer, which was to remain an undercurrent of his sensual and realistic story-telling all through his life'.[8] One of Maupassant's short stories (*Auprès d'un Mort* in the volume *Boule de Suif*) is about Schopenhauer, much of it in idolatrous terms.

Perhaps the greatest of all French writers to be influenced by Schopenhauer was Proust (1871–1922). From *A Reader's Guide to Marcel Proust*, by Maurice Hindus, we learn that Proust was 'an admirer of Schopenhauer' (p. 132), and that he had become so at an early age (pp. 3 and 44). He is said to have been given to 'language reminiscent of Schopenhauer's', for instance in describing the pleasure given by the presence of a lover as 'a release from suffering rather than a positive joy' (p. 129). It is noted 'how much his vision of life has in common with that of Schopenhauer' (p. 183), and we are told that 'nowhere is the influence of the philosopher Schopenhauer upon Proust's vision of the world clearer than in the delineation of the particular stage of Marcel's relationship with Albertine chronicled in *The Captive*' (p. 126). Maurice E. Chernovitz, in *Proust and Painting*, makes the point that Proust was not an original thinker, but rather that his capacious view of experience was a highly original synthesis of elements drawn from a wide range of sources: Chernovitz lists some fifteen of those sources, and among them he puts Schopenhauer first (p. 184). Patrick Gardiner, in his book *Schopenhauer*, judges (p. 202) that 'the kernel of Schopenhauer's account of the artist's approach to the world finds perhaps its most striking echo' in Proust.

English creative writers are often thought to be, by comparison with their counterparts in other cultures, less interested in abstract ideas, but a novelist more powerfully influenced by Schopenhauer than any I have so far mentioned was Thomas Hardy (1840–1928). In the Foreword to his book *Thomas Hardy's Universe* Ernest Brennecke writes (p. 9): 'If, indeed, one may attempt to come to grips with the intellectual content of Hardy . . . it is as impossible to succeed in such an attempt without indicating parallelisms from philosophers as it is to discuss his art without pointing out literary parallels. In particular, it is quite impossible, from the first, to ignore Schopenhauer, — and before one

---

[6] Josephson: *Zola and his Time*, p. 290.

[7] Robert Harborough Sherard: *The Life, Work and Evil Fate of Guy de Maupassant*, p. 269.

[8] Paul Ignotus: *The Paradox of Maupassant*, pp. 15, 236 and 78–9.

has proceeded very far, Schopenhauer is found to have usurped practically the whole discussion.' The rest of the book exemplifies this, which makes satisfactory quotation from it difficult. If Brennecke exaggerates Schopenhauer's importance it is by not allowing for the extent to which Hardy got his Schopenhauerism not only direct from Schopenhauer but also from his epigones. I suspect that Robert Gittings states the position more fairly when he stresses, in his book *The Older Hardy*, 'the breadth of his philosophic reading, and its effect on *The Dynasts*. There is, it has been shown, a great deal of Schopenhauer, whom he read and noted industriously in the late 1880s and 1890s, and still more of von Hartman, in particular, and of Haeckel, though the latter's philosophy has been seen not so much as an influence but as a reinforcement of what were already Hardy's own views' (p. 114).

J. O. Bailey in *Thomas Hardy and the Cosmic Mind* notes that 'Schopenhauer's *The World as Will and Idea* was translated into English in 1883, and it seems evident that Hardy read it during the composition of *The Woodlanders*, published in 1887. Dissertations and book-length studies have amply shown the influence of Schopenhauer upon Hardy's thought' (p. 88). Among these book-length studies Bailey picks out for special mention Brennecke's *Thomas Hardy's Universe*, which has just been cited, and also a book called *Thomas Hardy: An Illustration of the Philosophy of Schopenhauer* by Helen Garwood. What these books demonstrate is that Hardy was affected above all by the Schopenhauerian doctrine of the metaphysical will — the notion that the universe is the manifestation of a blind impersonal force which exists outside the human world of space and time and causal connection, and is utterly indifferent to it. He also accepted the doctrine that human beings do not, in the deepest sense, have free will, and that their character is therefore their destiny, a destiny which they are powerless to evade. These beliefs dominate what are probably his two most famous novels, *Tess of the D'Urbervilles* and *Jude the Obscure* — which were the two books which he wrote immediately after reading Schopenhauer. They also pervade what he regarded as his masterpiece, *The Dynasts*, a book-length dramatic poem which he wrote after he had finished with novels altogether. However, as with other major figures who have come under Schopenhauer's influence, the qualification needs to be entered that Hardy embraced the philosopher's work because it provided him with a solid and systematic intellectual foundation for insights which, to some extent, he held already on a basis of intuition, and which already informed his creative work. Nevertheless, the influence did change his practice, even to the extent of changing his nomenclature. To give just one example, 'he found it hard to use "He" or "She" for that vague purposeless blind thrusting which he found at the centre of everything. The nearest he could come to finding a satisfactory word was Schopenhauer's "Will". Hardy was quite ready to agree that "Immanent Will" did not perfectly fit the idea he wished to convey. But Schopenhauer and Hartmann had made the term more widely known than any other, and Hardy himself had no better one to offer as a substitute.'[9]

The book which Hardy wrote most immediately after his reading of Schopenhauer, *Tess of the D'Urbervilles*, is the one more widely regarded than any other as his masterpiece, and also the one most replete with Schopenhauerian allusions. Schopenhauer is even mentioned in it by name.[10] It recurrently harks back to the sentiment that it would be better not to have been born. On one page (134) we get, in different paragraphs, 'the plight of being alive', 'the world is only a psychological phenomenon', and 'She thought, without exactly wording the thought, how strange and godlike was a composer's power.' Listening to music, 'Tess was conscious of neither time nor space' (p. 179). We re-encounter our old friend the wheel of Ixion (p. 468 — see p. 171 of the present volume). Schopenhauer had written at length about our propensity to give unconscious expression to our true feelings, and had discussed somnambulism in this context: in the novel we get Angel Clare walking in his sleep and revealing his true feelings for Tess while doing so. Schopenhauer had argued that all weeping is caused, at bottom, by self-pity: in the novel we find Hardy specifying this connection not just on one but on most of the important occasions of weeping by his characters. The novel abounds in references to the fundamental indifference of both the natural and the human worlds to the lives of individual creatures (examples occur on pp. 141, 191, 244, 297, 305, 399 and 459). And there are whole passages which could have been written by the philosopher himself — for instance the following description (p. 363) of the 'strange birds from behind the North Pole [which] began to arrive silently on the upland of Flintcomb-Ash':

'. . . gaunt spectral creatures with tragical eyes — eyes which had witnessed scenes of cataclysmal horror in inaccessible polar regions of a magnitude such as no human being had ever conceived, in curdling temperatures that no man could endure; which had beheld the crash of icebergs and the slide of snow-hills by the shooting light of the Aurora; been half blinded by the whirl of colossal storms and terraqueous distortions; and retained the expression of feature that such scenes had engendered.'

[9] Carl J. Weber: *Hardy of Wessex*, p. 198.
[10] On p. 218 of the Penguin English Library edition. All subsequent page references are to this edition.

It is inconceivable that anyone can have read Schopenhauer and not be put in mind of him by passages such as this.

Another great novelist in the English language who was significantly influenced by Schopenhauer is Conrad (1857–1924). In his *Reminiscences of Conrad: 1924* (p. 52), his fellow novelist John Galsworthy says: 'Of philosophy he had read a good deal. Schopenhauer used to give him satisfaction twenty years and more ago.' But as Paul Kirschner says in *Conrad: the Psychologist as Artist* (p. 266), 'even if Conrad had not read a line of Schopenhauer, he would have absorbed much of his world-view from Maupassant. In a story about the German pessimist's death Maupassant paid tribute to "the immortal thought of the greatest devastater of dreams who ever walked the earth". When Conrad, in turn, praised Maupassant for his power "of detecting the one immutable quality that matters in the changing aspects of nature and under the ever-shifting surface of life", he was paying indirect tribute to Schopenhauer.' The book here quoted contains in its seventh chapter an extended discussion of Schopenhauer's influence on Conrad — as does William W. Bonney's *Thorns and Arabesques* in its first chapter, which is called 'Conrad, Schopenhauer and the Orient'.

In his introduction to Joseph Conrad's *Letters to R. B. Cunninghame Graham* (pp. 24–5) C. T. Watts characterizes the pessimism which is central to Conrad's letters, as it is to his novels: 'Conrad argues that reform is ultimately futile, because human nature is selfish and brutal . . . and because humanity is in any case destined to perish of cold, amid a mechanistic and soulless universe . . . so that even consciousness itself may be regarded as an evil, because its survey of our condition removes the illusion of freedom to improve our state.' Watts then continues (p. 25): 'Possibly the most direct literary contribution to Conrad's pessimism was made by Schopenhauer.' The impact of Schopenhauer on Conrad extends even to his use of individual words. As William W. Bonney puts it: 'An interesting example of the depth of influence Schopenhauer's *The World as Will and Idea* possibly had on Conrad is indicated by the fact that certain rhetorical patterns in Conrad seem to derive from Schopenhauer's writings' and he then goes on to give two extended examples.[11] Even the novelist's famous statement of what it was he was trying to do — 'My task . . . is, before all, to make you *see*' — is an instant evocation of Schopenhauer: 'The artist lets us see the world through his eyes. That he has these eyes, that he knows the essential in things which lies outside all relations, is the gift of genius and is inborn; but that he is able to lend us this gift, to let us see with his eyes, is acquired, and is the technical side of art.'[12]

[11] *Thorns and Arabesques*, p. 225.
[12] *The World as Will and Representation*, i. 195. It looks to me as if Conrad, who obviously

One of Conrad's novels, *Victory* — described by F. R. Leavis as 'among those of Conrad's works which deserve to be current as representing his claim to classical standing; and . . . the one that answers most nearly to the stock notion of his genius'[13] is centrally concerned with the same struggle as we saw Wittgenstein engaged in on p. 287. The main character, Axel Heyst, is the son of a philosopher who is modelled on Schopenhauer: he has grown up dominated by his father's ideas, and he tries to live his life in accordance with them. But he finds that the two main ethical principles — detachment and compassion — are incompatible with each other; and the story tells how his detachment from the world is breached by a compassionate tie which he forms with another human being, and how this brings about his destruction. As the narrator says early on, in the fourth chapter: 'His detachment from the world was not complete. And incompleteness of any sort leads to trouble.' Or, as Heyst himself puts it much later, 'he who forms a tie is lost. The germ of corruption has entered into his soul.'[14] In addition to this central theme, *Victory* contains other Schopenhauerian features. The three leading men embody what Schopenhauer regarded as the three available modes of human existence: Heyst is self-awarely detached from the world, Ricardo is engaged in living as on a battlefield, while for Mr Jones life is dominated by boredom; and of course this also means that the 'good' is trying to live outside the phenomenal realm while the 'bad' are wholly contained within it. Furthermore, these latter two are accompanied everwhere by a non-human embodiment of dumb, blind, inarticulate, amoral force in Pedro. Schopenhauerian references are recurrent in the dialogue. To give a couple of examples, at one point Heyst says: 'I don't think. Something in me thinks — something foreign to my nature.' At another the murderer who crashes in on his detached existence says to him: 'I am the world itself, come to pay you a visit.'

However, it is perhaps not surprising that the imaginative writer most influenced of all by Schopenhauer should be one who shared his mother tongue and the same specific cultural tradition. Even so, the personal affinities which Thomas Mann (1875–1955) had with the philosopher go much further than that. Indeed, they are startling. Mann too was born in one of the Hanseatic seaports, Lübeck, and into a family of rich and powerful merchants: his father was head of the

was much struck by this passage, was also consciously echoing it in his praise of Maupassant quoted a moment ago on p. 385.

[13] F. R. Leavis: *The Great Tradition*, p. 230 (Penguin edition).
[14] This quotation was later drawn on by Graham Greene in the epigraph for his novel *The Human Factor*.

ancestral firm and twice mayor of the free city. Mann too was brought up to go into the family business, and so, instead of being sent to university, was put to work in an office at the age of nineteen. There he, too, wrote in secret; but after a while he too threw over his job and took himself off to university, never to return to the family's traditional way of life but becoming instead a full-time writer. The story of his early life is the same as that of Schopenhauer's, and in the same small, highly specific social setting, but a hundred years later. This must, I think, have had something to do with the extraordinary degree of self-identification which Mann developed with Schopenhauer.

Mann's account of his discovery of Schopenhauer in his early twenties is reminiscent of Nietzsche's. He tells also how he wove the experience into his first novel, *Buddenbrooks*. The following account incorporates quotations from Mann and is taken from Nigel Hamilton's joint biography of *The Brothers Mann* (p. 63) — hence the reference to the writer by his first name:

'. . . the hour came that made me read, and I read day and night, as perhaps one reads only once in a lifetime.' It was a 'spiritual experience of absolutely first rank and unforgettable in kind', and it gave rise to serious thoughts of suicide — morbidity which was subtly transferred to the primary figure of *Buddenbrooks*.

Thomas had bought the Brockhaus edition of Schopenhauer's works at a sale some time previously, 'more to own it than to study it'. The volumes had 'stood a long time uncut on the shelves' when the day arrived. 'The little high-up room in the suburb sways before my eyes,' Thomas wrote in 1916, 'in which, sixteen years ago I lay stretched all day on the curiously shaped chair or sofa reading *The World as Will and Idea*. Lonely, undisciplined youth, yearning for both life and death — how it swallowed the magical potion of this metaphysics, whose deepest being is eroticism, and in which I recognized the spiritual source of Wagner's *Tristan* music! One only reads once like that, it never recurs. And what a stroke of fortune that I did not have to contain such an experience but had an immediate opportunity of expressing it, of showing my gratitude: a chance to give it a poetic rendering! For two yards from my sofa lay the impossibly growing manuscript — burden, honour, home and blessing of that strange period of my youth, highly problematic in terms of its chances of publication — which had just come to the point where Thomas Buddenbrook must be brought to death. To him, who was to me a thrice-related figure — father, descendant, shadow of myself — I gave the precious experience, the great discovery in his life, shortly before his end; I wove it into the story for it seemed to belong to him . . .'.

Another interesting thing about *Buddenbrooks* is that it is a saga about the kind of family that Mann shared with Schopenhauer. It expresses at one and the same time a lingeringly loving and an ironically detached attitude to these roots, and indirectly offers his justification for severing himself from them. As the above quotation has shown, Mann identified himself in more ways than one with his character Thomas Buddenbrook (and no doubt called him Thomas for that reason) and it looks to me as if, through him, he is living in imagination the life which he himself has forgone: Thomas Buddenbrook is what Thomas Mann would have been like if he had gone into the family business, an intelligent man not existentially engaged in what he was doing but playing a role from a sense of duty — and for that reason not very good at it, so that the firm would have gone downhill under him in spite of his superior ability.

There is a book devoted to Mann's Schopenhauerism called, appropriately, *Thomas Mann: The World as Will and Representation*, by Fritz Kaufmann. Of Mann's second full-length novel Kaufmann says: 'Schopenhauer's view is revived in *The Magic Mountain* . . . and it extends . . . throughout Thomas Mann's work' (pp. 40–1. On p. 104 he reiterates that 'Schopenhauer's point of view . . . is never quite absent in Thomas Mann'). Mann himself was aware of the all-embracing influence which Schopenhauer had come to have on him. In a letter to Paul Amann of 16 December 1916 he refers to Schopenhauer, Wagner and Nietzsche as 'the great Germans who were the shapers of my nature', and on 27 August 1917 he writes of 'the Wagnerian-Schopenhauerian, the Romantic realm, which, you know, is really the homeland of my psychic life'. Nor was he under the illusion that this influence was merely a general one: he saw it as extending to specific doctrines, including such as were bound to affect his practice as a novelist. For instance in a letter to Paul Amann of 25 March 1917 he writes: 'As a Schopenhauerian I am convinced of the metaphysical freedom of the will — and its empirical unfreedom.'

Comparatively late in his career, at the age of sixty-three, Mann published an essay on Schopenhauer. Its aim, he wrote in the essay itself, was 'to evoke today a figure little known to the present generation; and to reconsider and recapitulate his concepts'.[15] His reason for doing this, he said, was that although Schopenhauer might appear to be an only half-remembered figure he was in reality a philosopher whose full day had yet to come, and was therefore, rightly seen, a denizen of the future. 'I spoke of Schopenhauer as modern. I might have called him futurist . . . what I called his pessimistic humanity seems to me to herald the temper of a future time. Once he was fashionable and famous, then half-forgotten. But his philosophy may still exert a ripe and humanizing influence upon our age.'[16]

· · ·

[15] Thomas Mann: *Essays of Three Decades*, pp. 408–9.   [16] Ibid., p. 409.

Even in so short a survey as I have sketched in this appendix, one thing stands out: the creative writers influenced by Schopenhauer include a substantial number of the greatest since his day. Tolstoy, Turgenev, Zola, Maupassant, Proust, Hardy, Conrad, Thomas Mann — these figures, spanning the literatures of four different languages, with widely differing cultural traditions, must surely number among the tallest giants of imagination in the last hundred years and more. To these I could have added others who were in the same class as writers but less importantly touched with Schopenhauerian influence. For instance, in the footnote on p. 213 I gave reason for thinking that a Schopenhauerian doctrine surfaces at one point in the poetry of T. S. Eliot. Certainly the term 'objective correlative', which is universally attributed to Eliot, occurs in Schopenhauer,[17] and, as I have shown, Eliot studied Schopenhauer. There are also acknowledged to be traces of Schopenhauerian influence, direct or indirect, in the works of Rilke and Pirandello.

Furthermore, it is not only giants of world literature who were influenced: a host of minor, but some of them even more widely read, figures were affected too. To take one instance, Somerset Maugham, the best of whose short stories may well survive: his biographer tells us that he studied Schopenhauer when he was at Heidelberg University, that his outlook was influenced more by Schopenhauer than by anyone else, and that this profoundly affected the way he conducted the rest of his life.[18] Nor has Schopenhauer's influence been felt only by dead writers. I have confined my examples to the dead because their calibre is less controversial than that of the living; but I suspect that Schopenhauer's influence on significant writers is a continuing phenomenon. When I met Borges some time ago and remarked that I was about to embark on writing a book about Schopenhauer he became excited and started talking volubly about how much Schopenhauer had meant to him. It was the desire to read Schopenhauer in the original, he said, that had made him learn German; and when people asked him, which they often did, why he with his love of intricate structure had never attempted a systematic exposition of the world-view which underlay his writings, his reply was that he did not do it because it had already been done, by Schopenhauer.

All in all, especially when Wagner is taken into the reckoning, it looks to me as if the influence of Schopenhauer on creative artists of the very front rank surpasses that of any other philosopher since his time, and perhaps even that of any other philosopher since the ancient

---

[17] See *The Fourfold Root of the Principle of Sufficient Reason*, p. 119.
[18] Ted Morgan: *Somerset Maugham*, pp. 24, 25 and 615.

Greeks. The influence of Marx has unquestionably been wider, and the quantity of Marxist art is incomparably greater, but the only artists I can think of who are of obvious significance and have also had an intellectually serious relationship with Marxist philosophy are Brecht, Neruda, Malraux and Sartre — and these are fewer and of smaller calibre than the main figures I have been discussing. Marxist art is required by Marxist philosophy to function as an instrument of social change, and as such it is of merely immediate relevance, at best akin to high-class journalism and social analysis, at worst to group encouragement and propaganda. It must be difficult for a truly authentic artist to subscribe for long to Marxist philosophy, since its unqualified materialism, and hence its denial of the noumenal, are at odds with his direct experience.

Appendix 8

A Conjecture about Dylan Thomas

There is, I think, universal agreement among students of Dylan Thomas (1914–1953) that he established himself with one particular poem that was written and published when he was still in his teens.[1] It is a short lyric of four stanzas and a concluding couplet. The first two stanzas are as follows:

> The force that through the green fuse drives the flower
> Drives my green age; that blasts the roots of trees
> Is my destroyer.
> And I am dumb to tell the crooked rose
> My youth is bent by the same wintry fever.
>
> The force that drives the water through the rocks
> Drives my red blood; that dries the mouthing streams
> Turns mine to wax.
> And I am dumb to mouth unto my veins
> How at the mountain spring the same mouth sucks.

This is startlingly reminiscent of a passage in which Schopenhauer says that the reader who has understood him 'will recognize that same will not only in those phenomena that are quite similar to his own, in men and animals, as their innermost nature, but continued reflection will lead him to recognize the force that shoots and vegetates in the plant, indeed the force by which the crystal is formed, the force that turns the magnet to the North Pole, the force whose shock he encounters from the contact of metals of different kinds, the force that appears in the elective affinities of matter as repulsion and attraction, separation and union, and finally even gravitation, which acts so powerfully in all matter, pulling the stone to the earth and the earth to the sun; all these he will recognize as different only in the phenomenon, but the same according to their inner nature.'[2] Eight pages on there is a similar

---

[1] The manuscript is dated 12 October 1933, and the poem was published that same year. William York Tindall in *A Reader's Guide to Dylan Thomas* (p. 48) writes: 'This poem made Thomas famous.' Clark Emery in *The World of Dylan Thomas* (p. 269) says: 'This is the poem that started Thomas on his way'; and on the same page William Empson is quoted as saying that 'From that day he was a famous poet'.

[2] *The World as Will and Representation*, i. 109–10.

passage, containing some of the same images, which begins: 'Now let us consider attentively and observe the powerful, irresistible impulse with which masses of water rush downwards . . .' and ends: 'If we observe all this it will not cost us a great effort of the imagination to recognize once more our own inner nature, even at so great a distance.'[3]

Not only is there the same rhetorical repetition of 'the force' and 'the force that', and the same imagery of plants shooting through their stems and mountain streams driving through the rocks: the point they are making is identical, namely that it is one and the same force that constitutes and drives all the things that there are in the world, whether animate or inanimate, and that it is at one with what constitutes our inner nature as human beings. These similarities could be coincidental, but there are too many for this to be likely. It looks, rather, as if there may be a connection — especially if one realizes that such a connection could have come about quite easily through Thomas's interest in Hardy.

This interest was passionate. As Vernon Watkins tells us in his Introduction to *Dylan Thomas: Letters to Vernon Watkins* (p. 17): 'Hardy was his favourite poet of the century'. We know that Dylan Thomas read Hardy while still at school.[4] We know also that whatever he read in his early period as a writer went straight into his work. ' "The writers who influenced my earliest poems and stories were, quite simply and truthfully, all the writers I was reading at the time", Thomas told a student in 1951. He was seldom more simple or truthful. Particularly notable is the narrative influence of Thomas Hardy and A. E. Housman . . .'.[5] Given that the young Dylan Thomas was such a voracious reader, and that he had such an interest in Hardy, it would be unsurprising if he read *about* Hardy; it is what one would expect, in fact (just as, I cannot help remembering, I devoured at that age not only T. S. Eliot's poetry but any books and articles about it that I could lay my hands on). If he did, it is inevitable that he would have encountered discussions of Hardy's relationship with Schopenhauer. There were as yet comparatively few general books about Hardy, but, as one of them published in 1924 observed: 'It seems to be universally recognized at the present time by everybody interested in the subject that there is the closest intellectual affinity between Arthur Schopenhauer and Thomas Hardy.'[6] This fact alone could well have moved the book-mad young Dylan Thomas to pick up Schopenhauer in a library.

But in quoting Ernest Brennecke's *Thomas Hardy's Universe* we may

---

[3] *The World as Will and Representation*, i. 117–18.
[4] See *The Craft and Art of Dylan Thomas* (p. 22) by William T. Moynihan.
[5] Ibid., p. 23.
[6] Ernest Brennecke: *Thomas Hardy's Universe*, p. 14.

have hit more specifically on the vital clue. That book is devoted to an enthusiastic discussion of Hardy's connection with Schopenhauer, and it includes a great many quotations from the philosopher. In particular, it concentrates on the concept of 'Immanent Will', which Hardy derived from Schopenhauer *and which Dylan Thomas's poem is in fact about.* The book is one of very few devoted to Hardy's work which would have been effortlessly available to Thomas at that time, and, most important of all, it quotes the longer of the two relevant passages from Schopenhauer in its very first chapter (pp. 28–9). Given all these things, it seems to me much less unlikely that Dylan Thomas had read at least the quotation in Brennecke's book, if not some original Schopenhauer, than that the existence of such a many-levelled corre-spondence between his poem and Schopenhauer is coincidental.

Index